THE CREATIVITY CHALLENGE

THE
CREATIVITY
CHALLENGE

HOW WE CAN RECAPTURE
AMERICAN INNOVATION

KH KIM

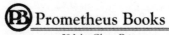
Prometheus Books

59 John Glenn Drive
Amherst, New York 14228

Cover image © art4all/Shutterstock
Cover design by Liz Mills
Cover © Prometheus Books
Interior illustrations by Steve Cyborski and Tom Alfaro © KH Kim

Inquiries should be addressed to
Prometheus Books
59 John Glenn Drive
Amherst, New York 14228
VOICE: 716–691–0133
FAX: 716–691–0137
WWW.PROMETHEUSBOOKS.COM

20 19 18 17 16   5 4 3 2 1

Library of Congress Cataloging-in-Publication Data

Names: Kim, Kyung Hee, 1964- author.
Title: The creativity challenge : how we can recapture American innovation / KH Kim.
Description: Amherst : Prometheus Books, 2016. | Includes bibliographical references and
    index.
Identifiers: LCCN 2016014246 (print) | LCCN 2016031676 (ebook) |
    ISBN 9781633882157 (paperback) | ISBN 9781633882164 (ebook)
Subjects: LCSH: Creative ability. | Educational psychology. | BISAC: PSYCHOLOGY /
    Creative Ability. | EDUCATION / Educational Psychology. | SOCIAL SCIENCE /
    General.
Classification: LCC BF408 .K526 2016 (print) | LCC BF408 (ebook) |
    DDC 153.3/5—dc23
LC record available at https://lccn.loc.gov/2016014246

Printed in the United States of America

CONTENTS

INTRODUCTION

When people ask me why I decided to write this book, I have a simple answer: I want to change the world. I want to help all people, especially parents, educators, and children, achieve their dreams through the power of creativity. This book fulfills a dream I have had my entire adult life. To me creativity isn't just a topic of research; it saved my life.

I was born in a South Korean mountain village and lived in Korea until I was thirty-three. Much of my Korean life was miserable, as I tried to live according to Confucian principles (the roots of East Asian culture), which trampled my desire for self-expression. However, an ember of my creativity survived thanks to my mother, one teacher, and one deliberate act of kindness that showed me glimpses of my creative future.

Approximately thirty minutes by truck from my home, on the very top of Palgong Mountain, there were two separate military bases: one American and one South Korean. Palgong Mountain always received a thin blanket of snow before our village did. The white powder was still there long after all of the snow in my village melted. I felt sorry for the soldiers who lived on the cold peak. The Korean soldiers' families lived close to my home and, in my eyes, these families were rich far beyond my imagination. The children in my village, including my siblings and me, were dirty and had lice in our hair. We could take baths only in the summer when we were able to swim in the streams and rivers. The military children bathed even in the winter, and their hair smelled like flowers. Some said the military children had bathtubs in their rooms, but I didn't believe them because I thought it would be strange to have that much water inside.

I didn't know where the American soldiers' families lived. I heard from my teachers that they lived on the other side of the earth, but I couldn't imagine where that was. The farthest places I could imagine were China and Japan. I didn't understand why the US soldiers would want to be on top of Palgong Mountain, in the cold and without their families.

One of my first memories of the US soldiers was when I was three. All of the little children in my village ran, cheering, behind military trucks that were driving up the dirt road toward their base. We tumbled and wrestled in the dust to catch the delicious caramel candies the soldiers showered down upon us. The caramels were soft and chewy; they stuck to my teeth while I ate them, and the taste stayed on my lips all afternoon. That was the first caramel candy I experienced in my life. We always had plenty of sweet fruits from the farms nearby, but there was nothing like caramel candy in my village.

There were 210 students in my middle-school class, but we spent most of our time divided into three separate groups of seventy students each. My elementary school was a ten-minute walk from home, but my middle school required an entire hour-long walk each way. Both public schools were for children who lived in the tiny villages on different mountains. In Korea at that time, teachers could earn extra points by teaching in remote places in order to become school administrators. Thus, most of the teachers in my schools were ambitious and energetic males who had a goal of becoming a principal by the time they reached their midfifties. These teachers were trained to educate the students and their parents by visiting their homes and instilling a vision and an understanding of what education and modernity could lead to; they were there to inspire us.

In December 1978, at the end of my first year of middle school, my homeroom teacher announced that I had received the highest grades in the class of 210 students. He told me that the US soldiers would visit our school to give a scholarship to me and a boy whose scores put him in second place. I had no idea what a scholarship was, and as the teacher was explaining this, a green US military Jeep with an American flag on its antenna drove into the schoolyard. Right behind it, a huge truck pulled in with four Ping-Pong tables in the back. All the boys in the school were ecstatic; they jumped up from their chairs and ran outside, shouting with excitement.

I was escorted into the principal's office to greet three US soldiers who arrived in the Jeep. They towered over us in their green uniforms, with their fancy buttons and gleaming smiles. Their skin looked so white to me—like lights. Their hands looked huge and hairy. They handed me an envelope with money in it, and they also gave one to the boy. I was shocked—why would powerful, huge superhuman beings like these Americans give anything to us? (No Korean people ever gave scholarships to my schools.) At that time, I could only imagine what we looked like to them. My face and clothes were filthy and smeared with mud, and my hair was matted. I had watched the lice on other children's heads and knew they crawled out of my hair too—fat and lazy from feeding on my blood.

Our English teacher pointed and told us to look over at one of the soldiers so that he could take our picture. As soon as we turned our heads, there was a big flash of light like lightning. There was a whirring sound and then, remarkably, a picture popped out of the little box. I had heard about cameras before but didn't know there was a camera that developed pictures right away. It was like magic! The boy looked at me with big eyes, and I looked at him with even bigger eyes. That was the first photograph I had ever seen in my life. Unfortunately, it faded over time—I thought I wore out the image by looking at it too often. I kept it in a special box and looked at it again and again, even after the image was gone.

After the US soldiers left the school, there were many changes, especially among the boys. They came to school early every day to play Ping-Pong before and after classes. They started studying because they realized that getting good grades could result in receiving money and Ping-Pong tables. The boy who got the other scholarship eventually went to the best military college and has been working at the Blue House, the home of the president of South Korea. He was inspired and had a vision of becoming like the US soldiers who had given us scholarships and Ping-Pong tables.

The experience was a life-changing event for me too. My parents invested all of the scholarship money—about $300 at that time—to improve my academic opportunities. They bought things for me that I had never imagined owning. They purchased an almost-new bicycle so that I didn't have to waste two hours a day walking to school. The extra time I gained would enable me to study longer each day. All of the villagers smiled and waved as I rode by, because they knew that the bicycle had been purchased with scholarship money. Next, my parents bought me a single bed and mattress so that I could sleep better and learn better. Normally, Koreans would sleep on their floors with thick blankets. From then on, I slept in my bed above the floor. That wasn't all. My parents also bought a cassette player, English cassettes, and English textbooks so I could learn to *speak* English better. With the leftover money, they bought five little pigs. We sold the pigs' babies countless times to pay for high-school tuition.

I don't think the US soldiers had any idea how much their gifts inspired my whole village. My teachers started encouraging me to study even harder to escape the poverty of my village so that someday I could help more people like me. I became attuned to other examples from the news and history that showed how noble passions can improve everyday life. Today, each time I guide a student, a teacher, a parent, or anyone, I've made a difference.

However, even as I became inspired and empowered to succeed *academically*, I struggled to envision my future *identity*. When I was little, people complained that I was too curious. Even in graduate school, I wasn't allowed to ask so many questions, because it was considered disrespectful to teachers or professors. I was different from other Korean women—a square peg in a round hole. When I became a teacher, I liked students who asked a lot of unexpected or unusual questions, even *troublemakers*. But my preference for those kinds of questions conflicted with Confucian principles. It took me a long time to understand the conflict between cultural values and creativity. It was only after I moved to America and studied creativity that I realized why the conflict existed.

After teaching English for ten years, I escaped from Korea with my two small children (ages four and nine). Every day was a tragicomedy of adventure, discovery, and improvisation. I struggled to raise my children in a very different environment than I was raised in. I made many mistakes as I discovered new approaches to foster their creativity. For this reason, I want to share my experience and research with those who face similar challenges and share similar desires.

I've spent my adult years studying creativity and innovators. For years I've researched and written extensively on various aspects of creativity for a specialized academic audience. This book, however, is about much more than just statistics and analysis. It is about surprising influences and factors in innovators' lives that everybody can understand and use to encourage creativity to flourish. I have developed three practical steps that produce innovation. The steps are:

Step 1: Cultivate Creative Climates
Step 2: Nurture Creative Attitudes
Step 3: Apply Creative-Thinking Skills

The Creativity Challenge is designed to empower three groups of people with skills and tools for creativity: parents and educators, organizations, and creative adults and students.

For parents and educators: The primary group this book is designed for is parents and educators. Although they can't control what children achieve, they *can* control many inputs for children's creative climates and creative attitudes. The development of creativity in individuals varies. My more than twenty years of creativity research suggests that this variation is due to differences in individuals' life experiences, not their inborn abilities/ talents or even IQ. I look closely at how parents and educators cultivate creative climates and nurture creative attitudes in children and how children apply creative-thinking skills. My extensive research is coupled with real-world examples that are easy to integrate into the plans and efforts parents and educators already make. They can help academic achievers become innovators. They can also help turn troublemakers around by understanding similar disruptive or distracted behaviors in the early lives of the innovators: Albert Einstein, Steve Jobs, Nelson Mandela, Georgia O'Keeffe, and Marie Curie.

For organizations including schools, governments, and businesses: This book provides background and courses of action to make organizations more efficient, effective, and capable of developing unique and useful ideas, services, or products.

For adults and students studying creativity or facing their own creativity challenges: I've used drafts of this book in my graduate courses. It's been successful for my students to understand creativity and improve their own. This book also provides insights and steps for individuals who want or need to break writers' block, pursue an artistic vision, fulfill their entrepreneurial dream, break out of a square-peg life, or simply move out of their parents' basement. It shows how they can improve their creativity by finding and/or growing an interest and turning it into a passion.

Helping individuals reach their full creative potential is very much like growing plants. I use original gardening metaphors to show the steps to innovation by cultivating creative climates, nurturing creative attitudes, and applying creative-thinking skills.

This book consists of four parts:

PART 1: WHAT IS CREATIVITY?

Chapter 1, "The Creativity Crisis," describes my research into what I have dubbed America's "creativity crisis," which spurred an explosive *Newsweek* cover story in 2010. This research has gained notoriety in the media because it revealed that American creativity has been declining since 1990. A brief description of the results of the study; the causes of, reactions to, and consequences of the creativity crisis; and the trend of American education *toward* test-centric climates—*against* creative climates—are presented.

Chapter 2,"The Creativity Solution," reveals the nature of creativity and presents my creative CATs (climate, attitude, and thinking skills) to achieve innovation. It starts with cultivating creative climates that nurture creative attitudes that enable creative-thinking skills, which are then applied to achieve innovation.

PART 2: WHAT ARE CREATIVE CLIMATES AND ATTITUDES?

Because I was raised in a farming village, I know what makes plants grow strong and productive: diverse soil, bright sun, fierce storms, and free space. Similarly, what I call "4S" climates are needed for children's creativity to flourish: Diverse resources and experiences (soil), inspiration and encouragement (sun), high expectations and challenges (storms), and freedom to be alone and unique (space). These climates emerged from my syntheses and factor-analyses of empirical creativity studies and great innovators' life stories.

In chapters 3 through 6, each chapter starts with an introduction about an early-life story of an innovator and how his or her early creative climates nurtured his or her creative attitudes and creative-thinking skills. In each chapter, step 1 shows research findings about how to cultivate creative climates:

Chapter 3, "The Soil Climate That Nurtures the Soil Attitudes": This chapter features Albert Einstein, who changed the way we see the universe; and it shows how parents and teachers of innovators (PTIs) cultivate the soil climates (diverse resources and experiences).

Chapter 4, "The Sun Climate That Nurtures the Sun Attitudes": Here we learn about Apple cofounder Steve Jobs, who made computers a part of everyday human experience; and how PTIs cultivate the sun climates (inspiration and encouragement).

Chapter 5, "The Storm Climate That Nurtures the Storm Attitudes": In this chapter we meet Nelson Mandela, who created democratic South Africa from a community that existed only in his imagination; and we see how PTIs cultivate the storm climates (high expectations and challenges).

Chapter 6, "The Space Climate That Nurtures the Space Attitudes": Here we study Georgia O'Keefe, who separated American modernism from imitative European art and pioneered a woman's artistic career in a man's world; and we see how PTIs cultivate the space climates (freedom to be alone and unique).

In chapters 3 through 6, step 2 is about nurturing creative attitudes: Step 2 starts with a brief anecdote from my life, illustrating how my own creative attitudes were encouraged or discouraged, or how I encouraged or discouraged these attitudes within my children. Then I summarize what research says about each of the attitudes and how each can contribute to creative-thinking skills. Finally, the end of each chapter presents examples from the innovators' lives to show how each of the attitudes seems negative.

PART 3: HOW DO CULTURAL CLIMATES AFFECT CREATIVITY?

Chapter 7, "Are Men Really More Creative Than Women Are?" shows the impact of gender bias on women's creativity. I use the life stories of Marie Curie (the first woman to win a Nobel Prize) and Mileva Marić (Albert Einstein's first wife) to understand its complexities and impacts. I compare how Curie's 4S climates nurtured her creativity and how Marić's patriarchal climates stifled her creativity. This can explain why Curie won two Nobel prizes while Marić's creativity was trampled, despite the fact that both were bright and rare female physicists with high creative potentials and early achievements.

Chapter 8, "Are Jews Really More Creative Than Asians Are?" explores how parenting/teaching in different cultures impacts creativity. I consider two specific parenting/teaching styles: Confucian (including "tiger-mother" parenting) and Jewish. I show how Confucian 4P parenting/

teaching affects Asians' creativity and how Jewish 4S parenting/teaching influences Jews' creativity. The differences between the two parenting/teaching styles explain why Jews have won a Nobel Prize 625 times more than Asians have.

PART 4: WHAT ARE CREATIVE-THINKING SKILLS?

Chapter 9, "ION Thinking Skills (Inbox, Outbox, and Newbox) within the ACP (Apple-Tree Creative Process),": focuses on creative process and creative-thinking skills. I present my Apple-tree Creative Process (ACP) that consists of four seasons (with eight stages):

1. Winter (stage 1: expertise development; and stage 2: needs identification)
2. Spring (stage 3: idea generation; stage 4: subconscious processing; and stage 5: idea evaluation)
3. Summer (stage 6: synthesis; and stage 7: transformation); and
4. Autumn (stage 8: promotion). I also present my ION thinking skills: inbox, outbox, and newbox. Both ACP and ION thinking skills emerged from my extensive analyses of creativity-test scores and empirical studies and theories of creativity and intelligence.

I believe this book can reverse the creativity crisis and recapture American innovation.

PART 1

WHAT IS CREATIVITY?

Chapter 1

THE CREATIVITY CRISIS

On July 10, 2010, a *Newsweek* cover story revealing my research on creativity "dropped like a bomb," as a newsletter at the University of Georgia put it.[1] As soon as the article—"The Creativity Crisis in America" by Po Bronson and Ashley Merryman—was published, scores of reporters wanted to interview me, spawning a flood of articles and news stories. The media frenzy was caused by my research finding that creativity in America was decreasing. According to *Newsweek*, "Kim found creativity scores had been steadily rising, just like IQ scores, until 1990. Since then, creativity scores have consistently inched downward." The article also explained how I found this decline was most serious among a particular group of individuals—children enrolled in kindergarten through sixth grade.[2]

To say that I, a college professor, was completely unprepared for the outpouring of interest in my research, sparked by a single magazine article, would be putting it lightly. But I had clearly touched a raw nerve within the American psyche—one that continues to be a sore spot today.

THE DECLINE OF CREATIVITY IN AMERICA

The study that triggered all this media attention was my analysis of 272,599 creativity-test scores using the Torrance Tests of Creative Thinking (TTCT for short). The TTCT is the most commonly used creativity test.[3] My analysis spanned individuals from kindergartners through adults, between the years 1966 and 2008, in all regions of America and some regions of Canada. The study demonstrated that creativity scores of Americans rose steadily from 1966 until 1990. After 1990, however, their creativity scores started significantly declining, while IQ scores continued to rise.[4]

The bottom line is this: Americans are less creative today than they were twenty-five years ago. Furthermore, this decline continues with no end in sight—Americans continue to become less creative over time. My analysis broke down each creative attitude and creative thinking individually, showing decreases in a variety of different aspects of creativity such as the attitudes or skills to:[5]

- Generate a large number of unique ideas
- Deal with hidden aspects of problems
- Work out the meaningful details of ideas
- Think in the big picture and distill ideas without losing essence
- Connect seemingly irrelevant ideas
- Articulate ideas and be a storyteller
- Be open-minded to opposing views and delay judgment
- Courageously defy or change existing norms, values, or traditions

To me, the most troubling aspect of this decreasing creativity is its prevalence in young children who should be actually improving their creative attitudes and skills. Not only that, but years after the study came out—despite all the concerns expressed by politicians, educators, and business executives—not much has changed. In fact, the decline in creativity continues unabated. My research shows that America has an increasingly limited number of individuals who are capable of finding and implementing solutions to problems the nation faces today. If this trend isn't reversed soon, America will be unable to tackle the challenges of the future.

Some argue that the fundamental structures that originally supported innovation in America are unchanged, and that the decrease in the number of creative individuals is an anomaly that will have no impact on America's global economic dominance.

I disagree. In the twentieth century, no other country in the world matched the United States of America's ability to turn ideas into innovative solutions to real-world problems. The country became a superpower thanks to the creativity of its people. This creativity was present in 1879 when Thomas Edison filed his light-bulb patent; in 1895 when Nikola Tesla partnered with General Electric to install electricity generators at Niagara Falls—the origin of today's home electricity; in 1927 when Philo Farnsworth *introduced* the electronic television; in 1958 when Jack Kilby *introduced* the integrated circuit; in 1971 when John Blankenbaker *intro-*

duced the first personal computer; and in 2001 when Apple *introduced* the iPod. (None of them really *invented*; they synthesized *existing* ideas, which they transformed into a new creation.)

Creativity is the key to creating highly skilled jobs and technological breakthroughs for future US economic success in international markets.[6] Without it, the economy will struggle to adapt to the changing world that moves quickly beyond its control; the next Apple, IBM, Google, Amazon, Microsoft, or General Electric will struggle to gain traction, as businesses in other creative countries gain momentum.

THE CREATIVITY CRISIS IN INDIVIDUALS

If America's parenting and educational system continuously condition children to think un-creatively, employers will struggle to hire creative individuals to solve real-world problems and create new opportunities. A significant part of America's economic success has been the result of dynamic young entrepreneurs who serve as incubators for new products or services. Creative individuals who are dreamers and risk takers are needed to keep this sector burgeoning, providing jobs and establishing entirely new industries.

Human beings have an unprecedented ability and potential to create, and many find that in the act of creating they fulfill their true purpose in life. It's this creative process that led to the invention of the simple hammer. The first hammers were simply stones attached to sticks with strips of leather and used to strike wood and animals. Much later, hammers were developed to drive nails into wood—and then clawed hammers, to easily remove them—thereby increasing the utility of this ancient tool. More recent variations include electric, hydraulic, or pneumatic hammers. The utility of the simple hammer continues to become more powerful and efficient. We expect and hope that hammers and other similar, simple tools will continuously evolve as human creativity enhances their design and utility.

When a hammer just sits in a toolbox and never gets used, it serves no purpose. Only when it is used to drive nails and build something—or demolish it—is the hammer fulfilling its purpose. It's the same with human beings. When people are able to express their creativity, they too are utilized to their full potential, which promotes their physical and psychological well-being.[7] When they use their creativity, they experience the joy of seeing their ideas and dreams become real. The excitement of artists or scientists engaged in unique and useful projects are vivid visions of creativity in action.

Individuals whose creativity is stifled become creative underachievers, frustrated, and unhappy with their lives.[8] Without a supportive climate, society is robbed of the potential achievements of those individuals. Despite all the innovation that has brought America to where it is today, the culture has changed in ways that have stifled creativity instead of encouraging it. America must reclaim what it does best: fostering creativity.

THE CAUSE OF THE CRISIS

The reporters who crowded on my front step after the *Newsweek* article had many questions for me, but mostly they wanted to know who was to blame for the latest American crisis. Unfortunately, there's no single person, entity, or institution that can be singled out. In fact, my research points to a gradual, society-wide shift away from the values that were the foundation of the American creativity. Understanding this shift starts with a look at what shaped American creativity in the first place.

The Home of the Brave

America was established initially by settlers who left behind everything they knew, including family, friends, churches, and businesses—in some cases escaping ideological oppression and tyrannical rule—in hopes of a better life. There were no guarantees that they would successfully find the new lives they were looking for after they arrived. They were risk takers and were optimistic that their hard work could create better futures. When others saw reason for doubt and feared the uncertainty of the future, they and subsequent generations of immigrants accepted uncertainty and saw opportunity. America assimilated newcomers better than most other countries, earning the "melting pot" characterization.[9] While each wave of newcomers initially faced harassment and exclusionary legislation—the Irish, the Eastern European Jews, the Chinese, the Italians, the Vietnamese, and others—most eventually became tightly interwoven within the American fabric. This multiculturalism contributed to America's creativity. Even today, immigrants arrive from across the globe, seeking a chance at *their* American dream.

The Founding Innovators

It's no accident that America became a beacon of freedom and opportunity. The Founding *Innovators* (not "Fathers"), including Thomas Jefferson, Alexander Hamilton, Benjamin Franklin, John and Abigail (woman) Adams, and Mercy Otis Warren (woman), built a foundation of entrepreneurial and legal systems that minimized corruption while protecting intellectual property. Subsequently, the early parenting and educational system reflected values important to American creativity, such as intellectual diversity, curiosity, risk taking, and nonconformity. The emergence of America's great entrepreneurial culture encouraged exponential innovation and economic growth.

Sputnik—Space-Age Competition for Creativity

American creativity accelerated after the Soviet Union successfully launched *Sputnik 1* in 1957, the first satellite to orbit Earth. America was humiliated, and its entire scientific and educational system came under intense scrutiny. Concerned for its national survival, leaders urgently sought a plausible explanation and decided that, compared to the Soviet Union, America suffered a lack of creativity in science and engineering. As a result, in the 1960s, federal research and development (R & D) spending was boosted to the highest level in America's history, above 2 percent of the gross domestic product (GDP). (Unfortunately, this amount has since decreased to just 0.78% of GDP as of 2014.[10])

During the 1960s, the American educational system followed suit, investing heavily in science and engineering education.[11] Students were eager to learn these subjects, not simply to get good grades, but to create something unique: technology to conquer the high frontier and explore space. Also, research-based teaching methods for fostering students' creativity were integrated into the US educational system. As a result, teaching methods changed from a teacher-controlled approach to a teacher-student interactive approach, which increased creativity from the mid-1960s to the mid-1980s.[12]

Americans' Insecurity

In the mid-1980s, America shifted into an age of creativity insecurity. *Domestic* insecurity (a desire for financial security and maintaining the status quo, instead of continuing to evolve) and *international* insecurity (a fear of global economic competition) have caused America's creativity to decline since then.[13]

Domestic Insecurity

As middle-class financial security becomes harder to achieve, American parents are more protective of their children and want them to pursue secure careers rather than follow their creative potential.[14] (They used to value children's imagination and originality.)[15] Today, education is seen primarily as a stepping-stone to a safe or lucrative career. Most of today's young Americans—64 percent—see "getting rich" as the single most important goal in life.[16]

Another indication of the decline in creativity in America is the decline in private and public R & D funds. The scientific and technological advances—which led to America's ability to create new industries and jobs, improve quality of life for all its citizens, and ensure its national security—were due to the outcomes of R & D. However, from 2000 to 2012, America increased its average annual R & D only 2.3 percent, while Asian countries increased theirs significantly: China (17.6 percent), South Korea (8.8 percent), Taiwan (7.7 percent), and Singapore (6.5 percent).[17] By 2019, China is expected to spend more on R & D than America is.[18] One result of the reduced US R & D spending is that the percentage of US inventors' patents in the US patent office dropped (from 57 to 49 percent) from 1996 to 2014, mainly due to the increased percentage of *Asian* inventors' patents.[19] China has become the number one country with patents in the World Intellectual Property Organization.[20]

US federal spending on R & D declined (15.4 percent) from 2010 to 2015—with spending on defense R & D declining the most (24.1 percent).[21] This is unfortunate considering the fact that defense R & D is important not only to national security, but also to the American economy through civilianized spin-off technology. Many innovative technologies were originally developed by the various military branches and organizations, such as the Defense Advanced Research Projects Agency (DARPA).[22] Some of DARPA's innovations, including the Internet, Global Positioning Systems (GPS), real-time speech translation, driverless cars, unmanned aerial vehicles, and invisible stealth aircraft, have made a huge impact on the American (and global) economy.[23] Many innovations developed by defense R & D began in someone's imagination, through science-fiction novels, movies, or video games, which were transformed into innovation through American creativity in engineering, business, and promotion skills.

Another indication of the decline in creativity in America is the decline in college and university research funds over the past two decades. The number of basic research articles published by US researchers in peer-reviewed journals has declined.[24] Budget cuts force the National Institutes of Health (NIH) to reject half of the high-quality research proposals it receives each year.[25] Even worse, the more creative a proposal for a grant is, the more likely it will be rejected, because funding agencies are reluctant to take risks with limited budgets.[26] This leads many of America's creative, young scientists to consider careers in foreign countries, including China, that have increased their investment in science.[27] Over the past decade, while the United States decreased funding for basic research, China increased its funding threefold.[28]

International Insecurity

During the twentieth century, America's strong economy championed globalization, spreading democratic and free-market values around the world. As the rest of the world developed, however, globalization led to increased competition. During the second half of the twentieth century, Asia emerged as America's greatest economic competitor and threat. Starting in the 1970s and reaching a fevered pitch in the brief US recession of the earlier 1980s, many Americans became afraid. They were afraid of Japanese competition, afraid of changes in American society, and afraid that Americans were falling behind the rest of the world.[29] Because of Japan's perceived economic success at the time, some American educational experts urged learning from or even copying the Japanese educational system.[30] The Georgia Department of Education, for example, revised its mathematics curricula to be more like curricula in Japan, as did others.[31] However, when the Japanese economy stalled during the late 1980s, Americans shifted their anxieties from Japan to other economies that were growing fast at the time. Today, China's economy is growing at such a rapid pace that Americans are once again afraid. This fear has led some to take a deeper look at the source of Asian academic achievements.[32]

ASIAN AND ASIAN AMERICAN ACHIEVEMENTS

The results of international assessments show that Asian students fifteen years and older consistently attain higher scores in reading, mathematics, and science than US students of the same age. Out of sixty-five participating countries, US students were seventeenth in reading, twenty-third in science, and thirty-first in mathematics; whereas China, South Korea, Hong Kong, and Singapore all ranked within the top five in these subjects.[33]

 Asian success has led Americans to examine their way of doing things in America, especially where educational paradigms merge: Asian students in American schools. Asian American students are outpacing other ethnic groups in academic achievement. As of 2006, Asian American students were over-represented (relative to their numbers in the population) in gifted/talented programs in forty-one of the fifty US states.[34] The Asian American college enrollment rate is also higher than that of non-Asian students. Based on the 2010 census, 52 percent of Asian Americans attended college or attained a graduate degree, while only 30 percent of whites did the same.[35] Further, Asian American students receive more advanced degrees in America than their population numbers would indicate. In 2010, Asian students accounted for 45 percent of doctorates in engineering, 38 percent of doctorates in mathematics and computer sciences, 33 percent of doctorates in the physical sciences, and 25 percent of those in the life sciences.[36]

 More Asian and Asian American students become spelling-bee winners, math wizards, and music prodigies than do non-Asian students. Asian Americans are most likely to fulfill occupations such as doctors, lawyers, or engineers. Despite being only 5.8 percent of the American population, statistics indicate that Asian Americans come from more stable home environments, go to better schools, and get better jobs than non-Asian Americans.[37]

So, flooded with data showing the academic prowess of Asians and Asian Americans, it's no surprise that US politicians and educational leaders decided that the best policy to address their *insecurity* was to emulate educational systems and culture from Asian countries.

AMERICA TAKES (THE WRONG) ACTION

Faced with an Asian populace that was significantly outperforming non-Asian Americans in so many different ways, US politicians and educational leaders concluded that the education system was broken and required a quick and dramatic change. Instead of focusing on outcompeting Asian countries in terms of creativity, however, they took a shortsighted action to *emulate* Asian education, and a flurry of supporting legislation soon followed: Former president Bill Clinton called for national education standards in 1997. Former president George W. Bush announced the No Child Left Behind (NCLB) Act in 2001. President Barack Obama announced the Common Core State Standards ("Common Core") with a federal grant program dubbed "Race to the Top" as a continuation of NCLB. These laws continue to exert immense pressure in American classrooms today.[38]

NCLB's stated goal is to ensure that *all* students receive high-quality education, and thereby to close the achievement gap between advantaged and disadvantaged students. It requires public schools to make Annual Measureable Objectives (AMOs) on state standardized tests in reading/language arts and mathematics for all children in grades three through eight—and once during high school—and then to report the test results.[39] If schools don't reach their AMOs for three consecutive years, state-approved "experts" are sent to the schools to implement *quick fixes* meant to get the schools on track. Schools are rewarded or punished through federal funds, and NCLB has become the most controlling and intrusive federal educational policy in American history.[40] The major result of these laws is a heavy-handed *test-centric* climate in schools.[41] (In a sad bit of irony, I left Korea with a hope that my children wouldn't experience the *exam hell*[42] of Asian education.) The legislation is generating outcomes that will haunt Americans for many years to come.

Focusing on Standardized Tests Instead of Standards

Today, the state-mandated standardized tests—rather than the state educational standards (Common Core)—exert the greatest pressure on classroom teaching practices.[43] Standardized tests don't measure everything,
and anything they don't measure—like creativity—becomes unimportant
in the classroom. To make sure their schools get proper funding, teachers
focus only on teaching the material included in the state-mandated tests.[44]
This naturally channels more time to tested subjects (reading/language arts
and mathematics), at the expense of non-tested subjects (such as science,
social studies, the humanities, physical education, arts, and foreign languages)[45] and reducing or eliminating recess.[46] NCLB also pushes English-
only acquisition and discourages preserving students' native language.
This runs counter to other nations' focus on language diversity to increase
global collaboration.[47]

Because schools are increasingly evaluated using students' performance on these inauthentic assessments (which don't measure *application* of what they've learned to a new situation), teachers have to teach to
the tests instead of utilizing more holistic real-world projects or assessments. Teachers squander time teaching test-taking skills, using previously
released questions provided by the state.[48] Schools are pressured to switch
to multiple-choice tests in all subjects, and students are molded into test
takers who only know how to fill in bubble choices.[49]

Leaving Disadvantaged Students Farther Behind

The decrease in time spent on non-tested subjects is especially harmful to
disadvantaged students who are already behind (those in poverty, minorities, the learning disabled, or those who have limited English skills). It
harms disadvantaged students in four ways:[50] First, because they must
devote extra time preparing for the tests, they have less opportunity to
actually master a subject or learn skills that help them in the long run.
Second, because they just memorize facts that are readily accessible with
today's computers and devices, they won't be competitive in the information age. Third, because they're not allowed to participate in enriched programs, they have less opportunity to find topics of curiosity or interest that

might lead to a lifelong passion. Finally, focusing on only tested subjects ignores developing the *whole* child, which inhibits teachers from incorporating multiple intelligences (such as music-smart, number-smart, body-smart, word-smart, picture-smart, people-smart, and nature-smart).[51] The lack of whole-child teaching further limits opportunities for disadvantaged students to learn according to their strengths or preferred learning styles. Ironically, spending extra time preparing for tested subjects harms the students that NCLB is supposed to help the most.

On a worldwide scale of funding for education, America is just average, especially with little funding devoted to instructional resources.[52] (In Asian countries, instructional resources, including teacher professional development, are highly funded. Teachers are highly respected and given better pay and financial incentives, and thus teaching careers are highly competitive.)[53] Since NCLB, ironically, the percentage of funds allocated for instructional resources actually *decreased*.[54] Because NCLB has been wasting money on the quick fixes, it hasn't supported real teacher professional development.[55] But teachers are forced to take on the responsibility for students' low scores, despite the fact that students' disadvantaged background has *four times* more impact on their scores than does their school's characteristics.[56] By age three, children from disadvantaged family backgrounds have heard thirty million fewer words (1,251 words per hour) than children from advantaged family backgrounds (2,153 words per hour), which predicts their achievement in school and standardized testing at age ten.[57] Using a one-size-to-fit-all yardstick, NCLB considers neither students' initial proficiency nor schools' initial standing when sanctioning schools that fail to meet the AMOs.[58] The sanctioned schools are those that work with the most disadvantaged students, which NCLB ends up punishing instead of supporting. Further, these schools are forced to spend an *even greater* proportion of money on administrative and testing-related expenses, instead of instructional resources.[59] Over time, their dependence on federal funding makes them even more bureaucratic, which not only limits schools' autonomy and creativity but also makes them even less responsive to their students' needs and decreases their students' test scores.[60]

Turning Teaching Professionals into Teaching Technicians or Even Cheaters

The legislation reduced teachers' autonomy over decisions such as curriculum adoption and teaching practices.[61] It also forces teaching practices that are inconsistent with teachers' own educational practices and enriched activities.[62] NCLB shapes what's taught in school, how it's taught, and in what language it is taught.[63] Teachers are given scripts for exact teaching—which turns teaching professionals into teaching technicians who follow predetermined and prescribed sets of rules.[64] Even worse, the legislation turns educators into cheaters. In 2015, for example, under extreme pressure to produce quick results, 178 teachers, principals, and district administrators in Atlanta school districts cheated by changing student answers on standardized tests to boost the scores.[65]

Improving Test-Taking Skills Instead of Achievement

Increases in achievement scores have been negligible while the costs to creativity are significant, measurable, and dire. In fact, NCLB has neither improved students' learning, nor reduced the achievement gap, leaving disadvantaged students even farther behind.[66] If some students' scores have increased, the actual reason may be that their test-taking skills have increased rather than their learning;[67] or it is that the tests have been made much easier than before.[68] More recently, in December 2015, the new legislation replaced NCLB with the Every Student Succeeds Act (ESSA) in order to "fix" NCLB problems. However, ESSA still focuses on testing mandates, and it just shifted from the federal control to the state control with a lot of fuzzy states' responsibilities.[69] Focusing only on increasing students' test scores and test-taking skills (instead of on developing their full creative potential) turns students into human bonsai trees. Bonsai trees are ornamentally shaped trees that are artificially pruned and wired, preventing them from reaching their full size. Likewise, American children are now pruned and wired to be un-creative, preventing them from reaching their full potential. The strengths that helped make America great have been "bonsaied," and the current test-centric climate is causing long-lasting, detrimental effects.

AMERICA IN FIFTY YEARS?

Following the worst trend line in creativity fifty years into the future, I can imagine a news article in 2066 like this:

Creativity Lost: America Left Behind

Like many short-lived, media-driven fads, Americans became bored with the so-called Creativity Crisis that erupted in the early years of this century, and it quickly faded into the background of Americans' collective consciousness.

Unfortunately, pretending the Creativity Crisis didn't exist didn't make it go away, in fact, it only got worse. In retrospect, this should really be no surprise. Instead of focusing their energy on becoming innovators, Americans were happy to become consumers of excess—choosing the gratification that comes from short-term pleasures over the hard work and sweat required to attain long-term goals. Many children became dependent on social media like never before—searching smartphones and computer screens for answers instead of experimenting and trying things own their own.

American parents and educators colluded to make children mentally weaker and more dependent than ever before. Instead of challenging children to confront a problem and sort through options to address it, they required rote learning. This produced a workforce unprepared for new jobs in the fast-moving, dynamic business world. These jobs required creative-thinking skills, which were sadly lacking within the US workforce. So instead of hiring American workers, companies hired workers from Asia—young men and women who not only cost less to hire but also were better educated and more creative than the majority of Americans.

One of the new economic stars was China. The Chinese copied the creative climates, creative attitudes, and creative-thinking skills that had once made America great, while the Americans copied Asian education methods—to their downfall. As China's economy rose, the Chinese government became less primitive and corrupt. At the same time, Chinese people continued their obsessive pursuit of expertise with the important addition of creativity. Although Americans became good test takers, Asians became better innovators. Without innovation, America was no longer able to compete in the world arena.

This glimpse of America's future doesn't have to happen. America has the power to recapture its innovation in the world. Each American can make a difference, starting right now.

AMERICA MOVING FORWARD

Creativity is declining; something must be done. The next chapter reveals the nature of creativity and presents the creative CATs (climates, attitudes, and thinking skills) to achieve innovation. They show three practical steps for cultivating creative climates, nurturing creative attitudes, and applying creative-thinking skills. Parents and educators can guide children to recapture the innovation that's being tested out of them.

Chapter 2

THE CREATIVITY SOLUTION

As a scientist, I make conclusions based on research. As an Asian, however, I'm superstitious. For example, I avoid the number four, which indicates the Chinese character death—many buildings in East Asia have no fourth floor for this reason. I never look into a broken mirror. I don't understand how fortune cookies work, but I trust that they do.

I started studying creativity because I had a life-changing experience with a fortuneteller, whom I also believe in, along with most Asians. One day an old man who had a long, grey beard and was dressed in a white Korean traditional costume and carrying a cane approached me. He told me that I'd have two very important children—because he knew I had two birthmarks in a certain area of my body—and that my children would contribute to the betterment of the world. I felt that he wasn't just looking into a crystal ball; he was reading my soul!

It wasn't a simple premonition. First, it meant I'd have at least two children. But until the mysterious man spoke to me, having children hadn't even crossed my mind. Second, for his premonition to come true, I'd have to be a good parent. I knew nothing about that, other than how my parents raised me. I started researching parenting so that I'd have the necessary skills to be a good parent. I read hundreds of books on both Korean and American parenting, which included many contradictory theories, ideas, and techniques. Eventually I began exploring the findings in scientific research studies in order to provide clear guidance for myself. Through this research, I learned a lot about intelligence, which led to my study of Nobel laureates because I discovered they contributed to the betterment of the world. This led to my deeper study of creativity because I found high intelligence isn't necessary to win a Nobel Prize or accomplish innovation, but creativity *is* necessary. Intelligence and creativity aren't the same.[1] My first study of a Nobel laureate was Marie Curie.

In time, I did have two children, just like the fortuneteller's premonition.

My goal was to raise them to be creative, so that they might have a chance of making great contributions to the world. This is when I encountered the challenges of teaching creativity. The actual act of teaching creativity isn't particularly difficult, but there's a lot of misinformation about what and how to teach children in order for them to become creative. Misinformation about creativity must be dispelled because it causes people to waste time on ineffective methods or prevents them from even trying. For example, if people believed the world was flat, they'd not dare to venture out to sea to discover unknown lands. If children believe that creativity is only a flash of brilliance from gods or by geniuses, or if they believe only artists are creative, they might not even try to explore their own creative potential.

Over the years I weeded through the overwhelming amount of misinformation as well as valuable knowledge. In the process, I've developed models to understand and teach creativity based on science, instead of traditions, superstitions, or false presumptions. Before I present the creative CATs, we should explore what I mean by "creativity" and "innovation."

WHAT IS CREATIVITY?

In the Western world, many people think that creativity is primarily artistic in nature—like painting a landscape, choreographing a dance, or writing a poem—and the terms *creative* and *artistic* are often used interchangeably.[2] In the Eastern world, however, creativity is considered to be scientific discoveries or inventions such as electricity, antibiotics, or the computer.[3] Overall, though, creativity is far broader than either of these interpretations. Creativity is making or doing something *unique* and *useful*. It is a *process* that leads to innovation in *all* fields. Creativity occurs in all social endeavors, including the arts, sciences, mathematics, engineering, medicine, business, leadership, parenting, teaching, and sports.[4]

WHAT IS INNOVATION?

Innovation is a *unique* and *useful* concept, intellectual property, invention, product, or service that results from a creative process. I say *unique* instead of *new* because nothing under the sun is really new. Every product is developed as an extension or a combination of existing ideas.[5] For example, Apple creates and releases the latest model of its iPhone, which actually consists of *existing* technologies combined in a unique way. This is innovation. Then, Samsung analyzes the iPhone and quickly synthesizes/transforms and sells a different-model phone that's better in some aspects. This is *also* innovation. The degree of uniqueness in both cases depends on whom you ask.

People may come up with many *unique* ideas, but unless they're applied in some way, they remain just ideas in the frustrated dreamer's head and are thus not *useful*, and not an innovation. An innovation must be unique *and* useful. For example, when an artist with great technical skills creates a realistic scene or replicates a popular style, it is *useful*, but is not unique. When an artist develops a technique for using materials differently or infusing emotions or ideas into a visible artifact, it is *unique*. An artist who can do both can become an innovator.

Innovation can be either tangible or intangible. Steve Jobs' creation of the iPhone and Georgia O'Keeffe's paintings are *tangible* innovations. Nelson Mandela's democracy for South Africa and Albert Einstein's relativity theory are *intangible* innovations. Both tangible and intangible must be unique and useful to others and/or the society to be considered an innovation.

Innovation ranges from small i to Big I.[6] *Small i* innovation examples are easy to come by. Their impact on the society is small, and they are created in everyday life, often without knowing it. When a chef puts together different ingredients and make a unique dish without following a recipe—a delicious dish that many customers appreciate (and thus useful)—is a *small i* example.

Big I Innovation occurs when an innovation affects the society in a big way. *Big I* Innovation examples include Nobel laureates' contributions to human knowledge and capability, such as Curie's discovery of radioactivity (1903); Einstein's discovery of the photoelectric effect (1921); and Mandela's ending of South Africa's Apartheid and leading a peaceful revolution to democracy (1993).

Both *small i* and *Big I* are important, yet the relative impact (*Im*) of an innovation can be determined, where $Im = T$ (time in years) $\times N$ (number of others affected). For example, if my unique creativity-development model is useful for 100 people's parenting or teaching for ten years, the impact of the innovation is 1,000 (*small i*). If the model is useful for 1,000,000 people for ten years, the impact of the innovation is 10,000,000 (*Big I*).

CREATIVE CATS
(CLIMATES, ATTITUDES, AND THINKING SKILLS)

Let's explore my creative CATs model to better understand the nature of creativity and, more important, how to best teach it to children. One of the reasons for the name *CATs* is that creativity is literally related to *cats*. More creative people identify as "cat people" rather than as "dog people," or they choose to own cats rather than dogs.[7] Perhaps creative people are too busy creating or traveling to take a dog out for a walk? Perhaps they're curious or independent like cats? (But hopefully not to the degree in the saying "curiosity killed the cat"—phrases like this actually kill curiosity; instead, say, "curiosity makes good cats," because curious cats are actually good at testing limits and determining what's harmful *or* beneficial.)

Another reason for the name is that CATs stands for three practical steps for innovation. They are: cultivate creative *Climates* (step 1); nurture creative *Attitudes* (step 2); and develop creative-*Thinking skills* (step 3). As Figure 2.1 shows, the *climate* is represented by the circle that surrounds the cactus, which nurtures the *attitude* represented at the heart of the cactus, which in turn develops the *thinking skills* represented at the mind of the cactus, which results in *innovation*, represented by the flowers of the cactus.

Figure 2.1. Creative CATs
(Climates, Attitudes, and Thinking Skills)

Step 1. The 4S Climates (Soil, Sun, Storm, and Space)

Surprisingly, the most critical part of a creative process is the *climate*, rather than the creation or the creator.[8] Fortunately, climates are the part parents and educators have the most control over. I use the term "climates" instead of "environments" because they're broader than the external, physical surroundings. Climates include both physical *and* psychological surroundings and conditions that influence individuals (including relationships, location, time period, etc.). The climates influence how individuals think and behave, including encouraging their creative potential (which promotes their emotional and psychological health[9]) or discouraging it.[10] Climates also include sources of feedback or evaluation for a final creation, which determines whether the creation is worthwhile. Only when the creation is recognized and valued by others/the society does it become an innovation.[11]

Diverse soil, bright sun, fierce storms, and free space are necessary for plants to grow strong and flourish. Similarly, 4S climates, first soil, second sun, third storm, and finally space climates in this order, are necessary for children's creativity to grow strong and flourish, as figure 2.2 shows.

1. Soil
(Diverse Resources & Experiences)

2. Sun
(Inspiration & Encouragement)

3. Storm
(High Expectations & Challenges)

4. Space
(Freedom to Be Alone & Unique)

Figure 2.2. 4S Climates (Soil, Sun, Storm, and Space)

The Diverse Soil Climate

First, the diverse soil climate provides individuals with *diverse resources and experiences*. "Resources" includes exposure and access to all kinds of diversity—things, people, knowledge, and views (rather than just financial resources). The soil climate also teaches individuals how to access and grow new resources instead of just consuming what's already available. Diverse soil is vital for plants' growth; one element can't compensate for another's deficiency. For individuals, an open-minded climate leads to thought-provoking experiences and conflicting and complex views from insiders and outsiders. Plants have greater fruiting success if their location enables cross-pollination with other plants. Likewise, resourceful individuals become more successful if their climate enables face-to-face interactions and collaborations with others.

When the soil climate initially nurtures young individuals' soil attitudes, they can encounter diverse subjects. The diverse soil climate is discussed in detail in chapter 3.

The Bright Sun Climate

Second, after the diverse soil climate, the bright sun climate *inspires and encourages* individuals. Sunlight attracts plants; inspirational figures and events attract individuals' optimistic curiosity. This nurtures their love of reading and learning. The sun shines on the *entire* world—even the most remote corner. Likewise, inspiring figures and events show the big picture and unlimited possibilities to individuals and draw them out of limited situations. Just as the sun gives plants warmth and energy, the sun climate gives individuals encouragement and excitement by inspiring and *playfully* introducing them to new subjects.

When the sun climate initially nurtures young individuals' sun attitudes, they can find a specific curiosity, preference, or interest (CPI) in a subject. The bright sun climate is discussed in detail in chapter 4.

The Fierce Storm Climate

Third, after the diverse soil and bright sun climates, the fierce storm climate provides individuals with *high expectations and challenges*. Gardeners set high expectations for plants to produce their maximum blossoms/fruits. Likewise, the storm climate sets high expectations for individuals to utilize their maximum potential. Gardeners prune early and consistently to prevent plants from growing out of control. Similarly, the storm climate early and consistently provides *both* positive and negative feedback to instill self-discipline and self-efficacy in individuals. Heavy winds and rain help plants grow stronger, just as challenges and adversity help individuals develop competitive skills to apply to increasingly difficult challenges.

When the storm climate initially nurtures young individuals' storm attitudes, they can develop useful expertise in a subject, which turns their CPI into a passion; only *after* they are truly good at something can it become a passion! The fierce storm climate is discussed in detail in chapter 5.

The Free Space Climate

Finally, after the diverse soil, bright sun, and fierce storm climates, the free space climate provides individuals with *freedom to be alone and unique.* Gardeners expect and respect that each plant will be different. In a similar vein, the space climate expects and respects that individuals will develop according to their own CPI. Gardeners provide plants with time and space to grow to their own shape and full size, and the space climate provides individuals with time and space to develop their uniqueness and grow to their full potential.

When the space climate initially nurtures young individuals' space attitudes, they can develop unique ideas based on their expertise. The free space climate is discussed in detail in chapter 6.

Step 2. The 4S Attitudes (Soil, Sun, Storm, and Space)

Attitudes—the ways individuals *react* to the climates—are also important. The soil climate introduces individuals to diverse people, cultures, religions, and opinions, but they must be *curious* or interested in some of the experiences in order to benefit from them. Two individuals exposed to the same climate may react differently, depending on their creative attitudes. Creative attitudes are individuals' characteristics, beliefs, and visions that compel them to create, which enable their creative-thinking skills.[12] I use the term "attitudes" instead of "personality" because attitudes are more *teachable* than personality is. About 40 to 55 percent of adult personality is inherited, but attitudes are less genetic and more changeable than personality is.[13]

The twenty-seven 4S attitudes (five soil, six sun, eight storm, and eight space attitudes) mirror the 4S climates. Attitudes are mainly influenced or changed by climates. This means that parents and educators can nurture children's creative attitudes by cultivating the 4S climates. Not every innovator possesses all twenty-seven of the attitudes, but the greatest innovators do. These attitudes predict innovation in *all* fields.[14] However, each of the attitudes might seem negative to some people.[15] Whether, why, and how these attitudes enable innovators' creative-thinking skills are discussed in chapters 3 (soil), 4 (sun), 5 (storm), and 6 (space) in detail.

The Five Soil Attitudes

The five soil attitudes are characterized by individuals' open and complex minds that best utilize resources. The soil attitudes help individuals become *resourceful cross-pollinators*, which enables their creative-thinking skills.

(1) The *open-minded* attitude involves considering others' views that are different from one's own. It's developed by early diverse experiences including exposure to other cultures. But open-minded individuals might seem "distracted" to some people.

(2) Having the *bicultural* attitude means embracing new cultures while maintaining one's own cultural identity. It's developed by *learning* from other cultures, and it matures by seeking diverse mentors. But bicultural individuals might seem "rootless" to some people.

(3) The *mentored* attitude comes from being mutually interested in and taught by experts and their constructive criticism. It's developed by individuals' trusting others and being *teachable*. Mentors share their expertise with mentees and guide them in developing mentees' own. Mentors and bicultural experiences help individuals understand complex views. But mentored individuals might seem "channeled" to some people.

(4) The *complexity-seeking* attitude is characterized by embracing equivocal and conflicting views. It's refined by dealing with or solving increasingly complex situations/problems, and it helps find and analyze unique opportunities. But complexity-seeking individuals might seem "overcomplicated" to some people.

(5) Having the *resourceful* attitude means finding and using all kinds of resources/opportunities effectively and efficiently to accomplish goals. It's developed by individuals' learning to prepare for or overcome financial, physical, or cultural challenges. But resourceful individuals might seem "opportunistic" to some people.

The Six Sun Attitudes

The six sun attitudes are characterized by individuals' self-inspiration and curiosity that sustain energy. Their sun attitudes help them become *curious optimists*, which enables creative-thinking skills.

(1) Having the *optimistic* attitude means seeing positive outcomes regardless of existing circumstances. It starts with positive attachment to others, which helps individuals confidently expand their world. But optimistic individuals might seem "unrealistic" to some people.

(2) The *big-picture-thinking* attitude comes from being inspired by others' words, deeds, or values and seeing the big picture beyond constraints. It draws individuals out of limited situations to pursue unlimited possibilities. Their optimistic and big-picture-thinking attitudes direct curiosity out toward the big world. But big-picture-thinking individuals might seem "dreamy" to some people.

(3) Having the *curious* attitude means thinking in a childlike manner and insatiably seeking new information. It leads individuals to unexpected opportunities, and it instills a desire to pursue them. But curious individuals might seem "annoying" to some people.

(4) Having the *spontaneous* attitude means being flexible and immediately acting on new ideas and opportunities. It starts with open-mindedness and curiosity, and it leads to playful approaches to experiences. But spontaneous individuals might seem "impulsive" to some people.

(5) Having the *playful* attitude means approaching situations in exploratory ways and seeing the lighter side of challenges. This helps sustain individuals' energy over time. But playful individuals might seem "mischievous" to some people.

(6) The *energetic* attitude comes from being motivated from within, regardless of external circumstances (by intense curiosity, self-inspiration, or other reasons). It starts with optimistic curiosity, and it sustains individuals' enthusiasm over time. But energetic individuals might seem "hyper" to some people.

The Eight Storm Attitudes

The eight storm attitudes are characterized by individuals' overcoming challenges and striving for goals. Their storm attitudes help them become *resilient hard workers*, which enables creative-thinking skills.

(1) Having the *independent* attitude means thinking and acting freely from others' influence, support, and control. It starts with thinking and doing things alone, and it helps individuals control their own behaviors. But independent individuals might seem "aloof" to some people.

(2) The *self-disciplined* attitude comes from individuals' motivating and controlling themselves to accomplish goals. It starts by adapting to existing expectations/limitations, and it develops by structuring their own situations while avoiding distractions and addictions. But self-disciplined individuals might seem "compulsive" to some people.

(3) Having the *diligent* attitude means exerting meticulous, steady attention to build skills to accomplish clear goals. It starts with self-discipline, and it results in skills necessary to pursue the goals. But diligent individuals might seem like "workaholics" to some people.

(4) The *self-efficacious* attitude comes from being confident to perform well on a *specific* task based on previous successful experiences. Self-efficacy (true confidence) across multiple areas builds individuals' resilience. But self-efficacious individuals might seem "arrogant" to some people.

(5) The *resilient* attitude comes from recovering and thriving after challenges or failures. It starts with self-efficacy and dedication to clear goals, and it helps develop skills that minimize the impact of setbacks or risks. But resilient individuals might seem "combative" to some people.

(6) Having the *risk-taking* attitude means leaving secure situations in pursuit of uncertain rewards. It starts with optimistic self-efficacy, and it develops as individuals plan for various outcomes. This helps them keep trying. But risk-taking individuals might seem "reckless" to some people.

(7) Having the *persistent* attitude means continuously striving for goals with commitment regardless of immediate rewards. It starts with individuals' self-efficacy and resilience, and it strengthens as they make progress toward their goals. But persistent individuals might seem "obsessive" to some people.

(8) Having the *uncertainty-accepting* attitude means acting without complete information regardless of potential challenges or outcomes. It helps individuals dare to attempt the impossible. But uncertainty-accepting individuals might seem "fearless" to some people.

The Eight Space Attitudes

The eight space attitudes are characterized by individuals' discovering and expressing their own uniqueness. Their space attitudes help them become *defiant dreamers*, which enables creative-thinking skills.

(1) Having the *emotional* attitude means recognizing, understanding, and expressing individuals' own feelings. It helps them communicate their own state of mind, and it develops empathy for others. But emotional individuals might seem "unstable" to some people.

(2) Having the *compassionate* attitude means internally empathizing with others and externalizing it by helping them in meaningful ways. It starts with understanding others and their situations and seeing the big picture. It helps individuals self-reflect about others' experiences and the big world. But compassionate individuals might seem "overreaching" to some people.

(3) Having the *self-reflective* attitude means enjoying solitude to understand the essence of individuals' own and others' experiences and views. It starts with enjoying time alone to work on goals, and it is facilitated by connecting with nature. It helps them be objective about their feelings and make their own choices autonomously. But self-reflective individuals might seem "withdrawn" to some people.

(4) Having the *autonomous* attitude means being independently and intrinsically motivated to pursue goals. It starts when individuals set

their own goals, and it matures as they enjoy achieving them. But autonomous individuals might seem "uncontrolled" to some people.

(5) Having the *daydreaming* attitude means sustaining unrealistic but goal-oriented thoughts while awake. It helps individuals disregard existing norms in their extemporaneous thoughts but capture useable aspects of the thoughts. But daydreaming individuals might seem "delusional" to some people.

(6) Having the *nonconforming* attitude means choosing to differ from mainstream patterns of thought and behavior. It develops by feeling comfortable being an outsider. It helps individuals reach their uniqueness beyond existing norms. But nonconforming individuals might seem "wild" to some people.

(7) Having the *gender-bias-free* attitude means rejecting stereotypes based on gender. It develops by using views and strengths from different genders. It opens the door to intellectual defiance across physical, financial, professional, and ethnic biases. But gender-bias-free individuals might seem "gender-free" to some people.

(8) Having the *defiant* attitude means courageously rejecting or changing existing norms, values, traditions, hierarchies, or authorities in order to pursue individuals' goals. Their defiance breaks the existing constraints, which enables them to see/do what others can't. But defiant individuals might seem "rebellious" to some people.

INNOVATORS' ATTITUDES: THE CACTUS AMONG US

Cacti exemplify attitudes of innovators and how they seem to others. People often admire both the cacti's ability to thrive in a desert and their flowers' vibrant colors. But people often do not want to be near cacti because their thorns (while necessary for the plants' survival) are painful to touch! Likewise, most people admire the achievements of innovators, but they often do not love the innovators themselves—especially when they are growing up—because their attitudes seem negative.

Soil attitudes—both cacti and innovators are resourceful cross-pollinators. Cacti learn to adapt to scare resources. They spread roots widely to capture miniscule moisture near the sandy surface and store water in porous or hollow trunks. They minimize water loss by opening stomata and blooming in cooler temperatures at night. Likewise, innovators learn to adapt to scarce resources by developing skills to seek out and find new resources to support their CPI. Cacti's sharp spines protect them from greedy predators but also provide protection for insects and birds that enrich their ecosystem. Cacti cluster together for protection against desert hardships. Likewise, innovators cross-pollinate with mentors and other experts to achieve innovation.

Sun attitudes—both cacti and innovators are curious optimists. Cacti enjoy the sunny side of life year-round. They optimistically draw curiosity and energy from the sun with their entire body and then multiply in sandy soil that other plants can't tolerate. Their vibrant, optimistic explosions of colorful blossoms transform an otherwise-bleak desert landscape into a rainbow of life, hope, and beauty. Likewise, innovators' optimism and insatiable curiosity turn challenges into opportunities and then innovation, which energizes themselves and others.

Storm attitudes—both cacti and innovators are resilient hard workers. Cacti become resilient by overcoming flash floods, lightning storms, fierce winds, dust devils, and locus swarms. They persistently protect trunks and roots with prickly spines and grow back when damaged. Likewise, by building self-efficacy, innovators withstand others' doubts and rejections and take risks to pursue their goals. Their resilience helps them consider setbacks and adversities as learning opportunities and overcome their flaws, weaknesses, and failures.

Space attitudes—both cacti and innovators are defiant dreamers. Cacti don't want to grow in flowerbeds with other plants and are content in a hot, dry desert. Nevertheless, cacti are compassionate oasis in the desert. From great distances, they guide insects, small animals, and thirsty travelers to shelter, food, and water stored in edible trunks. Likewise, innovators defy the crowd to pursue their goals and achieve what others can't even imagine. Their compassion to improve others' lives benefits the world and inspires future generations of innovators.

Step 3. ION Thinking Skills (Inbox, Outbox, and Newbox)

The 4S attitudes enable individuals' creative-thinking skills. Three ION thinking skills—inbox, outbox, and newbox—occur during the creative process, Apple-tree Creative Process (ACP). Inbox thinking is narrow and deep (inside the box) to gain or evaluate knowledge and skills; outbox thinking is quick and broad (outside the box) to imagine diverse possibilities; and newbox thinking combines elements of inbox and outbox thinking and transforms them into a new creation (new box). The soil and storm attitudes enable individuals' *useful* inbox and newbox thinking. The sun and space attitudes enable individuals' *unique* outbox and newbox thinking.

Inbox Thinking

Inbox thinking includes traditional ways of accomplishing tasks or choosing the right answer. Yet well-developed inbox thinking is essential for developing *expertise*—mastering a specific subject by understanding and applying knowledge and skills.[16] Expertise requires individuals to memorize, comprehend, and *apply* knowledge and skills. Inbox thinking also includes critical-thinking skills: analyzing and evaluating ideas that are generated later during outbox thinking. Inbox thinking works like a zoom lens that helps individuals zoom in on narrow knowledge and skills to look closely at details or evaluate them, which ensures usefulness of an idea or a creation.

Outbox Thinking

Outbox thinking is divergent or outside-the-box thinking that seeks nonconforming ideas. It generates fluent (*many spontaneously*), flexible (*different angles or kinds of*), and original (*novel*) ideas. Outbox thinking benefits from a readily accessible reservoir of expertise. It works like a wide-angle lens that helps individuals take a broad field of view and imagine many novel approaches to a problem or an opportunity, which ensures uniqueness of an idea or a creation.

Newbox Thinking

Newbox thinking combines elements of inbox and outbox thinking. It uses both the zoom and wide-angle lenses to uniquely combine/synthesize unrelated ideas and then usefully refine/transform the synthesized into a creation, which ensures both uniqueness and usefulness of the creation. Finally, newbox thinking promotes the creation so that it can be recognized as an innovation by others/the society.

4S Climates → 4S Attitudes → ION Thinking Skills

The 4S climates nurture the 4S attitudes in individuals so that they can apply ION thinking skills to accomplish innovation, as table 2.1 shows. Thus, innovation is dependent on individuals' creative climates, attitudes, and thinking skills (CATs), and it can be learned and practiced.[17] This is contrary to the common belief from both the East and the West that creativity is only a flash of brilliance from gods, geniuses, or artists.[18]

**Table 2.1. Relationships within the Creative CATs
(Climates, Attitudes, and Thinking Skills)**

CATs 4S	Climates (Climates facilitate individuals' initial creativity development)	Attitudes: Nurtured by Climates	Thinking Skills: Enabled by Attitudes
Soil	Diverse resources and experiences (help individuals encounter diverse subjects)	Open-minded, bicultural, mentored, complexity-seeking, and resourceful	*Useful* inbox and newbox thinking
Sun	Inspiration and encouragement (help individuals identify a specific CPI in a subject)	Optimistic, big-picture-thinking, curious, spontaneous, playful, and energetic	*Unique* outbox and newbox thinking
Storm	High expectations and challenges (help individuals develop *useful* expertise, which turns the CPI into a passion)	Independent, self-disciplined, diligent, self-efficacious, resilient, risk-taking, persistent, and uncertainty-accepting	*Useful* inbox and newbox thinking
Space	Freedom to be alone and unique (helps individuals develop *unique* ideas based on the expertise)	Emotional, compassionate, self-reflective, autonomous, day-dreaming, nonconforming, gender-bias-free, and defiant	*Unique* outbox and newbox thinking

CATS, SO WHAT? LET'S CULTIVATE THE 4S CLIMATES FIRST

Within the three steps of cultivating the 4S climates, nurturing the 4S attitudes, and applying the ION thinking skills, the first and the most critical step is to cultivate the 4S climates. Climates determine whether a creative idea or product becomes an innovation or nothing or a failure.[19] For example, I've studied an inventor who landed a job right after college with the most well-known high-tech company in Korea. Despite the fact that the company wanted to design innovative products, he was slammed for presenting unique ideas. He was told that his ideas were *nonsense*. However, he moved to America, where a company hired and promoted him because of his "nonsense" ideas. He later patented his ideas and became a vice president of another high-tech company. This was fortunate for America, but it was a loss for Korea due to its un-creative climate.

Climates also either encourage or discourage individuals' creativity development.[20] I've studied a child prodigy who was the focus of media attention since he was five.[21] At nine, he was admitted to a university's physics department. However, because his growth has been planned only around advancing his knowledge and skills in un-creative climates, although he's gained a lot of useful knowledge, he hasn't created anything unique. Unless he leaves the un-creative climate, I'm afraid that he'll never become an innovator.

Whether a prodigy or not, all individuals are born with creative potential, but their creative thinking depends on what's left over after their creativity is stifled or "bonsaied" by their climates. Their creativity is bonsaied by home climates first,[22] and then by school climates,[23] which are the most critical climates for individuals' creativity development. *Creativity is a gift, but it can be a curse* for individuals who are in un-creative climates (including test-centric climates).[24] They are scolded or punished for their creative attitudes and thinking.[25] This is because many parents and educators see children's creative attitudes as negative.[26] Some *believe* they value creativity, but in fact their actions are found to *de*value it.[27] For example, they often see the conforming attitude as indicative of children's creativity and the *non*conforming or defiant attitude as negative.[28]

While many parents and educators were staring only at a cactus's thorns, parents and teachers of innovators saw the cactus for its strength, its uniqueness, and its buds for potentially colorful blossoms. They cultivated creative climates and saw the positive aspects of children's 4S attitudes. They encouraged them to use their attitudes for applying ION thinking skills to achieve innovation, which eventually changed history. In this book, you will meet teachers such as Jost Winteler (for Einstein) at

Aarau; Imogene Hill (for Jobs) at Monta Loma; Reverend Cecil Harris (for Mandela) at Clarkebury; and Elizabeth Willis (for O'Keeffe) at Chatham, in addition to these innovators' parents. In my case also, without my teachers, especially Mr. Soon-Hyun Cho, I'd probably be trapped in a smelly sweat-shop—making socks all day—like all the other girls from my village.

Creativity has the power to transform the good to the best, and history has shown that it only takes a few parents or educators to make striking advances for humankind. If parents and educators learn to cultivate the 4S climates that nurture children's 4S attitudes at home and in school—rather than fostering un-creative climates that bonsai children's creative poten-tial—they can greatly increase future innovation.

PART 2

WHAT ARE CREATIVE CLIMATES AND ATTITUDES?

Chapter 3

THE SOIL CLIMATE THAT NURTURES THE SOIL ATTITUDES

Albert Einstein was born on March 14, 1879, to a Jewish family in Ulm, a large city on the River Danube in Southern Germany. Believe it or not, in terms of intelligence, he wasn't particularly smart.[1] However, he grew up in creative climates where learning was respected and excellence was expected.[2] His mother, Pauline Koch, was from an affluent family and was eleven years younger than her husband.[3] She was independent, resilient, and energetic.[4] She nurtured her children's self-disciplined and diligent attitudes for their studies.[5] She encouraged them to be ambitious and even embroidered the proverb, "Keeping busy brings blessings" on the family's tablecloth.[6]

Albert's father, Hermann Einstein, had a very different background and personality than Pauline.[7] He came from a poor family and loved mathematics from an early age. However, after graduating from secondary school, he became a merchant to make a living.[8] He was open-minded and defied Jewish traditions. His views and agnosticism diverged from the views of his wife and others,[9] and his example nurtured Albert's nonconforming and defiant attitudes. Hermann loved to read and shared this love with his two children by reading aloud the great works of Shakespeare, Schiller, and Goethe.[10] This nurtured Albert's curious attitude, and his love of reading and learning. Hermann sparked further curiosity by answering his endless questions and providing him with a variety of books and materials to enjoy with the necessary time to daydream.[11] Hermann often gave him opportunities to work through puzzles and build complex structures like houses of cards, and both he and Pauline encouraged Albert to always stick with his projects and challenges until completion, thereby nurturing his self-efficacious and persistent attitudes.[12]

Pauline was a talented pianist and wanted her son to love music as much as she did.[13] Despite her husband's business failures and lack of money, she bought Albert a violin and hired a tutor for lessons.[14] At first, Albert disliked violin lessons, which required repetitive practices.[15] However, Pauline motivated him by connecting music tempo to math, a subject that interested him.[16] She would accompany him on the piano when he practiced his favorite songs, and she also encouraged him to play in public.[17] Albert mastered the violin and also learned how to play the piano, eventually developing his love of music[18] (which later facilitated his newbox thinking, developing a theory that would connect everything in the universe musically and mathematically).[19]

Pauline also encouraged Albert's independent attitude early.[20] When he was only four years old, she took him to a busy street in town, left him behind, and instructed him to figure out how to get back home. He did so without knowing his mother followed him.[21]

At age five, Albert became ill and bedridden for a short time. To help him pass the time, Hermann gave him a compass and a playful story to go along with it. The story was about an old woodsman's wife who bought a compass for her husband because they lived deep in the forest and he kept getting lost. The way his father told the story was so captivating that Pauline almost burned their dinner that evening.[22] Albert was mesmerized by the magnetic needle within the compass, which sparked within him a lifelong sense of wonder about invisible forces at work in the universe.[23]

While Albert's parents stimulated his mind with various activities and experiences, they also nurtured his self-reflective and daydreaming attitudes. They let him spend plenty of time alone to think, walk, and daydream while observing the land, sky, trees, flowers, butterflies, and birds.[24] Sometimes he was so deep in thought that he wandered too far from home. Other times the wandering would occur only in his thoughts. When he was six years old, his family and cousins went to Oktoberfest in Munich. Everyone wanted to dance, but Albert wanted to hold on to their balloons instead. While the others were dancing, he let go of the balloons one by one. He watched in amazement and daydreamed where they were going and what invisible force pushed them up into the air instead of downward or sideways. When his parents discovered that he had let all of the balloons loose, they didn't get upset; instead, they let him share his fun daydreaming with them.[25]

That same year, Albert's parents sent him to a large Catholic school nearby—instead of a Jewish school farther away—so that he could walk to school and spend time thinking.[26] This nurtured his independent and self-reflective attitudes. They knew he'd be the only Jew among his seventy classmates, but they let him confront the challenges of anti-Semitism instead of protecting him from them. He was, indeed, frequently bullied for his religion, his lack of interest in playing sports or proving his masculinity, and his focus on reading.[27] Before then, he hadn't considered Judaism as a defining aspect of his identity, due to his parents' agnosticism. But he rebelled against the juvenile anti-Semitism and his parents' agnosticism by developing a deep curiosity, preference, and interest (CPI) in Judaism. He decided to start keeping kosher (a Jewish dietary tradition) and even composed hymns to sing to himself.[28] However, at twelve, he rebelled against what he believed, which he thought was manipulative aspects of religion, and abandoned his focus on Judaism in favor of new CPIs in science and math. Yet he did maintain his Jewish identity throughout his life.[29]

In addition to his parents, from an early age Albert benefited from two intellectually stimulating mentors, Uncle Jakob and Max Talmey, who recognized and developed his CPIs in math, science, and philosophy. Uncle Jakob was a successful engineer, inventor, and business partner of Albert's father.[30] For decades the two families shared a house together and took turns cooking and doing other chores.[31] This developed complex family interactions without friction and nurtured Albert's complexity-seeking attitude. Jakob patented electric meters, circuit breakers, and parts for electric generators. He dreamed of converting Munich's old-fashioned gaslights into electrically powered light bulbs, which nurtured Albert's big-picture-thinking attitude.[32] Jakob taught Albert that math can be fun by using everyday objects (trees, marbles, body parts, etc.) to show mathematical concepts and principles. He showed Albert the usefulness of those concepts and principles, for example, geometry for measuring and comparing things around him (lines, angles, surfaces, solid objects, etc.); how knees, elbows, and tree branches form angles; how honeycombs form a natural hexagon; how spider webs form an octagon; and how volcanoes form a cone.[33] He also turned algebra into games and word games (like "happy science goes hunting for a little animal whose name we don't know, called x").[34] He turned math into thought-provoking and fun activities so much that Albert preferred solving math problems to playing outside.[35] He also learned that mistakes forced him to seek out answers and new discoveries.

This nurtured his self-efficacious and persistent attitudes, strengthening his CPI in math.[36]

At age ten, Albert met Max Talmey (a twenty-one-year-old poor Jewish medical student) who was passionate about science. The Einstein family invited him for dinner every Thursday for five years.[37] He provided Albert with educational encouragement and enrichment, and different perspectives from his family. He shared with Albert both his books and his knowledge on the latest scientific breakthroughs. Those books included Aaron Bernstein's *Popular Books on Natural Science* (a twenty-one-volume set of fun, brightly illustrated books) on electricity, gravity, and other scientific information and experiments.[38] Albert devoured Talmey's books and energetically discussed them with him in an equal relationship. Albert was especially fascinated by exploring the speed of light, which combined his earlier CPI in math with his new CPI—in science—and started developing his expertise in space and time.[39] Talmey also introduced Albert to the work of great philosophers. Immanuel Kant became a favorite of thirteen-year-old Albert, building his abstract-reasoning and big-picture thinking skills.[40]

In school, however, Albert was viewed as a troublemaker.[41] His teachers thought he asked too many questions, and his bluntness often landed him in hot water.[42] One of them announced to Albert's class that he'd never achieve anything.[43] Other teachers announced that he was a bad example to other students, wasted others' time, and undermined teachers' authority.[44] Unlike his home life, where he was equal in his parents' eyes (a "guiding" parenting style), his teachers were rigid and militaristic (a "controlling" teaching style) and emphasized rote learning, which Albert was neither good at nor liked.[45] These dramatically different climates between his home and school nurtured his nonconforming and defiant attitudes, which his teachers didn't appreciate.[46]

Throughout his teenage years, Albert was distressed by his father's financial failures.[47] His family had to sell their home and move to Italy, leaving Albert to finish high school alone in Germany (while living with a distant relative).[48] His teachers and classmates continuously disliked him and treated him as an inquisitive outsider.[49] When he was fifteen, his teachers eventually forced him out of school, and he became a high-school dropout.[50] He suffered and almost had a nervous breakdown, but the experience built his resilient attitude.[51] After he left school, he hiked alone across the mountains from Milan to Genoa, Italy, for days, sleeping outside each night. One night during his trip, he was inspired by a sky full of falling stars, which rekindled his overwhelming CPI in space and in turn ignited his desire to graduate high school so that he could study physics in college.[52]

After visiting and helping with the family business in Italy, at sixteen Albert enrolled in Aarau High School near Zurich, Switzerland. The teachers at Aarau encouraged students to develop their own conclusions through exploration and experimentation—while accepting uncertainty (a guiding teaching style)—unlike his earlier militaristic German schools.[53] They encouraged him to ask questions (including those that constantly nagged his brain) and even to express criticisms.[54] Albert enjoyed mutual respect with his teachers, and he became popular among his classmates.[55] His CPI in physics flourished through readings and discussions and developed his expertise. With his early-developed daydreaming attitude, he imagined what it would be like to ride a light beam (which occupied his thoughts for the next ten years).[56] Also, at Aarau, he boarded with a teacher and mentor, Jost Winteler, whose family became Albert's lifelong family.[57] Winteler and Albert shared their love of philosophy and hiking in the mountains. Winteler strengthened Albert's optimistic, curious, and playful attitudes. One of Winteler's daughters became Albert's first girlfriend. She supported him in many ways, including washing his mailed dirty clothes after he went away to college and even when they didn't continue a romantic relationship.[58]

Albert eventually attended Polytechnic Institute in Zurich, but the professors' controlling teaching style following hierarchical relationships didn't suit his educational needs. After taking *fifteen* courses from Heinrich Weber (his physics professor) for two years, Albert complained that Weber didn't teach anything about new discoveries.[59] Albert was brutally honest in his complaints due to his early-developed nonconforming and defiant attitudes.[60] His seemingly arrogant attitude and frequently skipped classes annoyed his professors so much that not a single one wrote a recommendation letter for him.[61] Around the same time, he published a critique of a well-known researcher's theories—inviting rejection from every job he applied to—and became the only jobless graduate from his department.[62] Considering the conflict he experienced with many of his teachers and professors, how did he become an innovator?

Albert's soil attitudes enabled cross-pollination:

In his soil climate—including his mentors, Uncle Jakob, Talmey, and Winteler—Albert's soil attitudes had been nurtured. This enabled later cross-pollination with Mileva Marić (his first wife), Michele Besso, and Marcel Grossmann.[63] Without them, the Einstein name would be meaningless. Albert met Jewish-Italian Michele Besso in college, and they both worked at the Swiss Patent Office. Besso was six years older than Albert was, and he was like family to Albert for fifty years.[64] He was an expert engineer, yet he lacked ambition and big-picture-thinking and persistent attitudes compared to Albert.[65] Despite their differences, they shared the most sophisticated scientific notions and endless conversations about space and time and fed each other's minds.[66] Besso always gave Albert unique feedback and introduced him to other scientists' works, which helped build his famous theories.[67]

Albert also met Jewish-Hungarian mathematician Marcel Grossmann in college, and they became lifelong friends. Without Grossmann's help, Albert wouldn't have been able to graduate from college, get a job, or do the necessary complex math (non-Euclidean geometry) for his general-relativity theory.[68] Grossmann gave his class notes to Albert, which allowed him to pass the graduate exams.[69] It was Grossmann's father who finally got the patent-office job for him after Albert desperately tried to find work for two years.[70]

Albert's 4S attitudes enabled ION thinking for innovation:

At ten, Albert started developing expertise in his CPI in space and time when he met Talmey.[71] He used inbox thinking that was enabled by his soil and storm attitudes—which had been nurtured in his soil and storm climates—to learn from Talmey's expertise in space and time. At thirteen, he was especially fascinated by Kant's arguments that space and time are nothing but concoctions of the human mind. He also learned that mathematical concepts and principles could provide ways to connect between space and time.[72] He spent years discussing mathematical and scientific ideas with Uncle Jakob, Talmey, and Winteler, and then with Marić, Besso, Grossmann, and others.[73] His inbox thinking intensified during this period as he developed his significant expertise in space and time, which turned his CPI into a lifelong passion.

When Albert first daydreamed his theory—based on his expertise—he used outbox thinking that was enabled by his sun and space attitudes, which had been nurtured in his sun and space climates. He started developing a harmonious and mathematical theory to explain the universe.[74] At his first job at the Swiss Patent Office, his boss (Friedrich Haller) encouraged him to explore and develop ideas and skills by being critically vigilant and defiant, questioning everything. The job didn't give significant monetary benefits or social status, unlike the college professor Albert strived to become. However, it did give him plenty of time—more than professors were allowed to have—to improve his ION thinking (including daydreaming) to generate unique ideas.[75] Then he used critical-thinking skills to analyze and evaluate the unique ideas to make them useful.

When Albert combined his expertise in space and time with harmony in music and relativism, he used newbox thinking that was enabled by his 4S attitudes, which had been nurtured in his 4S climates. When he transformed his uniquely synthesized ideas into a useful theory—through refining with simplicity—he also used newbox thinking.[76] At age twenty-six—more than ten years after he began developing his expertise—he promoted his relativity theory by publishing it, which was recognized as an innovation by others/the society,[77] confirming the ten-year rule (the idea that ten years of immersion in a subject/field are necessary for innovation).[78] Yet his passion didn't stop, and at thirty-seven, he promoted another creation: his general theory of relativity, which explains the force of gravity in terms of a curving, four-dimensional space-time.[79]

While there were many other experiences in Albert Einstein's growth and fruitful success as an innovator, let's explore more deeply what the soil climate is and how it impacts individuals' creativity development.

According to the CATs model introduced in chapter 2, there are three steps for innovation. Cultivating the soil climate (step 1) and nurturing the soil attitude (step 2) are discussed in this chapter. Applying ION thinking skills is discussed in chapter 9 (step 3).

STEP 1: CULTIVATE THE DIVERSE SOIL CLIMATE

Grounding plants in firm soil is the first process in gardening, which provides an anchor for the roots that support and supply the plants. Diverse soil is also vital as it provides nutrients for the plants to grow. For gardening, the soil climate includes the characteristics of the soil such as the location, hardness, porosity, salinity, and nutrient content. For developing creativity, the soil climate provides individuals with diverse resources and experiences, which directly impacts the soil attitudes that they develop, which are described in step 2. The soil climate also provides individuals with a firmly grounded familial and cultural identity. It also provides exposure and access to diverse kinds of resources, including things, people, knowledge, and views (not just financial resources). It also teaches individuals how to access and grow new resources. While the soil climate initially nurtures the soil attitudes in individuals, they encounter diverse subjects that can become their CPI. Their soil attitudes help them become resourceful cross-pollinators, which enables useful inbox and newbox thinking for innovation.

Research Findings on the Soil Climate

1. Plant growth is enhanced by fertilizers and nutrients. Gardeners make sure they receive enough of them. A shortage of elements causes the fruit harvest to be low quality or nonexistent. Young innovators are like plants with hungry roots and sensitive leaves, absorbing resources from their climates. Resources include: friend and family interactions (including extended family), educational experiences (teachers, mentors, books, libraries, educational media, etc.), social experiences (community/religious/ cultural/artistic events, exhibitions, performances, etc.), and other diverse experiences and opportunities.[80] Parents and teachers of innovators (PTIs) encourage children to learn or do something that they don't know about (like taking a class, eating a new food, or reading a book they aren't initially interested in) and search for free events *on their own* (like music concerts, lectures, classes, extracurricular activities, and after-school clubs).

2. Plants flourish in open areas that get enough sunshine to grow. Culturally isolated and conformity-imposed rural environments limit young innovators' imagination.[81] Innovators grow up in or move to multicultural cities that are open to diverse nationality, ethnicity, religion, language, culture, and sexual orientation.[82] The physical proximity of densely populated large cities (that include large universities) promotes face-to-face interactions (cross-pollination) between diverse resources and experiences.[83] The openness and nonconforming climate of the city are more important than its economic or lifestyle opportunities when creative individuals make decisions to move to the city.[84] In multicultural cities, experts in diverse fields exchange, combine, and magnify their expertise through frequent formal and informal interactions.[85] They bounce off of and get insights from each other's ideas, and they grow from each other's inspirations, ideas, passions, and energies.[86] With children, PTIs decorate surroundings with objects that represent cultures from all over the world and visit large multicultural areas where diverse ideas, history, ethnicity, dress, lifestyle, religion, speech, culture, and sexuality can easily be observed—through live performances, open markets, ethnic restaurants, or seasonal festivals.

3. Soil must be porous enough to allow water to easily drain through. It must be loosely packed around the roots so that water doesn't stagnate and cause them to rot. PTIs are open to others' ideas while introducing children to diverse novel or unusual and intellectually or culturally stimulating activities and experiences.[87] They encourage children to go to unfamiliar events, places, and movies that show different ways people interact; befriend people who have dramatically different interests and backgrounds by expanding their group beyond their peer group (like different age groups, neighborhoods, cultures, countries, religions, and fields); and learn about other religions, as well as atheism.[88] This facilitates children's early exposure to wide ranges of CPIs, which starts creativity development.[89]

4. Soil must be packed tight enough for plants to be firmly rooted in the ground. Innovators grow up being firmly rooted in their family and culture, which helps them develop firm identity and overcome later challenges.[90] PTIs nurture children's positive familial, national, and cultural experiences by encouraging their involvement in such activities and traditions.[91] The parents make the family meal the most important time of the day without any distractions (from the television and computers); pass on family history and values; and help them visit grandparents and other older relatives and share experiences. Yet they teach children to avoid feeling that their family, race, culture, lifestyle, country, religion, food, or ideas are *better* or *worse* than others'.

Providing young innovators with secure loving relationships also enhances their curiosity, exploration, and open-mindedness, and it reduces dogmatic opinions and stereotype tendencies.[92] This opens their minds to learn about others' familial and cultural backgrounds.[93]

5. Firm soil must be regularly tilled to allow plants to absorb other nutrients. Young innovators develop bicultural identity by speaking foreign languages, getting to know people from different cultures, living in two distinctly different cultural regions (even within the same country), or living with parents who have different cultural backgrounds from each other.[94] PTIs support children's bicultural identity by introducing them to diverse people and encouraging them to learn from other cultures using multicultural communication skills. They encourage children to attend ethnic cultural events and get involved in activities that challenge racism, sexism, and other forms of prejudice. They also teach them that foreign accents are signs of courage and intelligence (displayed by people who were brave enough to make a foreign place their new home and are intelligent enough to learn a second language). With children, they watch foreign-made movies or the news from other countries, and they encourage children to explore their interests from the movie/news further and then discuss together. They do this while helping them maintain their own cultural identity. Young innovators' bicultural identity promotes their complex thinking, multiple perspectives, and ability to live as an outsider.[95]

Sadly, many immigrants remain even more traditional to their native culture than those still living in their home country.[96] For example, many Korean immigrants around the Washington, DC, area (where I currently live) raise children in more Confucian ways than those who live in Korea. Some of them have lived in America for twenty or thirty years, yet can neither speak much English nor understand other cultures. Even worse, when their children are in school, the test-centric climates force them only to adapt to American culture and to learn only English instead of supporting biculturalism or bilingualism.[97] This is a mutually exclusive situation that makes children either ashamed or confused about their own identity instead of developing bicultural identity. Also, even expatriates or TCKs (third-culture kids) who grow up living outside of their parents' original culture[98]—but as non-immigrants—can be culturally isolated. If they live only in a cultural bubble—surrounded only by other expatriates or TCKs—they develop ethnocentric worldviews instead of developing bicultural identity.[99]

6. *Too much of the same nutrient can kill plants, and one element in the soil can't compensate for another's deficiency.* Opinions or views that are too similar limit children's creativity development. Innovators' parents greatly influence children but also expose them to others' influence early, including mentors.[100]

In Greek mythology, *mentor* was a guardian of Telemachus who guided him throughout his life.[101] Today, mentoring is a cultivated and mutually respected relationship between mentors and mentees. Mentoring is focused on both personal and professional development where the mentors are trusted role models for the mentees in an equal relationship.[102] Mentors support mentees' goal setting by assessing their strengths and weaknesses and guiding them to career paths that align to the mentees' CPI.[103] They support mentees intellectually and psychologically and help develop or advance their expertise with both positive and negative feedback.[104] They eventually push mentees toward new opportunities to discover their own uniqueness by taking intellectual risks or defying the crowd.[105]

Mentoring helps young innovators develop their expertise on their own by remaining teachable.[106] PTIs identify children's CPI early by recognizing their excitements/strengths, likes/dislikes, beliefs, what's important to them, what they enjoy, and the people they look up to; and then they together explore the pathways within their CPI. They teach children to be mentored by *trusting* others, allowing others to teach them, listening to others' advice, and practicing self-disclosure while *not* leaning on others. Young innovators search for mentors through spending time with extended family members and adult friends. Different mentors at different times are the best:[107] A *playful* mentor first to help discover young innovators' CPI, then an *outstanding* mentor in the near area to develop their expertise, and finally a *master* mentor in the field (who works with only outstanding mentees) to stimulate their uniqueness. Einstein's parents introduced their son to two mentors early: Uncle Jakob (a playful mentor) and Max Talmey (an outstanding mentor). PTIs also help children find formal or informal skill/apprenticeship training for their CPI.[108] Emphasizing the importance of mentorship, Nobel laureates have searched for mentors early in their creativity development and often traveled far to work with the best in their field (a master mentor).[109]

7. Soil must have complex interactions between nutrients for plants to flourish. Innovators grow up in complex living environments. They often live with others—in addition to their family—who have different values and views. Their family interactions show complex, even chaotic relationships rather than hierarchal.[110] Their families (and cohabitants) often agree with each other on fundamental values but differ from one another in personality, attitudes, interests, and other views.[111] They often agree to disagree and are considerate of multiple perspectives. This facilitates children's creativity development more than their family's socioeconomic status or even encouragement.[112] PTIs value children's invisible/internal qualities such as curiosities, interests, and values—more than visible/external qualities such as cleanliness, good manners, or carefulness.[113] They encourage children's active, complex play and solving puzzles (not passive play like watching television or doing computer games); teach skills for complex arguments; and foster literature-rich environments.[114] They encourage asking "how" questions (instead of questions that require only "yes" or "no" answers) and thinking in gray (instead of thinking in black-or-white or right-or-wrong like "the good guy" or "the bad guy"). They discourage making oversimplifications in situations or thinking with absolutes (like "always" or "never," "all" or "nothing," and "everyone" or "no one"). PTIs also encourage children to express opinions with objective and flexible positions (like saying, "From my perspective . . .," "One way of looking at it is . . .," or "I'd like to hear your ideas") and to make friends with people whom they don't like or with whom they don't seem to be compatible. Young innovators' interactions and experiences with mentors and other cultures also build complex thoughts.[115]

   8. Soil that's too rich can be harmful to plants. Innovators grow up experiencing financial difficulties or existential challenges and hardships. Their complex interactions and relationships with their family are more important than their parents' possessions or occupation/education level, or the size of their home.[116] If children grow up with many privileges, they have few opportunities to learn resourcefulness and resilience that are necessary for creativity development.[117] (All of the innovators focused on in this book—Einstein, Jobs, Mandela, O'Keeffe, and Curie—were economically disadvantaged.) PTIs teach children how to manage and save money; how to use time wisely; how to maximize their resources by being organized and making plans in advance; how to find information (like online, local libraries, bookstores, etc.); and how to maintain and grow relationships (human resources). They encourage children to find and use materials and ideas in new/unique ways and to use technologies productively.

   9. Cross-pollinating apple trees bear fruit more heavily and regularly than self-pollinating trees. Cross-pollination is more important for good apple growth than proper light, location, pruning, spraying, or spacing is. For effective cross-pollination, at least two different types of apple trees with the *same* bloom season must be planted near each other. They must be located in places with pollination helpers (like bees, birds, animals, or wind). Similarly, cross-pollination between innovators who have different expertise and backgrounds—while understanding each other's work—is necessary for innovation.[118] Cross-pollination is sharing, adapting, and building on each other's diverse expertise across subjects/fields through formal and informal face-to-face interactions. It is most effective when individuals have already developed their own expertise in a subject, which enables them to realize how to add or improve their ideas or creations when cross-pollinating. To enhance cross-pollination skills, PTIs encourage children to develop expertise in their CPI and magnify their strengths more than improve their weaknesses. They encourage children to get involved in teamwork situations while maintaining a balance between time spent alone and with others. They teach children respectful questioning and attentive listening skills (like letting others finish their sentence or listening without second-guessing or countering them). They also teach children to give honest compliments by finding the best in others and acknowledge others' views and values even when they disagree. Encouraging children's resourcefulness of self, others, and the world through cross-pollination also builds healthy and supportive relationships that lead to greater innovation.[119]

STEP 2: NURTURE THE FIVE SOIL ATTITUDES

The soil climate—providing diverse resources and experiences—nurtures the soil attitudes (step 1). The soil attitudes form the foundation for all of the innovators' other sun, storm, and space attitudes. Step 2 explains what the five soil attitudes are, and how they nurture resourceful cross-pollinators who apply useful inbox and newbox thinking. It starts with a brief anecdote from my life, illustrating how my own soil attitudes were encouraged/discouraged or how I encouraged/discouraged these attitudes within my children. Then I summarize what research says about each of the attitudes and how each can contribute to useful inbox or newbox thinking. Each attitude can be learned and further developed through practice. The five soil attitudes (with the seemingly negative side in parentheses) are:

1. Open-Minded (and Distracted)

When my daughter was in first grade, she told me that there was a girl in her class whose parents were divorced. The girl was living with her father and grandparents and wasn't allowed to see her mother. That was the first time my children and I experienced a child whose parents were divorced. Divorces were rare in our city (Daegu).

Figure 3.1. Open-minded (and Distracted) Soil Attitude

I explained to her that the child's parents were terrible and selfish because they didn't consider how that child would suffer from the divorce. Although my own marriage was continuously on rocky ground, I didn't get divorced because I cared about my children's well-being more than my own happiness. I was convinced that every parent should feel that way, too. I was extremely closed-minded and even told my daughter not to be friends with the girl because I assumed that she'd be a bad influence.

Research findings on the open-minded attitude

The open-minded attitude (see figure 3.1) involves considering others' views that are different from individuals' own. *Open-mindedness is one of the most consistent attitudes found among innovators.*[120] Innovators embrace people, ideas, and views that are even radically different from their own. This doesn't mean they accept opposite viewpoints as truth, but that they recognize how others arrive at their conclusions. It gives them large mental and emotional reservoirs from which to generate and evaluate ideas, enabling critical-thinking skills.[121] It allows them to constantly learn and find new understanding by questioning and changing ingrained beliefs, which strengthens critical-thinking skills while developing expertise in a subject.[122]

Innovators pursue flexible ways of life, are daring, and travel extensively.[123] They are open to broad experiences and interests including fantasy and imagination.[124] They're open and sensitive to aesthetics and enjoy artistic stimulation through diverse activities.[125] Steve Jobs was a well-known champion for aesthetics; as he expressed, "The best companies pay attention to aesthetics. They take the extra time to lay out grids and proportion things appropriately, and it seems to pay off for them."[126]

Unique ideas often come after problems are considered from many different perspectives and after obvious/readily available ideas have been examined and discarded.[127] Innovators take in information and experiences to understand the world and stay flexible regarding final decisions to get new and more information.[128] This flexible openness avoids systematic focus, while embracing distractibility, which allows more distantly associated thoughts to enter the mind, which enables newbox thinking.[129] The innovators switch from their flexible openness to systematic focus, and vice versa, depending on the particular stage of the Apple-tree Creative Process (ACP).[130]

2. Bicultural (and Rootless)

I went from one of the most remote rural areas in Korea to a high school in one of Korea's largest cities (Daegu). Then I became an English teacher in the largest city (Seoul) and finally moved to America. Since then I've moved from the West Coast (California, where I didn't look very different from others due to the many Asians there) to the East Coast (Florida and Georgia, where I looked like a foreigner); from a warm place to a cold place; and from the open-minded North (Michigan) to the conservative South (Virginia). I've finally settled down in Maryland near Washington, DC, for now. Whenever my children and I moved to a different state in America, it was like moving to another foreign country; each state was so different!

Part of my son's college application essay went something like this:

In second grade, I befriended a girl named Claire who was my first crush, but I moved the next year. In sixth grade, I met my first favorite adult, who was my geography teacher and first wrestling coach, but I moved the next year. In ninth grade, I met my absolute best friend, Nick, the first friend my mother allowed sleepovers with, but I moved the next year.

Figure 3.2. Bicultural (and Rootless) Soil Attitude

Research findings on the bicultural attitude

Having the bicultural attitude (see figure 3.2) means embracing new cultures while maintaining one's own cultural identity. Innovators develop bicultural identity by being open and adapting to new cultures while keeping their own cultural identity intact.[131] When innovators are in Rome, they learn *what* Romans do and *why* they do it.[132] So their cultural knowledge and sensitivity extend to flexible thoughts, perspectives, and behaviors, which promotes not only newbox thinking but also psychological well-being.[133] They also notice contrasts between cultures, grapple to reconcile them at a deep level, form an alternative combination of ideas, and synthesize seemingly incompatible ideas, which advances newbox thinking.[134]

Innovators develop bicultural identity even when living in one country, because they learn from and are deeply impacted by another culture.[135] For example, Mandela's innovation was deeply impacted by Indian freedom movements—by Mahatma Gandhi and Pandit Nehru—while living in South Africa.[136] Both Jobs and O'Keeffe lived in America, yet Jobs' innovation was deeply impacted by Eastern philosophy, spirituality, Hinduism, and Zen Buddhism—and he visited India for nine months and Japan many times. Afterward, he remained a Zen Buddhist throughout his life.[137] O'Keeffe's innovation was deeply impacted by Arthur Dow's theory based on Japanese aesthetics, in which artists express themselves by form simplicity, symbolic color, and painting size or format.[138]

3. Mentored (and Channeled)

I always tell my children that my career success is due to my mentors who guided me along the way, which I value more than anything in my life. My English teacher, Mr. Soon-Hyun Cho, persuaded my village elders to send me to high school, believing that even a girl could become a professional if she was educated. He visited my village several times before my extended family finally agreed to send me to high school. Yet they were still convinced that I'd have a "tough" life; I'd become too educated to be obedient. But I became the first girl from my village who ever graduated high school, while all the other girls were working—having tough lives— in the sweatshops near the city.

There was Dr. Kofi Marfo, a Ghanaian professor at the University of South Florida, who recommended that I study under Dr. Torrance. Dr. Marfo guided me even after I left for the University of Georgia. He convinced me that I could become a great researcher despite my linguistic and cultural barriers, as he'd done before me.

I arrived at the Torrance Center, where I embarked on another PhD program. Dr. E. Paul Torrance—who was a humble, thoughtful, affectionate mentor yet, sadly, passed away in 2003—and Dr. Bonnie Cramond became my mentors. I've never met anyone who is as open, funny, honest, and trusting as Dr. Cramond. She accepted who I was 100 percent— including my differences, mistakes, weaknesses, and failures. I was able to talk with her about anything including interests, research, relationships, emotions, finances, and anything else that was on my mind; she's become my American mother! Under her guidance, for the first time, I realized research could relate to my real life, which made my research relevant, exciting, and fun for me.

Figure 3.3. Mentored (and Channeled) Soil Attitude

Research findings on the mentored attitude

The mentored attitude (see figure 3.3) comes from being mutually interested in and taught by experts and their constructive criticism. Although two experts may be successful in their respective fields, the one with more expertise on a particular subject can become the mentor within the relationship. To achieve their full potential, innovators need mentors more than any other influencer.[139] They earn mentors—who recognize, understand, and support mentees' CPI or passion—by remaining teachable and continuously evaluating themselves. Mentors help innovators focus on specific high goals to improve specific aspects of their performance by giving brutally honest feedback that compares their actual performance to their goals.[140] Mentors constructively criticize, recognize, and support mentees in a nonhierarchical relationship, and they help develop and/or advance mentees' expertise and critical-thinking skills (inbox thinking).[141] Most Nobel laureates in science earned at least one master mentor who was a previous laureate and who provided intellectual and research guidance and facilitated their creativity development.[142] These innovators attribute their success to their mentors.[143] Yet mentors also benefit from new perspectives and stimulation from their mentees, revitalizing their own creativity.[144] Both mentors and mentees stimulate questions and feed off of and grow from each other's energy and ideas, and their debates and arguments challenge conventional thoughts and spur their knowledge forward, which further strengthens inbox and newbox thinking.[145]

4. Complexity-Seeking (and Overcomplicated)

When I was little, every Sunday after church (while my parents were still busy with their services), I enjoyed listening to the life stories of lonely old ladies. They'd lost their husbands in their twenties or thirties from Japanese colonization or the Korean War. They intrigued me in the same way my Buddhist grandmother (who had lost her husband to the Japanese military in her twenties) did. Many of their worldviews were different from, or even opposite to, those of my peers, which helped me think in multiple perspectives.

My children deeply love their grandmother (my mother-in-law) even though she tried to train me as her servant for ten years, which deeply hurt my self-worth. But I never tell my children only my view of the painful experiences with her. I don't want them to see any events or experiences from only one simple perspective, and I want them to understand the complexity of the culture in which they lived. I explained—based on *her* view—that she'd been trained to behave in certain ways by her own mother-in-law many years before she trained me. (But I believe there is more to it than that: I suspect that my mother-in-law was a lonely wife who didn't receive attention from her husband, which made her even more attached to her first son, my husband. She—like most traditional Korean mothers-in-law—thought she owned her first son. He, being her first son, also believed that he was the only hope for her, and he grew up seeing it as his duty to live up to his mother's expectations and wishes.)

I've also learned that there are many complex, gray areas between black and white, especially since the first day of my career as a professor in America. On that day, I was introducing my research about innovators' creative attitudes to the faculty members and graduate students. As an example for the risk-taking attitude, I used Rudolf Nureyev who (at twenty-three) risked his life to move to the West. He was a Soviet-born modern dancer who created a new role for male ballet dancers, as ballet was a field that was previously reserved only for females. He was also bisexual—and, at the all-too-young age of fifty-four, he died of cardiac complications from AIDS. At the time, I thought of sex as a simple dichotomy and made a joke, "Nureyev ran away from Russia to seek freedom, yet he did that so much that he got AIDS." The next day Dr. Katherine Beuvais—who has become my mentor and my children's "Grandma B"—explained that my joke was so offensive that it made another faculty member very upset (who used to be a ballet dancer and whose personal hero was Nureyev). Without Grandma B's efforts to help others understand my *simple binary* concept from my cultural background, I could have lost my job on the first day!

Figure 3.4.
Complexity-Seeking
(and Overcomplicated)
Soil Attitude

Research findings on the complexity-seeking attitude

The complexity-seeking attitude (see figure 3.4) is characterized by embracing equivocal and conflicting views. Open-minded individuals' creativity depends not only on their flexible thinking but also on complex thinking.[146] Innovators develop complex thoughts by being open to more categories of information from more perspectives than are non-innovators.[147] They are multidimensional in their thinking and use complex structures in their minds to approach problems and create solutions.[148] They are intrigued by inconsistencies and/or exceptions to rules and enjoy overcoming conflicts and complexity rather than avoiding them.[149] Their complex minds further explore and recognize potential similarities/differences and patterns/relationships among many elements of information, which advances newbox thinking.[150] Innovators are complex and contradicted to themselves:[151] Depending on a particular stage of a creative process (ACP), they are narrowly focused or widely open-minded; are systematically persistent or flexibly spontaneous; are diligent or playful; are resilient or sensitive; are intensely curious or relaxed; are humble or self-efficacious; are self-disciplined or defiant; realistically evaluate or imaginatively daydream; and are socially isolated, self-reflective introverts or energetic, cross-pollinating extroverts.

5. Resourceful (and Opportunistic)

I learned resourcefulness since I was a little girl. For example, I can't throw anything away, especially food, because I grew up watching my parents sacrifice to grow anything. I'm not a hoarder; I find unique/useful uses for everything I keep. When fruits/vegetables get old, I freeze them and make smoothies later. If food garbage or some morsel escaped my efforts and spoils, it goes into the crab trap, the worm farm, the chicken pen, or the compost pile. Worn chopsticks become garden markers. I wash, dry, and reuse plastic bags and straws. I cut seemingly empty tubes of toothpaste in half to use the remainder inside. My children and guests tear paper towels in half to make the roll last longer or to use them as napkins.

Figure 3.5. Resourceful (and Opportunistic) Soil Attitude

Research findings on the resourceful attitude

Having the resourceful attitude (see figure 3.5) means finding and using all kinds of resources and opportunities effectively and efficiently to accomplish goals. This is as important for creativity development as *having* resources in the first place. If creativity is a muscle, resourcefulness is a workout, training and improving to overcome limitations. Initially, structures, limitations, and constraints provide a framework in which innovators develop their resourcefulness (as the saying goes, "necessity is the mother of invention"). Then, their resourcefulness matures into ability as they seek and grow resources beyond the limitations and constraints. This leads to more useful ideas or solutions beyond what they could achieve with only their own resources.[152]

Innovators are interdependent, yet they are resourceful so that they aren't afraid to ask for help. Also, they have limited time and energy, and thus to make the most of their resources, they seek out those experts who already have the desired expertise. They utilize the resources of others and also make themselves available as resources.[153] They are proactive about following their passion and are aware of the vast resources, possibilities, and opportunities for their passion.[154] For instance, Steve Jobs dismissed the myth of the innovator as a lone wolf by finding that innovators cross-pollinate with experts, but not with low performers.[155]

Cross-pollination includes formal and informal face-to-face interaction, networking, sound-boarding (good listening and offering feedback), collaboration, and collaborative competition (which is more effective for innovation than winner-take-all competition is[156]). Successful cross-pollination starts with the resourceful and mentored attitudes. Through cross-pollination, innovators magnify their own and others' strengths by feeding on and growing from each other's expertise.[157] Collaboration and cross-pollination are not synonymous. Collaboration is under the larger umbrella of cross-pollination. Collaboration involves purposeful planning toward a common goal. Cross-pollination occurs naturally, is more spontaneous, and can also result in learning from mild group competitions.[158] Expansive and diverse networks that readily embrace competitors or outsiders make even more resources, experiences, and expertise available to others.[159] The most unique ideas are generated when cross-pollinated by the widest variety of people with the widest perspectives.[160] Cross-pollination enhances access to others' expertise and experience-based know-how, which results in useful synthesis of knowledge/skills through newly observed or learned insights, which advances cross-pollinators' expertise and newbox thinking.[161]

Yet innovation is often a matter of sequencing resources.[162] The best approach to the creative process (ACP) combines unique individual thinking in depth *first* and then useful group thinking through cross-pollination *later*.[163] So, innovators tolerate isolation and enjoy working and generating unique ideas alone without distractions *first*, before they cross-pollinate.

INNOVATORS' SOIL ATTITUDES: THE CACTUS AMONG US

Innovators display the soil attitudes that might seem negative—such as distracted, rootless, channeled, overcomplicated, or opportunistic. For example, innovators who devote a lot of mental resources to being open-minded may seem distracted from the main effort. Jobs was so immersed in Zen Buddhism that he considered becoming a monk. In that instance, his behavior seemed distracted. But his lifelong spiritual mentor, Kobun

Chino Otogawa, advised him to find the Zen in his own life by dedicating himself to his passion for invention, which helped Jobs found Apple.[164]

Innovators are so bicultural (or even multicultural) that they seem rootless. Einstein held three citizenships by age thirty-two and five citizenships throughout his life. He thought of himself a citizen of the world and encouraged the formation of a world government to preserve peace.[165] He might seem *rootless*, but he sought firm roots in the world.

Innovators follow their mentors' advice so much that they seem channeled by the mentor. Under Alfred Stieglitz's mentorship, O'Keeffe established her career in a field that belonged to only men at the time. To continuously attract media attention, he diplomatically controlled her public image and mediated, or even manipulated, between her and her critics.[166] She might seem *channeled*.

Innovators seek complexity so much that they seem overcomplicated to the people around them. If Mandela had preferred a simple life, his first wife may not have left him; his second wife may not have had an affair; and he'd not have had to find his third wife. He might seem *overcomplicated*.

Innovators are so resourceful that they seem opportunistic. Einstein, in college, continuously mailed his laundry to his ex-girlfriend to wash.[167] He also used Grossmann's class notes to pass the exam, and Grossmann's father to get a job.[168] He might seem *opportunistic*.

Parents and educators must be able to see the long-term positive aspects of behaviors that seem *prickly* in children; so they can encourage the underlying soil attitudes instead of seeing the children as troublemakers. Also, such children must be able to view their own soil attitudes positively. When parents and educators succeed in cultivating the soil climate and nurturing children's soil attitudes, they are following the footsteps of the PTIs who encouraged, taught, and mentored the greatest innovators in history.

Chapter 4

THE SUN CLIMATE THAT
NURTURES THE SUN ATTITUDES

Steve Jobs was born on February 24, 1955. His mother, Joanne Carole Schieble, was a Swiss American working on a degree in speech language pathology at the University of Wisconsin (UW). His father, Abdulfattah John Jandali, was a Syrian immigrant who earned a PhD at UW and became a political-science professor and eventually a restaurant owner. As graduate students at UW, the two dated and Joanne became pregnant. They wanted to get married, but Joanne's father forbade it. Subsequently, Joanne moved to San Francisco, where Steve was born and adopted by another family a week later.[1]

The infant was adopted by Paul and Clara Jobs, high-school dropouts who were unable to have their own children. Originally, college-educated Joanne put a stipulation on Steve's adoption that he be placed with parents who were college graduates. She agreed to relax this requirement after Paul and Clara signed a written pledge promising to fund a college savings account for their new son. Steve grew up knowing that education was important to his biological parents. This helped him value education and nurtured his diligent attitude for learning. Since Steve was six or seven, throughout his life, he grew up with the pain of feeling abandoned by his biological parents and was always curious about them, which contributed to a feeling that he was a loner.[2] This made him grow up different from other children, feeling and thinking alone and pursuing his own identity. This nurtured his early independent, self-reflective, and defiant attitudes. Steve's endless curiosity and general defiance made raising him a challenge.[3] Paul was gentle and disciplined him in a calm but firm manner, making expectations clear without resorting to a harsh temper or physical punishment.[4]

Steve's parents taught him how to read long before he started school, and they encouraged him to explore and ask questions. As a little boy,

Steve only wanted to do two things: read books and chase butterflies.[5] His parents gave him plenty of time to both and to *think*—which nurtured his love of reading and learning.[6] His parents were open-minded and nurtured his complexity-seeking attitude by discussing various topics including what they were currently reading. They exposed him to various stimulating activities and experiences for finding his curiosity, preference, or interest (CPI).[7] They never had much money and couldn't afford new belongings or vacations. Steve witnessed them make real-world sacrifices to provide opportunities for him.[8] Steve had a daily newspaper route and worked summers and weekends at other jobs.[9]

Paul was a role model to Steve. He was a Coast Guard veteran with a knack for mechanics and worked as a machinist for a laser-manufacturing company. As much for fun as for money, he purchased wrecked cars, fixed them up, and then sold them.[10] Paul taught him how to take things apart and put them back together. Steve gained a love for mechanics and building things from Paul, who set aside a portion of the workbench in his garage for Steve to use and gave him his own set of tools—sized smaller than usual to fit a child's hands.[11] Steve grew up watching Paul's attention to design and detail as they worked on projects together. Paul emphasized excellent craftsmanship on *all* parts of a project, even those that remain unseen. This nurtured Steve's self-disciplined and diligent attitudes. He kept these important lessons in mind throughout his life.[12]

Steve wasn't as fond of working on cars as was Paul, but he did learn valuable future lessons—his resourceful attitude and promotion skills for selling. According to Steve, "Every weekend, there'd be a junkyard trip. We'd be looking for a generator, a carburetor, all sorts of components. He was a good bargainer, because he knew better than the guys at the counter what the parts should cost."[13] While in the school electronics club, Steve worked at an electronics store. He salvaged and sold valuable computer chips and components at electronics flea markets, where he learned about negotiating, making profits, and saving money.[14]

Steve had mentors—most notably Larry Lang, a neighbor. Lang was an engineer for Hewlett-Packard (HP). He showed Steve, at age six or seven, interesting components that fascinated him, like how a carbon microphone produced sound without an amplifier. He often invited Steve over for dinner to talk electronics and eventually inspired him to find his CPI in electronics. According to Steve, "He was my model of what an HP engineer was supposed to be: a big ham radio operator and a hard-core electronics guy. He'd bring me stuff to play with."[15] Lang gave him ham radio circuit-board kits and other gear. By playing with them and taking them apart, Steve gained an understanding of what was inside finished products and how they worked.[16] This was a confidence-building exercise for him—nurturing his playful and self-efficacious attitudes. When Steve was ten years old, Lang encouraged him to join HP's Explorers Club, a program for children who had an interest in electronics. For one project, Steve needed parts that HP made, so he boldly called the CEO of HP (David Packard), whose name and phone number were in the phone book. Packard took Steve's call, supplied the parts he wanted, and eventually offered him a summer job! He also became an early inspirational role model.[17] Further, when Steve saw the first desktop computer in the world (called the 9100A), which HP was developing, it was love at first sight.[18] These inspirational experiences nurtured Steve's big-picture-thinking and energetic attitudes and intensified his CPI in electronics and further specified into computers.

At school, however, Steve faced authoritarian learning (that was based on a "controlling" teaching style) for the first time, which was very different from his early learning environment, which was based on curiosity and variety by a "guiding" parenting style. Also, he had already learned so much before he started school that he was bored and became a risk-taking troublemaker.[19] With a friend, he committed all kinds of pranks and transgressions at school before becoming a fourth-grader: he made posters announcing a pet day, which led to dogs, cats, and snakes all over school; switched the other children's bike-lock combination numbers; and set off an explosive under a teacher's chair. Steve was often sent home from school, but his parents didn't criticize him. They blamed the school for taking the curiosity out of him instead of challenging and stimulating him.[20]

His fourth-grade teacher, Imogene Hill, recognized and guided Steve's defiant energy into learning. He was never good at memorizing facts yet loved reading. She gave him candy and money incentives to learn (which are effective for short-term goals), and before long he developed a respect for her and for learning that sparked his own desire to learn.[21] Hill provided him with a hobby kit for grinding a lens and making a camera. This was another confidence-building exercise for him.[22]

Taking advanced classes from Hill rekindled his love of reading and learning. He learned so much by the end of the year that his teachers recommended he skip fifth grade and advance directly to middle school.[23] However, this wasn't a smooth transition. He was younger than the other students in his new school and was bullied. He refused to be timid or beaten down and came up with a solution: at only age eleven, he demanded his parents move to another school district in Los Altos, the heart of the future Silicon Valley.[24] Although moving was his idea, he still faced being an inquisitive outsider at the new school, which nurtured his resilient attitude. But by high school, he didn't even try to fit in to any teenager groups and was proud of being different and nerdy. This reinforced his nonconforming and defiant attitudes.[25]

While Steve was developing his expertise in computers and marketing, America was undergoing rapid social and technological changes with epicenters in the San Francisco Bay Area. The area was ground zero for countercultural hippies who rejected America's 1950s conformity, materialism, and militarism. At the same time, the future Silicon Valley was quickly growing deep technological roots. In the area surrounding Stanford University, companies such as HP, Xerox PARC, Shockley Semiconductor, and Bell Telephone were leading the way.[26] The soil climate was strong for Steve's prepared mind, allowing his creative thinking to blossom. He cofounded Apple Inc. in his parents' garage and was instrumental in Apple's long-term success. The revolutionary Macintosh computer, iPod digital music player, iPad tablet computer, and iPhone smartphone were all developed, produced, and promoted under his watchful eye. In 2014, Apple's annual sales topped $182 billion.[27] Today, he's considered one of the most creative and successful people in US history.

His career wasn't one long string of successes, however; there were many defeats. Nine years after cofounding Apple, he was ejected from the company. Fortunately, his goals remained strong because of his well-developed resilient, persistent, and big-picture-thinking attitudes. Also, being fired from his own company gave him the opportunity to exercise his open-mindedness again and start even more unique and useful companies with his early-nurtured, beginner-like, curious attitude.[28]

Steve's soil attitudes enabled cross-pollination:

In his soil climate—including his mentors, Lang and Hill—Steve's soil attitudes had been nurtured. This enabled later cross-pollination with

Steve Wozniak, Mike Markkula, and Jonathan Ive. Without them, the Jobs name would be meaningless. At sixteen, Steve met Steve Wozniak, who was almost five years older than Steve Jobs and already had expertise in computing and software, fifty times better than any engineer Steve had ever met.[29] Compared to Steve Jobs, Steve Wozniak lacked big-picture-thinking and resourceful attitudes. Despite their differences, they both shared playful and energetic attitudes and passions for electronics, computers, and music.[30] After dropping out of college when Steve was working at Atari, his colleagues at Atari disliked his seemingly-arrogant attitude, so he was allowed to work at night when nobody was there. This enabled Wozniak to visit Steve at night and assist him with difficult tasks. During that time, they also invented and sold illegal blue boxes, a type of telephone equipment used to hack phones. This illegal/defiant adventure helped them establish a foundation for their future partnership, founding Apple.[31]

Mike Markkula was the first major venture capitalist for Apple. He excelled at pricing strategies, distribution networks, marketing, and finance. He taught Steve how to promote products in unique ways that had a powerful impact on customers. He agreed with Steve that their primary goal wasn't to make money but to make something that they could believe in and that would last forever.[32]

Jonathan Ive was the design chief at Apple and helped the company transform computing, phones, and music into unique and useful products. He led the human-interface software teams and the design teams for the iPod, iPod Touch, iPhone, iPad, iPad Mini, iMac, MacBook Pro, MacBook Pro Air, and iOP 7. He was gentle and easygoing, whereas Steve was intense and energetic. Despite their differences, both shared curious, emotional, and compassionate attitudes.[33] Both also shared self-disciplined and diligent attitudes, making the inside of Apple's machines look as good as the outside.[34]

Steve's 4S attitudes enabled ION thinking for innovation:

At age ten, Steve started developing expertise in his CPI in electronics and eventually computers, when he met Lang. He used inbox thinking that was enabled by his soil and storm attitudes, which had been nurtured in his soil and storm climates. His CPI was intensified especially when he saw the first desktop computer.[35] Through Lang's guidance, the HP Explorer

Club, the electronics club at Homestead High School, and the Homebrew Computer Club (an early computer hobbyist group in Silicon Valley), Steve continuously learned about new electronics, and his expertise matured.[36]

At his first job at Atari, Steve was encouraged by his boss, Al Alcorn, to explore and develop more ideas and skills. This improved Steve's outbox thinking, as he examined newly designed games and experimented with their different functions.[37] When Steve first imagined the future personal computer—based on his expertise—he used advanced outbox thinking that was enabled by his sun and space attitudes, which had been nurtured in his sun and space climates. When the rest of the world was thinking computers were only huge devices in offices, he imagined computers as small in-home appliances. To achieve this vision, he explored and developed unique, rudimentary human-centered interfaces. Then he used critical-thinking skills to analyze and evaluate them to make them useful.

When Steve combined his expertise in computers with business skills and Zen Buddhism, he used newbox thinking that was enabled by his 4S attitudes, which had been nurtured in his 4S climates. When he transformed his uniquely synthesized technology into a useful creation— through refining with simplicity—he also used newbox thinking. At twenty-one—more than ten years after he began developing his expertise in computers—he promoted his creation by cofounding Apple, which was recognized as an innovation by others/the society[38] (confirming the ten-year rule, just as Einstein had done).

Steve's passion never ceased, and at age fifty-one he synthesized many emerging technologies (MP3 players, GPS navigation, cameras, and touchscreens) into a single device—the iPhone. After he uniquely synthesized many complex technologies and functions, he transformed them into a useful, simple device.

Steve's pursuit of simplicity in all Apple products originated from Zen Buddhism. His interest in Zen Buddhism developed as a result of his continuous search for his biological parents—to reconcile the pain of abandonment while developing his personal identity. In his search, he immersed in Eastern spirituality—including Indian and Japanese culture and Zen Buddhism—which continued for the rest of his life.[39] This nurtured his bicultural and complexity-seeking attitudes. (Steve eventually met his biological mother and sister, but he refused to meet his father, knowing he had also abandoned his biological sister. Yet they'd already accidentally met several years before, when his father ran a restaurant in Silicon Valley. Without knowing their real identities, his father bragged to others that he'd met Steve Jobs, "a great tipper.")[40]

While there were many other experiences in Steve Jobs's growth and fruitful success as an innovator, let's explore more deeply what the sun climate is and how it impacts individuals' creativity development.

According to the CATs model introduced in chapter 2, there are three steps for innovation. Cultivating sun climates (step 1) and nurturing sun attitudes (step 2) are discussed in this chapter. Applying ION thinking skills is discussed in chapter 9 (step 3).

STEP 1: CULTIVATE THE BRIGHT SUN CLIMATE

Once plants are rooted in diverse soil, they require bright sun, as it provides warmth and light for plants to grow. Once individuals are in the diverse soil climate, the bright sun climate must inspire and encourage them for creativity, which directly impacts the sun attitudes that they develop, which are described in step 2. When the sun climate initially nurtures the sun attitudes in individuals, they find a CPI in a specific topic/subject by a playful introduction. Their sun attitudes help them become curious optimists, which enables unique outbox and newbox thinking. The best predictor of future innovation is young innovators' energy and enthusiasm for their early CPI.[41]

Research Findings on the Sun Climate

1. Plants keep their head pointed toward the sun and grow out of dark moments; they look at the sunny side of everything. Innovators grow up optimistic, expecting and working on the best outcomes. Their initial optimistic worldviews (seeing the world as a bright place) often start with their early positive attachment to others.[42] This leads to their positive interactions with and adjustment to new people and situations instead of being afraid or shy. Further, parents and teachers of innovators (PTIs) provide children with activities and experiences to increase their positivity and reduce negativity. For example, they help children find reasons to dwell on the good—by noticing little snapshots of kindness that they find themselves and others doing—instead of longing for a *big* happiness (that'll eventually emerge). They encourage children to count their blessings; *express* gratitude—verbally, in writing, or through actions; and be generous to others, to give others something to be grateful about. They encourage children to spend time with funny people who make them laugh and to find a reason to laugh. They also encourage children to avoid spending time with cynical/pessimistic entertainment and to reduce gossip, sarcasm, negative news, and intake or discussion of media (like TV, the Internet, newspaper, and radio) because the media fosters negativity. They also encourage children to forgive themselves for things that they regret or can't control; and they smile big in any situation—even when nobody's around—because optimism is attractive and spreading, while avoiding making unpleasant faces, crossed arms, tapping feet, rolling eyes, condescending smirks, and sighing. They also provide lessons and strategies to learn from mistakes and failures, so children believe in positive outcomes and approach opportunities with flexible thinking. Young innovators hold their heads high and imagine a bright future. Even when they're wrong, they stay positive, correct, improve, and succeed.[43]

2. *Plants grow* toward *the sun.* Innovators aspire to grow toward their CPI or to be like their role models. Their initial inspiration often starts with attending a great concert or event or reading a biography of an innovator.[44] PTIs introduce the idea of role models and help them find one. They're often early role models of children's CPI, sharing their experiences, activities, and materials with them.[45] Young innovators' knowledge about their role models' or inspirations' challenges, failures, and triumphs motivate and energize them. For instance, Einstein was inspired by Isaac Newton, who was inspired by Galileo Galilei (who died in the same year Newton was born). Jobs was inspired by Einstein (who died in the same year Jobs was born). The next great innovator might be a child who was born in 2011 and inspired by Jobs (who died that year).

3. *The sun shines on the* entire *world—lighting up even the most remote corner.* Innovators are optimistically self-inspired to grow outward and improve the entire world with their CPI and subsequent passion.[46] PTIs encourage children to be ambitious while not pressuring them to pursue a particular career. They encourage children to think with an abstract mind-set (something that can't be seen, heard, touched, tasted, or smelled—like democracy and love) rather than just a concrete mind-set (actual substances

or things like computers and classrooms). This helps children think and pursue a bigger value, mission, or vision beyond immediate rewards, narrow self-serving goals, or family interests. They also teach them to aim to be respected as innovators in their field by offering their expertise in ways that benefit others; spend time doing something *meaningful*, instead of just trying to be successful. They encourage big-picture thoughts—thinking in big, distant, futuristic, and imaginative ways, which enables abstract reasoning, outbox thinking, and newbox thinking.[47] Innovators maintain early inspirations, through which they later inspire the world.[48] PTIs help children find role models, idols, or heroes whom they can look up to and who inspire them; research things that they did; and emulate them. They share innovators' (including Nobel Prize winners') childhood stories on the child's level, through fiction or nonfiction books, videos, or movies, while not just focusing on the actual innovations. They encourage children to learn about the greatest people in national and world history; and they go to events that feature inspirational people whom they admire and become inspired by the quotes, sayings, or the hurdles that they've overcome.

4. *Plants need warmth to germinate their leaf* buds. On even the coldest day, sunshine can warm the surface of plants enough for cells to transfer water and nutrients. PTIs' warmth and encouragement germinate children's *curiosity* (or preference or interest) *buds*. Children's optimistic worldviews and inspirations broaden their perspectives and are also sources of their curiosity.[49] This is because the world becomes a safe and exciting place, and they're unafraid to explore, seek new information, and learn.[50] PTIs' warmth encourages children to actively ask questions and take risks to explore the unknown.[51] They encourage children to learn about nature, music, art, and people; find that the world is a wonderful mystery and full of things they don't yet know about; and get excited by the simplest wonder by keeping their beginner's mind. They let children's curiosity determine the pace and direction of learning; help them learn through experimenting; and encourage their argument and debate, which may often be noisy and disorganized. They let children explore without readymade toys and give them opportunities to learn through non-structured learning (like learning by doing, building, interviewing, storytelling, or cooking). They elicit children's questions and encourage them to ask questions even when they think they know everything they need to know; and pose new questions of *why*, *what if*, and *why not* to themselves and

others every day. They answer their questions with great care, researching matters in depth to spark subsequent questions and how to find answers instead of just providing one answer.[52] (Sadly, test-centric climates make children only answer questions instead of asking them; they're trained to memorize and recall the right answer; unusual/unique questions are ridiculed.) Innovators' initial CPI for a specific topic or subject grows into a lifelong passion through their continuous curiosities and diligent reading and learning.[53] Even after becoming experts, they still maintain a beginner's curiosity, which makes their long and laborious creative processes (Apple-tree Creative Process: ACP) exciting.[54] Einstein didn't think that he had any special talent, but only that he was passionately curious.[55]

5. *Plants increase the surface of their leaves as they grow; successful growth promotes more growth.* Curiosities promote more curiosities. Reading is a central activity for satisfying young innovators' curiosities and is often their parents' favorite leisure-time activity.[56] Innovators' parents let children see them reading to themselves and read aloud to them, often even after the children can read on their own. They share interesting things, entertainment, imagination, and fantasy experiences from books with children. They discuss learning and long-term educational planning with children for attaining high levels of education.[57] Yet they emphasize the importance of and the love of learning rather than just promoting formal schooling.[58] PTIs provide activities and strategies to make learning relevant to everyday life. They create environments to explore something further and together.

Great innovators didn't attain high levels of formal schooling; they learned and developed expertise mostly through reading:[59] Alexander Graham Bell was educated mostly by his father;[60] Thomas Edison had only three months of formal schooling and was taught by his mother;[61] Abraham Lincoln had less than a year of formal schooling;[62] Benjamin Franklin had formal schooling only to age ten.[63] One critical trait shared by *all* innovators is their love of reading and learning—being deeply engaged in their own self-education/self-training in their passion and goal.[64]

6. *In the bright sunshine, plants work spontaneously.* Even the slightest breeze helps spread petals, fragrance, and seeds. Likewise, in an optimistic and inspirational climate, young innovators work spontaneously for their curiosities, which helps them generate unique ideas. PTIs don't overly plan or program children's lives but give them general structure (which provides

limits and demands to ensure children's physical and emotional safety/ security and their self-control/self-responsibility). They reward children's spontaneity and encourage them to act on their thoughts or ideas and try or improvise things[65] (such as to act like superheroes/famous people; draw or color to express feelings at the moment; trim bushes into new shapes; switch accents; and make or play musical instruments).They help children mix spontaneity with productive and comfortable routines. They some-times make immediate plans and just go do it—instead of talking about it; and encourage children to change regular routines or established patterns to do things they don't usually do, especially if the repetitive behaviors limit their beliefs or willingness to experience new things. They encourage themselves and children to do things that provide exciting stories to tell, starting small and slow, and keep experimenting with new ways of doing something to surprise others at the outcome.

7. *While playing, plants work with pollination helpers (like bees, but-terflies, birds, or animals).* Innovators grow up with their love of reading and learning for fulfilling curiosity in a playful way, not as a chore.[66] They learn and work best in a playful environment, where their mentors/ adults make the subject fun and playful—sparking more curiosities.[67] Their CPI in a topic/subject often starts with a playful introduction to the topic/subject, in which they are instantly hooked. For example, Her-mann's playful introduction of a compass to Einstein at age five, and Lang's playful introduction of a carbon microphone to Steve at age six or seven. (Sadly, as most Asian parents/educators do, I focused too much on my children's *proficiency* in their piano and art skills and not enough on *playfulness* when they first started their lessons.) PTIs see fun and playfulness as important factors for children to learn and create—even as a good practice for life—and teach them that creative expression starts with imperfect results.[68] They resist the work-play dichotomy.[69] (Sadly, test-centric climates are hardly playful and are eliminating children's play times, which stifles children's outbox and newbox thinking.[70]) PTIs encourage children to play with their tasks instead of using external rewards (which are effective for short-term goals) to reach long-term goals.[71] Comedy and humor are also easy-to-grasp tools for making the creative process (ACP) more playful, so PTIs introduce children to funny people and activities like improv. They encourage children to read funny books or watch funny movies, standup gigs, or comedians/comedies.

They make age-appropriate jokes with children and laugh at what they think is funny. They encourage themselves and children to make at least one person laugh each day. They also encourage them to write and tell jokes that make points or have purposes; practice punch-line timing; and be funny with words or physical comedy (like impressions of other people, mime, or slapstick). They provide children with opportunities for silliness through projects (like arts, sciences, or building projects) by incorporating playful elements in their presentations (like adding humor to titles or descriptions or using funny props) or making comic strips or drawing cartoons with funny caricatures and puns. They sometimes throw a costume party for children and help them make a costume to look like their favorite animal, idol, superhero, food, or literary character.

8. Plants generate internal energy by making food in their leaves by combining air, water, and sunlight. Young innovators generate internal energy by combining external, inspirational figures/events and/or playful introductions to their CPI. They're known for their physical energy, excitement, intellectual and personal intensity, and concentration, even though some of them face physical limitations.[72] Their energy is generated internally by their intensely focused mind for their CPI, and then by their diligent/persistent work to actualize it, and finally by their passion throughout life, while often sacrificing their immediate pleasures.[73] This energy is the best predictor of future innovation.[74] In order for children to find their CPI, PTIs encourage children to choose three words to describe the kind of person they'd love to be; and to make lists of what they'd do if they could do only one thing for the rest of their life, or what they dream about doing regardless of money, location, ability limitations, or practicality.

PTIs are energetic,[75] and they foster children's energy and energetic mind/life by promoting an active physical life, including healthy activities and lifestyles. They help children effectively use their energy by teaching them to avoid multitasking or scattering among many tasks; take time to concentrate on a project/challenge in a deliberate/focused manner; and then think about it in unfocused ways while doing something else simple and easy. They also encourage children to spend time with others who can bring out the best in them and from whom they can draw strength; maintain regular contact to motivate and excite one another while avoiding insulting, complaining, participating in petty gossip, or looking down on others. They also continuously look for role models or sources of inspiration for pursuing healthy activities. Young innovators discover inspirational figures and events throughout their lives. PTIs also encourage children to express and utilize their high energy by sharing joys of small creative accomplishments, being enthusiastic about others' achievements, and enlarging their future career plans.[76]

Sadly, test-centric climates kill children's high energy, instead of utilizing it: Test-centric climates force teachers to identify energetic children as troublemakers rather than as future innovators.[77] Some creative attitudes are the same as some descriptions of Attention-Deficit/Hyperactivity Disorder (ADHD): being spontaneous/impulsive, energetic/hyper, risk-taking/reckless, and emotional/unstable.[78] America's recent trend of over-diagnosing and over-prescribing ADHD medications dopes young innovators in misguided attempts to control their seemingly negative creative attitudes.[79] Medicating them not only stifles their creative attitudes but also tragically makes them believe that they're neither *allowed* nor *able* to harness their own energy to pursue their CPI or passion.

STEP 2: NURTURE THE SIX SUN ATTITUDES

The sun climate—providing inspiration and encouragement—nurtures the sun attitudes (step 1). The sun attitudes are characterized as innovators' optimism and curiosity that sustain their energy. Their sun attitudes help them become curious optimists, which enables unique outbox and newbox thinking. Step 2 explains what the six sun attitudes are and how they nurture curious optimists who apply outbox and newbox thinking. It starts with a brief anecdote from my life, illustrating how my own sun attitudes were encouraged/discouraged or how I encouraged/discouraged these attitudes within my children. Then I summarize what research says about each of the attitudes and how each can contribute to outbox and newbox thinking. Each attitude can be learned and further developed through practice. The six sun attitudes (with the seemingly negative side in parentheses) are:

1. Optimistic (and Unrealistic)

I used to have a severe test anxiety, like most Asian students do. When I was in high school, I was preparing to take the Korean equivalent of the SAT/ACT—the Korean college entrance exam. In America the SAT/ACT can be taken multiple times, but in Korea the test can be taken only once. All seniors take the exam at the same time. The country enters a state of mass hysteria as every student's future and family expectations hang on the result of a single score.[80] Each student prepares for the exam for years, dedicating at least sixteen hours a day taking classes and working on practice exams.[81] By the time of the exam, I had studied tens of thousands of hours.

On the exam day, I, with my worst test anxiety, was checking my work in the math section when the proctor announced that there were only two minutes remaining. Deep in concentration, I thumbed at the corner of the page and suddenly I made the heart-wrenching discovery that there was another page of the exam that I hadn't seen! (The practice tests I had been working on for years always had only a single page of math questions; I could not finish the second page of the real test!) My life was over. I had studied all those days and nights for nothing. I would not get into my dream college.

My failure definitely shut certain doors, and at the time I could see only the negative repercussions. However, my mother was genuinely grateful that I, despite my test anxiety, still earned enough scores from the other subjects to get a full-ride scholarship for the best state university in the region. For me, it was hard to think like that at first, but I came to understand her view. She had been the most optimistic person I knew despite the fact that she had suffered many misfortunes, including the deaths of her three sons. She had remained grateful for many

Figure 4.1. Optimistic (and Unrealistic) Sun Attitude

things in life, thanked God *every* day, and stood up again. (She was certain about seeing her dead sons again in heaven.) Since then, I've learned to be optimistic, and much good and ultimately my path in life came out of that "failure." Today, like her, I do my best at highlighting my positivity and strengths instead of worrying about my weaknesses or the results.

Research findings on the optimistic attitude

Having the optimistic attitude (see figure 4.1) means seeing positive out-comes regardless of existing circumstances. Innovators jump on oppor-tunities, meet new people, dare to explore new ideas and experiences, venture into uncertain and "risky" endeavors, and discover doors of oppor-tunities out of difficulties.[82] They don't avoid challenges in pursuing their unguaranteed goals, because they believe in positive outcomes.[83] When they can't find a solution, they redefine the problem to make it more approachable. Focusing on what's going well and seeing negative events in a positive light promotes their psychological well-being by reducing their stresses, and it enables them to persist despite setbacks and failures, to create opportunities out of challenges, to enhance their flexible perspec-tives and thus outbox and newbox thinking, and to achieve unique ideas and/or solutions.[84]

2. Big-Picture-Thinking (and Dreamy)

My younger sister inspires me. She's a fine example of eminence without material riches. She went to the best college in Korea and then pursued a life helping others in need. While other college students enjoyed their freedom for the first time after the exam hell, she was changing diapers for disabled adults who had no families. Once she graduated college, she worked while earning a graduate degree. But after graduation, instead of making and spending money for herself, she diligently and persistently worked to found a multicultural library for children in Seoul, funded only by private donations. Many immigrants from impoverished countries have moved to Korea with children, where there are not many books in their native languages. A multicultural library is a new concept in Korea because books are usually available only in a few languages (Korean, Chinese, Jap-anese, and English).

My sister is an innovator. She identified a need, saw the big picture, turned her CPI into a passion, created a new version of an existing public institution, and gave it what it needed to fly. However, although many donate time and money to her causes, most Koreans can't understand what motivates her. According to my hometown villagers, her life is a failure, not only because she's poor, but also because she's unmarried. They often ask her "Why?" and even "What's wrong with you?" To a society that celebrates conformity—where everyone gets married and where success is defined as getting rich or increasing status—her life *is* a failure. But according to my Americanized children, she's admirable. I'm proud of her innovation, but I still dislike her suffering. I blame my parents for my sister's suffering. When we were growing up, every day they told us to study hard and become 'the light and salt of the world,' which we did not understand at the time but has become deeply ingrained in our minds. Yet I thank them for nurturing our big-picture-thinking attitude. My brother (a pastor) also serves others.

Figure 4.2. Big-Picture-Thinking (and Dreamy) Sun Attitude

Research findings on the big-picture-thinking attitude

The big-picture-thinking attitude (see figure 4.2) comes from being inspired by others' words, deeds, or values, and seeing the big picture beyond constraints. Innovators think in distant and futuristic ways.[85] They think away from *me* (people or things different from *me*),[86] away from *here* (faraway problems),[87] away from *now* (future plans),[88] and away from *reality* (unlikely or imaginative things).[89] Innovators' big-picture thoughts transcend the concrete constraints and limitations, which promotes outbox thinking, and they enable them to recognize patterns and relationships among the various parts of a context or system, leading to unique connections between unrelated things, which promotes newbox thinking.[90] For instance, when innovators were deeply in love with someone, inducing a long-term perspective (by eternal love!) and thus enhancing outbox and newbox thinking, they achieved innovations such as the greatest paintings, novels, songs, plays, and architecture.[91]

Innovators are inspired to do what they love by their big-picture goal.[92] Their inspiration sparks energy that shines brightly throughout their lives. Their big-picture goal enables them to sustain their optimistic view of how their creation may benefit the world (even as the details transform over time).[93] By seeing their big-picture goal with the compassionate attitude, they take greater risks and become even more creative, leading to a bigger impact on more people.[94] Albert Einstein, Steve Jobs, and Benjamin Franklin were all inspired by their big-picture goal—to change the world—which led to a big impact on many people.[95]

3. Curious (and Annoying)

According to my mother, my first question was, "Why don't I have a penis like my big brother?" She told me a rabbit took mine. My second and third questions were, "Why only mine?" and "How can I get it back?" I'd already observed gender inequality, which is part of the fabric of Korean life. I knew a penis granted many opportunities, but not for me. The irreconcilable issue dogged me throughout my schooling in Korea. I always asked many questions, and many of the answers kept leading back to Confucianism. Confucianism in Korean society is like water that fish swim through. It is subconscious but pervasive; if you ask a fish, "How is the water?" the fish will in turn ask you, "What is water?" It was impossible for me to grasp what life would be like without Confucianism, but I was curious to know. My curiosity for and frustration with it eventually led me to my dissertation topic: Confucianism.

Figure 4.3. Curious (and Annoying) Sun Attitude

Research findings on the curious attitude

The curious attitude (see figure 4.3) is characterized by thinking child-like and insatiably seeking information. Innovators approach situations and problems from a childlike beginner's mind that's unconfined to rigid ways of thinking.[96] They ask many "crazy" questions, as creativity begins with curiosity. Their expertise grows as they develop a love of reading and learning and diligently learn to actualize their CPI. Their CPI and prior knowledge—in addition to curiosity—alert them to details that others miss, which leads to even more curious questions.[97] They don't give up easily because curiosity reveals new options even at dead ends.[98] Curiosity that's continuously rewarded and renewed helps turn their CPI into a lifelong passion. Even as adults, they're still in close communication with their inner child. They're able to ignore (or at least attenuate the effect of) social restrictions and conventions, and their childlike beginner's curiosity fends off stagnant thinking, which opens them to more possibilities and promotes outbox and newbox thinking.[99]

4. Spontaneous (and Impulsive)

In my second month in America, I attended a conference for the Home Instruction for Parents of Preschool Youngsters (HIPPY) program in California. It's designed to help parents—who are less educated and poor—break the cycle of poor education and poverty. This was the topic of my Korean doctoral dissertation because I wanted to help poor and uneducated parents like mine. (My father completed only his first grade due to the Japanese taking his father away; my mother completed only third grade due to the Korean War. I grew up ashamed of this because education is extremely important in Asia.) At the conference, I met a board member of HIPPY who was implementing research on the program, which I wanted to learn. I spontaneously invited myself to visit her home in Tampa, Florida over our first American Christmas. My children and I, without any forethought or planning, flew there. After returning to California, I decided to move to Tampa so that I could learn more about the program and conduct research.

Visiting her and moving to Tampa was spontaneous! I hired a moving company for our furniture, packed my car with my children and food, and found the interstate highway that would take us from the West Coast to the East Coast. The deserts in Arizona, the hills in Texas, the big rivers in the state of Mississippi all looked never-ending. We got lost many times. The first time was in Texas late at night. After I put gas in my car, I went inside the gas-station convenience store. Three men were joking around with the cashier. Instead of giving me directions, one of them smirked and said, "Asian chicks turn me on." I didn't (and still don't) understand many American slang words, but I could tell that they weren't interested in helping me. After that, I didn't bother to ask anyone for help with directions, even when we got really lost.

Figure 4.4. Spontaneous (and Impulsive) Sun Attitude

When we crossed the Mississippi River, I was scared because the bridge was very long, hilly, and narrow. I drove so slowly on the bridge that a policeman pulled me over. But after he looked at everything—

including my children (who were shaking) and all of our blankets, pillows, and food—he let us go without a ticket! When I lived in Korea, the longest I'd driven was for four hours. From California to Florida took *sixty-four* hours.

Research findings on the spontaneous attitude

Having the spontaneous attitude (see figure 4.4) means being flexible and immediately acting on new ideas and opportunities. People often think too much to be spontaneous; paralysis by analysis is commonplace. Innovators prefer a flexible, spontaneous way of life to a set path.[100] They're willing to say "Yes!" and uproot a stable life at any moment to follow the opportunity whenever it comes up. A short-fused willingness to fulfill immediate desires is a childlike behavior and is unacceptable to most adults.[101] However, it helps innovators be less self-conscious and generate ideas more spontaneously—even subconsciously—promoting outbox and newbox thinking.[102]

Innovators balance spontaneity with persistence as a technique for generating and evaluating ideas.[103] Their spontaneous thinking is chaotic and flexible rather than systematic and rigid. They think spontaneously, using random and subconscious thoughts without giving much thought to practicality, to generate ideas (during the idea-generation stage of an ACP). After taking a break, they critically and persistently evaluate those ideas for merit and utility (during the idea-evaluation stage of the ACP).[104]

5. Playful (and Mischievous)

I wasn't allowed to be playful as an adult when I was in Korea. It wasn't until I met the people at the Torrance Center in the United States that I discovered my playful side. I was allowed to look at things without thinking about what others might say and without feeling judged. They let me be myself; I was born again there.

Humor is culture-bound.[105] When students make a joke in my class, I often fail to understand it. I ask them to explain, and then after they explain it, it isn't funny anymore. Often when I make a joke, my students don't respond. Other times, when I'm serious about something, they think I'm hilarious. Once I accidentally pronounced "presidential election" as "presidential erection" because, like most Asians, it's hard for me to pronounce *L* and *R* differently. Then one student asked, "You mean Bill Clinton?" I said, "No." All of my students laughed to no end. I still don't get why it was *that* funny.

Asian people don't think playfulness or humor is creative.[106] It's even against Confucians' value on formality, where playfulness or humor is considered imprudent or flippant.[107] Humorous candidates are never elected in Korea. To my knowledge, no official, and certainly no president, is allowed to joke in public. Not only presidents, but also employers and employees must be serious at all times because they're expected to be respectable.

Figure 4.5. Playful (and Mischievous) Sun Attitude

Research findings on the playful attitude

Being playful and humorous are creative actions.[108] The playful attitude (see figure 4.5) involves approaching situations in exploratory ways and seeing the lighter side of challenges. Innovators are more playful and humorous than are non-innovators.[109] They are focused on their passion and goal, while using casual and flexible thinking, including humor.[110] (I use playful cactus illustrations in this book, which were created by my daughter's playful ideas.) They don't take themselves too seriously, and they maintain a level of good humor that helps them overcome creative blocks, absorb criticism, and keep their egos in check during periods of success.[111] So, playfulness and humor promote their health and coping.[112]

Innovators' humor and playfulness structure their work as fun and/or play in a way that frees their outbox thinking—which is limited by work-play dichotomy—and finds ideas/solutions that might not have been thought of using pure logic or common sense.[113] Their provocative approaches that deliberately mock analytical top-down approaches facilitate newbox thinking and reveal surprising connections and/or opportunities.[114]

Group humor reinforces unity of effort. Workplace humor helps reframe situations from fresh perspectives. Its spontaneity, experimentation, and fun prompt outbox thinking.[115] It also cultivates a sense of community and shared intimacy, promoting healthy social interactions in the group.[116]

6. Energetic (and Hyper)

When I was little, I didn't have the opportunity to take any lessons in sports or the arts. However, I learned how to swim in the river when I was six, playing with the older children in the village. While I was learning, I was told to swim only in the shallow part of the river. But I was so curious that I went into the deep part and nearly drowned. I tried to cry for help, but by doing so I drank in so much water that I lost consciousness. When I awoke, my uncle was trying to get the water out of me by pushing on my stomach and blowing in my mouth. I learned later that a fifth-grade girl saved me from the water. I still remember her name but never had the opportunity to thank her.

When spring came the next year, I went to pick wild flowers in the mountains with other children (mostly boys). The bright azaleas made the entire mountain look like it was on fire. All of us were eating azalea petals, so our lips were pinkish-red. When I was full, I noticed an unusual flower on the cliff. Although my friends told me not to, I climbed up the cliff and finally reached the stem of the flower. As soon as I reached it, though, I fell off, and my body plummeted all the way down to the bottom of the cliff. I thought I was dead. But when I came to, I was inside a bush. Lots of leaves from the previous years cushioned my fall. The other children were horrified and crying because they were certain I was dead; their streaming tears washed lines of clean skin through the dust and pinkish-red azalea color all over their faces.

My explorations in nature were possible because my grandmother wasn't with me. At that time, she lived in Daegu city with my older brother to get him a better education. If she'd been home, she'd never have allowed me to act like a boy. My mother let me play outside with boys because she knew that I had too much curiosity and energy to be stopped by anyone.

Ever since I was little, I've always had so much energy that I think if I had grown up in America, I'd have been diagnosed with ADHD and medicated. I still have so much energy that my students describe me as the most energetic professor—ever.

Figure 4.6. Energetic (and Hyper) Sun Attitude

Research findings on the energetic attitude

The energetic attitude (see figure 4.6) is typified by being motivated from within, regardless of external circumstances (by intense curiosity, self-inspiration, or other reasons). Innovators are tremendously energetic, because they're curious about or inspired by something and must examine it further (which is called "curiosity tension").[117] Their energy matures throughout their journey. It begins as they discover a curiosity, a preference or an interest (CPI); it accelerates as they develop expertise; and when their CPI ignites into a full-fledged passion, they devote sacrificial, obsessive energy to accomplish their clear—but unguaranteed—goal.[118]

Innovators learn to manage or channel their seemingly limitless energy in order to fulfill their passion or goal. Sometimes they sleep very little. But a lack of sleep impairs short-term memory that's critical for creativity, so sometimes they sleep a lot or take power naps.[119] They incorporate regular walks in nature and maintain health for their successful creative process (ACP). A more physically fit body supplies better nutrients and more oxygen to the brain. No amount of excessive drudgery can replace the power of a healthy body and a rested mind for developing creative thoughts.[120]

Creativity doesn't decrease with age.[121] Innovators' productivity depends on the length of time they have been actively engaged in a field—not how old they are.[122] Career changes rejuvenate creative energy.[123] Also, creativity is facilitated by factors that postpone mental decline and retain mental energy, including healthy diets and exercises, social activities and networks, and intellectual engagement.[124]

INNOVATORS' SUN ATTITUDES: THE CACTUS AMONG US

Innovators display the sun attitudes that might seem negative—such as unrealistic, dreamy, annoying, impulsive, mischievous, or hyper. For example, innovators are often so optimistic that they seem unrealistic. For instance, Mandela's pursuit of democracy while he was in prison for twenty-seven years might seem unrealistic.

Innovators are often so big-picture-thinking that they might seem dreamy, just as Einstein's hope to create a theory that would explain the entire universe might seem dreamy.

Innovators are often so curious that they might seem annoying. For example, in elementary school, O'Keeffe had so many questions that her teachers sometimes were unable to answer, but Aunt Lola answered all of them.[125] Her teachers might have considered O'Keeffe annoying.

Innovators are often so spontaneous that they might seem impulsive. At twenty-three, when Mandela discovered Dalindyebo's (his guardian) arranged-marriage plan for Mandela, he ran away to Johannesburg without any plan, which made him suffer from no food and no place to live until he met Walter Sisulu.[126] Such a move could be deemed impulsive.

Innovators' playfulness might seem mischievous. When young Steve Jobs caused others to bring their dogs and cats to school by making posters for a fictional pet day, and when he swapped others' bike-lock combinations,[127] he was considered mischievous.

Innovators are often so energetic that they might seem hyper. O'Keeffe's energy for painting when she was able to see; then for charcoal after she could barely see; and then for sculpting after she became almost blind at eighty-four[128]—might seem hyper.

Parents and educators must be able to see the long-term positive aspects of behaviors that seem prickly in children; so they can encourage the underlying sun attitudes instead of seeing the children as trouble-makers. Also, such children must be able to view their own sun attitudes positively. When parents and educators succeed in cultivating the sun climate and nurturing children's sun attitudes, they are following the footsteps of the PTIs who encouraged, taught, and mentored the greatest innovators in history.

Chapter 5

THE STORM CLIMATE THAT
NURTURES THE STORM ATTITUDES

The history of the people of South Africa is similar to the history of other peoples who were subjugated, marginalized, persecuted, and sometimes enslaved by European colonists. In 1910, Cape Colony was unified with three other British colonies to create the Union of South Africa, and three years later, the new government passed the Natives Land Act. This law made it illegal for black and "mixed-raced" people to own land—immediately dispossessing hundreds of thousands of people from their land.[1]

Nelson Mandela was born on July 18, 1918, in Mvezo, a village in the Cape Province. His birth name was Rolihlahla, which colloquially means a *troublemaker*.[2] On the first day at a missionary school, his teacher gave him the name Nelson. At the time, it was common for children to be given new Anglicized first names to make it easier for British colonials to address the African people.[3]

Nelson was born into a lesser royal family within the Thembu tribe, where excellence was expected of him.[4] His father, Hendry Mandela, was a local chief and served as the principal counselor to the king regent of the Thembu people. Unfortunately, he lost both his title and his fortune due to a disagreement with a governing British colonial magistrate in the area. Hendry stood up to the magistrate, was charged with insubordination, and was removed from his principal counselor position. (After that, Nelson's family became poor and moved to the homestead of his mother, Nosekeni Fanny, in the village of Qunu.) Nelson identified with Hendry's proud defiance and stubborn sense of fairness, which nurtured his nonconforming and defiant attitudes.[5]

Nosekeni's home consisted of three separate round huts. One was for cooking, another for storing food, and a third for sleeping. She constructed the huts with molded bricks from local clay and the roofs from bundling rope around grass. Everyone slept on mats on the dirt floor without pillows.[6] Nelson learned to be a shepherd and spent a lot of time outside playing with other boys. He grew up learning essential knowledge, techniques, and skills: how to swim; how to drink milk straight from a cow; how to quietly stalk a bird and kill it using a slingshot; how to find and gather honey, fruit, and edible roots; and how to use a sharpened piece of wire to catch fish. He made toys using the things around him, including clay and tree branches, and playfully fought with sticks.[7] This early experience of playing with and adapting to nature built his physical strengths and self-efficacious and risk-taking attitudes. He sustained these strengths for almost his entire life with long-distance running, soccer, and boxing for ninety minutes a day.[8] This nurtured his self-disciplined attitude. The security and simplicity of his early rural upbringing also nurtured his optimistic and playful attitudes. At twenty-three, he moved (actually ran away) to the bustling city of Johannesburg—a stark contrast to his early country life—but he would always consider himself a country boy.[9]

Nelson had a large extended family. Following the precepts of the Xhosa tradition, Hendry was a polygamist with four wives. His wives lived miles away from each other, and he periodically visited each of them. He had thirteen children with his four wives: four sons and nine daughters. Nelson was the youngest of the four sons and spent time living with each of his father's wives. Nelson thought of each as his own mother and treated them with respect, and each one of them loved and supported him in return.[10] Accepting his four mothers' views and advice nurtured his complexity-seeking and gender-bias-free attitudes. Additionally, Xhosa tradition made Nelson consider his cousins as brothers and sisters. This tradition of possessing a large number of close influences shaped how Nelson influenced others, which nurtured his mentored and resourceful attitudes.[11]

From Hendry and his relatives, Nelson grew up listening to proud stories of his forbearers' rebellions and battles against the waves of white European settlers, and the military troops that eventually subjugated the Xhosa people and brought them under British colonial rule. He consistently learned about African culture and history at home, building his cultural identity, and he also learned *Ubuntu*, which is the African notion of human brotherhood and compassion.[12]

Nosekeni became a devout Christian, and at age seven Nelson was baptized in the Methodist church and sent to a missionary school. He became the first of his family to go to school, as both of his parents were illiterate.[13] Nelson's entire formal schooling was by European missionary institutions. But he continued his African home education, which he used as a source of wisdom. His curiosity for both European and African traditions developed his love of reading and learning, which made him an Afro-European. This helped him build his bicultural identity, but Nelson also felt conflicted because he hated learning about the people who oppressed his own South African people.[14]

At twelve, Nelson's world drastically changed when his father died of lung disease.[15] Nosekeni decided to honor Hendry's wish for Nelson to go live with another family that had an established father figure, for a better upbringing and future opportunities. It was a tough decision because she would desperately miss Nelson. Suddenly, Nelson had to mourn the death of the entire world he knew and loved unconditionally, but he knew Hendry had wanted him to be educated and prepared for a bigger world.[16] (Throughout his life, his mother supported Nelson's revolutionary efforts and encouraged his education until her death, which unfortunately occurred while he was imprisoned.)[17] Finding strength in his father's vision, when he arrived at his new family's home, he let his mother leave without shedding a tear.[18] This nurtured his big-picture-thinking and independent attitudes.

Jongintaba Dalindyebo, the Thembu king regent, accepted Nelson into his home and treated him like his own son. He became Nelson's guardian and mentor. However, Nelson still felt like an outsider because his new family and world were very different from his original family and world. He eventually became an integral part of the new family as he was given the same status and responsibilities as Dalindyebo's own children.[19] Dalindyebo and his wife were stern, but they guided and reprimanded him in fairness. Nelson never doubted their love. He had a lot of household chores, but among them he enjoyed pressing Dalindyebo's Western suits the most. He pursued this task with excellence, taking great pride in carefully making the creases in his trousers.[20] This nurtured his diligent attitude.

Dalindyebo never told Nelson how to behave, but Nelson observed him and followed his example.[21] Learning about leadership and democracy from Dalindyebo's court and regular tribal meetings was Nelson's main focus as a teenager.[22] He was fascinated by Dalindyebo's leadership style, which was characterized by listening silently and impassively to people until he needed to elicit a consensus from contrasting views.[23] This nurtured Nelson's big-picture-thinking and self-reflective attitudes. Dalindyebo's openness to diverse points of view nurtured Mandela's open-minded and complexity-seeking attitudes. This helped him later be open to the diverse views and ideologies from the Communist Party, Indians' nonviolent resistance movements, and even prison guards and workers. It also shaped his own leadership style of consensus building.[24]

Nelson learned early how to recognize the good in others and tried to emulate their behavior as best as he could. He looked up to Dalindyebo's son, Justice, in every way. He thought Justice (who was four years older) was more intelligent than he was, so he worked diligently to keep up with him. (Nelson's new aunt examined and helped with his homework most nights.)[25] Justice became another mentor for Nelson.[26] Nelson accepted his uncertain future, as opposed to Justice, who was in line to become the regent of the Thembu tribe following Dalindyebo.

Nelson criticized missionary institutions' imperialism but still maintained respect for the missionary traditions and teachers who were often opposed to other white administrators, which strengthened his defiant attitude.(He'd often write letters to his former teachers to thank them when he was in prison.)[27] Nelson and Justice attended Clarkebury secondary school. The school governor/teacher, Reverend Cecil Harris, became Nelson's first white role model. He planted the seeds in Nelson for racial harmony and a lifelong love of gardening.[28]

At twenty-one, Nelson joined Justice at the University College of Fort Hare, and at twenty-three he was elected to the Student Representative Council (SRC). When the students boycotted the poor food quality and SRC's lack of power, he resigned from SRC to support them. But the college expelled him for insubordination and told him he could return only if he served on the SRC again. To support the students' view, he proudly defied the college, like his father had defied the British magistrate.[29] Sadly, this decision caused him to become a college dropout.[30]

When he returned back to Dalindyebo's home, he found two arranged-marriage plans by Dalindyebo: one for Justice and the other for Nelson, according to the tribal custom. But Nelson and Justice decided to defy the custom, stole two oxen for money, and ran away to Johannesburg.[31] In Johannesburg, after struggling with no food/money for several months, a cousin introduced Nelson to the future African National Congress (ANC) leader Walter Sisulu, who aspired to change South Africa for the benefit of black Africans.[32] Sisulu helped Nelson get a job at Lazar Sidelsky's Jewish law firm as an articled clerk (apprentice to lawyers). Giving a job to a black man was extremely rare, but Sidelsky had been involved in African education, donating money and time to African schools. Sidelsky, Nelson's new mentor, repeatedly insisted that Nelson become a role model for other Africans by becoming a successful attorney, not a politician.[33]

Despite Sidelsky's advice, at twenty-six, Nelson joined the ANC and became actively involved in its movement against Apartheid, a racial segregation system that restricted non-white people's basic human rights from 1948 to 1994. He cofounded the ANC Youth League (ANCYL) with Sisulu and Oliver Tambo. At thirty-three, he became president of ANCYL. The police massacre of sixty-nine unarmed black South Africans and the subsequent banning of the ANC changed Nelson's commitment from nonviolent protest to advocating sabotage and guerilla tactics to end Apartheid. This eventually put him in prison for twenty-seven years.[34]

Instead of deflating his spirits, however, being in prison gave him the time and space to think and reflect. He read of great leaders who overcame challenges and adversities and rose to greatness.[35] This inspired him and helped him realize the potential greatness in every ordinary individual. He even became a fatherlike figure to some of the prison guards and workers.[36] He, decades after, believed that if he hadn't been imprisoned, he would not have gained the leadership skills to end Apartheid.[37] His future eventually vaulted him to the top ranks of the world's greatest heroes.

Nelson's soil attitudes enabled cross-pollination:

In his soil climates—including his mentors Dalindyebo and Justice—Nelson's soil attitudes had been nurtured. This enabled later cross-pollination with Walter Sisulu and Oliver Tambo. Without them, the Mandela name would be meaningless. Through his friendship with Walter Sisulu, who was six years older than Nelson was, Nelson began to see that his duty wasn't just to his tribe or region but to Africans as a whole. He moved in with Sisulu, who became a role model, mentor, and lifelong friend; and his first wife was Sisulu's cousin.[38]

Nelson met Oliver Tambo at Fort Hare, and they cofounded South Africa's first black law firm. Tambo helped him during his long years of imprisonment from ages forty-four to seventy-one. When Nelson was sixty-one, Tambo furthered an intense campaign to free him, which fueled the growing international outcry against Apartheid. This brought popular and international attention to Nelson's imprisonment. More and more people condemned Apartheid and eventually helped set him free.[39]

Nelson's 4S attitudes enabled ION thinking for innovation:

At twelve, Nelson started developing his expertise in his CPI in leadership, when he met Dalindyebo.[40] He used inbox thinking that was enabled by his soil and storm attitudes, which had been nurtured in his soil and storm climates. While observing Dalindyebo's leadership, Nelson learned democracy meant everyone must be heard and decision making must include everyone.[41] Nelson's involvement in the ANC and its movement against Apartheid, under Sisulu's mentorship, advanced his expertise. Cofounding ANCYL with Sisulu and Tambo and eventually becoming its president further matured his expertise.

When Nelson first imagined the future of South Africa—based on his expertise—he used outbox thinking that was enabled by his sun and space attitudes, which had been nurtured in his sun and space climates. He represented a community with the view that a nation belongs equally to all of its different people. This ideology was a radical shift from the *we* versus *they* mentality (in-group vs. out-group).[42] Most politicians at that time sought power by highlighting the differences between these groups and served only the people within those groups who voted for them. However, Nelson represented a broader community that existed only in his imagination.[43] Through his experiences with missionary-school teachers and Sidelsky (at his first job), he had learned that black and white people have far more in common than they have differences. This improved Nelson's outbox thinking instead of strengthening a (literal) black-and-white dichotomy.

When Nelson synthesized oppositional views and situations from African and European cultural experiences, he used newbox thinking that was enabled by his 4S attitudes, which had been nurtured in his 4S climates. He synthesized (1) African culture and history with *Ubuntu*; (2) European missionaries' compassion; (3) European oppressors' views, history, and literature; (4) Indians' philosophy of peaceful-resistance; (5) the Communist Party's philosophy; and (6) his imprisonment experience.

When Nelson transformed his uniquely synthesized ideas into his democracy, he also used newbox thinking. At age seventy-two—far more than ten years after he started developing his expertise, also confirming the ten-year rule—he promoted his ideas of democracy by leading the ANC in negotiations with President Frederik Willem de Klerk to end Apartheid.[44] He prevented a seemingly inevitable bloody racial war and led a peaceful revolution, which transformed into South Africa's nonracial democracy.[45] In 1993, at age seventy-four, Nelson and de Klerk jointly won the Nobel Peace Prize.[46] Finally at seventy-five he became South Africa's first democratically elected president (with de Klerk serving as his first deputy).

While there were many other experiences in Nelson Mandela's growth and fruitful success as an innovator, let's explore more deeply what the storm climate is and how it impacts individuals' creativity development.

According to the CATs model introduced in chapter 2, there are three steps for innovation. Cultivating the storm climate (step 1) and nurturing the storm attitudes (step 2) are discussed in this chapter. Applying ION thinking skills is discussed in chapter 9 (step 3).

STEP 1: CULTIVATE THE FIERCE STORM CLIMATE

Although sun is necessary, too much of it in the absence of storms damages plants' buds, blossoms, or young fruits. Likewise, the bright sun climate is necessary, before providing individuals with the storm climate, but too much of it in the absence of the fierce storm climate makes them become frustrated dreamers. In a forest, fierce storms are vital for providing water, thinning weak plants, and introducing genetic variety that helps strong plants survive even greater adversity. The storm climate sets high expectations and challenges for individuals, which directly impacts the storm attitudes that they develop, which are described in step 2. When the storm climate initially nurtures the storm attitudes in individuals, they develop expertise that turns their CPI into a passion. Once they are truly good at something, it can be their passion. Their expertise contributes to usefulness of their creation. Their storm attitudes help them become resilient hard workers, which enables inbox and newbox thinking.

Research Findings on the Storm Climate

1. An apple tree won't bloom just because it's warm; it must also be mature to reproduce. Innovators' parents value learning and hard work, and, compared to others, they marry later in life. Usually they wait until they're in their thirties to have their first child, when they're emotionally mature and have access to resources for the benefit of their children.[47]

2. Apple trees grow well in a warm, safe greenhouse, but they also require a certain number of cold hours outdoors—independent from the greenhouse—for their successful fruit production. Gardeners protect outdoor young trees from winter storms and support them with trunk guards, but they also allow the trunk to move and grow without restraint. Similarly, through early positive attachment, innovators' parents prepare children for the real world before they leave home. They nurture children's emotional resources and optimism to overcome challenges, and independence to develop their own identity instead of clinging to their parents.[48] In time, innovators' parents emphasize independence rather than doing things as a family, and their children enjoy experiences apart from their families.[49] Parents and teachers of innovators (PTIs) teach children independence by encouraging them to do tasks on their own, starting small, and to not feel as if they need a buddy to do every task. PTIs also teach children to avoid depending on others or GPS for directions and to know the basic route before going anywhere. They also encourage children to learn to be handy around the house by watching adults, videos, or reading instructions or manuals; and to learn to cook and engage in other household matters (like planning for the future, balancing budgets, understanding expenses, and finding ways to save money). Young innovators' transition from security to independence helps them discipline themselves, build self-efficacy, and accept uncertainty in an ambiguous world.[50]

3. The earlier pruning starts, the less likely trees grow askew. Preventing trees from growing in the wrong direction early is easier than correcting them later. The right amount of pruning (neither over-pruning or under-pruning) channels trees' energy into blooming and fruiting. Likewise, the right amount of discipline channels children's energy into creativity development. Too little discipline wastes children's potential, but too much discipline—based on compliance and obedience—limits their independence, self-discipline, risk taking, and thus creativity development.[51] Regarding disciplining children, there are four major parenting styles, which I have modified into parenting/teaching styles: controlling (also called "authoritarian"), guiding (also called "authoritative"), permissive, and neglectful. Controlling parents/teachers dictate how children behave while showing little warmth; guiding parents/teachers set high behavioral expectations for children while showing warmth; permissive parents/teachers exert little control over children's behavior while showing warmth; and neglectful parents/teachers demand little and are detached from children.[52] The guiding parenting/teaching style is best for children's creativity development and used by PTIs.

Using the guiding parenting/teaching style, PTIs nurture children's self-discipline by setting limitations and behavioral frameworks.[53] PTIs teach children boundaries through punishment or criticism and explain how these will keep them safe (without self-discipline, they're like a wagon rolling down a mountain with no brakes; with the proper controls, speed can lead to all sorts of opportunities—and even flight). They teach them how to invest in long-term values (ethics, principles, purposes, delayed gratification, etc.), instead of short-term pleasures (such as shopping and using drugs). PTIs have logical discussions for important issues with young children before the issues arise (like the dangers of alcohol and drugs, sexuality, and teenage pregnancy) while sharing accurate statistical facts. They also teach children to increase big-picture emotions (like hope and pride) that motivate long-term goals like career achievements; and to decrease shortsighted emotions (like instant happiness) that motivate short-term goals like leisure and immediate gratification. Young innovators' early independence gives them strength to discipline themselves and focus on their goals, removing distractions and addictions (to drugs, alcohol, gadgets, etc.).[54] Note that alcohol and marijuana are the most commonly abused substances; a common misconception is that they enhance creativity.[55] While experimenting with them for the first time can facilitate generating *unique* ideas, true innovation requires attention to detail and follow-through to become useful.[56] In addition, alcohol and marijuana slow down thinking, and regular use can alter several brain areas.[57]

They teach children to learn that achieving expertise over time through hard work is a beautiful and powerful feeling; and to invest effort for long-term results to make their own luck by becoming the right person *ahead of time*. To teach this PTIs use examples such as Jonas Salk and Alexander Fleming: Jonas Salk studied viruses from kindergarten through medical school because they sparked his curiosity; then he worked in university labs for another decade, becoming an expert in research methodologies and viruses; finally, he discovered the polio vaccine by having a prepared mind, not by pure chance. Alexander Fleming's familiarity with bacteria-killing agents, after years of intensive research, enabled him to appreciate his accidental discovery of penicillin in a dirty petri dish.[58]

Consistently, persistently maintained apple trees produce higher-quality fruit. PTIs get the best results from consistently, persistently practicing small efforts. They discipline and guide every day for ten minutes rather than have a huge and lengthy discussion once a month for five hours. Many adults pay attention to children's academics and negative behaviors more than their social growth and positive behaviors, which increases negative behaviors.[59] But PTIs pay attention to both positive and negative behaviors and to both academics and social growth. They guide children with thoughtful flexibility instead of relying on rigid rules.[60] They don't expect children to obey rules without choices or options, discussions, or questions. They provide explanations for their decisions and rules and encourage children to be a part of the process of making decisions and rules.[61] This improves children's flexible thinking and self-discipline.[62] They inspire a vision—not fear—in children by letting children disagree with them; listening to children's argument; and letting children understand why PTIs think the way they do. They discipline in an immediate and proportional manner with clear expectations and reasons for those expectations.[63] They use two-way communication for discipline—not only giving but also taking feedback—that's open, expressive, and logical.[64] They're neither forcefully strict nor use physical punishment.[65] When children fail to meet expectations, PTIs make the expectations clearer and demand adherence to them while respecting children's free will.[66] They facilitate, instead of being controlling or restrictive, so that children engage in exploratory behaviors and correct their own mistakes.[67] They consistently, persistently monitor children to ensure that the right lessons are learned and maintained to nurture their self-discipline and diligence.

4. Gardeners start with early high expectations for great blossoms and fruits, even before planting seeds. Likewise, PTIs set high expectations for children early. However, compared to Asians, many Americans lack a strong work ethic, and 93 percent of Asian Americans describe other Asian Americans as very diligent, whereas only 57 percent of non-Asian Americans said the same about their fellow non-Asian Americans.[68] About 62 percent of Asian Americans say that non-Asian American parents have low expectations for their children, whereas only 9 percent said the same about Asian American parents.[69] Children's expectations are formed early in pre-school or kindergarten through their parents' expectations, which affect their achievements not only in childhood but also in later years.[70]

PTIs instill high expectations and diligence in both themselves and young children, and they grant children great responsibility early.[71] They, together, make chore charts for children to follow and complete weekly. They encourage children's organization and focus by creating structured environments.[72] They teach organization skills and time management and prioritizing skills to children; encourage them to give everything a *home* where it belongs; help arrange their own schedules and make to-do lists using a board or a calendar to visualize tasks that need to be done today, next week, or this month. PTIs also help children set specific goals rather than just urging them to do their best.[73] Children who achieve superior results without great effort haven't truly excelled and have wasted their potential. PTIs encourage excellence within the children's own potential while valuing their freedom and playfulness.[74] They specify their expectations for knowledge/skill acquisition and mastery while giving interesting tasks/activities and avoiding repetitive ones.[75] They accurately assess children's readiness and challenge them accordingly.[76] PTIs help children set high goals based on individual mastery of knowledge and skill rather than socially desirable goals or for others' recognition or for just achieving scores, while making the goals realistic. They encourage children to write down short-term, intermediate, and long-term goals; display writings or photos of their goals somewhere they can always see them and visualize achieving them; and draw/create pictures of themselves in five years and constantly reflect on them to become more like their future self. PTIs also teach children what it takes to reach their goals, help them know where to focus, and motivate them (like amount of effort, particular problem-solving approaches, or percentages of questions answered correctly). They encourage children to use time lines to self-monitor their progress for their goals daily in journals/calendars; record what they've achieved and have yet to achieve, share their goals with others (which makes them more obligated to achieve them), and ask others to check on their progress. PTIs give feedback regarding progress toward goals; and reward or have them reward themselves for achieving milestones or small goals toward the big goal along the way (like movies or theater, a spa treatment, or trips). Young innovators grow up diligently pursuing and achieving higher goals.[77] Their high achievements accompany internal high satisfaction and (possible) external rewards, which leads to setting future goals even higher.[78] They utilize their maximum potential through diligence.

5. *Trees develop confident roots and stalks by overcoming hard storms.* Young innovators build self-efficacy (true confidence: knowing what they are good at) for performing specific tasks by overcoming challenges through their self-discipline and diligence. Self-efficacy is different from self-esteem (general sense of self-worth, like "I am important") or self-confidence (general belief in themselves, like "I am smart").[79] Only their self-efficacy—neither self-confidence nor self-esteem—enhances their resilience, persistence, and subsequent expertise in their CPI.[80] Accurate self-efficacy is also useful to decide what difficulty levels and what courses or careers to pursue.[81]

However, self-esteem/self-confidence is often inflated in today's America,[82] and it is inflated more in Westerners than in Asians.[83] This might suggest that the permissive parenting/teaching style is popular among American parents and educators. Giving everybody trophies for mediocre accomplishments actually hurts children in the long run. Constantly sugarcoating feedback will deprive them of reality and what it truly takes to accomplish goals.[84] Children need to be criticized for harmful or unethical behaviors and lazy or deficient performances.[85] Inflated self-esteem can actually magnify antisocial or ethnocentric tendencies (as it has for many notorious criminals including Adolf Hitler).[86]

PTIs teach children that happiness will come from pursuing and achieving goals. They provide children with information and inspiration to achieve their goals. Young innovators are engaged in beneficial extracurricular and social activities for their goals rather than only spending time with friends, playing video games, or watching television and hoping for the best.[87] PTIs nurture children's accurate self-efficacy in their task through successful experiences, which helps achieve children's goals.[88] They praise children sincerely, specifically, immediately, and contingently on positive behaviors, which makes their expectations clear.[89] They won't say, "That's great!" when children feel that they could have done much better.[90] They praise for effort during the process, on what's good and why—to help them improve—including persistence, strategies, methods, self-corrections, or thoughtful concentration during the execution of a task ("Good attention to detail!" or "You worked very hard!"), not the child as a whole ("Good boy!"), his or her intelligence ("Smart!"), or just the result ("Good job!").[91] PTIs also teach them to gracefully accept compliments instead of countering or contradicting them.

PTIs discover and foster specific strengths in children by giving both positive and negative feedback.[92] By learning their specific strengths and weaknesses, young innovators develop an internal locus of control instead of an external one, so they know that success/failure depends on themselves instead of on something out of their control.[93] They don't perceive tasks to be too difficult, and they foresee success and adopt thoughtful approaches to accomplish them.[94] They are committed to high goals by putting in the effort and persisting over time.[95]

6. Trees' resilience prepares them to withstand the hardest gales and support heavy fruits. Young innovators' resilience prepares them for the tensions and isolation during their lengthy and bumpy creative process (the Apple-tree Creative Process: ACP).[96] PTIs spend more time challenging, disciplining, and cultivating children's minds than coddling them. They nurture children's resilience by helping them enjoy their greatest strengths and take pride in developing their expertise.[97] They often use positive feedback when children are beginners or are uncertain about their commitment.[98] After children gain more expertise and are committed, PTIs use negative feedback when they show a lack of progress toward goals.[99] They teach them how to accept and respond to critiques and give them brutally honest but constructive feedback.[100] PTIs give children *negative* feedback after establishing a close relationship with children, and they plan ahead to ensure enough time for a sufficient *in-person* discussion. To give negative feedback to children, they choose a thoughtful time and a private, neutral, comfortable place; create a warm socio-emotional climate; and maintain close physical distances while engaging in eye contact. They listen before they speak and be objective and supportive with a smile and positive body language; communicate expectations to convey realistic objectives for future success; and focus on concrete and achievable objectives regarding only things that children can improve. They give negative feedback that's focused on task-based rather than person-based qualities, and that they see as necessary and feasible. They start with honest compliments and then give negative feedback, while not overwhelming them with the negative feedback. They start small and share a few criticisms and discuss others next time. They focus on future goals and discuss past events only when relevant. They give negative feedback for making goals/objectives clear; help children set goals based on the feedback *themselves*, by asking them to generate their own ideas for improvement. At the *next* meeting, they discuss and praise their efforts or progress first and then give more negative feedback.

They expose children to the real-world challenges for them to succeed and fail instead of being overly protective.[101] For example, they teach children not to be afraid of falling down or failing. They let children play outside and explore, stumble, trip, get dirty, fall, get hurt, get bruised, even cry, and then bounce back. They also let children falter or fail their projects early and often; learn from mistakes; and get up on their own and try again. They share Michael Jordan's words, one of the world's most celebrated athletes, "I've missed more than 9,000 shots in my career. I've lost almost 300 games. Twenty-six times I've been trusted to take the game-winning shot and missed. I've failed over and over and over again in my life. And that is why I succeed."[102] They teach them how not to fear failure and instead to use it as a positive motivator. They provide support and guidance and also show them how to support others. By overcoming challenges/adversities—including family failures/financial crisis, physical/mental disabilities, or even a loved one's death—young innovators develop resilience to overcome challenges in their work and extend their compassion to the big world.[103]

7. *Outdoor apple trees take more risks than those in the greenhouse, yet thrive and fruit more successfully.* PTIs encourage children to actively experiment, explore, risk, and modify their surroundings instead of just sitting and accepting what is taught.[104] With nurtured self-efficacy and resilience, young innovators take risks in the real world.[105] PTIs discourage children's perfectionism, which prevents them from accepting mistakes/failures and taking risks.[106] Instead, they encourage children to take physical and intellectual risks. They help children discover and express their CPI in a playful climate without threats of immediate evaluation of final products; and they encourage children to regularly cook with adults, create

new recipes, and make a mess. They enjoy what they cook (even if it tastes awful). Further, PTIs encourage children to put themselves into situations where they're likely to fail; outline ways they can mitigate the failure; prioritize what needs to be done first and later; be confident with their plans and proceed without worrying; and apply lessons they learn from it. They also channel children's Type-T (Thrill-seeking) personality into responsible risk-taking behaviors. (Innovators have a Type-T personality [they seek and enjoy thrills, are restless or distractible, are hungry for constant variety, resist repetition, and think about numerous things in parallel ways, not in serial ways]. Ironically, so do daredevils, delinquents, and criminals.)[107]

PTIs teach children to do good things (like run for office or get involved in student government, charity work, or a cause they believe in)—instead of just complaining about problems or avoiding them; and to stand up for others who can't stand up for themselves or someone who isn't popular but is in need or in danger. They share stories of those who were courageously risk-taking and listened to the needs of others, including Mahatma Gandhi, Ludwig van Beethoven, and Jonas Salk: Mahatma Gandhi continually reminded the world that *non*violence could be the means to ending conflict even though it made him subject to violence; Ludwig van Beethoven had the courage to create great music even after he became deaf; and Jonas Salk, inventor of the polio vaccine, had the courage to give the vaccine to himself and his family before making it public.

8. *Trees eventually achieve fruits by their persistence.* Innovators eventually achieve innovation by their persistence rather than being prodigies.[108] Child prodigies' early success often comes too easily to them, which inhibits them from building the necessary resilience and persistence to persevere against challenges and frustrations during their creative process (ACP).[109] (Or their parents push them too hard, overprotect them, or limit their interactions with others, so there's little room for independent thought or cross-pollination.)[110] To encourage children to reach their goals, PTIs nurture children's persistence early by providing an easy task or one that involves low risk and then gradually proceeding to a challenging one.[111] PTIs also help them build something or solve a problem by developing strategies to solve a piece of the problem instead of tackling the whole thing at once.[112] They gradually increase the duration and intensity of children's tasks by breaking them into smaller, easier pieces, enjoying a sense of accomplishment by completing each of the pieces. They also teach chil-

dren to switch between two projects instead of quitting or getting distracted by net-surfing or chatting; and to examine the reasons that led to failure and try different ways instead of just doing the same thing again and expecting different results. By accomplishing the task or solving the problem, children learn that they're physically and mentally able to do something they originally thought they couldn't do, which further increases their persistence.[113] PTIs teach children to turn disadvantages into advantages by stepping back from the situation and objectively looking at their errors/ mistakes; and use mistakes/failures positively for different purpose and better results, while sharing examples of William Perkin, Spencer Silver, Brian Klee, John Pemberton, and Marc Chavannes and Alfred Fielding: William Perkin's experiments failed to cure malaria, but he used his failure positively and developed the first synthetic dye, which was bright in color and didn't wash out; Spencer Silver failed to invent a strong adhesive, but he used his failure positively and developed sticky notes, which uses a temporary glue that doesn't stick for long; Brian Klee failed to develop a drug to lower blood pressure due to the *side effect* of creating long-lasting erections, but later he used his failure positively and developed Viagra, which is used for treating erectile dysfunction; John Pemberton failed to cure headaches, but later he used his failure positively and succeeded in developing Coca Cola; and Marc Chavannes and Alfred Fielding failed to invent textured plastic wallpaper, but they used their failure positively later and succeeded in developing plastic bubble wrap as packaging material.[114]

9. Trees overcome drought and uncertainty by digging their roots deeper. Young innovators overcome doubt and uncertainty by finding deep meanings and purposes (like when Einstein dropped out of high school, Jobs was ejected from Apple, Mandela's father died, O'Keeffe's family faced financial crisis, and Curie's older sister *and* mother died). Young innovators' doubt and uncertainty become catalysts for their creative process (ACP) when they seek emotional compensation, self-reward, or refuge from painful emotions, through safe, expressive activities (reading, writing, learning, drawing, making, building, etc.).[115]

PTIs teach children not to fear uncertainty, by adapting to new situations and experiences. They encourage children to try something that they've never tried before; to attend events or parties where all of the attendees are strangers; and to experience unpredictability and uncertainty by traveling to extremely different places than their own town or city.

They provide examples and lessons to build flexible thinking in order to go beyond the safe limits, cope with uncertainty, and take risks again. For example, they share innovators' stories of accepting uncertainty and the unknown in order to invent a new business, including those of Walt Disney, Colonel Sanders, and Henry Ford: Disney was fired from a newspaper for being uncreative but, believing in his own creativity, he—despite multiple bankruptcies along the way—founded a new industry—animated motion pictures—and became one of the best-known motion-picture producers in the world. Sanders—despite over one thousand rejections—was still passionate about his dream of creating a new industry—franchise—and he, at sixty-five, used his Social Security check to save Kentucky Fried Chicken and finally found a restaurant that was willing to work with him. Ford—despite his first, second, and (almost) third company's bankruptcies—kept manufacturing, while making and learning from countless mistakes and failures, toward his dream of creating a new industry—mass-produced automobiles—and he finally created the Model T.[116]

PTIs also teach children that rules can have exceptions and some rules apply to different people at different times/situations; and that they should respect the rules but respectfully question them. They give vague assignments, questions that don't have a clear answer, or open-ended problems or real-life questions that have multiple answers or no solution (like exploring underlying problems and potential solutions for a thirty-years-later future scenario); and encourage them to consider *all* answers as incomplete or insufficient while welcoming different ideas or ways of thinking.

Young innovators learn to accept uncertainty by the joy and pride that come from pursuing their CPI—through self-efficacy and persistence—while expanding their compassion toward the world.[117] They eventually turn their CPI into their passion by achieving expertise. They prepare for subsequent stages of their creative process (ACP) by incorporating uncertainty as they pursue uniqueness.

STEP 2: NURTURE THE EIGHT STORM ATTITUDES

The storm climate—setting high expectations and providing challenges—nurtures the storm attitudes (step 1). The storm attitudes help innovators overcome challenges while pursuing high goals. Step 2 explains what the eight storm attitudes are, and how they nurture resilient hard workers who apply inbox and newbox thinking. It starts with a brief anecdote from my life, illustrating how my own storm attitudes were encouraged/discouraged or how I encouraged/discouraged these attitudes within my children. Then I summarize what research says about each of the attitudes and how each can contribute to useful inbox and newbox thinking. Each attitude can be learned and further developed through practice. The eight storm attitudes (with the seemingly negative side in parentheses) are:

1. Independent (and Aloof)

The only scholarships in Korea were for academic achievement. Most semesters in college and graduate school, I earned scholarships. I also worked as a private tutor for many students of wealthy families. From 1980 to 2000, there was a national law that prohibited private tutoring, to help make it fairer for poor students whose parents couldn't afford private tutoring. Given the risk of prosecution, private tutoring became even more expensive and so I (illegally) made more money, which enabled me to support my siblings and my parents. In Asia, because all high-school students study extremely hard to try to get into highly ranked colleges, they don't have enough time to eat or sleep. But once they're in college, they enjoy socializing and dating rather than studying. However, I had no time for such activities due to tutoring every afternoon and night. But it enabled me to be financially independent at an early age.

I've also been religiously independent since my brother's death because, despite my intense prayers, God took him. I also begrudged the church because my father gave more time to it than to his family. I thought that the people there took him away from me. Also, I hated the fact that my mother had time to sleep for only about three hours a night because, in addition to her household work, she was also burdened with what my father was supposed to do. As I grew up, religion continued to be a thorn in my side. My husband's family was Buddhist, but I rebelliously refused to convert. I'd not bow at the ancestors' shrines with them. My mother-in-law repeatedly criticized me by saying that all Korean

Figure 5.1. Independent (and Aloof) Storm Attitude

Christians are wicked because they worship a strange white man (Jesus) who isn't even related to them, instead of their own ancestors.

Research findings on the independent attitude

Having the independent attitude (see figure 5.1) is thinking and acting freely from others' influence, support, and control. Innovators strive to be physically, emotionally, spiritually, financially, and intellectually independent.[118] Although they learn from mentors, they remain free to choose what to do with their advice. Among non-innovators, social information from newspapers, television, and popular media is often regurgitated (which is non-independent), which many accept without questioning. But innovators seek proof instead of accepting given facts and make sense of the world based on their own personal observations and experiences.[119] They devote their energy and time to develop expertise in the subject of their *own* CPI by staying away from negative social influences or others' controls.[120] Their own unique inbox thinking skills including critical-thinking skills are developed through their independent thoughts and actions.[121]

2. Self-Disciplined (and Compulsive)

My father was the most self-disciplined and diligent person I knew. He was always quiet, always organized and clean, always diligent, and always working. He was also the most kind and polite man in the village, especially to older people such as his mother and church people. Every morning he entered her room, greeted her with a big bow, made her bed, took out her chamber pot, and emptied and cleaned it for her (because we had only an outhouse). There were so many routines that he did precisely the same way in the same order every day, and he worked on the farm and served in the church as an elder. During cold winters, when other farmers were resting from their yearly work, gambling with cards, drinking alcohol, and smoking, he was reading the Bible and serving for the church and its older people. Fortunately, and unfortunately, he believed childcare was only the mother's responsibility, so all of his reli-

Figure 5.2.
Self-Disciplined
(and Compulsive)
Storm Attitude

gious rules didn't interfere or control us too much. But I learned how to discipline myself by watching him. For years, I've completely focused on perfecting my model of how to develop creativity. I always think about it—when eating, dreaming, and possibly even after this life has ended!

Research findings on the self-disciplined attitude

Following the self-disciplined attitude (see figure 5.2) means motivating and controlling oneself to accomplish goals. Innovators are self-disciplined and committed to improving their expertise and achieving their goals.[122] They direct their efforts toward goal-relevant activities—away from goal-irrelevant activities—by setting clear, high goals.[123] They learn organizational and time-management skills while avoiding distractions and addictive behaviors. Their self-discipline teaches them that overcoming frustrations and failures requires more diligence and persistence.[124]

In their storm climate, innovators' self-disciplined attitude enables them to improve expertise by more learning, understanding, and by conforming to the existing rules, constraints, and traditions in their field, even when they *disagree* with them.[125] Rules and constraints often help innovators shape and define useful solutions and ideas, which further advance their expertise.[126] Later, innovators' defiant attitude enables them to challenge or *break* the rules or constraints and to start making changes—in their space climate—(yet still) *within* the system or tradition.[127]

3. Diligent (and Workaholic)

When I sought employment while I earned my PhD from the University of Georgia, some universities invited me for on-campus interviews (I had applied to forty-nine places!). Afterward, to my surprise, I wasn't offered a single job. To help me discover what I was doing wrong, Drs. Cramond and Hébert did mock interviews with me. They asked me exactly the same questions from my failed interviews, such as "What are your strengths and weaknesses?" I gave my standard answer based on my Confucian humility and strong work ethic, "I've no strengths but work hard." I also added proudly, "People call me a workaholic." They laughed loudly, and

Figure 5.3. Diligent (and Workaholic) Storm Attitude

then helped me make a different list of my five strengths. I wrote down, memorized, and recited them for my next job interview. I was immediately hired by Eastern Michigan University. If I had continued to spout Confucian values, I might never have been offered a job in America!

Research findings on the diligent attitude

The diligent attitude (see figure 5.3) is characterized by exerting meticulous, steady attention to build skills to accomplish clear goals. There's no secret trick or shortcut to developing expertise and subsequent innovation.[128] At least ten years—according to the ten-year rule—of diligent work and deep immersion and ten thousand hours of practice are necessary for developing expertise in an innovator's chosen field.[129] Innovators experience a lot of drudgery during years of deliberate practice before emerging as an expert and then finally an innovator.[130] They sacrifice present happiness for their pursuit of self-growth. They *create* their own luck by preparing for the opportunity to become the right person, in the right place, at the right time.[131]

4. Self-Efficacious (and Arrogant)

Figure 5.4.
Self-Efficacious
(and Arrogant)
Storm Attitude

Asians often exhibit less self-esteem or self-confidence than Americans[132] because Confucianism discourages confidence and individualism.[133] Natural talent and physical appearance invoke self-confidence in Westerners but are less significant to Confucians, who value hard work above anything. I am not self-confident (generally). Although I am self-efficacious (specifically) in my expertise in creativity, I will *never* be self-efficacious in driving a car. Before I admitted how bad my driving was to my students, I didn't know the stereotype that Asians are bad drivers. I'm not sure whether it's true, but I know in my specific case, the stereotype holds true: I'm a terrible driver.

Research findings on the self-efficacious attitude

Having the self-efficacious attitude (see figure 5.4) entails being confident to perform well on *specific* tasks based on previous successful experiences.

Innovators are not necessarily self-confident, but are self-efficacious, which is one of the most critical predictors of innovation in all fields.[134] Innovators' diligence over time through self-discipline leads to mastery of specific knowledge/skills and thus self-efficacy. They know their specific strengths and weaknesses and how well they perform on specific tasks, which motivates them to persist and advances expertise.[135] Through their self-efficacy and subsequent expertise, their CPI finally ignites a lifelong passion. They're also optimistically self-efficacious; they expect the best while learning how to handle the worst.[136] Their self-efficacy across multiple areas becomes a foundation for resilience, risk-taking, and persistence. They take on all sorts of opportunities, perceive difficulties as challenges, and strive to achieve their passion and goal during their Apple-tree Creative Process. This also promotes their general well-being.[137]

Innovators maintain high self-efficacy with deep intellectual fulfillment[138]—while maintaining their humility: They're humble—perhaps shy or awkward—even after their innovation and contributions to change the world because they know their innovation was built on the shoulders of giants. They recognize their own mistakes and failures, which they actually make more of than others, because they try more and fail more.[139]

5. Resilient (and Combative)

Even though I grew up in a farm town, everyone was hungry. The Korean government provided bread to children when I was in elementary school (using wheat given by America, which I didn't know at the time). The teacher would hand it out every morning, and the children would devour it as quickly as possible, except me. My four-year-old baby brother walked to my school to get the bread I got. When he couldn't come, I took it to him after school. My classmates stared at the bread on my desk all day long (they still remember this, even forty years later!), but it never occurred to me to eat it myself, because my brother enjoyed it so much. However, when I was ten, he died after two years of many surgeries and treatments for diseases that were unknown to me. He was only seven. This changed my life; I became a ten-year-old adult, as his death robbed me of my childhood.

After my brother died, my mother was more distraught than she was when he was sick. She was hospitalized for three months and wished she had gone with him! But she had to take care of my two-year-old sister. Two years later, happily, my parents had another son. But he was born sick, so my mother focused a tremendous amount of energy on him. It was hard, but her attention on the new baby was good for her, as it eased the pain of her loss. I did everything I could to help her so she'd not be sad again, and the baby wouldn't die. I helped raise my baby brother and sister. I dressed them and bathed them. I cleaned their clothes, but because we didn't have water indoors, this meant breaking the ice in the winter and using my little hands to rub the clothes in the freezing river until I couldn't bear it.

After I grew up, I paid for my brother's and sister's high-school and college tuition. To this day, we've never had a conversation about why I did this for them. They think I just had too much money. But to be honest, I often didn't have enough money to pay for the bus to college after I paid their tuition. Sometimes I had to borrow money from my friends' parents or had to sell things to meet my obligations. I'd do anything for them because I loved my mother, who lost her son, the brother they never met or don't remember.

Research findings on the resilient attitude

The resilient attitude (see figure 5.5) is characterized by recovering and thriving after challenges or failures.[140] Extreme trauma doesn't necessarily beget disorder.[141] For example, Holocaust survivors displayed stress-related symptoms but also resilience and even psychological growth.[142] This was thanks, in part, to their commitment to something or someone, to their sense of control or self-efficacy, and to their interpretation of adversities as a challenge.[143]

Figure 5.5. Resilient (and Combative) Storm Attitude

Despite challenges and adversities, innovators build resilience by setting clear goals and maintaining self-efficacy through:[144] first, committing to and taking actions for goals instead of dwelling on bad things; second, considering troubles as temporary, controllable, and specific to the troubles; third, using a wide range of flexible coping strategies; and fourth, turning failures into lessons, believing every experience is a learning opportunity, and failure is better than no experience.

Innovators' resilience prepares them for uncertainty by thinking of multiple possible scenarios and figuring out what to do in each case. They find and use resources; actively seek and ask for support and assistance; and build trusted alliances and networks through their resourceful attitude.[145] They're realistic about threats and risks and make plans.[146] They seek balanced views between their own perceptions and outside views. They seek feedback for their weaknesses, mistakes, or failures rather than strengths or successes.[147] They're resilient to and *seek* negative feedback— brutally honest advice, ruthless objections, and ferocious criticisms—to calibrate their perception of reality and further refine their inbox and newbox thinking for their creation.[148] They improve themselves by distinguishing between task-related negative feedback and personal attacks.[149] Their critical thinking and newbox thinking are further enhanced when their climate frames criticism and negative feedback as contributions.[150]

The creative process (ACP) involves uncertainty and risks, and innovators' resilience overcomes their frustrations and failures.[151] Focusing on their passion and goal fills their emotional needs and is a form of self-reward or a refuge from their adversities.[152] Their self-efficacy, resilience, and persistence for the goals overcome bad luck.[153]

6. Risk-Taking (and Reckless)

In 2000, I decided to move to America. All of my friends warned me not to, for three reasons: first, all Americans had guns; second, Americans had sex on the first date; and third, Americans had AIDS. In South Korea, only soldiers and police officers have guns. My friends had these images of a dangerous America because of the movies and the news they'd seen. (Strangely, the American soldiers who gave us scholarships and Ping-Pong tables or who threw caramel candies—still my favorite candies—to us were never portrayed in the movies or in the news.) I was willing to risk these dangers in America!

Figure 5.6. Risk-Taking (and Reckless) Storm Attitude

Most Korean immigrants who move to America either are married to an American or know other earlier immigrants who can help or support them. Without either luxury, I arrived at the Los Angeles Airport in California with only my nine-year-old daughter and four-year-old son. I'd signed a lease for an apartment in La Jolla through the Internet, but by mistake, the lease didn't begin until two days after we landed. So, we rented a hotel room that we were too afraid to leave. When my children got hungry, I cooked ramen noodles in the microwave and fed them using the back ends of our toothbrushes; there were no chopsticks in the hotel! Everything looked different and dangerous in America.

Research findings on the risk-taking attitude

The risk-taking attitude (see figure 5.6) involves leaving secure situations in pursuit of uncertain rewards. Innovators are optimistically self-efficacious to venture into uncertain and risky creative endeavors.[154] They are adventurous, jump on opportunities, and dare to explore instead of being pessimistic and finding fault with opportunities.[155] They take social/emotional risks (like embarrassment or loss of respect) and intellectual risks by presenting new/different ideas. This invites resistance because new/different ideas often conflict with others' interests.[156] Although they seek information before taking a risk—as having more information reduces risk—there can never be enough information to completely eradicate risks.[157] So they're willing to risk negative feelings, failure, and others' ridicule in pursuit of their goal.[158] Their optimism for their goal enables them to ignore noise and interference.[159] They aren't dissuaded by errors, mistakes, and failures on their way to innovation because they learn from them.[160] Risk-taking enhances their skill mastery and self-efficacy, goal achievement, and taking subsequent risks.[161] Innovators who take high risks are more successful than those who take low risks—*nothing ventured, nothing gained.*[162]

Risk takers usually take risks for monetary gain/social status, but *innovators* take risks for a bigger purpose.[163] The values in their hearts (principles, ideals, or beliefs)—from their inspiration, big-picture thought, and/or compassion—are the source of their courage. For most people, sticking with the status quo is easier than taking risks and sacrificing their conventional life.[164] But for innovators, timidity entails the biggest risk of all: denying their personal passion or goal.[165] Their courage isn't the absence of fear, rather that they feel that something's truly worth taking risks for.[166] Fear usually inhibits action, but to innovators, acknowledging fear motivates action.[167] They push limits and come up with something new or do things differently. They champion their creation and share their passion with an unwilling, unkind, or even hostile world. They're willing to be rejected and face adversity head-on to transform their wild dream into reality.[168]

7. Persistent (and Obsessive)

Our fourth day in America, my children and I met a neighbor who told us he was a graduate student at the University of California at San Diego. He was very nice to us and helped us go to a furniture store and furnish our empty apartment. My children even started calling him "Uncle." (It's a Korean custom to call *close* adults "Uncle" or "Aunt.") He introduced me to the idea of loyalty cards and encouraged me to get a Vons supermarket card for discounts on food. He told me to give him a blank check so that, in his words, he could give the check to the store manager, who'd issue me a loyalty card. When he finally gave me the Vons card, I was so happy I almost cried. I felt like I became an American citizen.

We took Uncle and several of his friends to fancy restaurants on that day and the next day. On the third day, Uncle disappeared with my wallet. When I went to my bank, I found $3,600 missing from my account. One of the employees at the bank showed me a copy of the check with a phony signature. She did nothing to help me.

Another neighbor of mine, the son of an immigrant, found out what happened and called the police. The next day, two huge policemen and an investigator came to my apartment. They wore uniforms with guns holstered in their black leather belts, handcuffs, radios, and all sorts of dangerous-looking equipment. My children and I were so nervous because of the police that we could barely speak! Impatient with my lack of English-speaking skills, they only feigned interest in what had happened and hardly investigated the matter.

The monetary loss was insignificant compared to the overwhelming fear that gripped us. We worried that Uncle would seek retribution because he might think *we* called the police. Every night we pushed the dinner table against the front door and stacked all of the glasses we had on it so we'd hear if he broke in. I kept a telephone in my hand even when I slept.

With the danger and fear that we experienced, why didn't I go back to Korea? Simple: I couldn't and wouldn't quit. I was persistent and remained optimistic about my future life in America. Even then, I believed there were more good people than bad; I had just not met them yet.

Research findings on the persistent attitude

The persistent attitude (see figure 5.7) is characterized by continuously striving for goals with commitment and energy, regardless of immediate rewards.
We *are* what we repeatedly do; persistence is innovators' habit. For example, Einstein didn't think that he
was smart, just that he tackled problems persistently
and seemingly obsessively. (Note that persistence
facilitates or results in productivity, but neither obsession nor addiction does.) Innovators' passion (which
evolved from their CPI by their self-efficacy) and commitment to their
goal compel them to persist physically and mentally.[169]

Figure 5.7. Persistent (and Obsessive) Storm Attitude

They persist through failure *and* success, which is the biggest difference between innovators and non-innovators.[170] An antonym for an innovator is a quitter, not a copier or an imitator (copying or imitating is good
as long as improving follows).

Persistence is necessary at most stages of the creative process (ACP)
such as:

- At stage 1 (expertise development) for thoroughly understanding a
  subject and endlessly applying that understanding to new and real-
  world situations;
- At stage 2 (needs identification) for finding the hidden, underlying
  need;
- At stage 3 (idea generation) for searching for original ideas that come
  later than obvious ideas;
- At stage 5 (idea evaluation) for analyzing (to thoroughly understand)
  and systematically evaluating the ideas; and
- At stage 7 (transformation) for working out the details of the synthesized idea/creation while inviting others' brutally honest feedback
  and overcoming failures.

Instead of quitting, innovators *switch* their persistence into spontaneity
to allow their conscious mind to be flexible,[171] because their persistence
and the narrow focus of their conscious mind inhibit its flexibility and

seeing a bigger picture.[172] This is why, at the stage 4 (subconscious processing)—*after* persistently working/generating ideas and *before* persistently evaluating them again[173]—they take a break from their main work to allow their conscious mind to be flexible, which in turn allows their subconscious mind to find a better idea (an Aha! idea).[174] Thus, even when their conscious mind takes a break, it is the persistence of innovators that enables their subconscious mind to process continuously. This indicates that persistence is also required at stage 4.

The creative process (ACP), especially the transformation stage, is long and laborious and filled with anxiety, frustration, and failures.[175] But innovators persist until they achieve a final creation, while their mind continues learning through a mistake or a failure consciously and sub-consciously, whether or not they think they're focused on it.[176] Their per-sistence overcomes bad luck, lack of resources, and all possible excuses, regardless of their age.[177] Even after the final creation, their persistence does not decrease; in fact it increases.[178] They keep thinking and improving their creation, which leads to many other creations. Their creations may be of high *quality*, but it is the quantity of innovators' creations that allows at least one of their many creations to be recognized as an innovation; they produce more than non-innovators or quitters do.[179]

8. Uncertainty-Accepting (and Fearless)

My son was diagnosed with ADHD by *his teachers* in first and ninth grade *only* when he was in private (and expensive) schools. The principal and his teachers said that he asked too many disruptive questions in class. I asked, "Does he do so intentionally to disrupt the others, or did he honestly want to know?" They answered that he was genuinely curious, but they didn't have time for his endless questions, and even other students' parents had complained about it.

Figure 5.8.
Uncertainty-Accepting
(and Fearless)
Storm Attitude

I decided not to send him to those private schools again. I chose uncertainty by sending him to Korea to live with his father. I made him stay out of school in his tenth grade, and I wondered how it would affect him. His father patiently answered all of his questions and let him do whatever he was interested in doing, including learning to cook in a culinary school, playing lacrosse, and playing computer games, sometimes without eating or sleeping.

A year later, however, my son missed his friends in America. He also wanted to learn computer programming. I let him come back. We moved to Arlington, Virginia, to find an open-minded public school and a mentor to support his CPI in programming. Under an expert's mentorship, he enjoyed programming so much that he, along with two of his friends, created the Yorktown High School Coding Club. They worked intensely on programming a fall-detecting and emergency-contact device for those who live alone, fall, and are unable to move. During that time, he neither studied for the SAT/ACT nor put effort into applying for universities. I reminded him that he didn't *have to* go to college, but that going to college would ensure more certain life courses. He chose the uncertainty of pursuing his programming project over the certainty of going to college. Fortunately, in the end, he not only won the 2015 US Microsoft's Imagine Cup—among 500,000 applicants—but also went to college to study nano-engineering and computer science.

Research findings on the uncertainty-accepting attitude

The uncertainty-accepting attitude (see figure 5.8) calls for acting without complete information regardless of potential challenges or outcomes. Creating something that's never existed before entails uncertainty, and innovators welcome the journey into the unknown.[180] Nothing about the creative process (ACP) follows on a straight line. When a creative idea is presented to people, most don't recognize it as creative, nor do they like it.[181] They feel more comfortable with the status quo than with the unknown, uncertainty, or possibility of change.[182] They're inclined to latch on to *any* attractive answer or reject the uncertain too quickly and trade possibility for certainty.[183]

Innovators sacrifice a content and conventional life for their clear, but unguaranteed, future goal.[184] They learn to tolerate ambiguity and accept anxiety and psychological discomfort. Also, their playfulness helps them embrace and even value problems that have no easy or clear-cut answers, which they consider an exciting opportunity to explore.[185] Innovators remain open-minded while pursuing their passion, and playfully grapple with future ideas, enjoy exploring complex problems, and find unique solutions.[186] When Steve Jobs cofounded Apple, little was known about future personal computers. Nobody was certain whether homes and offices would use computers like small home appliances, especially when businesses were using computers the size of rooms. The personal-computer market didn't exist, but Jobs strongly believed in his vision of the future. Innovators who learn to accept and leverage greater uncertainty are more successful than those who don't.[187]

INNOVATORS' STORM ATTITUDES: THE CACTUS AMONG US

Innovators display the storm attitudes that seem negative—such as aloof, compulsive, workaholic, arrogant, combative, reckless, obsessive, or fearless. For example, innovators are often so independent that they might seem aloof. At an early age, Jobs emotionally detached from his parents after learning he was adopted.[188] He wondered about how his biological parents' genetics would influence what he'd become, and he drifted emotionally further away from his family over time. He believed this made him a loner.[189] He might seem *aloof*.

Innovators are often so self-disciplined that they seem compulsive. Jobs studied meditation, became a vegetarian, and followed many extreme diets. He believed these behaviors—in combination with his practice of Zen Buddhism, meditation, and Eastern spirituality—would help empower his mental well-being.[190] For this reason, he might seem *compulsive*.

Innovators often work so diligently that they're called workaholics. Jobs told those who wanted to become like him that they must work *diligently* until they are really good at something before finding their passion.[191] He demanded Apple employees work as diligently as he—until he was completely satisfied—no matter how long that took. Some loved and others *hated* his work ethic.[192] He pushed them with brutally honest feedback and believed that his duty was making them better, not making things easier for them, to elevate their expertise.[193] He might seem like a *workaholic*.

Innovators are often so self-efficacious that they seem arrogant. Einstein's professors in college thought that he was *arrogant*. Jobs' coworkers' at Atari thought that he was *arrogant*.

Innovators are often so resilient that they seem combative. At twelve, Mandela lost his father and had to leave his family. At twenty-three, he was expelled from the University College of Fort Hare. At twenty-six, he married Evelyn Mase (his first wife) and had four children with her, but she left him (at thirty-nine) while he was imprisoned. He was allowed to be out of the prison to marry Winnie Madikizela (his second wife) and had two daughters with her, but he wasn't allowed to watch them grow up because he was imprisoned.[194] At fifty, his mother died, and Winnie was also sent to prison, leaving their two daughters behind. His first son was killed in a car accident at twenty-five, leaving his two small children behind (Mandela's grandchildren). At seventy-one Mandela was freed from prison, and at seventy-five he became the president of South Africa. At seventy-seven he divorced Winnie, and at eighty he married Graça Machel (his third wife). At eighty-one he finished his presidency and wanted to retire, but at eighty-seven he decided to fight the AIDS epidemic when his second son died of AIDS. Mandela publicly acknowledged his son's disease and insisted that fighting AIDS was a human-rights issue.[195] All of this might seem *combative*.

O'Keeffe's relationship with Alfred Stieglitz (her husband) started as an affair, as he was a married man, and he divorced his wife and married O'Keeffe. While they were married, he had another affair with a young poet, Dorothy Norman, which made O'Keeffe combative at first. But it eventually helped her resilience by channeling her pain into independence from him, which led to a stronger commitment to her art. This pain caused a dramatic turn in her work, revealing new beauty in lifeless objects and desolate landscapes in the Southwest.[196] Some might consider her *combative*.

Innovators are often so prone to risk taking that they seem reckless. Young Jobs took a lot of risks playing all kinds of pranks at school, which caused him to be sent him home many times.[197] He might seem *reckless*. But his parents knew that he was bored without challenges and stimulations.[198] He loved taking new and unique risks on his own and getting others to take risks throughout his life.[199]

Innovators are often so persistent that they seem *obsessive*. For instance, when Marie Curie's second daughter, Eve, was little, she thought that Einstein was obsessive, because whenever his family was with her family, the only thing he talked about was his relativity theory.[200]

Innovators accept uncertainty so much that they seem fearless.

Mandela was willing to spend the rest of his life in prison fighting for *his* democracy, a form of government that had never existed in South Africa. It confined him to a prison for twenty-seven years, and for that he might seem *fearless*.

Parents and educators must be able to see the long-term positive aspects of behaviors that seem prickly in children, so they can encourage the underlying storm attitudes instead of seeing the children as trouble-makers. Also, such children must be able to view their own storm attitudes positively. When parents and educators succeed in cultivating the storm climate and nurturing children's storm attitudes, they are following the footsteps of the PTIs who encouraged, taught, and mentored the greatest innovators in history.

Chapter 6

THE SPACE CLIMATE THAT
NURTURES THE SPACE ATTITUDES

Georgia O'Keeffe was born on November 15, 1887, in the farm-house of a large dairy farm near Sun Prairie, Wisconsin. She was the second child and first daughter of her parents, Francis and Ida. Francis's family emigrated from Ireland, and Ida's family emigrated from Hungary. Georgia's grandfather, George Victor Totto, was a Hungarian count and the inspiration for Georgia's name.

Ida's family had a long tradition of educating women. Ida was independent and self-disciplined and a powerful role model for Georgia. She was demanding and persistent, and she never spoiled her children.[1] She set high expectations for them and spent more time challenging and cultivating their minds than coddling them.[2] As Georgia once recalled, "As a child, I think I craved a certain affection that my mother did not give."[3] However, Ida was very involved in her children's intellectual development. She was a talented storyteller and would regularly read entire books to them.[4] She particularly favored adventure and historical stories such as *The Adventures of Kit Carson*, *The Last of the Mohicans*, and *Stanley's Adventures in Africa*. The heroes she read about conveyed powerful messages about individual strength, the ability to change oneself and others, and persevering against adversity.[5] This nurtured Georgia's big-picture-thinking, resilient, and risk-taking attitudes. Ida also used amusing games and music to stimulate her children's minds.[6]

Ida and Francis had different personalities and religions, but both strongly believed in developing their children's potential. They consistently built their children's' diligent and self-efficacious attitudes. They supported unique conditions that facilitated each child's learning. For example, Georgia's sister (also named Ida) decided that she would no longer attend school because she detested her teacher. Instead of forcing her to return to school, her parents homeschooled her.[7] They allowed their children to have some levels of freedom *while* demanding responsibility.

Francis was open to new ideas and inventions. He acquired the first telephone in Sun Prairie and persuaded other farmers to erect poles for telephone wires. He used a newly invented harvest machine in his fields.[8] He took his children on spontaneous and adventurous trips to the wilderness and to see string bands and magic shows, which nurtured Georgia's playful attitude.[9] Georgia liked her curious and spontaneous father and his farm more than her mother's aloof world of learning.[10] The farm was where Georgia discovered the wonders of scenery, sounds, colors, and textures of the four seasons. This fostered her close relationship with nature, understanding its processes and noticing its details through her self-reflective attitude.[11] Her respect and intense observation of nature as a child became her primary source of inspiration for her art, as she became known for expressing naturally unashamed sensuality in her colorful and close-up paintings of flowers.[12]

Living on a farm, each child had chores and responsibilities *every* day. There were only a few rules on the farm, but they were critical because they were directly related to the livelihood of the family. They took care of dairy cows and draft horses and large vegetable gardens. Subsequently, they grew up with a love of gardening. They learned how to sew and cook, and they even made their own clothes. According to Georgia's sister Catherine, "We learned to sew as soon as we could hold a needle."[13] The demands of farm life nurtured Georgia's self-disciplined and diligent attitudes.

Georgia never met her grandfathers, and two of her father's three brothers died of tuberculosis, so her father's only living brother, Bernard, lived with Georgia's family. Since Georgia was a baby, Ida's Aunt Jenny also lived with the family and became another role model for the children. She was very affectionate and supportive of them, and they were attached to her. Living with her provided another opportunity for Georgia to experience different beliefs and opinions. Living with Uncle Bernard and teachers who rented rooms from her family also introduced her to various views. This showed her parents' way wasn't the only way of doing things, and it nurtured her complexity-seeking attitude.[14]

Georgia grew up believing her brother was her parents' favorite, which made her competitive, independent, and athletic because she was constantly trying to out-run and out-climb him.[15] She was surrounded by autonomous, nonconforming, and gender-bias-free *female* role models. She strongly believed that God was *a woman*.[16] Her two strong grandmothers were resilient and kept their large families together even after losing their husbands. They made everything by hand and loved art and music—painting flowers and fruits—which inspired Georgia artistically.[17] Ollie and Lola, Georgia's mother's sisters, also were nonconforming women and frequent visitors. They (especially Aunt Lola) encouraged Georgia's curiosity by answering her unlimited questions.[18] She often visited Aunt Lola in Milwaukee—which gave her an opportunity to spend time in a big city. She later lived with Aunt Lola when she was in high school and with Aunt Ollie when she was in college. Her continuous interactions with these two strong mentors impacted her worldviews and career.[19]

Georgia's family's nonattached, independent relationships facilitated her attention to surroundings rather than to personal relationships.[20] She had plenty of time alone, beginning in early childhood when one of her main sources of pleasure was playing make-believe with her homemade dollhouse.[21] This nurtured her self-reflective and daydreaming attitudes. Her family allowed her to be different—even to be a troublemaker—and accepted her embarrassing clothing and hairstyle, choice of friends, and boylike behaviors.[22] This nurtured her autonomous, nonconforming, and gender-bias-free attitudes.

Like the mothers of Einstein and Curie, Georgia's mother was musically talented and enjoyed singing and playing the piano. In time, Georgia became an accomplished piano and violin player herself. Later in her life, she recalled her own love for music, saying, "Singing to me has always seemed to be the most perfect means of expression. It's so spontaneous. And after singing, I think the violin. Since I cannot sing, I paint."[23] At eleven, she began taking drawing classes. Art became so important that every Saturday, the girls were driven to the home of Sara Mann (a local watercolorist) in a buggy—a seven-mile round-trip to Sun Prairie—for watercolor painting lessons.[24] Ida encouraged Georgia by framing her work.[25]

Ida and Francis paid an extra twenty dollars above the expensive eighty-dollar tuition for Georgia to continue art instruction when she was admitted to Sacred Heart boarding school in Madison.[26] Although the art instruction was hard at first, she incorporated the nun's brutally honest criticism as she progressed. At one point she was criticized for drawing *too tiny*, so she started drawing everything *big*.[27] Within the strict rules of the boarding school, she found great freedom in her art because she was focused on improving her drawing, while enjoying classical music concerts and exciting intellectual classes.[28] Due to her family's financial constraints, the next year she enrolled in a public high school in Milwaukee and lived with Aunt Lola.

Uncle Bernard died of tuberculosis when Georgia was eleven. The family was terrified that Francis would also die from it, so they finally moved to Williamsburg, Virginia, when Georgia was living with Aunt Lola in Milwaukee.[29] Although her early farm life was peaceful and economically stable, her father had continuous financial failures after the move, which made the family suffer. Also, moving to Virginia (in the South) was a culture shock for her. Independence and education were valued in her family (in the Midwest) as a means of success, but Southern girls were dependent on their family lineage in preparation for their future roles as dependent wives.[30] Their mothers had few responsibilities because they depended on servants.[31] This dramatic contradiction with her previous world helped Georgia define her self-identity and who she would become. This nurtured her nonconforming and defiant attitudes. Also, frequent moves and adapting to culture shocks nurtured open-minded and bicultural attitudes. Whenever others made fun of her Midwestern accent, she handled it playfully, even mischievously.[32]

At fifteen, Georgia started at her new school, Chatham, in Williamsburg, Virginia, and met an outstanding art teacher, Elizabeth Willis. Willis recognized Georgia's creative potential and became another mentor. She allowed Georgia the freedom to work at her own pace. Sometimes Georgia worked intensely, and other times she didn't work for days.[33] Willis had a critical impact on getting Georgia (and her parents) to focus on her art as a potential career, even after high school. Georgia's parents sent her to the Art Institute in Chicago, which was unusual for girls at that time.[34]

Georgia lived with Aunt Ollie while in Chicago for a year and then studied at the Art Students' League in New York City for a year. Then she gave up her study for four years and lived with her family in Charlottesville, Virginia due to her family's financial crisis, her own illness, and her career barriers within the male-only artistic world.[35] But her family encouraged her to attend Alon Bement's art classes. Bement mentored and introduced her to his own mentor, Arthur Dow. Dow developed methods based on his expertise in Japanese aesthetics, which rejected the imitative European art and advocated the artist's own expressions. This inspired

Georgia to overcome challenges in her life and in her art.[36] She started expressing her own feelings and ideas through her drawing and painting, and she started working as an art teacher in Texas.[37]

Georgia's soil attitudes enabled cross-pollination:

In her soil climate—including her mentors, Aunts Lola and Ollie, and Willis—Georgia's soil attitudes had been nurtured. This enabled later cross-pollination with Anita Pollitzer and Alfred Stieglitz. Without them, the O'Keeffe name might be meaningless. Georgia's friendship and correspondence with Pollitzer lasted forty years. Pollitzer was seven years younger than Georgia was, and her letters connected Georgia to the artistic world of NYC. This was critical to her artistic direction—motivating and giving her diverse perspectives—especially when working in Texas and isolated from the outside world.[38] Pollitzer became an influential women's rights movement leader, which influenced Georgia's work. Most important, she connected Georgia with Alfred Stieglitz, her future husband.[39]

Stieglitz was a pioneer in photography and a sponsor of newly emerging American modern art. His skillful management was critical for Georgia's fame and income. He became her critic, agent, and mentor, and he controlled her public image and promotion, staging one-woman shows of her work every year until his death.[40] His mentorship enabled her involvement in the male-only avant-garde artistic movement in NYC.[41]

Georgia's 4S attitudes enabled ION thinking for innovation:

At eleven Georgia met a local artist, Mann, and started developing her expertise in her CPI in drawing and painting. She used inbox thinking that was enabled by her soil and storm attitudes, which had been nurtured in her soil and storm climates. At thirteen she developed her skills further by incorporating the nun's criticisms at Sacred Heart (drawing everything big). At fifteen, she matured her expertise under Willis's mentorship.

When Georgia first imagined unique abstract charcoal drawings—based on her expertise—she used outbox thinking that was enabled by her sun and space attitudes, which had been nurtured by her sun and space climates. Her continuous connections with diverse rural settings (Sun Prairie in Wisconsin, Williamsburg and Charlottesville in Virginia, Amarillo and Canyon in Texas, etc.), and urban settings (Madison, Milwaukee, Chicago, NYC, etc.) enhanced her outbox thinking.

While at her first job teaching art in Texas, she expanded her outbox thinking by developing more ideas, being inspired by the southwestern landscape, and corresponding with Pollitzer about NYC artists' new ideas. She exercised outbox thinking to incorporate Dow's expertise (in Japanese aesthetics) in her work (simplistic form, symbolic color/shape use, size/format variation, etc.) instead of the imitative European realism. Then, she used critical-thinking skills to analyze and evaluate the results and to decide how to best incorporate new techniques into her work.

When Georgia synthesized her visual images of nature and emotions with Japanese aesthetics, she used newbox thinking that was enabled by her 4S attitudes, which had been nurtured by her 4S climates. She filled her drawings with vivid images of the places where she had lived, and synthesized Asian and American forms and ideas (influenced by Dow's methods), unlike others' drawings at the time. When she transformed her uniquely synthesized ideas into useful charcoal drawings—through refining them with simplicity—she also used newbox thinking. At age twenty-eight—more than ten years after she began developing her expertise, she promoted her drawings by persistently sending them to Pollitzer, who in turn sent them to Stieglitz. As soon as Stieglitz hung them in his Gallery 291, the unknown O'Keeffe became known to the artistic world in NYC (again confirming the ten-year rule).[42]

Georgia's passion didn't stop, and she imagined her best-known large-format flower paintings by synthesizing her early styles with *photographic* manipulations. She painted magnified blossoms precisely rendered and close up to emphasize shape and color, as if seen through a magnifying lens—an artistic approach influenced by Stieglitz's photography.[43] At forty, her calla-lily paintings sold for the largest sum ever paid for a group of paintings by a living American artist. She became one of America's greatest innovators and most commercially successful modern artists—disseminating American modernism in which artists express their own feelings and ideas—which helped American art become independent from imitative European art.[44]

While there were many other experiences in Georgia O'Keeffe's growth and fruitful success as an innovator, let's explore more deeply what the space climate is and how it impacts individuals' creativity development.

According to the CATs model introduced in chapter 2, there are three steps for innovation. Cultivating the space climate (step 1) and nurturing the space attitude (step 2) are discussed in this chapter. Applying ION thinking skills is discussed in chapter 9 (step 3).

STEP 1: CULTIVATE THE FREE SPACE CLIMATE

After plants are rooted in diverse soil, get bright sun, and become strong by overcoming fierce storms, they need their own space. Free space is vital for plants, as it provides room and time for them to grow. Similarly, after individuals are exposed to diverse experiences, get warm encouragement, and become strong through overcoming challenges, they need their own space to find and be themselves. The fierce storm climate is necessary, but too much of it in the absence of the space climate makes individuals become boring technicians who don't have their own unique skills. The space climate provides individuals with freedom to be alone and unique, which directly impacts the space attitudes that they develop, which are described in step 2. When the space climate initially nurtures individuals' space attitudes, they develop unique ideas. Their space attitudes help them become defiant dreamers, which enables outbox and newbox thinking.

Space climates remind me of my impatience and my mother's patience. When I was in first grade, I scored 30 percent right on a math test, but I didn't care because school was unimportant to me. That day, just like every day when I came home from school, I went outside to play marbles with the neighborhood boys while my parents were still working on the farms. After dinner, my mother continued working around the house, and then she found my test. The look on her face will be forever imprinted in my memory. Suddenly, I realized how important my education was to her. She told me to bring my marbles and showed me a fun addition and subtraction game with them. Whenever I got a right answer, she raised me up so I could reach the traditional homemade pumpkin candies that were on the top shelf. We also played games using sticks, chopsticks, grains, nuts, fruits, and other things (that no other Koreans would use) for practicing addition and subtraction. This continued every night, even when I started getting perfect scores on my tests. She also emphasized how learning was useful to my everyday life rather than just the scores. I have never met any parent who is as patient as my mother was.

I'm embarrassed to admit that I didn't learn my mother's patience.

Once I furiously yelled at my four-year-old daughter, "You're too stupid to learn!" Though twenty years have passed since this incident, my daughter still reminds me of my harsh words. For being so "stupid," she sure has an excellent memory!

Research Findings on the Space Climate

1. Plants need their own space to grow. Without space, plants become stunted or suffer from diseases due to limited airflow over their leaves and a lack of nutrients for their crowded roots. Following similar reasoning, parents and teachers of innovators (PTIs) give children free space to recognize, understand, and express their emotions—instead of just conforming to the current situation or adults' values or consensus. This is in contrast to most other adults—who often teach children to curb emotional expressions, which are considered unreasonable or childish tactics.[45] This makes children feel shameful about their expressions, so they hold them back, which limits their creativity.[46]

Instead, PTIs express emotions and accept their own and children's strong emotions.[47] Controlling emotional outbursts starts not with repressing the emotion but by developing the ability to articulate emotions verbally, artistically, or other ways. For example, they teach children to practice communicating negative feelings in positive ways by calmly explaining how they feel when they're upset or by writing down situations that caused an emotion and finding its origin and recognizing their strengths and limitations. They also encourage children to make songs, draw, or dance to communicate the saddest, happiest, or angriest moment they've experienced; and to express or act out stories with gestures, facial expressions, or body movements. They further teach children to avoid wanting to feel loved by everyone, and to distance themselves from others who bring them down or make them feel bad about themselves (unless they're giving constructive criticism). PTIs are patient; they emphasize children's self-exploration and self-expression—even when making messes—instead of organization, clean environments, or perfect results.[48] They also avoid interrupting children when they're immersed in their creative process (like writing songs, poems, lyrics, or short stories, or making art or building something) and help them focus on it without any distractions or interruptions (like e-mails, phone calls, computer, social media, text messages, TV, or video) by choosing a designated start and stop time so that they can experience *flow*, where nothing else matters to them. As a result, young innovators become aware of their own feelings/emotions and are comfortable self-regulating them.[49]

2. Plants, especially fruit trees, can be considered compassionate because they share their flowers and fruits with others (animals and people). Sympathy is feeling sorry for others but not experiencing their emotions. In contrast, empathy is experiencing others' emotions by imagining their perspective and situation.[50] Compassion goes further by taking action to ensure positive outcomes, which is a means of externally expressing internal empathy. Most adults reward rationality and competition more than empathy and compassion. But PTIs encourage children to be sensitive and self-reflective of their own and others' emotions.[51] For example, they help children read both fiction and nonfiction books that emphasize characters' emotions and develop insights on others' problems and situations. They encourage them to consider and understand others' viewpoints, feelings, attitudes, and motives through exercises like role-reversal or role-play. They teach communication and cooperation skills so they can consider and incorporate others and others' viewpoints in their actions.[52] For example, they teach children to listen and respond after others finish speaking; use encouraging words to show they're listening (like "Tell me more" or "Let's talk about it"); and validate others' emotions by agreeing with what they said while helping others find answers to their problems *by themselves*. They play make-believe with young children to teach how to extend children's empathy not only to other people, but also to objects and events, such as nature, animals, things, and causes.[53]

High levels of empathy and compassion result in many positive outcomes in life, including increased social interactions, more successful relationships, higher levels of maturity, greater life satisfaction, and physical and emotional well-being.[54] However, empathy in America is declining, and young adults are more self-centered than ever.[55] Compared to the 1970s and 1980s, today's American college students don't connect with statements such as "I often have tender, concerned feelings for people less fortunate than me," or "I sometimes try to understand my friends better by imagining how things look from their perspective."[56] Among American adults (ages 18–25), 64 percent say getting rich is the most important goal in life; another 17 percent say it is the second most important goal; and only 30 percent choose helping others as their ultimate goal.[57]

PTIs, however, encourage children to learn about others and recognize when others do something that's worthy of recognition and promote it. Further, they help children learn about tragedies in national and world history caused from insensitivity, cruelty, prejudice, ethnocentrism, xenophobia, and racism and discuss (and plan) how to reduce such tragedies. They help children experience self-efficacy (true confidence) and a true sense of pride and empowerment, from accomplishing small goals and triumph over obstacles and improving conditions for themselves and others in need.

3. Plants need to be left alone. Plants require a balance between nutrition they're fed by fertilizer versus nutrition they process alone. Some gardeners over-fertilize plants, which causes plants to look lush and green during the growing season, but they will neither bloom nor bear fruit during harvest. Many of today's parents overfeed children with stimulating extracurricular activities but deny them downtime to be alone to think—to digest and process what they've learned.[58] PTIs are self-reflective themselves, encourage children's self-reflection in solitude, and support their slow, considerate learning.[59] For example, they support children's deep thoughts by encouraging them to move away from distractions; control the noise around them (like turning off any electronics); and avoid multitasking (which interrupts deep thinking and wastes time by incurring switching time). They help children spend lots of time freethinking and playing alone; feel independent in solitude (*not* lonely, bored, needy, or afraid); and entertain themselves through pondering, writing, reading, beading, building, or art-making. During children's alone time (or before going to bed), PTIs encourage children to think about what happened that day and try to remember beautiful things they've heard, seen, read, said, or done; focus on one event and think how they feel about it and why; let go of negative feelings they hold; or write down three things they're grateful for. They also teach children relaxation and anti-stress techniques and to be kind to themselves by sharing responsibility with others. PTIs regularly visit rural areas for children to have different experiences, explore outdoors, and be connected to nature. They help children appreciate life by stopping to smell wild flowers, admire the world around them, and learn from and respect nature (developing humbleness). As a result, innovators grow up enjoying being alone, analyzing their experiences, and incubating ideas.[60] They're like eagles that don't flock and are content to be alone, which enables unique perspectives and ideas to form.[61]

4. Even if gardeners prefer roses to azaleas—no amount of fertilizer, sunlight, or pruning will change an azalea into a rose. PTIs don't try to change children to take on adults' dreams. Young innovators' self-exploration and self-expression autonomously lead to their own CPI— which can be different from their parents' or others'.[62] PTIs are flexible and encourage children to pursue their own CPI, first by allowing children's emotional identity to be separate from the adults'.[63] It continues by demonstrating each parent's independent interests and activities outside the home (also, innovators' mothers have wide interests and activities, separate from the husband and household).[64]

5. Gardeners don't make flowers but patiently control conditions, so plants can autonomously produce blossoms. Even if they plant sun-loving plants in the shade and try to force them to be shade-loving, the plants still need the sun. Cacti thrive in sunny desserts, while ferns thrive in shady wetlands. Gardeners respect these differences and won't plant them in the same flowerbox. Each plant is different. And each child is different. PTIs support differences in children and their autonomy.[65] For example, they incorporate young children's responsibility in everyday activities.[66] Then they develop longer-term activities that require them to make consequential decisions to prepare for life-determining decisions later.[67] Using the guiding parenting/teaching style, they aren't controlling or micromanagers who tell children what and how to do every detail and dismiss the idea that there's only one way to do something.[68] They create general structures and don't over-structure children's tasks/experiences, allowing them to construct on their own.[69] Further, PTIs teach children to avoid others' dominance by encouraging children not to allow their world to revolve around others' needs; plan their day according to their own schedule; maintain solid friendships (if friends need a favor, help them), but avoid letting others dominate their own plan; and depend on others for emotional support, but avoid letting others determine their level of happiness. This also facilitates children's positive psychological/emotional health.[70] With observation, patience, and respect for children's autonomy, they help children explore, express, and develop their own CPI.[71]

6. Even seeds from the same pod grow to be different. Some seeds grow tall and willowy, while others grow to be short and compact. Siblings share the same parents, home, and neighborhood, but their experiences differ. They may have different temperaments, different interactions with parents, different access to resources, different teachers or friendships, and other relationships. These non-shared experiences shape children's creativity development more than their shared experiences.[72] Innovators' parents encourage each child to develop creativity autonomously. PTIs let children take the time and space to find themselves and their CPI—by understanding their own skills/talents, strengths/weaknesses, likes/dislikes, habits, biases, expectations, fears, and prejudices. They let children choose topics for assignments and delivery modes for presentations of final products, and they let them show and discuss their creation to others. They encourage children to combine more than one CPI if they have multiples (like poetry and dance can be writing poems about dance; painting and animals can be creating paintings of animals). They help sustain children's CPI and achieve self-efficacy by inspiring and supporting them through being around people with the similar CPI or watching movies and reading books or magazines that are inspiring or supportive of their CPI. For example, for beginner pianists, they inspire children through piano concerts, or movies or biographies about pianists; or they plan music recitals or talent shows among several families that have children with a similar CPI, or they find receptive and inviting audiences at nursing homes.

    7. Each plant takes a different amount of time to grow. Plants (and creative thinking) take time and patience to grow; some more than others.[73] Immature plants can't be forced to blossom early. Healthy roots, strong stems, and better results (and innovation) require long-term decisions. Young innovators' slow starts might look like procrastinating, but their unrushed pace often leads to better results.[74] PTIs value learning according to children's own initiative and help them autonomously work at their own pace. Their patience demonstrates trust and causes children to trust their own potential, so children don't feel rushed into producing quick outcomes. (Test-centric climates might achieve short-term improvements on children's test scores, but they cost children's long-term creative thinking.)[75]

    8. Plant growth is happening even when they look dormant or unproductive. During winter, gardeners patiently wait out dormancy. It appears that there's no growth, but gardeners who trust their expertise and understand the plants will eventually see fruit. Through this kind of trust and understanding, PTIs encourage children to play, daydream, and imagine.[76]

They facilitate children's play, instead of dictating it, and encourage them to play physically and wildly, actively interacting with others/objects in new scenarios (like puzzles, board games, storytelling, and outdoor activities—not passively like watching TV). They encourage make-believe (like pretending that they're monkeys, dinosaurs, dragons, machines, princesses, or villains, or pretending, "this refrigerator box is an delivery truck" or "this stick is a magic wand") and role-play (like acting out dramatic plays; creating puppet shows; projecting themselves into new worlds, different times, and improbable situations)—outdoors when possible—that explore, discover, and stimulate fantasy and unique expressions.[77] They teach imaginative word games (like listing all imaginative ways to use common objects, playing with wild and crazy ideas, or approaching problems in fanciful ways); imaginative story-making and storytelling (like playing with improbabilities, abandoning logic/logical thoughts, and using their dreams to think of what-ifs, hows, and whys); or imaginative folklore (like collecting and modifying myths, legends, folk music, riddles, and folk art). They encourage children to change events around in books or movies; or add in characters they made up or from different books. They also encourage children to draw/paint what doesn't exist (like a penguin's hairpiece). PTIs help children play with objects or hand-made toys with no specific features (like dolls without faces, balls made of cloth, or cars without tires) to let their imagination invent new toys or games. Further, they support children's futuristic thoughts by encouraging them to see mirrors, pictures, TVs, or computer screens as gateways to the future. They also encourage them not to accept what they read or see as complete; identify gaps in knowledge; ask futuristic questions; or work on future scenarios in which they can identify underlying future problems and solve them.

Appealing to fantasy and futuristic thoughts stimulates children's imagery, storytelling, and spatial abilities.[78] Through imagination, they develop skills for modulating their circumstances, emotions, and happiness.[79] Young innovators' exposure to classic fables, fairy tales, nursery rhymes, and fantasy books increases the uniqueness of their future creation.[80] (Sadly, the decline of active play in school and at home is killing creative potential.[81] Overscheduling academics at the expense of playtime stifles children's unique ideas.[82])

9. *Plants that escape bonsai gardeners become the plants they're destined to be.* PTIs emphasize children's personal choices that don't conform

to society's expectations.[83] They accept children's different ideas/behaviors (like putting tree branches in a vase, incorporating pet food into an art project, shoveling snow with a spatula, coloring outside the lines, having a backwards day by doing things in reverse order, or valuing things that others throw away and converting them into something useful). PTIs teach children to find their uniqueness by encouraging them to name a favorite thing, person, animal, color, number, hobby, song, motto, or philosophy by which they live; look at the answers and themes and descriptors of themselves to find how they're different from others; and do *more* of this list to create their uniqueness.

Innovators' parents are nonconformists themselves; and they encourage children to be comfortable with marginality and being an outsider; think dramatically different than their contemporaries/peers (like Galileo, whom nobody believed and who was considered crazy); avoid trying to be mainstream in their sexuality, profession, language, religion, how they live, or what they eat; spend time to be an observer, without joining the group, to remain an outsider; be unconventional and intellectual minorities in school, clubs, and online; join groups that are unfamiliar (like schools where they'll be a minority, or a traditionally African or Greek church); or find a like-minded friend or an intellectual stimulator who can understand them. [84] They teach children that it's okay to think/act like nerds (who have passion for academics) or geeks (who have passion for a specific activity/subject), and that nerds and geeks are responsible for nearly all innovations that we all enjoy. They help children view their imagination and nonconformity as strengths for turning their passion and goal into unique future creations.[85]

Sadly, children's nonconformity frustrates teachers—especially in test-centric climates—who see them as troublemakers.[86] Even though teachers *say* they identify and reward creativity, they mostly identify conforming achievers as gifted children.[87] They inadvertently discourage or punish children's creative attitudes and tease, scorn, or isolate them from peers.[88] Pressure to conform, which reduces children's curiosity and outbox thinking, occurs most between fourth and six grades;[89] this reduction in creativity has been creeping earlier for two decades.[90] Some, especially males, eventually drop out due to pressure to conform.[91] Training to identify and harness creativity, instead of punishing it, is necessary for teachers who want to reverse this trend.[92]

10. Apple trees that cross-pollinate—between male and female blossoms—bear fruit better than trees that just self-pollinate. Innovators use nonconformity as a strength by accessing and learning from *both* males and females.[93] PTIs reject gender-biased roles, expectations, and stereotypes and encourage children's gender-bias-free interests.[94] They let children find their own comfort level regarding the gender and sexuality spectrum; become independent, dominant, and tough girls, or sensitive and soft boys; and pursue future dreams regardless of their gender. They accept children's personality and choose a variety of colors for clothes/projects, let them pick colors for their clothes/projects, and let them make personal choices as if they were the other gender.

Young innovators incorporate the opposite gender's strengths. For example, young male innovators pattern their mothers' creative attitudes, whereas young female innovators pattern their fathers' creative attitudes.[95] They don't sacrifice their creativity to live up to others' expectations for their gender.[96] They connect their softness and sensitivity (traditional femininity) with independence, self-efficacy, and assertiveness (traditional masculinity).[97] Also, cross-pollination across genders foreshadows cross-pollinating across different professional realms, which is critical for innovation. Many artistic innovators have science backgrounds, and many scientific innovators have art backgrounds.[98] Over time, they connect the dots and bring these two worlds together.[99]

11. Plants grow bigger and healthier free from others' control. Once they learn alternatives to conforming, young innovators develop defiance against inconsistent or unjust rules, norms, or values. PTIs support children's uniqueness and teach them to be assertive with their original ideas. For example, they elicit children's assertiveness by encouraging them to do their own thing for their own reasons and avoid letting others tell them what to do; find something small to firmly and politely say "no" to; create an opposite argument to one of their strong personal beliefs and present it to an audience; and *ask* others to help them do something and express their needs/desires (because no one can read others' minds).

PTIs support children's nonconformity, ability to challenge the status quo, and willingness to defy socially desirable behaviors—so that they can achieve beyond what others can see.[100] For example, they encourage children to ask questions about widely accepted knowledge; to not automatically accept rules, authorities, or paradigms; to challenge by asking *why*; to challenge adults' opinions with respect, and responsibly break the rules; and to challenge the beliefs of stereotypes about the world and what makes it work, and break those stereotypes.

Yet PTIs also balance nonconformity/defiance (for uniqueness) with conformity/self-discipline (for usefulness) that is necessary for innovation.[101] For example, they support children's productive defiance by encouraging them to stand alone against the crowd or expectations—*while* respecting others' opinions—and learn skills for compromising and negotiating (or working with someone who has such skills.); think objectively about what they're trying to change to see if it's of true benefit; direct their defiant thinking into revolutionary outcomes (like changing public opinions effectively for what they believe); be proud of their work and appreciate their strengths *while* observing what they like in others' work; and constantly assess their own work to make it better, finding their style and then shifting it over time.

STEP 2: NURTURE THE EIGHT SPACE ATTITUDES

As the space climate nurtures individuals' space attitudes (step 1), they discover and use their own uniqueness. By combining their sun and space attitudes (for uniqueness) with the soil and storm attitudes (for usefulness), they make their creation both unique and useful—*innovative*. Step 2 explains what the eight space attitudes are, and how they nurture defiant dreamers who apply outbox and newbox thinking. It starts with a brief anecdote from my life, illustrating how my own space attitudes were encouraged/discouraged or how I encouraged/discouraged these attitudes within my children. Then I summarize what research says about each of the attitudes and how each can contribute to unique outbox and newbox thinking. Each attitude can be learned and further developed through practice. The eight space attitudes (with the seemingly negative side in parentheses) are:

1. Emotional (and Unstable)

Confucianism discourages expressing emotions; affectionate expression is considered inappropriate.[102] My parents met for *the first time* on their *wedding* day, and I've never seen or heard them being affectionate with each other. They showed their affection for me by doing a lot for me, but they never verbally said they loved me. It isn't something I say to my children either. I'm trying to grow beyond this limitation by *texting* affectionate messages. This is less awkward for me than to say them face-to-face. Still it's hard—my Confucian roots run deep.

Verbal and emotional abuse and physical punishment were acceptable disciplining methods where I was from because most Asian parents and teachers follow the controlling parenting/teaching style.[103] I endured all three in my own childhood. Physical punishment to control behavior is one of the biggest differences between Confucian and Western parenting.[104] Yet despite the harshness, I, like most other Asians, never doubted my parents' unconditional love for me. Since I came to America, however, my children have observed the permissive parenting style from our friends and neighbors. Due to the confusion between Korean and American discipline, I changed my behavior in accordance with research: I started reinforcing my children's positive behaviors through rewards while disciplining them for negative behaviors with explanation and justification, without physical punishment.[105] I don't criticize them about who they are or their abilities, but I do give them brutally honest criticism for what and how they do (or don't do), and whether they do their best regardless of the results.

Figure 6.1. Emotional (and Unstable) Space Attitude

Research findings on the emotional attitude

The emotional attitude (see figure 6.1) is characterized by recognizing, understanding, and expressing one's own feelings. Innovators experience deep emotions and are sensitive to the environment.[106] They're emotionally expressive and can be over-reactive or oversensitive to stimulation: physiologically, intellectually, sensually, or imaginationally.[107] Emotions affect creativity often more than cognitive or other rational factors—positively and negatively.[108] Many creative attitudes (big-picture-thinking, compassionate, optimistic, spontaneous, playful, energetic, etc.) involved in the creative process (Apple-tree Creative Process: ACP) start with emotions. Innovation also *evokes* emotions within both the innovator and the audience.[109] Although artistic innovators are often more emotionally expressive than scientific innovators are, emotions are involved in all creative endeavors (painting, invention, science, leadership, sport, etc.).[110] Science Nobel laureates are also emotionally sensitive and use emotions in their creative process (ACP).[111]

Innovators' intense emotions and reactions enhance outbox thinking, but they can inhibit inbox thinking (especially critical thinking).[112] Their emotions can make them exposed, vulnerable, misunderstood, or isolated, but it isn't a sign of mental illness.[113] Overall, innovators enjoy superior mental health, *despite* the myths about tortured artists and mad scientists.[114] Both mental illness and creativity involve imagination, but they're very different thought processes.[115] The emotions for creativity cause *goal-oriented* craziness and are healthy and productive.[116] Although innovators can be unstable or unpredictable, they're controlled.[117] Also, their resilience prevents sustained erratic or self-destructive behaviors.[118] In contrast, mental illness is a distortion of adjustment to life and reduces creative capacity.[119] Innovators who indeed suffer from mental illness can be quite successful if they undergo treatment, because creativity is conducted by healthy mental processes.[120] Creativity enables innovators to function and flourish despite their mental illness because they *are* innovators.[121] Innovators' mental health is improved by their creative expressions.[122] The brain mood is positive, optimistic for creative thinking, and their creative process (ACP) is a source of joy and energy, reaching a state of mind described as *flow.*[123]

Positive emotions (happiness, joy, playfulness, being in love—not just lust, etc.) enhance outbox thinking.[124] Most unique ideas occur when innovators are happy and excited about their work (although sad individuals can generate unique ideas if they see the work as interesting/pleasant).[125] Positive emotions help innovators increase the scope of attention and see the big picture instead of just the details; direct interest out toward the big wide world; learn new things and build relationships; and free the mind to increase fluent, flexible, original outbox thinking.[126] But positive emotions can also inhibit persistent focus and inbox thinking (like working out details/calculations and critical thinking).[127] Positive emotions can lead to Aha! moments and new box thinking only if the subconscious mind is willing to persist in finding unique/useful ideas.[128]

Negative emotions (fear, anxiety, anger, etc.) inhibit outbox thinking but can enhance inbox thinking through persistent focus and critical thinking especially if they're used as motivation.[129] Relaxation/rest reduces negative emotions and improves creative climates. But despite the assumption that relaxation/rest is useful for Aha! moments, it's useful only if it's preceded by an intense period of work and followed by another intense period of work.[130]

2. Compassionate (and Overreaching)

The village I grew up in is on the largest flat plateau in the mountain. I thought it was civilized and modern because we had government offices; people from other villages had to walk a very long way to visit them. I thought my village was the center of the universe—but in reality I'd never even seen a small city.

For as long as I can remember, my parents rented out rooms in our house to boarders. One of them was a newlywed couple by (of course) an arranged marriage. The wife didn't hear well, which might have frustrated her husband (Mr. Hong). But I communicated well with her by being compassionate, and we became friends as we talked a lot while he was at work. I loved listening to her stories about the big city that she came from, especially a shocking *television* that would show people even though they weren't inside the box. Despite Mr. Hong's kindness and politeness to my family, he often beat his wife and dragged her around the yard by her hair. Her knees bled from scratching the ground. "How come I'm not allowed to even pinch my brother, but Mr. Hong can beat his wife?" I asked my parents, and I learned that this was part of the legacy of Confucianism; a husband needed to discipline a wife, and thus neither my parents and neighbors nor the policemen would stop him. This traumatic experience made me start thinking that the world isn't always fair and that something must be done.

One of the other renters was a single man who had a chronic illness that prevented him from getting married. Additionally, his face was scarred from severe chicken pox he had as a child. He breathed harshly and sometimes couldn't walk. I'd run errands for him and pick up his medicine from the pharmacist. He was different from other men: he was the only unmarried adult man I knew; besides him, I'd never met a man who cooked; he showed traditionally feminine characteristics; he was emotionally expressive, sensitive, and self-reflective; and he read a lot and liked to tell stories, which I listened to with great interest. I learned a lot from him and his perspective of the world,

Figure 6.2. Compassionate (and Overreaching) Space Attitude

which nurtured my compassion for him. His thoughts were meaningful and deep. Although I was little, I learned from him that people who think deeply and speak intelligently are attractive even if they have a scarred face or are considered ugly in appearance.

Research findings on the compassionate attitude

Having the compassionate attitude (see figure 6.2) entails empathizing with and helping others in meaningful ways. Creativity requires expressiveness to emotionally touch and move others.[131] Innovators are sensitive to others' emotions and develop skills to articulate their own emotions and thoughts.[132] Their empathy allows them to bond with mentors, meet and learn from unique people, and understand what others (such as their audience or customers) really want and need.[133] Emotional empathy is beneficial for creativity yet can lead to preferential treatment to those they feel for.[134] For this reason, taking others' perspectives (perspective-taking empathy) is better than just emotional empathy.[135] It reduces bias and helps understand verbal and nonverbal cues for effective negotiations and problem solving.[136]

Innovators' curiosity and compassion for humanity often drive their creative endeavor.[137] Their passion is strengthened by compassion for others' needs, which inspires their big-picture goal and promotes outbox and newbox thinking.[138] The compassion of Einstein, Jobs, Mandela, and Curie for humankind was more pronounced than their compassion for their own families; and O'Keeffe's compassion for nature was bigger than her compassion for humankind. So innovators are often misunderstood by those closest to them. Although their compassion and desire to improve humankind is at the heart of their creativity, their visionary dreams aren't always understood or accepted by the world, either. They may not ever be understood, but they pursue their creativity anyway. Through their compassionate and big-picture-thinking attitudes, they sustain their optimistic view of how their final creation may benefit the world.[139] This enables them to take greater risks and achieve Big I.[140]

3. Self-Reflective (and Withdrawn)

Figure 6.3. Self-Reflective (and Withdrawn) Space Attitude

I left my village for high school in Daegu. Every exam week, my mother would come to where I lived after she had worked on the farms all day. The trip took her three to four hours, including waiting for buses, transferring, and walking. She cooked dinner for me (but not for herself, which I didn't know until she was diagnosed with malnutrition years later), watched me studying and sleeping, and then woke me up and fed me breakfast. Before the sun was up, she'd be back on the bus, heading back to my hometown to attend the early-morning church service and then work on the farms. She never told me why she did all of these things. My self-reflection on her life and work made me work hard to make her happy (and to become the light and salt of the world, of course!) instead of expressing my gratitude verbally. I feel that *any* time in my life is much easier than any time in hers.

Research findings on the self-reflective attitude

The self-reflective attitude (see figure 6.3) is characterized by enjoying solitude to understand the essence of one's own and others' experiences and views. Both introverts and extroverts can be creative, yet self-reflection is necessary for Big I.[141] Innovators are introverted at times during their creative process (while reading, practicing, daydreaming, capturing thoughts, formulating hypotheses, etc.).[142] But being self-reflective is more than simply being introverted. Self-reflection is beneficial for innovators because:[143] first, it helps them focus on the demanding creative process (ACP) in the absence of distractions; second, it helps them maintain their independent mind, staying away from negative social influences; third, it helps them bulwark their self-efficacy against others' doubt and skepticism; fourth, it helps them assess their own beliefs, work objectively/critically, and think persistently; and finally, fifth, it facilitates the uniqueness of their creation. Yet they switch from self-reflection in social isolation into social integration depending on the specific stage of a creative process (ACP).[144] They're vocal and animated when discussing topics of their expertise or promoting their creation in ways others can understand and appreciate—by being social and communicative—like extroverts.[145]

Innovators appreciate and learn from nature. A relaxed state of mind that's stress-free and distraction-free is vital for self-reflection and the creative process.[146] Innovators throughout history have demonstrated the importance of utilizing nature to enable self-reflection. Often they love solitary walks and appreciate nature. They enjoy gardening—Jobs, Mandela, O'Keeffe, Curie, and Einstein (although he wasn't good at weeding) were avid gardeners. In fact, Mandela even created gardens on the roof of his *prison* and grew all kinds of vegetables! Innovators' affinity for gardening is one reason I use gardening metaphors in this book.

4. Autonomous (and Uncontrolled)

Right before I earned my American doctorate, Dr. Lee (my husband) visited a famous fortuneteller in Seoul, Korea, who told him, "Your wife won't come back to Korea." Dr. Lee was distraught. I'd already lived in America for four years. "How can I make her come back home?" he asked. The fortuneteller answered, "If she returns to Korea, her bones will ache with extreme pain." Dr. Lee remembered the precise words and asked him how to change my fate. "Her name, Kyung ('auspicious')-Hee ('girl'), is too out of control to be a woman's name," said the fortuneteller. "The Chinese character to spell Kyung that her family chose means *auspicious* (that's only for males) instead of the character pronounced the same way but meaning *obedient*."

"So we just change the spelling of her name?" asked Dr. Lee.

"No. She needs a new name and must hear it aloud more times than she's heard her own name. Then her destiny will change, and she can return home to you."

Dr. Lee was very excited. Although it was before sunrise in America, he called and told me everything. I bolted upright in my bed—shocked.

Finally, I knew the answer: my parents had spelled my name with the wrong character. I should've known! It made complete sense to me, and I believed it. My life would've been simple if I had changed my name long ago. Dr. Lee wanted to start my new name right away before my old name was used any more. I told him it was a bad time due to my final exams, but he couldn't be dissuaded.

A few days later, he arrived at my doorstep in Georgia with a suitcase in one hand and a mini cassette player in the other. On the cassette he'd recorded himself calling out my new name again and again. I asked him to stop it because I had to study, but he wouldn't. He played the tape again and again. I was afraid of what I would become when I had heard my new name called out more times than my old name. But I was also relieved that I had an answer about why I couldn't conform to Korean society.

He played the tape and followed me around the house while I did chores, in the kitchen while I prepared dinner, and in the car when I went to pick the children up from school. He played it all through the night when I slept. After a week, he was packed and ready to leave. He said, "Play the tape over and over." "No," I replied sincerely. I wanted neither to go back to Korea, nor to be controlled by anyone or any Korean rules or customs again. I wanted to live my own life for my own passion and goal. Upon earning my PhD and becoming a professor, I divorced him. I wanted to live as an autonomous human being.

Figure 6.4. Autonomous (and Uncontrolled) Space Attitude

Research findings on the autonomous attitude

Having the autonomous attitude (see figure 6.4) means being independently and intrinsically motivated to pursue a passion or a goal. *Extrinsic* motivation is doing tasks/activities because they yield rewards/benefits upon completion (money, fame, grades, etc.), which often hurts creativity because it just controls people and is effective only for simple/rote tasks or short-term goals.[147] In contrast, *intrinsic/autonomous* motivation is doing a task purely because of the enjoyment derived from doing it.[148] Autonomous motivation comes from self-efficacy and a passion, which enhances learning and persistence.[149] Innovators are autonomously engaged in their work for their passion or goal. They autonomously expand sacrificial, (seemingly) obsessive energy to accomplish their clear—but unguaranteed—goal.[150] In this pursuit, their work is incorporated into their identity.[151] Their extreme intensity often causes them to sacrifice their personal life, so they seem hyper or like workaholics.[152] But this intensity by their autonomous motivation promotes outbox and newbox thinking and thus the uniqueness of their creation, and it also promotes their energy to overcome obstacles in their work and life and their happiness.[153]

5. Daydreaming (and Delusional)

Like most Koreans, I grew up hating Japanese people (until I met my Japanese babysitter for my children in America). Korea has a tragic history of being colonized and brutally abused—in ways similar to the Holocaust—by the Japanese for thirty-six years (1910–1945). Many Koreans, including my own grandfather, were tortured, killed, or enslaved by the

Japanese. I grew up daydreaming about my grandfather who never returned after the Japanese captured him. He never died in my fantasies, and I was sure that if he knew he had a granddaughter (me!), he'd come home right away because I looked just like him (which my grandmother always told me).

Since my baby brother died when I was ten, I have daydreamed that he's a seven-year-old angel in heaven. I didn't want to grow up nor for my mother to grow older because otherwise (I thought) he'd not recognize us in heaven. So I persistently helped my mother dye her grey hair black.

Figure 6.5. Daydreaming (and Delusional) Space Attitude

Research findings on the daydreaming attitude

The daydreaming attitude (see figure 6.5) is characterized by sustaining unrealistic but goal-oriented thoughts while awake. I include mind-wandering (having random thoughts, feelings, or fantasies) within daydreaming. There are advantages and disadvantages to daydreaming. Daydreaming impairs the ability to perform complex tasks (and impairs reading comprehension more than low vocabulary capacity does; it is especially detrimental when driving).[154] It can occur anywhere and anytime (15–50 percent of people's time), even when individuals are engaged in high-demanding tasks like taking important tests.[155] Boring reading material can encourage daydreaming because other thoughts are more interesting, although interesting material can also encourage it if it provokes related thoughts.[156] Both individuals with ADHD and frequent daydreamers have difficulty paying attention and experience daydreaming-related disruptions.[157] But being able to quickly divert attention (similar to daydreaming) to follow discovered information is also beneficial for outbox and newbox thinking.[158]

Although many dismiss fantasies and daydreams as nonsense, there are advantages to unplanned, distracting daydreaming because it facilitates Aha! moments. *The most unique idea and Aha! occurs while innovators are spontaneous, unfocused, and daydreaming.*[159] Both daydreaming and subsequent Aha! discoveries occur especially when innovators engage in low-demanding tasks. Having the persistent attitude and doing focused work is critical to inbox thinking and thus innovation, but too much focus can act as a blinder that blocks outbox thinking and Aha! inspiration. Innovators will persist to achieve an idea or a goal even when they fail; then they engage in low-demanding tasks—rather than completely resting—become spontaneous and daydreamy; and then they achieve the idea or the goal by increasing subconscious processing and outbox and newbox thinking.[160] Their daydreams are *goal-oriented*.[161] After daydreaming, they practice mindfulness of the present to capture and evaluate and follow through the idea or the goal using their persistent attitude.[162] Innovators constantly seek unique ideas while taking advantage of daydreams to achieve a goal, which often leads to Big I.[163]

6. Nonconforming (and Wild)

When I was four, my parents' new apple orchard yielded the first two apples on the sapling trees, which looked perfect. I picked and devoured both of them. They were crisp and sweet, and the juice dribbled down my chin. The next day, my grandmother was furious that I ate them—not because she wanted them, but because a girl shouldn't have been the first one to eat them. Tradition requires boys to eat the first fruit, so that the trees would yield fruits *every* year; otherwise, they'd yield only every *other* year. Nobody told me this until it was too late, and I worried about the apple trees every year after that. I observed as floods, droughts, and frost depleted our expected harvests. For my parents' entire lives, they didn't make much money from the apple orchard even though they worked themselves nearly to death. I blamed myself for my inability to resist the apples.

I enjoyed wearing skirts, knitting, and cooking, but also playing marbles, sword fighting, and hunting rabbits on the snowy mountains. As I got older, I felt threatened by the expectations of what girls must look like, act like, and talk like. To be beautiful, women had to conform to the traditional role and appear fragile and delicate—never strong or tough. I earned a black belt in the Karate club in college and was strong and persistent. When I married, my in-laws did all they could do to discourage such behavior. Confucians strongly believe that everyone should be like everyone else, and eccentricity is of no benefit to anyone.[164]

I hope my daughter will continue to be an independent, self-sufficient, and strong woman. I don't want her to conform to the traditional norm. In America, she can choose her own path and make her own future.

Figure 6.6. Nonconforming (and Wild) Space Attitude

Research findings on the nonconforming attitude

Having the nonconforming attitude (see figure 6.6) involves choosing to differ from mainstream patterns of thought and behavior. Conventions and traditions hardly inspire innovation. Innovators listen to what their heart yearns for and shut out others' expectations. They sacrifice conventional definitions of success for their self-convictions, not trying to measure up or prove anything to others.[165] They're prepared to face the consequences of following unconventional paths.[166] They develop new concepts, approaches, and products using outbox thinking by breaking conventional/ traditional ways of thinking; they reject the limits imposed by others and set their own rules; and they find their strengths and pursue their own goal instead of others'.[167] They're unconventional and unsubmissive nonconformists who push the known boundaries to change the world.[168]

More innovators are from nonconforming/individualistic cultures than from conforming/collectivistic cultures.[169] Individualistic Westerners often think in terms of *I* (which encourages uniqueness), whereas collectivistic Easterners often think in terms of *We* (which encourages conformity and harmony).[170] Innovators emphasize *I* and uniqueness.[171] Those who don't belong to an existing group and don't share a *We* identity with the group members are also nonconformists. They may feel uncomfortable but it enables unique outbox and newbox thinking.[172]

Innovators are often outsiders—nonconformists by circumstance. They come from nonmainstream familial, educational, professional, economic, or cultural backgrounds.[173] They don't share a *We* identity with the mainstream. As outsiders, they experience two different norms/traditions and must adapt to the mainstream, which causes insecurity and self-doubt but enables unique outbox and newbox thinking.[174] They are not necessarily self-confident, but they are driven to overcome their outsider status by developing self-efficacy in their subject/field. While feeling that they have nothing to lose because they are outsiders anyways, they take risks by stepping out of their comfort zone, which facilitates the creative process.[175] In addition to their common economical disadvantages, the innovators discussed here faced different circumstances that made all of them outsiders, including Einstein's Jewish heritage, Jobs's perceived abandonment by his biological parents, Mandela's living with Dalindyebo's family, and O'Keeffe's and Curie's being women in a man's world.

More innovators are left-handed than are right-handed—nonconformists in the right-handed world.[176] They use both hands to cope with the world, which engages their whole brain.[177] This promotes newbox thinking, which is a whole-brain process. Innovators' brains show more interactions between the left and right sides than do non-innovators'.[178] Sadly, more females and people from conforming cultures are forced to conform to the right-handed world, which stifles their creativity.[179]

7. Gender-Bias-Free (and Gender-Free)

I grew up with no such thing as gender-bias-free. Everything was based on gender. I wasn't allowed to celebrate my daughter's 100-day-birthday party, nor her first-year-birthday party, because her grandparents didn't want to acknowledge a *girl* as their first grandchild. (The tradition of a 100-day-birthday party began long ago when infant mortality rates were high.)

Educating women had long been opposed by Confucianism.[180] This is why all the girls from my town worked in sweatshops while the boys were in school. Patriarchal cultures emphasize leadership and skills for males and obedience for females.[181] Accordingly, most Asian females don't achieve their potential, and their professional careers are limited.[182]

Many Asian students go abroad to improve their ability to speak English, which is required to get better jobs. (But only speaking English, without expertise in anything, never leads to innovation.) Their mothers will quit their jobs and go abroad with them to support their education. Meanwhile, the fathers work extremely hard to support the family and education and see the family only once or twice a year. Koreans call these fathers "Goose Dads" because geese migrate, like the fathers who must fly a long distance to see their families.[183] There were more than 100,000 goose dads in South Korea in 2008.[184]

On American Valentine's Day, boys/husbands give gifts to girls/wives, which is opposite to Korean Valentine's Day, where only girls give gifts to boys. In America, when I go into a bank or a grocery store, even older men open the door for me. When I visited Korea last time, I was walking into a department store and expected this young man to open the door for me. My nose was almost broken when he allowed the door to slam in my face, which reminded me that I wasn't in America. When I talk with my American students who are married, I find that husbands and wives often share household responsibilities. As my personal experience shows, America is gender-bias-free compared to Asia.

Figure 6.7. Gender-Bias-Free (and Gender-Free) Space Attitude

Research findings on the gender-bias-free attitude

Following the gender-bias-free attitude (see figure 6.7) means rejecting stereotypes based on gender. It's about diversity and removing limitations to gender expressions. Innovators are gender-bias-free—psychologically rather than physically—and exhibit *both* masculine and feminine attitudes and characteristics, which they use in their creative process (ACP).[185] Nonconforming to the conventional gender norms and resisting gender-role expectations make them flexible and adaptable, which promotes outbox and newbox thinking.[186] It also enables their variety of thinking strategies/

techniques beyond those prescribed for their own gender.[187] This further nurtures their resourceful attitude to get more social support during difficult times, which strengthens their resilient attitude.[188]

8. Defiant (and Rebellious)

I was defiant since I was a child, but I wasn't allowed to express my defiance at any level until I entered graduate school in America. Torrance Center's creative climate encouraged my defiance. In my Korean doctoral program, I learned and memorized many theories about intelligence and creativity to prepare for exams. Upon starting my American doctoral program, I found that my memorized theories had grown obsolete and became mental clutter. In Korea, I'd only been taught the strengths of the theories, but in America, I *critiqued* them and learned not to memorize anything, as new research brings new theories.

My defiance sparked many unique research hypotheses by questioning established knowledge, conclusions, or theories. I questioned my own Asian culture (Confucianism); the TTCTs (the most widely-used creativity tests); the theory that only highly intelligent people can be creative; and the theory that creativity is steadily increasing in America. Yet I also expect that my research findings will be supported only until new research disproves them.

Figure 6.8. Defiant (and Rebellious) Space Attitude

Research findings on the defiant attitude

The defiant attitude (see figure 6.8) is shown by courageously rejecting or changing existing norms, values, traditions, hierarchies, or authorities to pursue one's goal. Innovators aren't typically the most intelligent or educated people in their field.[189] Using only knowledge/conclusions from the past to try to solve future problems stifles creativity.[190] Creativity requires outbox thinking and must go beyond current expertise, and too much knowledge can restrain it. *An idea must be unique to be creative, which requires deviating from the norm or the tradition.*[191] Creativity is both destructive, to be unique, and constructive, to be useful.[192] The more unique a creation is, the more it engenders opposition/resentment, because uniqueness is defiant in nature.[193] Thus, innovators must take risks and act defiantly toward governing or controlling powers.[194]

Many innovators start their innovation as defiant troublemakers (even criminals) by violating norms or laws.[195] For example, Jobs and Wozniak invented and sold illegal blue boxes that made free long-distance calls. This defiant venture established a foundation for their future partnership. Jobs stated, "Experiences like that taught us the power of ideas. . . . And if we hadn't have made blue boxes, there would've been no Apple."[196]

Many innovators are defiant later-borns. First-borns use more inbox thinking, attain higher degrees from better schools, enter higher-status occupations, and are more conventional than their younger siblings—striving to fulfill their parents' expectations.[197] Later-borns use more outbox thinking and are more defiant—even rebellious—and revolutionary than first-borns.[198] (For females, birth order isn't as significant—because females' gender-bias-free attitude is more significant for their creativity development than their birth order is.[199])

Defiance, however, has limits. If an idea seems too radical by the society, it'll be rejected. Creativity isn't anarchy—it's unpredictability within limitations and surprise within familiarity; the flair of a creation's uniqueness is limited by its usefulness, and the benefit of its usefulness is limited by its uniqueness.[200] Respecting the status quo—to be useful—must come before defying it—to be unique. Innovators first learn, understand, and conform to the existing rules or traditions/constraints or systems in their field—even when they disagree with the rules. (Rules and constraints often help shape and define useful solutions/ideas.) And then they challenge or break the rules/constraints and make changes still *within* the system or tradition. For example, O'Keeffe is known for intense close-up flower paintings that are abstract art. But she was first used inbox thinking and trained to draw realistic scenes of nature and traditional/classical figures. Then she was schooled in classical painting skills and achieved expertise in painting realism. Then she used outbox thinking and was inspired to try abstraction, which was defiant and revolutionary at that time. And finally she achieved uniqueness of her creation in addition to usefulness.

The pattern of innovators' journey is, first, developing expertise and practicing inbox *realism* and achieving usefulness (using their soil and storm attitudes); second, developing defiant *optimism* to go outside the box and achieving uniqueness (using their sun and space attitudes); and finally, developing newbox *realistic-idealism* and achieving both uniqueness and usefulness (using their 4S attitudes).

INNOVATORS' SPACE ATTITUDES: THE CACTUS AMONG US

Innovators display the space attitudes that might seem negative—such as unstable, overreaching, withdrawn, uncontrolled, delusional, wild, gender-free, or rebellious. For example, innovators are often so emotional that they might seem unstable. Jobs was often extremely emotional about music and deeply touched by artists.[201] He wore his emotions on his sleeve, and he wept or cried in public—when he was fired from Apple, when Disney agreed to buy Pixar, when employees missed deadlines or lost in negotiations, and when he learned that there was a CD tray in the iMac, not a slot.[202] He might seem *unstable*, but his emotions showed that he was passionate about everything he did.

Innovators are often so compassionate that they might seem overreaching. Mandela understood nonblack people's views and emotions by connecting and empathizing with the guards in the prison, and he even learned Afrikaans (the language of the oppressors). His compassion helped him negotiate the new South African constitution,[203] and speaking Afrikaans to Afrikaners—including the Apartheid leaders—helped them be open with and be fond of him.[204] He might seem *overreaching*.

Innovators are often so self-reflective that they might seem withdrawn. Einstein spent time with his two sons by making toys/cars, telling stories, or playing lullabies on his violin. But when pondering his relativity theory, he was aloof and neglected them.[205] While his wife was taking care of the crying baby and keeping house, he escaped for long walks to self-reflect, often wandering absentmindedly and getting lost.[206] He loved sailing because it gave him a chance to be away from people and think in depth.[207] He might seem *withdrawn*.

Innovators are often so autonomous that they might seem uncontrolled. Einstein started worshiping Judaism intently in elementary school, but by age twelve when he started becoming deeply immersed in science, he gave up Judaism, becoming religiously autonomous.[208] His parents let him make his own decisions about his education, career, and citizenship. After dropping out of high school at fifteen, he traveled alone on foot from

Milan to Genoa, Italy, crossing mountains with only a few books. He loved the Italian way of life so much that he gave up his German citizenship.[209] Then he decided to become a Swiss citizen while at Aarau in Switzerland. He might seem *uncontrolled* by many other parents.

Innovators daydream so often that they might seem delusional. At Aarau, Einstein imagined what would it be like to ride a light beam or what would happen if he ran as fast as the speed of light.[210] These questions persistently occupied his thoughts for more than ten years before he found the answers.[211] He might seem *delusional.*

Innovators are often so nonconforming that they might seem wild. O'Keeffe was the only great woman artist of her generation who posed nude (for Stieglitz), which he exhibited at his gallery in NYC in 1921. This caused a public sensation and elicited sexual interpretations of her work.[212] She might seem *wild.*

Innovators are often so gender-bias-free that they might seem gender-free. Stieglitz created a sexualized image of O'Keeffe and a sexually liberated woman's aura to her work. However, she denied either gendered or sexualized interpretation of her work because she wanted to be known as a good artist, not a good *woman* artist. She might seem gender-free. Yet her denial established a mystique, which made people even more curious, and today she's best known for her suggestive, sensual, expressionist paintings.[213]

Innovators are often so defiant that they might seem rebellious. While attending the rigid culture of the German schools, the fervent German nationalism and militarism made Einstein hate authority, which contributed to his defiance.[214] His relativity theory went against conventional scientific dogma that had defined science for centuries; against religious dogma; and against all other forms of dogma and authority. He might seem *rebellious.*

Parents and educators must be able to see the long-term positive aspects of behaviors that seem prickly in children; so they can encourage the underlying space attitudes instead of seeing the children as troublemakers. Also, children must be able to view their own space attitudes positively. When parents and educators succeed in cultivating the space climate and nurturing children's space attitudes, they are following the footsteps of the PTIs who encouraged, taught, and mentored the greatest innovators in history.

PART 3

HOW DO CULTURAL CLIMATES AFFECT CREATIVITY?

Chapter 7

ARE MEN REALLY MORE CREATIVE THAN WOMEN ARE?

C ulture—a major part of creative climates—has a critical impact on parenting and education for creativity because parents raise their children according to the values and norms endorsed by their own culture.[1]

Previously I discussed the 4S climates (soil, sun, storm, and space). In this and the next chapter, I'll discuss the impact that cultural climates—*patriarchal culture*, *Jewish culture*, and *Asian culture*—have on creativity. This can help parents and educators determine their own attitudes toward children's creativity and in what ways the culture climates in which they work and live affect their beliefs, expectations, and parenting/teaching practices.

THE MAJORITY OF NOBEL PRIZE WINNERS ARE MEN

Differences in mental strategies between males and females have emerged from my extensive empirical studies and analyses of creativity-test scores (including divergent-thinking test scores). Due to their attention to the details and their persistence, females are often good at inbox (or verbal) thinking (and the elaboration skill of newbox-thinking), whereas males are often good at outbox (or visual) thinking.[2] This might be because of traditional roles in their patriarchal cultures where females are expected to be more conforming (inside the box).[3] However, males and females are born with similar creative potential, and neither is born more creative than the other.[4] In fact, both traditional masculine and feminine traits, such as independence and sensitivity, are necessary for creativity.[5]

In reality, however, female innovators are extremely rare compared to the abundance of male innovators.[6] The Nobel Prize is the highest and most prestigious honor for creativity, symbolizing the highest degree of creative achievement.[7] Yet as of 2014, only 5.3 percent of Nobel laureates were female. Most female Nobel laureates are in nonscientific fields, and only 2.6 percent of laureates in the scientific fields were female.

Madame Marie Curie, the first woman to win a Nobel Prize, won two Nobel Prizes in science: one for physics in 1903 and the other for chemistry in 1911. There have been only two female physics Nobel laureates, so Marie alone represents half of them. There have been only four female chemistry Nobel laureates, so Marie and her daughter, Irene, represent half of *them*.

Before diving deeply into the subject of women and creativity, it would be helpful to first consider the lives of two brilliant women physicists with equally high creative potential: Marie Curie and Mileva Marić.

CREATIVE POTENTIAL ENERGY:
LIFE STORIES OF TWO FEMALE PHYSICISTS

Marie Curie

Marie Curie (née Maria Salomea Skłodowska) was born in the Kingdom of Poland on November 7, 1867. She was the fifth and youngest child of her father, Władysław, and her mother, Bronisława. Władysław and Bronisława had different personalities and religions (he was an atheist, and she was a devout Catholic). Yet both were teachers and strongly believed in developing their children's potential. Education was valued and excellence was expected in the home, nurturing Marie's diligent attitude. After the Russians prohibited laboratory instruction in Polish schools, Władysław brought home the equipment that wasn't being used anymore, and he introduced his children to playful science and scientific experiments, nurturing Marie's curious attitude. However, Władysław was fired from teaching math and physics for supporting the Polish national resistance movement against Russia. This put the family in a difficult financial situation. To make ends meet, the family rented out rooms in their home to students. The revolving door of students caused her mother and one of her oldest sisters to contract tuberculosis when Marie was little.[8]

Marie, a toddler, didn't understand the disease and why she wasn't allowed to hug or even touch her mom—who played the piano and sang beautifully to her children. Sadly, when Marie was eight, the oldest sister died, and then two years later her mom also died, which caused Marie to go into a deep depression. The deaths, despite Marie's intensive prayers, also caused her to abandon Catholicism and become agnostic and defiant toward God. Fortunately, this life-changing experience motivated Marie and another older sister to find a cure for the disease that took their two loved ones. These experiences nurtured Marie's resilient and big-picture-thinking attitudes. In this devastation, Władysław took on the role of both mother and father. He taught his children about nature, math, and physics, and he answered all of their questions with great care. He'd read aloud his original poetry and literary classics translated into Polish such as *David Copperfield* and *A Tale of Two Cities*.[9] This nurtured Marie's love of reading and learning and her curious attitude. Despite Russia's ban on teaching the Polish language, history, literature, customs, and even speaking Polish, Władysław instilled in his children a hope for Polish nationalism by teaching them Polish history and literature. Marie grew up patriotic and hated the Russians, which nurtured her defiant attitude, but her Russian teachers didn't appreciate it. When Marie was fifteen, Władysław was concerned about her depression. so he had her stay with her two uncles' families in the country for a year. She absolutely enjoyed outdoor activities and recuperated while developing her love of nature and (seeming) obsession with reading. This nurtured her resilient and self-reflective attitudes.[10]

Marie neither had money for dresses nor liked going to parties and dances like other girls. She hid her insecurity as a poor outsider with her intellectual superiority. Women weren't allowed to attend Polish universities, so Marie and her sister Bronisława attended the illegal, secret Flying University at night. Then they agreed that Marie would first support Bronisława's education in Paris and then Bronisława would support Marie's. Marie got a job as a governess (private live-in tutor) in the provinces where room and board were free and sent half of her salary to Bronisława for her education. At nineteen Marie was a governess for the Żorawskis family and passionately fell in love with their son, Kazimierz. But his family disapproved of her because her family was poor. She was heartbroken, so she vowed to never love any man ever again, and she moved to France and enrolled at the Sorbonne—the University of Paris—where she studied physics, chemistry, and math. She tutored in the evenings while living in an attic where it was suf-focatingly hot in summer and freezing cold in winter. She eventually over-came her linguistic and cultural barriers and adapted to the French culture and learned the language, yet she maintained her Polish identity for the rest of her life, which nurtured her bicultural attitude.[11]

At age twenty-six, she earned a degree in physics and began work at an industrial laboratory. While searching for a place to conduct her lab-oratory experiments, Marie was introduced to Pierre Curie, whom she would eventually marry. Pierre came from a long line of medical doctors, including his father, uncle, and grandfather, who expected excellence in the family. Pierre was thirty-four when he met twenty-six-year-old Marie. He had already made contributions to science, including his expertise on measuring minute amounts of electricity using his electrometer (which was invented with his brother). This enabled her search for elements and minerals that produced rays. Without cross-pollinating with him, her inno-vation would have been impossible.[12]

Marie encouraged Pierre to finish his doctoral dissertation at the Sor-bonne. At that time, Marie moved back to Poland to get a job at the uni-versity where her first love, Kazimierz, was a math professor. But she was denied because of her gender, and she returned to Paris. After Pierre com-pleted his doctoral degree, he finally convinced Marie to marry him, and a year later they wed.[13]

The Curies rarely left their laboratory, but both did enjoy nature, gar-dening, and bicycle rides through the countryside. At twenty-nine, Marie gave birth to their first daughter, Irene, whom her father-in-law—Dr. Curie—delivered and helped care for. Although the Curies needed addi-tional income for their growing family, Pierre encouraged Marie to pursue a doctorate instead of getting a job. Marie saw her husband as a cross-pollinator rather than a lover. With help with the baby and the household from Pierre and Dr. Curie, Marie worked toward her doctorate, which was extremely rare for a woman at the time.[14]

Pierre arranged a space for Marie's experiments. He invented, sup-plied, and adjusted instruments and equipment for her work. He also provided her with his expertise on magnetism and materials including mountains of pitchblende rocks. For four years, she (seemingly) obses-sively isolated radium by extracting only 0.1 grams of it through grinding and boiling *one ton* of pitchblende. She made the impossible task possible by her resilience/persistence and cross-pollination with Pierre, and her love and admiration for him grew in the process. They loved their work even though the working environment was unbearable; they worked in a smelly, cold or hot, leaky, and dusty shack. In 1903 when Marie was thirty-six, the Curies finally won a Nobel Prize in Physics.[15]

The Curies cared deeply about Irene's education. They wanted to convey to her their curiosity for and desire to explore nature and science. Pierre took Irene for long walks, during which they talked and talked, and he answered her questions with great care. Sadly, Pierre never got the opportunity to truly know their second daughter, Eve. At age forty-six, he unexpectedly died from a skull fracture when he fell beneath the wheels of a horse-drawn carriage. His constant overexposure to the radioactive element radium had made his bones weak. Eve was just fourteen months old, and Marie was thirty-eight at the time of his death.[16]

Marie was devastated, but the elder Dr. Curie helped her and took care of the children by providing optimistic, playful climates and lively conversations. She eventually overcame Pierre's death and became a role model for her daughters. Marie accomplished small goals every day and kept journals of her daughters' growth and important events, in addition to those of her research. She taught her daughters Polish and made science fun for them just like Władysław had done for her. Marie never pushed her daughters to follow her career, but exposing them to great scientific mentors (including Albert Einstein) inspired Irene to become a scientist and eventually another Nobel laureate.[17]

Marie's innovation was enabled by her 4S attitudes that had been nurtured in her 4S climates.

Mileva Marić

Mileva Marić was born in Serbia on December 19, 1875 (eight years after Marie Curie was born). She was the oldest of three children and from a wealthy family. Her father's encouragement and support helped her become dedicated to math and science at an early age, which was rare for a girl then. Mileva excelled not only in math and science but also in handicrafts, painting, singing, playing the piano, and foreign languages.[18]

After great effort by her parents to secure special exemptions, Mileva became one of the first girls admitted to the all-male Royal Classical

High School in Zagreb in 1891. Later, at twenty-one, Mileva enrolled as a foreign-exchange student at Zurich Polytechnic, where she was the only woman in the Physics Department. She met and began a romantic relationship with one of her classmates, Albert Einstein, who was only seventeen.[19]

Mileva captivated Albert's imagination, and they spent long hours discussing exciting scientific ideas and physics theories. They wrote each other love letters full of excitement about the latest theories in physics. Both were nonconforming and defiant thinkers who shared a love of reading, math, physics, nature, and hiking. Both were musically talented, and he would play the violin while she sang or accompanied him on the piano.[20]

Mileva insisted that she had no intention to ever marry because she firmly believed that it wasn't possible for a woman both to be a housewife and to maintain a career. Albert was so consumed by his study that he took little interest in his clothing and appearance (like wearing slippers or no socks) and even eating. This activated Mileva's maternal instincts, which further attracted her to him. She eventually abandoned her own needs in favor of Albert's—bowing to the patriarchal cultural norm of the dutiful housewife.[21]

Overwhelmed by her growing love for Albert, Mileva decided to move far away from Albert and audit classes at the University of Heidelberg in Germany. It only lasted one semester, but when she returned to Zurich, she brought back Philipp Lenard's theories that shaped Albert's relativity theory. When she originally left for Heidelberg, Mileva was big-picture-thinking, self-efficacious, independent, and strong. But when she returned to the arms of her beloved Albert, she had become a self-doubting, defeated, dependent, and emotional woman in love. Albert's parents never supported their relationship. Pauline hated her because, first, she wasn't Jewish; second, she was too intelligent to be a housewife; third, she was four years older than Albert; and fourth, she walked with a limp (due to hip damage when she was born). But Hermann eventually accepted Mileva.[22]

Mileva's academic relationships with her professors were damaged because of her romantic relationship with Albert, who had intellectual conflicts with the professors. Also, being the only woman in the department made the situation worse. This influenced her failure on the oral section of the graduation exam.[23] Even worse, in 1901, an unmarried Mileva became pregnant with Albert's child and was ill during much of her pregnancy. Albert was unemployed and neglected her. He couldn't afford to marry Mileva and lacked the financial wherewithal to support a family. At twenty-seven, Mileva gave birth to Lieserl—little Lisa—who was soon given up for adoption. (Coincidentally, Lisa is also the name of Steve Jobs' daughter, whom he denied first.) Mileva failed her graduation exam for a second time. She also suffered from the social stigma of being an unwed mother. The loss of her daughter plagued Mileva for the rest of her life. All of these situations shattered her dream of becoming an innovator.[24]

Albert and Mileva eventually married in 1903. The wedding did little to lift Mileva's spirits. She tried to fill the void of her daughter by focusing her attention on Albert. They had a son, Hans, born in 1904. She had no help in caring for Hans, and Albert's lack of financial stability forced her to take in boarders. Mileva completely subsumed her dreams for Albert and dedicated herself to his success. She continued to assist Albert with his work—talking through his ideas (sound-boarding) and checking his mathematical calculations. Albert published four famous papers in his "miracle year" of 1905. This was only possible because for the previous ten years he had been cross-pollinating his ideas with Mileva and Michele Besso. Even though Mileva made major contributions to his work, Albert acknowledged only Besso's help as "the best sounding board"[25] in his publication. This is the exact opposite stance of Pierre, who refused to accept the Nobel Prize in 1903 unless Marie was also considered.[26]

The Einsteins' second son, Eduard, was born in 1910. He was a talented pianist but suffered from schizophrenia, which made him extremely unstable. Now that they had two sons, Albert demanded that Mileva focus entirely on housekeeping and raising their sons, and she agreed. Marcel Grossmann taught Albert math and helped him with the calculations for his general theory of relativity. Ironically, Mileva was considered to be just as accomplished in the mathematical field as Grossmann was.[27] Soon after, Albert began having affairs with women—including his cousin Elsa. Albert and Mileva separated in 1914 and divorced five years later; five months after that, he married Elsa. The divorce and her son's declining mental health took a toll on Mileva in her later life. In 1933, at age fifty-four, Albert immigrated to America under the threat of the Nazi German government. (Hans also immigrated to America with his wife five years later, and right after their arrival, their son died, which meant Hans as the last of the Einstein lineage.) Albert never visited Mileva or Eduard again. She took care of Eduard alone, and when he destroyed everything in their home, she had a mental breakdown, was hospitalized, and died alone at seventy-two.[28]

Mileva's creative potential was forced to wither by her anti-creative attitudes, which were nurtured in her anti-creative climates. But the 4S climates cultivated Marie's 4S attitudes, which enabled her creativity to fully blossom.

Seven Ways to Kill Women's Creativity in Patriarchal Cultural Climates

1. Patriarchal climates throughout the history of humankind have brainwashed women to be the inferior sex.[29] Many powerful *men* have promoted and perpetuated the idea of female inferiority.[30] Confucius, for example, claimed that God granted men superiority over women.[31] Aristotle believed that females were naturally deficient and weak compared to males.[32] These beliefs have made it difficult for women to break out of their traditional roles as wives and mothers.[33]

2. Patriarchal climates provide different resources and expectations for girls and boys.[34]

Male dominance in innovation is caused by the way children are raised.[35] Perhaps without meaning to, parents raise boys and girls differently. This is especially true when girls have a brother in their family—*unless* a father purposely raises his daughter the same as a son.[36] Female innovators often don't have a brother (especially an older brother).[37] First-born daughters are raised with fewer gender-bias than later-borns.[38] Female Nobel laureates, including Curie, fit into the unusual category of either being the first daughter or being raised by fathers who encouraged the CPI (curiosity, preference, or interest) of their daughters (like Carol Greider[39] in 2009 and Christiane Nüsslein-Volhard[40] in 1995) or taught them how to use tools or build things and participate in activities that were normally reserved for boys (like Linda Buck[41] in 2004).

3. Patriarchal climates push females to keep their focus inside the home and pressure them to be submissive and sensitive to others' needs. But they encourage males to be independent and focus on achieving goals in the wider world.[42] Females have fewer opportunities in higher education even when they academically outperform males.[43] Females are often in lower-paying and lower-status occupations than males.[44] Due to their patriarchal beliefs, successful males consider their academic/career achievements as their greatest achievements, whereas successful females consider their children as their greatest achievements.[45]

4. Patriarchal climates inhibit females' nonconforming attitude. However, innovators use nonconformity as a strength; for example, non-conforming to the patriarchal climates' gender norms enables them to access and learn from *both* males and females by incorporating the opposite gender's strengths; male innovators adopt their mothers' creative attitudes, such as softness and sensitivity; female innovators adopt and emulate their fathers' creative attitudes toward work and achievement such as indepen-dence, self-efficacy, and assertiveness.[46] Only nonconformists who resist many social norms and expectations—in addition to the gender norms—can accomplish innovation, because nonconformity enables intellectual autonomy, defiance, and thus outbox and newbox thinking.[47] However, resisting social norms is especially hard for females.[48] Therefore, females are successful only in areas that demand less social and gender-bias con-formity, such as literature.[49] Those areas also require fewer resources, for example, writing a great novel requires a small writing desk instead of a well-equipped scientific laboratory.[50]

5. Patriarchal climates force females to choose between pursuing a career or starting a family.[51] Male Nobel laureates are more likely to marry and have children than their female counterparts; female laureates and innovators often have fewer or no children; they also bear more respon-sibility for marriage and childcare than their male counterparts.[52] Mileva didn't have help with household tasks and childcare, and both Albert and her mother-in-law, Pauline, caused her stress.[53] But Marie received both physical and emotional support from Pierre and her father-in-law, Dr. Curie.[54] This, in part, resulted in Mileva's miserable life, while, in com-parison, Marie experienced a fulfilling life with two Nobel Prizes.

6. Patriarchal climates stifle cross-pollination for females. There are few female role models and mentors.[55] Most Nobel laureates have mentors who are often previous laureates.[56] Nobel laureates are hesitant to mentor females because they assume that females will lose their career ambition; but in our patriarchal climates, in a man's world, creative individuals, espe-cially females, excel when they meet a mentor.[57] In addition to mentors, females also don't have other cross-pollinators such as close colleagues and collaborators.[58] Even when they get an opportunity for cross-pollina-tion, they often don't receive acknowledgment.[59]

Both Curie and O'Keeffe had their husbands as cross-pollinators who facilitated their wives' creativity development and promoted their creation. Without this, there might have been no innovation for either of these women! Unfortunately, Mileva never had a cross-pollinator.

7. *Patriarchal climates ignore females' professional accomplishments.*[60] The media and the public often don't recognize female's innovation, even the greatest females'.[61] Four years after Pierre's death, Marie had a relationship with one of his former students, Paul Langevin, who had been separated from his wife. In 1911 when Marie was nominated for her second Nobel Prize at forty-four, French newspapers portrayed her as a "Jewish home wrecker"[62] (note that she was Polish, not Jewish) instead of recognizing and celebrating her innovation. This was due to the public's sexism and xenophobia (fear/hatred of foreigners and outsiders).[63] The media coverage led to public outrage, influencing the Nobel committee to regret its decision.[64] Marie was pressured not to come for the Nobel Prize award ceremony. But she went anyways and stood by the integrity of her work and captivated the audience with her genuine award-acceptance speech.[65] She was self-efficacious, resilient, and persistent! Her life and work inspired generations of innovators, especially when they were growing up, including Nobel laureates such as Rosalyn Yalow[66] (1977) and Elizabeth Blackburn (2009)[67] in physiology/medicine and Ada Yonath (2009) in chemistry.[68]

Only a small fraction of females has accomplished innovation in a man's world (in patriarchal climates). Patriarchal climates nurture anticreative attitudes, which disable outbox and newbox thinking. If men and women are represented equally when proposing opportunities or solutions, innovation doubles!

Chapter 8

ARE JEWS REALLY MORE CREATIVE THAN ASIANS ARE?

JEWS WIN 625 TIMES MORE NOBEL PRIZES THAN CONFUCIANS DO

I discuss Jewish parenting/teaching and Confucian parenting/teaching in this chapter. Note that although I cite statistical differences in creative achievements of people from the two cultures, I do so only to compare approaches to cultural parenting/teaching. I'm not making a judgment about the creative potential of individuals from either culture.

The Nobel Prize symbolizes the highest degree of creative achievement.[1] Jews constitute only 0.2 percent of the world population as of 2014,[2] yet 194 Nobel Prize winners have at least one parent who identifies as Jewish. Between 1901 and 2014, Jewish Nobel laureates account for 22.6 percent of the 860 total individual worldwide recipients.[3] To break it down further, Jews have 8.7 percent of the Nobel Prizes in peace, 12.6 percent in literature, 21.3 percent in chemistry, 25.6 percent in physics, 26.6 percent in physiology/medicine, and 38.7 percent in economic sciences. Within Nobel Prize awards, their contribution to the scientific fields is even higher: Jews won 26.3 percent of the scientific fields (chemistry, physics, physiology/medicine, and economic sciences) worldwide.

When I refer to Asian culture in this book, I focus on the Eastern part of the continent—the countries of cultural East Asia, which includes China, South and North Korea, Japan, Taiwan, Hong Kong, Macau, and Vietnam. Because of their large number of Chinese immigrants, I also include Singapore, parts of Malaysia, and Mongolia. Although each of these countries has its own unique history, their people share a common culture that springs from the teachings of Confucianism, Taoism, and Buddhism. Of these three areas of thought, Confucianism is the most powerful unifying influence within Asian culture.[4] I address people from this Confucian culture as "Confucians" in this book.

As of 2015, Confucians constitute 23.4 percent (almost one fourth) of the world population.[5] But between 1901 and 2014 only 37 Confucians won a Nobel Prize, accounting for only 4.3 percent of the total recipients.[6] Considering the sizes of the populations, the ratio of winning a Nobel Prize for Jews, per person, is about 115.092, whereas that of Confucians per person is about 0.184; a Jew is about 625 times more likely to win a Nobel Prize than a Confucian is—a shocking number!

Many claim that Jews' winning Nobel Prizes and other innovations are due to their high intelligence.[7] This isn't true, because Confucians' IQs are as high as Jews'.[8] High national IQs correlate to high *test scores* internationally, but not to high numbers of Nobel Prize winners (based on IQ data from 108 countries).[9] Jews win Nobel Prizes for reasons other than high IQs. Innovators didn't necessarily have high IQs either,[10] and some of them had low IQs.[11] Instead, innovators, including Jewish innovators, had their 4S attitudes and ION thinking skills that had been nurtured in their 4S climates.

WHAT'S JEWISH 4S PARENTING/TEACHING?

There are some similarities in developing creativity between Jewish and Confucian parenting/teaching. Both emphasize and support high education, and children have early exposures to family interests in learning.[12] Both make high expectations clear for children's achievements and nurture diligence in them. Both teach resourcefulness and how to earn, save, and manage resources. Both respect elders and their wisdom. Both go back thousands of years into history. However, after extensive research, I've also found significant differences in the ways creativity is developed between Jewish and Confucian parenting/teaching. Jewish 4S parenting/teaching is more successful for innovation than Confucian 4P parenting/teaching is.

As a researcher, I don't have any particular personal emotions or thoughts toward Jews or their parenting/teaching. Because many Nobel laureates have a Jewish background, I interviewed many Jews to get an understanding of their culture. I lived with a Jewish family for three years;

I researched influential Jewish texts; I visited synagogues and participated in Jewish ceremonies and holidays such as bar mitzvahs, Passover seders, and Hanukah. I was on a mission to discover the unique features of Jewish parenting/teaching and how it might affect Jewish innovation. When I started my research, I knew next to nothing about Jewish parenting/teaching. I've learned that some consider discussions about Jews to be taboo, and even Jews are reluctant to publicly discuss these kinds of issues.[13] However, because I came from another culture, I didn't know that it was taboo. That's why I studied and wrote about it. Likewise, innovation comes from a beginners' mind. Those who know too much can't or won't go beyond the box.[14]

1. Jewish Soil Parenting/Teaching: Diverse Resources and Experiences

1. Jews nurture children's open-minded attitude by exposure to
and adaptation to diversity and varied experiences:

Throughout history, Jews were often violently expelled from their homes/countries because of their beliefs.[15] This forced them—culturally—to be exposed to all kinds of people, experiences, areas, cultures, languages, and arts. The survivors, who chose resilience over surrender or death, often developed open-mindedness, which freed them from their own prejudices and opened their minds to other perspectives and ways of life.[16] (Having the open-minded attitude enables inbox thinking—expertise development and critical thinking—and newbox thinking.)

2. Jews nurture children's bicultural attitude by
developing bicultural identity:

Jewish identity is more cultural than it is either genetic or religious.[17] (Most American Jews consider Judaism to consist more of attitudes/behaviors than a religion.)[18] Much of Jewish innovation is from their bicultural identity: keeping their own culture while learning from a main culture.[19] Jewish identity has strengthened in response to horrific events of the twentieth century, including the Holocaust.[20] Their identity has also been strengthened by the establishment of the modern State of Israel.[21] Since the Holocaust, American Jewish philanthropies have extended the Jewish concept of family. Through their overseas philanthropic activities, they unite Jewish identity together across the cultural, racial, or political barriers that previously divided Jews.[22] These events have shaped the Jewish parenting/ teaching style and children's unique bicultural identity.[23]

Jews traditionally married Jews, which helped maintain Jewish identity.[24] But today's America is multicultural, and intermarriage is becoming normative, which has modified Jewish attitudes toward intermarriage. At least half American Jews agree with intermarriage,[25] and 44 percent of married American Jews are married to non-Jews.[26] However, Jews still maintain their cultural identity while learning from other cultures, ideas, languages, and religions. In Jewish homes, parents build children's Jewish identity by being role models and supporting Jewish practices inside and outside the home.[27] In Jewish communities, children build their Jewish identity through classes, school systems, and short-visit and long-stay programs in Israel.[28] Jews also publish guides for integrating non-Jews who marry Jews. They build support centers for non-Jews who want to nurture their children's Jewish identity. As a result, intermarried Jews who were previously alienated or who abandoned their Jewish identity are increasingly reintegrating into the Jewish community and developing a bicultural identity.[29] (Having the bicultural attitude enables inbox and newbox thinking.)

3. Jews nurture children's resourceful attitude early:

Jews provide children with training and education and teach how to find and utilize resources. Their children learn to enjoy and utilize books, art, music, libraries, museums, and other resources (in the soil climate). Historically, Jewish intellectual culture was reinforced by being allowed only to pursue intellectually demanding vocations like international trade, banking, and finance, which weren't pursued by the mainstream culture in the countries where they lived.[30] One long-term effect (after many generations) is that these vocations have provided Jewish children with family resources.[31] Moreover, Jews often get married later than non-Jews, so they're more financially and emotionally established when they marry and have children.[32] (Having the resourceful attitude enables inbox and newbox thinking.)

4. Jews nurture children's cross-pollination early:

When children gather together to learn and discuss the Torah and the Talmud, they learn a sense of belonging not only to their local community but also to the broader Jewish community. They debate controversial topics, give one another feedback, and cross-pollinate ideas.[33] During the Jewish coming-of-age ceremony, the bar mitzvah boy or bat mitzvah girl leads the service. The performance isn't competitive—it's collaborative.[34] The child receives a lot of support and encouragement before and after the event. This nurtures Jewish children's self-efficacy and cross-pollination. (Cross-pollination enables inbox and newbox thinking.)

5. Jews nurture children's mentored attitude early:

Jewish children are surrounded by small i or Big I innovators in their community, which makes mentors more accessible.[35] Jews introduce children to mentors who provide them with diverse expertise and perspectives. At the same time, they aren't afraid to hold theories that are different from those of their mentors. Their debates and arguments with mentors challenge conventional thought and spur their knowledge forward.[36] (Having the mentored attitude enables inbox and newbox thinking.)

Science Nobel laureates often work at prestigious universities that have many resources for research.[37] Access to these universities *and* these mentors is statistically more likely for Jews than for Asians. This is because these universities reduce Asian applicants' SAT scores by 140 points—to adjust for inflation of certain racial groups' test scores.[38] But Jewish students are an "invisible minority"[39] within white students whose scores aren't reduced.[40]

2. Jewish Sun Parenting/Teaching: Inspiration and Encouragement

1. Jews nurture children's big-picture-thinking attitude by pursuing
Tiḳḳun olam *("repairing the world"):*

Tiḳḳun olam exhorts Jews to leave the world a better place than they found it.[41] Jews create a sense of belonging to a more important and higher ideal, teaching children to be compassionate for people who are in need.[42] Jewish parenting demands children give to charity, and charity becomes a religion for non-religious Jews.[43] Jews establish generosity as a norm within their identity by giving 10 percent of their income to charity, for example.[44] Despite many religions' emphasis on caring for the poor, religious people aren't more charitable than nonreligious people.[45] But Jewish families give charitably more often (8 percent more) and larger amounts (20 percent more) than religious or non-religious families (Protestant, Catholic, Muslim, Buddhist, non-traditional religions, etc.).[46] This fact emerges from the data regardless of different levels of income/wealth between Jewish and non-Jewish families.[47]

Jews also devote more time and money to non-Jewish causes than to Jewish causes.[48] Jewish mega-philanthropies (which donate more than $10 million a year to charity) have supported primarily non-Jewish causes (like local charities, education, and the arts).[49] Although Jews make up only less than 2 percent of the American population, they make up 30 percent of the most generous charitable donors; and 25 percent of all mega-philanthropies are Jewish.[50] The facts of Jewish philanthropic giving reveal their big-picture-thinking and compassionate attitudes, which Jews instill early in their children. (Having the big-picture-thinking and compassionate attitudes enables outbox and newbox thinking.)

2. Jews nurture children's spontaneous attitude by
engaging and performing in the arts:

Jews' love of the arts contributed to the survival of their culture and has become an integral part of their parenting/teaching.[51] Jews traditionally revere music, and Jewish composers and instrumentalists have made significant contributions to Western classical and popular music.[52] For example, Jews account for one-fourth of the one hundred greatest conductors of the twentieth century.[53] They also account for 40 percent of the pianists, 50 percent of the cellists, and two-thirds of the violinists of the one hundred greatest players of the twentieth century.[54] Musical training and other nonverbal artistic skills (like painting or choreography) not only nurture children's spontaneity through self-expression but also develop a synthesis skill through pattern finding.[55] (Having the spontaneous attitude enables outbox and newbox thinking.)

3. Jews nurture children's playful attitude through humor:

Jews were traditionally separated from the majority culture, which helped them to see things from a distance (which is a major characteristic of humor).[56] Jewish playfulness is found even in the Torah and the Talmud.[57] Throughout history, humor has contributed to Jews' resilience and survival, which nurtured children's playful attitude.[58] Although traditional Jewish humor isn't entirely joyful about the present, it still has enough inner optimism to be playful.[59] (Having the playful attitude enables outbox and newbox thinking.)

4. Jews nurture children's curious attitude by
  developing children's love of reading:

Jews provide children with a model for inquiry and questioning.[60] Interpreting the many meanings of the Torah and the Talmud teaches Jewish children to be willing to explore unanswered questions and defer judgment.[61] Doubting, constant questioning, and loving arguments are valued in Jewish parenting/ teaching, which nurtures children's curiosity.[62] Jews further develop children's curiosity by sharing their own joy of reading and by reading out loud to children, which nurtures children's love of reading early. Traditionally, Jews were known as the "People of the Book" because they immersed themselves in reading and learning.[63] Their purpose of learning is to satisfy their curiosity for knowledge, connect with their history, bond with their community, and pass on the curiosity.[64] Their literacy has enabled Jewish communities and people around the world to communicate even when they're separated by geography, political ideology, or local language. (Having the curious attitude enables outbox and newbox thinking.)

3. Jewish Storm Parenting/Teaching: High Expectations and Challenges

1. Jews nurture children's resilient and persistent attitudes:

Most Jews were subjected to anti-Semitism into the 1940s, and although discrimination declined after World War II, it still continues around the world and even in America today.[65] Some American Jews experience marginalization, alienation, bias, or discrimination.[66] Jewish identity has been shaped by tragedy, survival, and triumph. Despite invasions, the Inquisition, Soviet pogroms, persecutions, the Holocaust, and other genocidal threats to Jews, they have survived and have become resilient and persistent.[67] More important, instead of focusing on fear of repetition or the memory of tragedy, they've transformed their collective memory into social-justice movements.[68] These social-justice movements have become important opportunities for nonreligious Jews to contribute to the resilience and survival of Jewish values and culture, especially since the Holocaust.[69] (Having the resilient and persistent attitudes enables inbox and newbox thinking.)

2. Jews nurture children's risk-taking and uncertainty-accepting attitudes:

Jews traditionally maintained a strong storytelling culture.[70] (Storytelling is a newbox thinking skill and encourages verbal fluency and imagination.[71]) Storytelling based on morals, irony, and humor is a major source of Jewish families' entertainment. The weak overpowering the strong—which recurs throughout Jewish scripture and history—is a main theme in Jewish storytelling, which is instilled in Jewish identity.[72] The Christian Old Testament story of King David, who, as a little shepherd boy, killed the Philistine giant Goliath with his faith, a sling, and a stone is an example of the theme.[73] Jews identify themselves as a seemingly weak minority (like David) but eventually survive against oppression (like that of the Philistines) and captivity throughout history. It's in the Holocaust (exemplified by Auschwitz and Anne Frank), where Jews were slated for total extermination but ultimately survived.[74] The stories from Auschwitz and from Anne Frank's diary affected Jewish identity: she symbolizes the struggle of the weak against the strong and longing for justice and, in contrast, Auschwitz symbolizes injustice, dehumanization, and death.[75] From these and other excruciating tragedies, Jews instill in their children's identity strength for overcoming obstacles and contributing to social justice in the world.[76] This helps them take risks and accept uncertainty. (Having the risk-taking and uncertainty-accepting attitudes enables inbox and newbox thinking.)

3. Jews nurture children's self-efficacious attitude:

Jews emphasize efforts more than results, and doing one's best rather than being *the* best.[77] Children learn that each mistake is a gift for getting better.[78] Their communities' encouragement and emphasis on diligence lead to children's achievement and self-efficacious attitude.[79] Children learn that with persistence, they're capable of high achievement and taking on responsibility—including developing their own skills and making contributions to the world.[80](Having the self-efficacious attitude enables inbox and newbox thinking.)

4. Jewish Space Parenting/Teaching: Freedom to Be Alone and Unique

1. Jews nurture children's autonomous attitude:

Jews practice the guiding parenting/teaching style rather than the controlling, permissive, or neglectful style, and they focus on nurturing children's autonomy.[81] They set clear rules and expectations to young children while being responsive to their needs.[82] They negotiate with children rather than rely on force.[83] They discourage physical punishment and protect children's rights and freedom of choice.[84]

Jews encourage children's autonomy and pursuit of their own aspirations and dreams more than non-Jews do.[85] They encourage children to use their own judgment and responsibility to pursue their own curiosity, preference, or interest (CPI).[86] They reinforce children's curiosity and interest in how and why things happen—rather than cleanliness, order, social rules, or good manners—more than non-Jews do.[87]

Jewish teachers traditionally nurtured students' autonomous attitude in a nonhierarchical relationship in which they questioned, argued, and debated with them. This kind of teaching environment partly comes from Jewish tradition in which teaching the Torah was an unpaid position; teachers would take whatever jobs they could get to earn a living.[88] The title *Rav* (translating to "rabbi" or "teacher") also refers to an artisan or a tradesman.[89] (Having the autonomous attitude enables outbox and newbox thinking.)

2. Jews nurture children's gender-bias-free attitude:

Jewish boys consider gender less dichotomously than do non-Jewish boys, and they are freer from homophobic conventions and gender-stereotypes than non-Jewish boys are (for instance, Jewish boys are freer to express their emotions).[90] Their mothers don't emphasize masculine or feminine attitudes, which are common to other cultures.[91] Boys' gender-bias-free attitude is reinforced by the fact that Jewish lineage is passed on through mothers rather than through fathers.[92] Also, both parents transmit strong

Jewish identity to their children, but mothers are more responsible for keeping Jewish identity than fathers are.[93]

Additionally, Jewish girls benefit from traditions that encourage women's education. A long time ago, when educating girls wasn't mandatory in many cultures, schools for girls were common in Jewish culture.[94] Jewish girls are also more involved in keeping Jewish identity through community events than Jewish boys are.[95] Educating and empowering women have resulted in higher percentages of Nobel laureates among Jewish women than among Jewish men. Jewish women account for 35 percent of world women Nobel laureates and 50 percent of US women laureates in the scientific fields.[96] (Having the gender-bias-free attitude enables outbox and newbox thinking.)

3. Jews nurture children's nonconforming and defiant attitudes:

Some Jews don't publicly identify as Jewish, and they feel alienated from mainstream culture and internalize anti-Semitism they experience.[97] They avoid disclosing their Jewish identity for fear of stereotyping or prejudice.[98] The stronger their Jewish identity is, the more discrimination they perceive.[99] Fortunately, being on the margins of society nurtures the nonconforming attitude and helps them bond with other Jews who feel the same way.[100] For example, instead of obsessing about football or video games, Jewish boys often hold different values and discuss their lives and the world with other Jewish friends.[101] Their sense of purpose and their unique role in the world helps them take their personal interests more seriously than their non-Jewish peers do.[102] They identify themselves as a nonconforming outsider who has a different mind-set from insiders.[103]

In addition to historical accounts, some American Jewish children directly experience anti-Semitic attitudes.[104] (This might range from societal bias from adults or, to a lesser degree, childish teasing.) Through this shared experience, Jews develop a sense of representing the Jewish minority to the non-Jewish majority and rise to the challenge of confronting anti-Semitic attitudes and behaviors.[105] They defy the norms, stereotypes, and authorities that they perceive as unjust.[106] They come to self-identify as a defiant outsider, which drives them to support underdogs and the victimized.[107]

Jews nurture children's CPI and uniqueness while nurturing the nonconforming and defiant attitudes.[108] They support children's defiance to pursue their CPI, including questioning and rejecting the norms and even aspects of Jewish heritage.[109] Their children's defiant attitude helps them understand complicated relationships and generate revolutionary ideas.[110] They learn from many defiant Jewish role models, including Albert Einstein, Sigmund Freud, Karl Marx, Baruch Spinoza, and many others.

Jewish 4S Parenting/Teaching, So What?

Statistically, Jewish 4S parenting/teaching nurtures children's 4S attitudes, which enable ION thinking skills. Understanding the strengths of Jewish parenting/teaching is useful to non-Jewish families and educators who want to implement the CATs model. Compared to Jewish 4S parenting/teaching, I discuss Confucian 4P (Principles) parenting/teaching in the next section. I start with my personal experiences with Confucianism.

CONFUCIAN IMPACT ON ASIAN PARENTING AND EDUCATION

I grew up in a culture that was deeply rooted in the principles of Confucianism. One characteristic of this culture is the overbearing control that the husband's parents exert over the daughter-in-law. I entered into a marriage with a successful dentist, Dr. Lee, whose family was originally from Andong (the most aristocratic city of Korea). Despite the fact that he told my parents not to worry about a wedding dowry, his parents expected a fortune from my family. In a traditional Korean wedding, if the groom was highly successful (like a doctor or a lawyer), it was custom for the bride's family to give the groom's family three keys—one for a house, one for a new car, and one for a business office. However, my family was too poor to give anything to his family. My parents and I hoped that my education and successful career (as a high-school English teacher—a highly respected position in Korea) were enough *to prove my worth*. But my mother-in-law didn't seem to care about me, my degree, or my career. She emotionally tormented my mother and me by constantly reminding us of what other daughters-in-law brought to their husbands' families. Eventually, my mother became depressed because she wished she could send everything and anything to my husband's family to please them, but she had nothing to give. Ever since then, I've carried enormous guilt about my mother's depression. Even now, as she rests in her grave.

In 1991, I gave birth to a little girl. Because the child wasn't a boy, my mother-in-law expressed to me and others that I was deficient—because she had a boy on her first try. She didn't even consider my daughter to be her grandchild. Two years later, when I became pregnant with another girl, she demanded that I have an abortion. I begged and pleaded with my husband to persuade his mother that I would definitely have a son next time. But he was no help and told me to obey her. After being coerced to get an abortion, I wanted to never look at him again. I understood why he sided with his mother, but I hated him for it.

Soon after that, I started graduate school and began teaching at a middle school in Seoul (far away from home in Daegu) to escape from my married life. I lived there over two years with only my daughter, and I chose not to be with Dr. Lee, who still wanted to have a son to please his parents. My father knew the immense amount of pressure I was under to have a son, so he searched for and sent me all kinds of Chinese medicines that were supposed to help me have a son. Meanwhile, in her sleep, my daughter started crying out for her dad, "Appa," with tears on her face. This made me feel so guilty that I finally relented to try to have a son and go back to my married life. Because my menstrual cycle was regular, I arranged on one specific Sunday to take a bus to meet Dr. Lee at a hotel in Daejeon (a city between Seoul and Daegu). Even though he was my husband, I wouldn't even allow him to open the curtain to let any light in the hotel room, because I despised my hopeless fate. As soon as the intercourse was over, in tears, I took a bus back to Seoul.

Immediately after that day, I got pregnant, and I delivered a son in 1995, and my life drastically changed. My mother-in-law bowed deeply to me in the delivery room. I was finally treated with respect—like a legitimate daughter-in-law—and not a servant anymore. I was given presents, encouraged to shop, travel, and even to continue my PhD program.

I didn't understand it at the time, but all of my actions and the actions of those around me took place beneath a smothering blanket of Confucianism. Everyone was supposed to dress and act the same: predictable and polite, except to those beneath in the pecking order. My parents-in-law didn't allow me to discipline my son because he was their *only* grandchild (too precious to discipline). Outwardly my life was improving, but inwardly the hopelessness of my fate was worsening. I felt I would never be able to be myself or be free from the control of my parents-in-law and the traditions. I didn't want to be somebody's or some culture's human bonsai.

One day I felt so hopeless that I took a handful of sleeping pills. Unfortunately, and fortunately, it didn't kill me. After two weeks in a coma, waking up in the hospital, I had a dream about the American soldiers who threw caramel candies and gave us scholarships and Ping-Pong tables. I started thinking that in America I might be able to live and raise my son the way *I* wanted to. My friends had told me that America is dangerous, but what could be more dangerous than dying?

I knew some women who had a similar married life as I did, but they accepted the control of the culture without question. I wanted to discover what made me different and what made me reject the luxuries, protected lifestyle, and successful husband that seemed to be other women's dream. But I faced significant challenges for turning my dream into reality. Even though I knew my conversational English was limited, I felt certain that my grammar and vocabulary would suffice for my escape. I felt I had nothing to lose and everything to gain by leaving the only world I had ever known. Dr. Lee agreed to help me move to America only if I'd promise to stay alive. With his help, I convinced his parents that their precious grandson must learn to speak English to guarantee his success in life. Eventually, I got my wish and escaped to America.

What Is Confucianism?

Confucianism is the principles and values based on Confucius's philosophy and ideas, which continue to serve as the ethical and moral foundations for most Asians' everyday life even today—more than two thousand years after his death.[111] Confucius is the Westernized name given to Kong Fuzi by Jesuit missionaries.[112] Kong Fuzi was a diligent student. He was tall but unattractive, which supposedly made him study harder because he lacked a social life.[113] He started his socio-political teaching in his early twenties. At age fifty-four, he left home and traveled for thirteen years with his disciples, sharing his philosophy and ideas.[114] His followers referred to him as Master Kong. After his travels, Master Kong devoted the rest of his life to instructing his disciples and editing his works until his death at seventy-two. *The Analects of Confucius* are the main books of Confucianism.[115]

In China during Mao Zedong's Cultural Revolution (1966–1976), Confucianism was criticized as a roadblock to modernizing China.[116] Its influence within school systems decreased as the government tried to modernize education through math, science, and Western methods of learning.[117] However, in Korea, a succession of presidents throughout its modern history has reinforced Confucianism—due to the political power of the aristocrats (called *yangban*) who supported Confucianism.[118] Along with business conglomerates, presidents of Korea have used Confucian principles (like "Loyalty to the Country and Filial Piety to the Parents") as propaganda to manipulate their people and have reinforced the principles through the educational curricula.[119] Because of the institutionalization of Confucianism, Korea has become the most Confucian country in the world.[120]

What Is Confucian 4P Parenting/Teaching?

The four Confucian parenting/teaching principles (4P) include, first, hierarchical relationships; second, academic diligence and achievement—instead of inborn ability; third, filial piety and loyalty; and finally, harmony and conformity.[121]

The first Confucian parenting/teaching principle: Hierarchical relationships

1. Confucians stifle children's independent attitude.

The stability of society is based on five *unequal* relationships between ruler and servant; parent and child; husband and wife; older and younger siblings; and friends—where one is older/wiser than the other, so the other must obey.[122] Confucians practice the controlling parenting/teaching style in a hierarchical relationship,[123] and physical punishment is an acceptable disciplining method.[124] They instill obedience and dependence in children, but the independent attitude is necessary for critical thinking.

Confucians use one-way communication instead of open and two-way communication with children, which emphasizes listening instead of expressing opinions or discussing alternatives.[125] Children's verbal restrictions and hierarchical parent-child and teacher-student relationships force children to accept and memorize what's taught without critical thought, which is necessary for inbox and newbox thinking.[126]

On the traditional social pyramid, Confucian scholars/aristocrats are at the top; second, farmers; third, artisans/craftsmen; fourth, merchants; and, finally, slaves (including butchers, monks, shamans, and entertainers) are at the bottom (slaves are inherited).[127] Merchants fall toward the bottom because buying and selling things for a profit is considered deceptive (lying).[128] (But promotion skills are critical in the creative process [ACP] to achieve innovation.) Societal respect for scholars (and their rote learning) but disrespect for artisans/craftsman and merchants contributed to the late development of business, science, and modern technology in Confucian cultures.[129]

In hierarchal relationships, age is a mark of personal prestige and wisdom, and the older generation has the right to exercise discipline and control over the young.[130] Although respecting elders' wisdom can contribute to developing expertise, hierarchy discourages the autonomous, nonconforming, and defiant attitudes, which are necessary for outbox and newbox thinking. The detriment of hierarchy is exemplified by the Korean Air Flight 801 crash in 1997. An engineer wouldn't challenge the captain's authority (the captain was much older than the engineer), which led to the crash and death of 228 people.[131]

2. Confucians stifle children's gender-bias-free attitude.

Traditional Confucian hierarchy instills obedience in females even more than in males. A woman is expected to be obedient to her parents when she's a child, to her husband when she's married, and to her son in her old age.[132] Confucian bias against women and educating women forces women into submissive roles, limiting their potential and careers,[133] and the gender-bias-free attitude is necessary for outbox and newbox thinking.

The second Confucian parenting/teaching principle:
Academic diligence and achievement

1. Confucians instill in children the importance of education and respect for teachers.

Scholars (and teachers) are at the top of the social pyramid and are respected *much* more than they are in America.[134] In Taiwan, Confucius's birthday is celebrated as Teachers' Day (a national holiday).[135] In Korea, many wedding ceremonies are administered by former teachers/professors, and the government has a program to help adults find their former teachers. Confucian countries offer significant financial benefits for teachers, including better pay and incentives (like low or no-interest mortgages on their homes in Japan, and no income tax in Taiwan),[136] which promotes competition for teaching positions. This results in a highly qualified body of teachers.[137] When a problem arises, Confucian parents ask, "What's wrong with my child?" whereas American parents often rush to blame the teacher by saying, "What's wrong with the teacher?"[138] In Confucian educational systems, mutually respectful and helpful relationships between parents and teachers provide united support for children,[139] which nurtures children's mentored attitude, enabling inbox and newbox thinking.

2. *Confucians instill a hard work ethic and willpower in children instead of waiting for an inborn ability/gift/talent.*[140]

Whereas American parents believe inborn talents/gifts are greater predictors of children' success than diligence, Confucians believe otherwise.[141] This Confucian principle nurtures children's diligent and persistent attitudes, which enable inbox and newbox thinking.

The miracle of the Asian Five Dragons (immense economic growth in Japan, South Korea, Taiwan, Hong Kong, and Singapore) in the 1980s was due to hard work, thrift, persistence, and pursuing diplomas and higher degrees.[142] The Confucian principle that contributed to that growth is also vital to developing expertise, which is the foundation of ION thinking.

Westerners' (including Americans') belief in inborn ability can inhibit their hard-work ethic and self-criticism for further improvement, while inflating their self-esteem. Compared to Confucians, Westerners often exhibit less self-criticism, higher self-esteem,[143] and more self-enhancing biases.[144] This is especially detrimental as it prevents Westerners from accepting and applying negative feedback to their tasks. When Confucians receive negative feedback, they work hard to improve themselves by correcting their weaknesses according to the negative information. They consider that negative feedback helps themselves identify their shortcomings or deficits, which causes them to not only pay attention to negative feedback but also to take it very seriously.[145] In contrast, because Westerners often consider that their tasks are performed by their inborn ability, when they receive negative feedback, they feel offended or threatened (as they see the negative information is on themselves, not on their tasks), which causes them to not only see negative feedback as unfavorable, inaccurate, or a personal attack, but also to be less persistent in their tasks.[146] However, Confucians seek, rather than avoid, negative feedback.[147] While Confucians focus on improving their work, Westerners focus on recovering their self-esteem by thinking about positive information or past successes (or consoling themselves with the thought that they are at least better than average), all of which serve self-serving biases, inflated self-esteem, and thus inaccurate self-efficacy.[148] Westerners' belief in their inborn ability stifles the self-disciplined, diligent, self-efficacious, resilient, and persistent attitudes, which prevents them from striving toward fulfilling even greater creative potential. However, because Confucians live in exam hell, children focus mostly on the lowest-order inbox thinking skill (memorization) measured by their exams, which limits not only their expertise development and critical thinking (inbox thinking), but also outbox and newbox thinking.

3. Confucians force children to memorize others' written words in exam hell.

There is much pressure to pass exams—instead of exploring, questioning assumptions, or discussing their own ideas.[149] To prepare for the college entrance exam, Confucian students endlessly memorize textbook information. They're pushed into tutoring sessions and exam-preparation courses, and their parents invest in private tutoring or cram schools (private test-prep institutions), even when this can cost half of some households' income each year.[150]

The origin of an exam hell dates back to China's civil service examination system in the 600s.[151] It was when millions of men (and no women) from the middle class were allowed to rise to the upper class by passing the exams. Passing the exams brought them—and their entire extended family and ancestry—many advantages, such as financial rewards, prestige, and power.[152] The exam system stabilized the social hierarchy and status quo.[153] To pass the three-year cycle exams, candidates sought and purchased previously successful exam essays (mostly based on Confucian classics), which they memorized by rote.[154] Due to the extremely high rewards from passing the exams, teenagers started taking the exams and kept trying every three years until they died; some of them did nothing but preparing for the exams in their lives, while experiencing extreme test anxiety,[155] which led to suicide for some.[156] Even after the exam system ended officially in 1905, exam-induced suicides in the exam hell are still found in today's Confucian countries.[157]

4. Confucians enforce a work-play dichotomy.

Confucians teach that play is unproductive and worthless, and their parenting/teaching is a practice-intensive, homework-heavy, and product-driven enterprise, which values only academic work while devaluing play or fun.[158] Pursuing awards and high marks contribute to ION thinking *only if* they encourage children's CPI. But Confucians don't allow children's CPI in nonacademics (arts, sports, etc.),[159] because these don't help with college applications.[160] Focusing only on academic achievement allows no time for play, deep thoughts, or fantasy, which inhibits children's spontaneous, self-reflective, and daydreaming attitudes.[161] But these attitudes are necessary for outbox and newbox thinking.

Confucians instill a goal of getting into the best college. Once their children/students are admitted into a college, Confucians consider their parenting/teaching mission accomplished.[162] The success or failure of their parenting/teaching is judged by their children's/students' college ranking. However, parental involvement and support is essential to college students' academic success, emotional/mental health, and creativity—often more than it was in middle or high school.[163]

The third Confucian parenting/teaching principle:
Filial piety and loyalty

1. Confucians instill filial piety—
   parents' unquestioned authority—in children.

Filial piety is the most essential value in Confucians' minds.[164] It's the students' main writing topic throughout their education (whereas American students are given various topics for creative writing). Filial piety entitles parents to strongly influence their children's decisions (about things like a profession and a spouse).[165] Confucians often think of filial piety in terms of debt and obligation:[166] Parents do their best to educate their children while children are expected to obey their parents and repay them by being academically and occupationally successful and then supporting their aging parents financially.[167] Parents maintain high involvement for their children's education and show their affection by sacrificing or doing their best for their children's academic achievement.[168] In return, they set high expectations and demand obedience and self-discipline from their children. When their children fail academically, they feel anxiety, shame, and guilt. They see their role as a controller or a director who *teaches* and *trains* children to prepare for the future while Western parents see their role as a facilitator.[169]

Children who disagree with parents or question parental authority are considered a family disgrace, but children who conform to the filial-piety principle often learn in passive, uncritical, and uncreative ways, and they become authoritarian, dogmatic, and conformist,[170] which stifles outbox and newbox thinking. Additionally, to repay the debt they owe for their parents' sacrifice, children's goals become wealth and high family status, which further stifles the big-picture-thinking attitude, which is necessary for outbox thinking and newbox thinking.[171] (Also, older parents with strong filial-piety attitudes often expect more support from their children and report lower life satisfaction than those without strong filial piety.)[172]

2. Confucians require loyalty at work as an extension of filial piety.

Filial piety is a prototype behavior, which transfers to loyalty at work and social organizations where subordination, unquestioned authority, and paternalistic leadership are expected.[173] This contributed to the Asian Five Dragons' economic miracle through social paradigms such as lifelong commitment to one's job.[174] However, this loyalty can lead to unquestioned allegiance to authority and the rejection of ideas from the out-group, which stifles outbox and newbox thinking.

3. Confucians instill an in-group-only mentality in children.

The importance of similarity and blood relationships causes a sharp distinction between in-group and out-group members (*we* vs. *they* mentality).[175] Confucians see the world as an arena of endless competition against non-family or out-group members. They teach children to work hard to beat their peers, and they openly compare their children to others. They emphasize results more than efforts, and being the best instead of doing one's best. A child is often considered a failure if he or she doesn't rank first, which sorts humanity into only winners and losers,[176] which limits not only children's true confidence (self-efficacy), but also their cross-pollination. Confucian education focuses on competition so much that in my entire schooling in Korea (from elementary school to the doctoral program), I never had *a single* group project. But self-efficacy and cross-pollination are necessary for creativity development.

4. Confucians encourage children to copy others' work.[177]

There are high occurrences of plagiarism and low originality among Asian students in their countries and overseas.[178] Their plagiarism can be a way of respecting the author of respected texts without criticizing or improving,[179] or it can be a reflection of their collectivist view of text ownership in which information is shared and owned by the whole society.[180] However, since the beginning of the civil service exam system in the 600s, plagiarism for the exams has continuously occurred due to extreme competition.[181] Confucian children's plagiarism often arises from their fear of failure and extreme pressure to do well for their family.[182] The pressure of competition is so great that, without thinking about the moral impact, some Confucians support their children's cheating in class to get better results.[183] Confucian education values ethics and manners, but any behavior that sustains the model of filial piety is excusable.[184] Children who feel more filial obligation to excel cheat more willingly than those who feel less so.[185] But plagiarism is conducive to ION thinking only if the original work is improved or transformed in some way.

The last Confucian parenting/teaching principle: Harmony and conformity

Confucians teach children that they exist only in relation to others, especially to families and in-group members.[186] They overemphasize the value of harmonious relationships and teach children how to be liked by others. They teach children to avoid disagreement and conflict to save face, while encouraging indirect communication and formality.[187] Their formality discourages playfulness because playfulness and humor are considered flippant.[188] Children are overly concerned with parents' and others' views and lack autonomy in the decision-making process, and their self-expressions are squashed and pruned like bonsai trees.[189] Confucians strongly believe in conformity, in which children's individuality and uniqueness are discouraged or punished.[190] They value humility and conformity at the expense of self-efficacy and originality.[191] But supporting children's playful, emotional, autonomous, self-efficacious, and nonconforming attitudes is necessary for ION thinking.

Confucian 4P Parenting/Teaching, So What?

High levels of Confucian parenting/teaching are directly related to low levels of creativity.[192] Confucians are often less creative than Westerners,[193] but Confucian children can become creative if they're in the 4S climates.[194] Confucian education has begun to copy aspects of the previous American educational system that fostered creativity.[195] But Confucian parents and educators are mainly interested in tricks and strategies that *claim* to foster creativity.[196] They don't realize that the 4S climates must be cultivated and that the 4S attitudes must be nurtured first, before children develop and apply ION thinking skills.

Confucian Parenting/Teaching Today: Tiger-Mother Parenting/Teaching

In 2011, Amy Chua—a Chinese American who is a professor of law at Yale University—rattled many American parents with the publication of her book, *Battle Hymn of the Tiger Mother*. In this book, Chua blasted American parents for their permissiveness and low expectations for children. Drawing on her own parenting experience, she advocated unrelenting discipline and boasted of how she had raised her children, who seemed very successful. Chua refers to this parenting style as being the Chinese or "tiger-mother" style, but the same approach is used throughout all Confucian countries today. Tiger-mother parenting/teaching is today's version of Confucian parenting/teaching. The outcome from tiger-mother parenting/teaching is a large number of Asian and Asian American children excelling at many academic measures. Some non-Asian Americans see this as a threat to their children's opportunity and potential success.

Chua described how she applied her tiger-mother rules to keep her children focused on their studies. For example, in her home, earning less than an A or earning second place was unacceptable except in gym and drama. Her children were only allowed to participate in extracurricular activities in which they could win a medal, and they were, of course, expected to win first prize. Activities such as crafts, theater, play dates, sleepovers, school plays, dating, and even playing any instrument other than the piano or violin were considered to be *loser activities*, which were forbidden.[197]

Chua says that whereas Western parents make their children practice piano or violin for an hour a day, tiger mothers make their children practice *at least* three hours every day. Even when traveling internationally, she would find a place for her children to practice for three hours without food or bathroom breaks. When her second daughter was three years old, she resisted learning a piano piece, so Chua made her stand outside in freezing weather. When she was five, Chua slapped her when she practiced poorly and threatened to burn all her stuffed animals. When she was seven and gave up on a piano piece, Chua threatened that she would get rid of her dollhouse piece by piece and take away birthday parties for years.[198]

When I was tutoring in college, *every* mother was a tiger mother. There were minor differences in tiger mothers, and I enjoyed analyzing the relationship between a child's attitudes/thinking skills and the mother's parenting. While the fathers worked late into the night, the mothers were ferociously pushing their children to study more and focus all of their attention and energy toward the big college entrance examination that would determine their future. Tiger-mother parenting is mostly a maternal behavior. Fathers may participate but mainly support mothers in that role.

Some American parents think that tiger-mother parenting/teaching is the best because it pushes children to academic achievements. They believe tiger-mother parenting is especially better than *permissive* American parenting—which establishes few rules for children and exerts little control over their impulses and desires.[199] Some American parents fear that their grandchildren will wind up working for low wages, assembling future iPhones designed by the tiger mothers' children. In contrast, others think that tiger-mother parenting is child abuse and that tiger children are emotionally scarred time bombs waiting to explode.[200] Although many Americans are shocked by Chua's book, many others embrace its perceived core message.

Is tiger-mother parenting/teaching good for raising eagles?

In 2005, I published a study called "Learning from Each Other: Creativity in East Asian and American Education."[201] In this article, I reported that Confucian parenting/teaching is good for boosting rote learning and test-taking skills, but perishable knowledge gained this way isn't good for creativity.[202] The 4S climates and attitudes welcomed in America are what make ION thinking skills and healthy lives flourish.[203]

Tiger-mother parenting/teaching is like making plants into bonsais by forcefully pruning and wiring. Although clipping branches doesn't hurt the plants, the purpose is mainly for the enjoyment of the bonsai keepers, not for the self-actualization of the plants themselves. Tiger-mother parenting/teaching is also like the process of clipping birds' wings, which keeps the birds safe. It's a painless procedure for the bird and causes no long-term physical harm. The feathers will grow back after a few months. But it prevents them from flying.

Children who don't develop their creative potential are like chicks that never learn to fly. They know to hop in and out of the coop, but they never think to leave the coop or barnyard to try new foods or new things. They peck and scratch among what's given to them and even live well. They might even be able to get to the top of the pecking order in the barnyard with perfect test scores. They might be able to read and play music flawlessly, preening their long feathers and enjoying the admiration of the rest of the flock. However, the birds (children) can't do what they were born to do—*fly*.

There's no such thing as a standard "eagle" parenting/teaching style (described in the next paragraph) in America. However, it does display characteristics that are distinct from tiger-mother parenting/teaching in the East. Compared to tiger-mother parenting/teaching that roars ferociously at children who don't achieve as ordered, America's traditional ("eagle") parenting/teaching style provided children with opportunities for exploring various career avenues to express their creativity themselves. American parents and educators were comfortable with the fact that some of the answers couldn't be found on standardized tests. They cultivated the 4S climates, nurtured the 4S attitudes, and produced resourceful cross-pollinators, curious optimists, resilient hard workers, and defiant dreamers who applied ION thinking skills for innovation. The defiant spirit—not

standardized tests—is what motivated generations of Americans to inno-
vate in scientific research, discovery and inventions, business, leadership,
sports, technology, entrepreneurship, and the arts.

Eagle parents and educators don't clip children's wings. Instead, they
build nests in thriving ecosystems and nurture chicks that are struggling to
use their wings. They teach them the survival skills that are required to live
on their own and encourage them to take that first leap on their own. They
stimulate their imagination about the world outside the nest and inspire
them to find their own reasons to take the risk of flying. They teach them
how to use their sharp eyesight to cut through the fog of uncertain futures.
They inspire them to use their wings to soar by showing how eagles soar
high above the land (sometimes with other eagles), instead of flocking with
small birds. The chicks learn to fly by becoming resourceful cross-pollinators and resilient hard workers. They travel to new places and expand
their horizons by becoming curious optimists. They eventually soar to new
heights in new ways by becoming defiant dreamers.

Teaching young birds how and where to fly (which areas are safe),
and reasons why they should fly, is time-consuming. It's risky parenting/
teaching—compared to the standardized tiger-mothers' approach to
keeping chicks safe by clipping their wings. Teaching creativity is a riskier
investment with less-certain payoffs than focusing on test scores.[204] Academic achievers with clipped wings become successful in *established* companies and systems, but not in innovation. The fact that Chua's daughters
are academic achievers is wonderful. It's always good to learn from others
(including tiger mothers) through open-mindedness. However, a complete
adoption of tiger-mother parenting/teaching won't accomplish innovation.
It restricts the 4S climates while repressing children's 4S attitudes and ION
thinking skills. Only children in the 4S climates with the 4S attitudes and
ION thinking skills have the potential to become the greatest innovators.
American parents and educators must not sharpen their claws like tigers
or slip into orange-and-black-striped costumes to educate children. They
must not abandon their own traditional American ways of raising eagles.
Eagles soar, and so do creative minds. The world has been improved by
breakthroughs made by eagles, not by clipped-wing chicks.

PART 4

WHAT ARE
CREATIVE-THINKING SKILLS?

Chapter 9

ION THINKING SKILLS (INBOX, OUTBOX, AND NEWBOX) WITHIN THE ACP (APPLE-TREE CREATIVE PROCESS)

O ne sunny afternoon, my children and I go out to our garden. With scissors, we cut sweet-potato vines, chives, mung beans, purple eggplants, and shiny red bell peppers larger than my fist. My daughter discovers some asparagus that I've forgotten about, and my son brings in some green apples, which we eat while we clean and chop the vegetables. While my son peels garlic in the kitchen, I go back outside to cut tentacles of thyme, lacy plumes of dill, and robust lengths of basil that fill the kitchen with a heady, green fragrance.

We don't know exactly what we're making yet, but we'll use everything we picked. We'll make some sort of soup, side dishes, and of course we'll have rice. We decide to make pickles, which we've never done before, so my son finds instructions on the Internet. It's a lot like making kimchi, but with vinegar instead of fish sauce.

While reading about the canning process to make pickles, my son is inspired. He goes back outside and collects more apples, pears, and figs. He begins to clean them and boils them in a pot to make jam—something I never would've thought to do. We're making something *unique and useful*, using a lot and a variety of different ingredients. More ingredients don't necessarily make a better dish, but more options do improve the quality of a creative process. (Generating more ideas leads to better ideas; the quantity of creations leads to higher quality; innovators just produce many creations, some of which become recognized as innovation!)[1]

CREATIVITY IGNORED: FAULTY SELECTION OF GIFTED AMERICANS

Most schools in America increasingly ignore creative thinking. Most college and graduate-school admission procedures rely only on tests like the SAT, ACT, GRE, GMAT, MCAT, and LSAT, supposedly to measure students' academic readiness. However, those tests measure lower-order thinking skills (memorization/comprehension).[2] At least forty-nine states use IQ or a standardized achievement test when identifying gifted students,[3] but these tests identify only academic achievers, not future innovators. E. Paul Torrance, who is called the "Father of Creativity"[4] concluded that identifying giftedness based only on IQ or achievement test scores eliminated approximately 70 percent of future innovators from consideration.[5] In my own research I found that the number was even higher—that 80 percent of the top 20 percent would have been neglected.[6] For example, in 1925, Lewis M. Terman started the oldest and one of the longest running longitudinal studies in education and psychology.[7] His study selected gifted children based solely on their IQ scores, and this method made him miss future innovators such as William Shockley and Luis Alvarez (Nobel laureates).[8] IQ is different from creativity. Many agree that an IQ of about 120 is necessary for innovation,[9] but I found that at any level, creativity and IQ are weakly related.[10] The smartest child doesn't necessarily become an innovator,[11] but creative children do. Most children are born creative, but over time anti-creative climates foster their anti-creative attitudes, which kills their ION thinking skills.[12] We must cultivate the 4S climates for *all* children, not just for academic achievers, to nurture their 4S attitudes that enable their ION thinking skills.

WHAT ARE ION THINKING SKILLS?

Previous chapters described the *4S climates* (step 1) and the *4S attitudes* (step 2) that enable ION thinking skills. This chapter explains ION thinking (step 3) in detail, which innovators apply to produce something unique and useful. ION thinking consists of inbox, outbox, and newbox thinking in a hierarchical order, as the pyramid of figure 9.1 indicates. Higher-order thinking skills are built on lower-order thinking skills that must be developed beforehand.[13]

Many assume creative thinking is a single magical act that comes out of thin air, but this assumption is wrong.[14] J. P. Guilford (a pioneer of creativity research, whose presidential inauguration speech at the American Psychological Association in 1950 initiated "serious" creativity research in America and the world)[15] proposed that creative thinking consists of two mental processes that can be learned and practiced: convergent and divergent thinking.[16] Torrance developed Guilford's theory in greater detail. I've expanded on both of their theories through ION thinking. Inbox thinking is narrow and deep (inside the box) to gain or evaluate knowledge/skills; outbox thinking is quick and broad (outside the box) to imagine diverse possibilities; and newbox thinking combines elements of inbox and outbox thinking to create a new thing or a new process (a new box). ION thinking is necessary for the creative process (ACP): developing expertise (inbox); then generating ideas (outbox), and after a break, evaluating ideas (inbox); then connecting and synthesizing previously unrelated ideas (newbox); and then refining and transforming (newbox), and finally promoting them as something unique and useful (newbox)—an innovation, which defies the traditional categorization.

What Is Inbox Thinking?

Inbox thinking includes traditional ways of accomplishing tasks or choosing the right answer (which females are often better at than males are).[17] Well-developed inbox thinking is narrow and deep and is also persistent and systematic to gain or evaluate knowledge/skills. It includes *lower-order* thinking skills such as memorization, comprehension, and application, which are necessary for developing expertise.[18] (Memorization is the lowest inbox thinking skill, but most tests, including standardized tests, mainly measure memorization.[19]) Expertise is mastering a specific subject by achieving and understanding special knowledge and skills through instruction and practice, and then applying them in new and real-world situations.[20] Inbox thinking works like a zoom lens that helps innovators zoom in on narrow knowledge/skills, deciding what specific knowledge/skills to acquire, looking closely at details, and planning courses of action for developing more expertise. It is mainly developed through innovators' soil and storm attitudes that nurture resourceful cross-pollinators and resilient hard workers. They use inbox thinking and practice inbox *realism* to develop expertise by following or copying existing rules and norms.

As the middle part of the pyramid of figure 9.1 indicates, inbox thinking also includes *higher-order* thinking skills, such as analysis and evaluation, which are necessary for critical thinking.[21] Gaining expertise must come before either outbox thinking or critical thinking in the ACP, whereas critical thinking usually comes *after* a variety of ideas have been generated during outbox thinking. Critical thinking zooms in to analyze and evaluate those ideas, and choose the best one(s) or make decision(s).

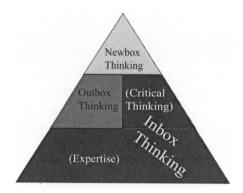

Figure 9.1. ION Thinking Skills (Inbox, Outbox, and Newbox)

What Is Outbox Thinking?

Outbox thinking is quick and broad for imagining diverse possibilities, and it is also spontaneous and chaotic for seeking nonconforming ideas (which males are often better at than females are).[22] The middle part of the pyramid of figure 9.1 indicates outbox thinking, which includes higher-order thinking skills such as fluent thinking, flexible thinking, and original thinking.[23] It benefits from a readily accessible reservoir of expertise. It works like a wide-angle lens that helps innovators take a broad field of view and imagine many, diverse, and unique approaches to a problem/opportunity. It may even redefine the problem itself. It is mainly developed through innovators' sun and space attitudes that nurture curious optimists and defiant dreamers. They use outbox thinking and defiant *optimism* to go beyond the box, break the rules/norms, and see/do beyond what others can.

What Is Newbox Thinking?

Newbox thinking combines elements of inbox and outbox thinking and transforms the combination into a new creation. The top part of the pyramid of figure 9.1 indicates newbox thinking, which includes the *highest-order* thinking skills such as synthesis,[24] transformation, and promotion. It uses both zoom-in and wide-angle lenses to connect and synthesize previously unrelated ideas; and then refine and transform, and finally promote them as a unique and useful creation.[25] Newbox *realistic-idealism* is developed through innovators' 4S attitudes, which are nurtured by their 4S climates.

Those with *only* inbox thinking become boring technicians while those with *only* outbox thinking become frustrated dreamers.[26] Inbox thinkers *borrow* information while outbox thinkers *imagine* ideas. Newbox thinkers *extract* and then synthesize the information (from inbox thinking) and the ideas (from outbox thinking), and then refine and transform them into a creation. Inbox thinking uses left-brain skills while outbox thinking uses right-brain skills.[27] Newbox thinking uses both left-brain and right-brain skills.[28] Innovators are newbox thinkers who are capable of both inbox and outbox thinking and switching between the two, depending on a particular stage of their creative thinking process (ACP). Brain CBF (cerebral blood flow), EEG (electroencephalography) tests, or fMRI (functional magnetic resonance imaging) indicate that innovators' brain halves are more interactive and cooperative than non-innovators'.[29] However, every individual *habitually* uses either more inbox or outbox thinking. Thus, cross-pollination between inbox and outbox thinkers increases a chance of innovation. All three ION thinking skills must take place in the creative process (ACP), making it a *whole-brain* process.[30]

WHAT IS ACP?

ACP (Apple-tree Creative Process)[31] is an eight-stage process analogous to the seasonal growth cycle of apple trees. Each stage represents activities that innovators must do, or interactions that they must have, to bring a unique idea to complete fruition. ACP begins with winter (expertise development and needs identification); then becomes spring (idea generation, subconscious processing, and idea evaluation); then becomes summer (synthesis and transformation); and finally becomes autumn (promotion). The order can be *changed* and some parts can be *repeated*, depending on the problem/opportunity.[32]

Winter ACP: Expertise Development (Stage 1) and Needs Identification (Stage 2)

During the winter stages of an ACP, innovators use inbox thinking to develop expertise in the long winter, and they use outbox thinking to identify needs in the late winter.

Stage 1 (Long Winter): Expertise Development   Stage 2 (Late Winter): Needs Identification

Figure 9.2. Winter ACP (Apple-Tree Creative Process)

Stage 1 (Long Winter): Expertise Development

Apple trees seem dead in the winter, as figure 9.2 shows, but they're actually dormant. They are growing and preparing for the spring. Their roots grow independently from the parts that are inactive during the winter. This allows them to expand their root systems in search of water and nutrients, which is critical for their health and growth later in the year. Gardeners keep roots healthy for future blooming by pruning and removing unwanted shoots and protecting the trees from squirrels and deer. When innovators are developing expertise, they are like apple trees—you can't actually *see* root growth or expertise growth, but both are happening. This becomes evident during blooming and fruiting in later stages.

What Is Expertise?

Expertise is the full and complete knowledge and skills of a particular subject. It requires sufficient comprehension and understanding to effectively apply the principles in real-world situations.[33] As the ten-year rule suggests, expertise isn't something anyone is born with, and it can't be developed overnight. It's developed over time by learning from your own experiences, mistakes, successes/failures, and from others' success/failures.[34]

Expertise provides the foundation of outbox and newbox thinking as the base of the pyramid,[35] as figure 9.1 shows. It enables the generation of multiple, viable alternatives and intuition by providing the foundational repertoire of raw materials for outbox thinking.[36] It enables critical thinking—evaluating of the results of outbox thinking. Then it facilitates synthesis of the results of the critical thinking by providing concepts and conceptual combinations during newbox thinking.[37] Finally, it facilitates the transformation stage by providing the knowledge for implementing ideas and predicting outcomes.[38]

Apple trees won't bloom if they are too immature to reproduce. Likewise, precocious children are not experts, so they can't achieve innovation yet.[39] Children's imagination is more intense and emotionally exciting than adults', but their imagination is built only on their limited knowledge and experience.[40] Additionally, they can't do big-picture thinking and abstract reasoning yet, thus they can't yet turn their creativity into innovation. Abstract reasoning develops in adolescence, which enables them to combine their true imagination with a potential creation to achieve innovation.[41] The more complex a field is, the more expertise is required for innovation within it.[42] For this reason, sports innovators reach the highest level of international achievement in their mid to late twenties; and in the arts and sciences, in their thirties and forties.[43] (Of course, this also depends on when they *started* developing expertise.[44])

How to Develop Expertise? The Long Winter

During the development of expertise, parents and teachers of innovators (PTIs) remove distractions. Exercising children's self-discipline and self-reflection creates the opportunity for their solitude and immersion, which are necessary for developing expertise.

PTIs don't wait for a sign of a gift/talent. They provide children with diverse resources and experiences, and inspire and encourage them to be curious or interested in something as early as before age three.[45] By that age, for example, children who have been provided with such resources/experiences have heard thirty million more words than children without such resources, which predicts their later learning (so no "baby talk"!).[46] PTIs expose children in *playful* ways to diverse subject and fields and other experiences.[47] After an initial sign of children's curiosity, preference, or interest (CPI), PTIs' purposeful planning and their analysis of and guiding of children's performance and practice leads to the children's self-efficacy in their CPI.[48] Mentors provide immediate feedback for children's gradual and steady improvements.[49] They help develop children's specific high goals to improve specific aspects of their performance by giving brutally honest positive and negative feedback that compares their actual performance to their goals while providing opportunities for practice and performance (for ten thousand hours).[50] This leads to innovators' expertise, which becomes their passion.[51]

Practicing and performing for extended periods of time leads to unique patterns of neurological development and physiological adaptations in children's minds.[52] This is the *real cause* of a gift/talent in children.[53] This rejects the common belief that inborn abilities are the source of passion and innovation. In fact, gifts/talents that appear early (like in prodigies) limit developing expertise and subsequent innovation.[54] Most parents wait for a sign of gift/talent in children *before* providing resources or inspiring/ encouraging and challenging them to develop expertise. But *reversing* this order leads to a better chance of innovation:[55] First, PTIs provide children with resources and experiences in the soil climate; second, they help them find their CPI in the sun climate; and third, they help them diligently build their self-efficacy (learn what they're good *and* bad at) and develop CPI expertise in the storm climate. Fourth, a gift/talent emerges in the children, which becomes their passion; and finally, they discover and develop their own unique ideas beyond their expertise in the space climate for their future creation, which can lead to an innovation.

The list below includes more specific ways to develop expertise.

(1) *Memorize knowledge and skills*: Innovators use lower-order inbox thinking skills, such as memorization, comprehension, and application, for developing expertise. Knowledge acquisition by memorization is the lowest-order thinking skill of the pyramid.[56] Develop concrete mind-sets (first learn something that can be seen, heard, touched, tasted, or smelled) before abstract mind-sets, and pay attention to relevant details. Use memory to absorb definitions, facts, and lists: for example, create outlines to organize learned information; *chunk* information (grouping information together) by creating meaningful/funny sentences, songs, or acronyms; and recognize and use a preferred learning style for auditory (learn by hearing), visual (learn by seeing), or body (learn by doing) learners. Recite or retrieve material or skills,[57] which individuals with normal intelligence are able to do.[58]

(2) *Build comprehension*: Comprehension is the second lowest-order thinking skill of the pyramid.[59] Fully and completely understand the information that comes from gaining knowledge. Then, convert it into a form that's personally meaningful, using words, illustrations, graphs, or other visual ways to diagram: for example, put information into your own words to explain what's happening in a story, summarize, or give your own example. Explain it in detail, not just reciting the information, and be able to add (or omit) (ir)relevant facts to it,[60] which anyone with normal intelligence is able to do also.[61]

(3) *Determine applications*: *Apply* the information (that is from building comprehension) to new and real-world situations and share it with others by creating models or prototypes. Apply abstract/theoretical concepts to solve concrete/practical situations, and create action plans.[62] Learn how it works (or doesn't work) in the new situations or environments, which also anyone with normal intelligence can do, but it takes a long time.[63]

(4) *Develop your CPI early, instead of just focusing on IQs/grades*: Early expertise development contributes twice as much to ION thinking skills than IQ does.[64] ION thinking skills don't require high IQs or grades, as long as you develop your CPI and subsequent expertise *early* in a subject/field.[65] In fact, those with super-high IQs/grades or photographic memories aren't always good

at outbox thinking.[66] Innovators who earned superior grades in school achieved only incremental or *evolutionary* innovation, but those who earned lower grades were good at outbox thinking and achieved radical or *revolutionary* innovation.[67]

(5) *Immerse yourself in a subject/field for a period of at least ten years,*[68] (preferably by age twenty):[69] Purposefully practice for ten thousand hours with clear, specific, high goals.[70] Practice and perform repetitively while taking opportunities for performance in public.[71] Ten years of intense immersion in their subject is necessary for even the most gifted/talented,[72] and others need much longer.[73] So children who are committed to their CPIs for only a few months or years will never approach what they're capable of achieving.[74]

(6) *Cultivate self-education rather than formal education*: Formal education is positively associated with innovation *only* up to two years of college. During this time, students take broad, diverse courses (including arts and humanities), which are conducive to outbox thinking. After two years of college, classes are specific to majors, which can lead to the development of blinders to new ideas.[75] The world's greatest innovators developed expertise in their CPI through *self*-education, not by attaining high *formal* education.[76] For example, Alexander Graham Bell,[77] Thomas Edison,[78] Abraham Lincoln,[79] and Benjamin Franklin[80] were elementary-school dropouts; Nelson Mandela and Steve Jobs were college dropouts; Einstein was a high-school dropout, but he was encouraged and inspired to go to college; further, without Grossmann's help, Einstein would have become a college dropout, yet he continuously educated himself. Even after high achievements, innovators' energy and drive to maintain improvement efforts through self-education does not decrease; in fact it often increases.[81]

(7) *Don't let too much knowledge limit fluent, flexible, original outbox thinking*:[82] A winter that's *too* long freezes apple trees, which prevents them from blooming. Oversaturation of knowledge leads to entrenchment or crystallization—when one becomes a prisoner of one's own knowledge. It prevents accepting different ideas or looking at things in a new, rebellious light.[83] Those who have encyclopedic knowledge can't make significant contributions to innovation. They can't or won't entertain alternatives because their

knowledge restrains them. Curious optimists who never lose the ability to ask basic, childlike questions, while seeking out others' perspectives and opinions, achieve revolutionary innovation.[84]

(8) *Develop the 4S attitudes*: First, become s resourceful cross-pollinator in the soil climate—using *diverse resources and experiences*—and learn diverse subjects.

Second, become a curious optimist in the sun climate—using *inspiration and encouragement*—and find a CPI in a specific subject by looking for a *playful* introduction to the subject.[85]

Third, become a resilient hard worker in the storm climate—pursuing *challenges* and meeting *high expectations* in the subject of desired expertise—and turn your CPI into a passion by your purposeful, persistent practice and resilience.

(However, expertise alone is not enough for achieving innovation; you must become a defiant dreamer in the space climate—using *freedom to be alone and unique*—and develop unique ideas—beyond your expertise—for a future creation. Combining the sun/space attitudes with the soil/storm attitudes makes the creation both unique and useful: *innovation*.)

Once innovators have developed sufficient expertise, they're able to start identifying needs, gaps, or problems, and potential approaches to solving them. This initiates the next stage of an ACP: Identifying needs.

Stage 2 (Late Winter): Needs Identification

After a long, cold winter, apple trees come out of dormancy. As figure 9.2 shows, leaves begin to emerge as soon as they *sense* the warm sun. After innovators are immersed in the expertise-development stage, their prior knowledge *alerts* them to details that others miss,[86] and their *sensitivity* to inconsistencies, problems, gaps, or missing information makes them curious.[87] Perceived gaps are the next step in needs identification because innovators develop further expertise to fill the gap, which is compelled by their *curiosity tension*. Curiosity leads to more curiosity, which develops thorough expertise because information gathered this way rapidly assimilates into the innovators' conscious and subconscious memory.[88] If it's impossible to fill the gap with existing information, it becomes a need.[89]

Practice identifying a need: Make a list of things that bother you or others and then try to find ways to cope with them. Look for inconsistencies, missing pieces, and incomplete information in everyday life, and recognize, examine, and verify gaps in your knowledge. Look for *un*obvious aspects of objects, materials, methods, steps, or processes (OMMSP); subtract something from or reduce/miniaturize them; or remove inefficiencies, materials, methods, or steps from objects. Look at faked images and images, pictures, or objects containing hidden bloopers, misspelled words, or differences between two pictures; images that contain optical—color, motion, shape, or size—illusions; or images that contain hidden animals, people, things, shapes, meaning, or messages to be found.

Innovators use outbox thinking to re-create the entire problem in their minds and consider many factors that might fulfill the need, which requires the open-minded and self-efficacious attitudes.[90] This enables them to identify the complex *underlying* need (and sometimes the moment the true underlying need is recognized, so is the solution).[91] Their observation and curiosity also enable them to visualize a *hidden* need.[92] The hidden need may emerge for the first time inside their imagination/intuition, which is enabled by their expertise and visualization (a newbox thinking skill).[93]

Meeting the underlying/hidden need requires outbox thinking to imagine potential solutions first; and then inbox thinking is required to determine *criteria* for the solutions.[94] Once innovators identify a need and determine the criteria to meet the need, they begin the next stage of an ACP: Generating ideas for the need.

Spring ACP: Idea Generation (Stage 3), Subconscious Processing (Stage 4), and Idea Evaluation (Stage 5)

During the spring stages of an ACP, innovators use outbox thinking for the idea-generation stage. Then they use both inbox and outbox thinking to coax Aha! moments from the subconscious-processing stage. Finally, they use inbox thinking for the idea-evaluation stage.

Stage 3 (Early Spring): Idea Generation   Stage 4 (Spring Break): Subconscious Processing   Stage 5 (Late Spring): Idea Evaluation

Figure 9.3. Spring ACP (Apple-Tree Creative Process)

Stage 3 (Early Spring): Idea Generation

After identifying needs and criteria in the previous needs-identification stage, innovators generate many ideas to solve/meet the problems/needs. Outbox thinking is like vigorous blooming because fluent, flexible, and original ideas pop out. The goal of the idea-generation stage is to generate and capture *unique* ideas. Innovators use higher-order outbox thinking skills, such as fluent thinking, flexible thinking, and original thinking, for idea generation .

In the center of the leaf group, apple blossoms pop out of their buds, as figure 9.3 shows. Cross-pollinating apple trees bear fruit more heavily and regularly than self-pollinating trees. Just as cross-pollination is critical for apple trees' fruiting success, cross-pollination is critical for innovators' idea-generation stage to generate *unique* ideas. Cross-pollination is sharing, generating, combining, adapting, and building on each other's diverse knowledge, skills, and experiences.

Fluent Thinking, Flexible Thinking, and Original Thinking

(1) *Fluent thinking is a skill to spontaneously generate many ideas.*[95] Apple trees bloom profusely and continuously once they start blooming. Likewise, fluent thinking doesn't begin with one specific thought, but rather many thoughts pop out spontaneously. If there's a lack of free flow, idea generation won't be effective. So innovators use spontaneous, childlike, and playful attitudes to enhance their fluent thinking. They generate many ideas based

on their deep exploration of relevant subject knowledge.[96] More idea generation leads to more unique ideas and better ideas, and thus fluent thinking is the foundation of both flexible and original thinking.[97]

Capturing *and externalizing* ideas by *visualizing* them on a sheet of paper (or screen, board, wall, etc.) is critical for fluent thinking. Innovators develop *capturing skills* early because if an idea isn't physically captured in detail, it will be lost forever. They improve capturing skills by identifying the activities, settings, and times (like early morning) that work best for their fluent thinking. Also, the best idea often comes when least expected, and thus they are always ready to capture it by carrying sketchpads, pens, or notepads (or small computers), which all innovators including those in this book did (and Einstein captured his ideas even when sailing—alone and without a life jacket even though he couldn't swim).[98]

Practice fluent thinking: Engage in open-ended or unstructured activities (like doodling, looking at pictures/paintings, or making art projects a major part of your life—not just for recess or playtime). Focus only on free flow, not quality (like listing as many answers as possible to describe the color *red* to a blind person).

(2) *Flexible thinking—a skill to generate different* kinds *of ideas from different angles*[99]—*is an even better predictor of innovation than fluent thinking is.*[100] It's a skill to consider multiple options and perceive a common object/situation in a different way—even after having seen it repeatedly before. Flexible thinking breaks patterns of thinking and looks at things from different perspectives and even opposing views. It requires the courage to think independently, disregard presumptions, and break through barriers.[101] A hypothesis that's never reconsidered, reformulated, or restated inhibits outbox and newbox thinking, but flexible thinking prevents that.[102]

Practice flexible thinking: See from other angles (like sitting in different chairs or lying on the floor to observe something) or turn a design upside down (like drawing animals upside down to discover other animals). Make non-peer-group friends or take roles with opposite perspectives or see events from others' perspectives (people, animals, or objects), from other times (past, present, or future), or from other places (like another city or country). Look at problems from the reverse/opposite perspectives (like "What would make me lose?"). Look for alternatives, options, and other possibilities (like using alternative materials, methods, steps, or processes for objects). Reverse OMMSP or consider multiple purposes for an idea (like putting OMMSP to an alternative use, or changing a function of objects). Review patents and patent applications in your subject/field of interests at the United States Patent and Trademark Office (USPTO: http://www.uspto.gov/). Use annoyances for a purpose, like George de Mestral, Alexander Fleming, and Henri Becquerel did: George de Mestral was annoyed by the prickly burrs of mountain bushes clinging to his pants, but he used the burrs for a purpose: after microscopic examination, he duplicated the natural hooks and loops of burrs, inventing Velcro—hook-and-loop closures and attachments! Alexander Fleming was annoyed by the unknown fungus that grew on his dirty equipment he left in the sink of his laboratory, but he used the fungus for a purpose: he found that this fungus stopped bacterial growth, later succeeded in developing, Penicillin—the first antibiotic! Henri Becquerel mistakenly left a photographic plate in a dark drawer with a uranium rock, and it exposed the plate, but he—with Marie and Pierre Curie—identified and used it for a purpose and named it *radioactivity.*[103]

(3) *Original thinking—a skill to generate new or unusual ideas—is an even better predictor of innovation than flexible thinking is,* although it is a skill based on both fluent and flexible thinking.[104] One can be creative without being flexible or fluent, but one can't be creative without being original.[105] To go beyond fluent and flexible thinking, original thinking requires mental persistence: when multiple ideas are generated, simple ideas emerge first and unusual ideas emerge later;[106] original thinking swiftly moves through all spontaneous, fluent ideas that are unoriginal, and then it generates more unusual ideas that otherwise would not have come up.[107] Also, when more kinds or different categories of ideas are persistently generated (by flexible thinking), the more unusual they're likely to be.[108]

Original thinking is the pinnacle of creativity, but it requires the sun and space climates to bring it forward. Original ideas/ behaviors are viewed as deviant because they are contrary to the norm.[109] Most people are resistant to change, the unknown, and uncertainty, and they question and crush original ideas.[110] Original thinking is especially at risk in test-centric climates where con- formity is forced and, sadly, students adapt by keeping original thoughts/ideas to themselves. Innovators generate original ideas using their sun and space attitudes, which they fight for with their storm and space attitudes.[111] They take risks and act defiantly toward governing or controlling powers.[112]

Original thinking is culture-specific.[113] A plain idea in one culture can actually be a stunningly unusual idea in a different culture. Therefore, cross-pollination across cultures is a good opportunity to generate more unique ideas.

What Are Nine Cross-Pollination Tips to Generate Unique Ideas?

Cross-pollination, especially for the idea-generation stage, may seem similar to *brainstorming*, but it's different. Brainstorming is usually a short-term, formal group activity intended to generate ideas. (Individual idea generation is often more effective than brainstorming for generating unique ideas.[114] This is partly because brainstorming is conducted without following the rules. For example, individuals must be encouraged for any ideas, not just good ideas,[115] and they must express ideas freely, [116] without being afraid of being evaluated[117] or judged.[118])

Cross-pollination occurs over time, in formal or informal face-to-face interaction in real-world settings (like casual meetings, networking, sound- boarding [my daughter was the sounding board for the cactus metaphor and the names of "soil," "sun," "storm," and "space"], collaboration, and com- petition). Using *both* individual idea generation[119] and cross-pollination[120] is best for generating unique ideas, especially when following the below tips. Cross-pollination not only combines or builds on each other's ideas (facilitating unique ideas), but also promotes group commitment.[121] It is most effective when individuals have already developed their own expertise in a subject, which enables them to realize how to add or improve their ideas or creations when cross-pollinating.[122] It enhances access to others' exper- tise and experience-based know-how, which results in unique synthesis of knowledge/skills through newly observed or learned insights.[123] Innovators' early-developed resourceful and mentored attitudes enable cross-pollination skills listed below, which leads to a greater chance of innovation:

(1) *Combine individual idea generation with cross-pollination*: Generate ideas alone and independently while externalizing them in a notebook or on sticky notes *before* cross-pollination.[124] This process helps capture the uniqueness of individuals' ideas without being prematurely influenced by groupthink (a social pressure from a majority group, which affects one's perceptions and stifles independent thought and personal responsibility).[125] *After* generating ideas alone, cross-pollinate with others and *externalize* each individual idea on a wall or a board, and then compare, contrast, merge, and regenerate ideas. The unexpected pairing of previously unrelated ideas helps generate more unique ideas.

(2) *Warm up before generating ideas*: Use physical exercises when generating ideas both alone and with others—simple body move-ment, relaxation and breathing exercises, or dance—even for just a brief period of time—to improve blood flow to the brain and generate more ideas spontaneously.[126]

(3) *Communicate and clarify goals*: Incorporating structure can lead to a better understanding of problems and generate more unique ideas.[127] A facilitator is helpful for formal cross-pollination,[128] especially when—rather than using broad goals—clarifying goals using subcategories and generating ideas *within* narrow, clear goals;[129] providing sequential goals, rather than simultaneous goals;[130] and focusing on a few goals rather than many goals.[131]

(4) *Develop the open-minded attitude without judgment*: Apple blos-soms pop out in warm air. Ideas spontaneously pop out in a warm, *psychologically safe* environment where every idea is welcomed without interruption or judgment.[132] Shout out and write down every idea. Don't stop to evaluate or try to control quality of ideas.[133] Gen-erating *and* evaluating ideas simultaneously is like driving with one foot on the brake and the other on the accelerator, so keep your foot off the brake and evaluate later. After each generated idea, a facili-tator should repeat and record each idea, without either *praise* or *criticism*.[134] Generate as many spontaneous ideas as possible for

fluent thinking; generate as many different kinds of ideas (concrete things, abstract concepts, construction materials, foods, colors, etc.) as possible for *flexible* thinking; and generate as many unusual, strange, wild, or crazy ideas as possible for *original* thinking.

(5) *Utilize a diverse group with different perspectives*: In the same way that cross-pollination between *different* types of apple trees (with the *same* bloom season) is beneficial, access to multiple perspectives is beneficial.[135] The most *unique* ideas are generated when cross-pollinated by a wide variety of people with wide perspectives (who have some understanding of the subjects/fields).[136] But pay attention to unshared or minority ideas and even small differences because original ideas are often obscure and unpopular.[137] This helps generate more ideas that are distinctly *unique* from each other.

(6) *Develop the resilient attitude that leverages debate, dissent, and conflict*: [138] Don't emphasize *harmony or cohesion*, which is especially emphasized during typical brainstorming.[139] Debate, dissent, and conflict stimulate subsequent ideas by confronting competing views or multiple perspectives.[140] This liberates participants from the worry of ridicule.[141] Present and enjoy genuine disagreement and constructive conflict among ideas instead of presenting ideas that are similar to others.[142] Be mindful that disagreement and conflict must be task- or subject-related rather than personal.[143]

(7) *Build on your own and others' ideas*: Be analytical and a good listener during cross-pollination because it can lead to piggybacking on others' ideas and new combinations.[144]

(8) *Increase positive emotions* (love, happiness, elation, joy, curiosity, playfulness, etc.): Positive emotions free the mind to elicit big-picture thinking and increase spontaneous, fluent, flexible, and original outbox thinking, [145] and enhance sensitivity when identifying problems.[146] Positive emotions can also increase distractibility,[147] which facilitates more distant connections/combinations between ideas.[148] Watch movies (even a short comedy video) or try new sounds or foods that can trigger or cause positive emotions. Yet positive emotions and distractibility often reduce focus and persistence.[149] Use positive emotions for spontaneous, fluent, and flexible ideas, but be aware of the possible negative impacts on persistence and original ideas.

(9) *Keep probing even after seemingly unique ideas appear*: Take time to harvest second- and third-order ideas, and be persistent for original ideas that come after common and obvious ideas.[150] Set an idea quota (like fifty ideas) or a time limit (like an hour) when generating ideas both alone and with others.

After innovators complete an intense effort to generate unique ideas (using the nine cross-pollination tips), they change their mind-set and environment to facilitate subconscious processing to coax Aha! discoveries.

Stage 4 (Spring Break): Subconscious Processing

As figure 9.3 shows, gardeners take a break to wait for the entire tree to bloom before blossom-pruning/fruit-pruning. Likewise, innovators wait for more unique ideas by taking a break from strenuous, conscious thinking for three reasons: first, to step back and see all the ideas generated (and they aren't attached to any particular idea); second, to let their subconscious mind process, incubate, and percolate ideas; and finally, to rest their conscious mind in preparation for the strenuous process of critically evaluating ideas (the idea-evaluation stage).

Subconscious processing is like a *search engine* in an innovators' mind. Within their wide range of expertise, it is sifting through their memory, comparing and understanding unsorted information, and then connecting unrelated thoughts to generate a new idea.[151] Innovators' subconscious processing is facilitated by their goal-oriented daydreaming, which is enabled by their daydreaming attitude, where the subconscious mind conducts outbox thinking with little concentration (of the conscious mind).[152]

What Is "Aha!"?

When innovators rest/daydream, they often arrive at a new perspective, insight, or sudden Aha!, which is an unexpected idea or a connection between ideas/thoughts. This is because the subconscious mind is often blocked by habits, stress, distractions, and rigid logic structures of the conscious mind.[153] Aha! can occur at any point during an ACP, but it usually occurs during a break (like a spring break!) *after* innovators try to achieve a specific goal such as solving a problem or generating a unique idea. It is not always as a complete solution for an entire problem, but it usually occurs as small Aha! moments relevant to the particular stage of an ACP.

How to Coax and Use Elusive Ahas!

Although many people think that experiencing Aha! is only the result of genius or luck, it's actually a voluntary and active skill that innovators learn, control, practice, and plan as part of their daily schedules.[154] Coax Aha!s throughout an ACP using the following procedures.

Before having a specific goal:

- With the self-disciplined/autonomous attitudes, achieve expertise in your *specific* CPI and have a prepared mind to recognize Aha! ideas.[155]
- With the curious/open-minded attitudes, seek and be responsive to new ideas/changes.
- With the bicultural/complexity-seeking attitudes, expose yourself to *broad* subjects/areas/fields that are mutually distant (conceptually) from each other.[156]
- With the risk-taking/nonconforming attitudes, think like a newcomer/ an outsider and extend/go beyond the existing boundaries/constraints.[157]
- With the big-picture-thinking/compassionate attitudes, see the whole unity rather than its separate pieces and find patterns/relationships among them.[158]
- With the resourceful/mentored attitudes, cross-pollinate with experts who are in different areas/fields.
- With the uncertainty-accepting/defiant attitudes, connect/combine at least two different subjects/areas/fields.[159]

When trying to achieve a specific goal:

- With the diligent/persistent attitudes, immerse yourself in a specific goal *before* planning a period of rest/daydream, which makes the subconscious mind persistently process the goal even when you (and your conscious mind) are resting/daydreaming.[160]
- With the self-reflective/complexity-seeking attitudes, think slowly

and deeply while taking a plenty of time and space for the goal (or the problem) and related thoughts (and ideas) to simmer and connect distant concepts. [161]

- With the self-efficacious/resilient attitudes, be confident to coax an Aha! moment to achieve the goal.[162]

After trying to achieve the goal *for a long time*:

- Leave the environment physically and mentally and relax[163] (like going for a walk, hiking, exercising, jogging, drawing, bathing, or traveling), with the emotional/optimistic attitudes (using positive emotions); [164]
- Switch from the persistent attitude to the spontaneous attitude to be unfocused,[165] and enjoy your daydream with the playful/daydreaming attitudes;[166]
- Daydream while taking a mental break from the current task by working on another *easy* or a low-demanding task,[167] and allow the subconscious mind to digest, simmer, and ripen its thoughts and increase its processing for the goal;[168] OR
- Have a good night's sleep and be an early bird (and learn new material in the morning), rather than a night owl;[169] yet with the goal in mind, before falling asleep, place a pen and paper next to your bed to capture dreams and an Aha! discovery.[170]

After capturing the Aha! idea:

- Immerse yourself in the idea to follow it through and turn it into reality with the curious/energetic attitudes.[171]
- With the open-minded/independent attitudes, critically analyze and evaluate the idea.[172] Because an Aha! idea is only a conscious realization of a subconscious event, it requires an idea-evaluation stage, which is the next stage.[173]

Stage 5 (Late Spring): Idea Evaluation

As figure 9.3 shows, at least a month after full blooming, gardeners blossom-prune/fruit-prune and leave only promising blossoms/fruit on the tree. This channels the trees' energy and nutrients to improve the size, color, and quality of the remaining fruit. Fruit-pruning too early doesn't allow gardeners to see all the blossoms, and fruit-pruning too late reduces the size of ripened fruit. Likewise, after consciously generating many *unique* ideas, and after subconsciously generating a *more-unique* idea(s) by taking a break, innovators analyze and evaluate the ideas to select the most *useful* ideas by thinking critically—fruit-pruning. They remove weak ideas to make sure resources are focused only on improving the quality of the most useful ideas.

What Is Critical Thinking (or Fruit-Pruning)?

Ideas/products that are unique but not useful are considered irrelevant or crazy.[174] *After a break*, innovators think critically and fruit-prune the ideas generated in the idea-generation and the subconscious-processing stages.[175] They use higher-order inbox thinking skills for critical thinking, such as analysis and evaluation. In today's world where information is cheap and only a mouse-click away, critical thinking is an essential skill to select useful information. It isn't a one-step process of simply criticizing something. It's analyzing ideas; then comparing them to objective criteria; then systematically evaluating them; and then selecting the most useful ideas,[176] which anyone with normal intelligence is able to do.[177] Just as gardeners leave only a few, fast-growing apples while pruning the others, innovators use five fruit-pruning tips to leave a few, useful ideas.

What Are Five Fruit-Pruning Tips to Select Useful Ideas?

(1) *Defer decision-making until seeing the forest (whole picture)*: With the open-minded attitude, never *assume* anything, and keep thinking even after seeing the readily available or seemingly useful ideas.[178] With the independent attitude, track down the original source and check the reliability and validity (by comparing, contrasting, and deciding whether it is true/false, sometimes true, or partly true) of an idea—or products, news, opinions, statements, or arguments— before accepting it or them. Do not jump to a conclusion and look for further evidence to support your conclusion about the idea, and do change your mind or consider alternative explanations if the

evidence changes the conclusion. Aggressively seek and patiently discover more ideas before fruit-pruning the options and selecting useful ideas.

(2) *Persistently analyze to thoroughly understand an idea*: Investigate underlying origins, causes, and circumstances, and gather facts for an idea. Demonstrate your mental process by saying aloud what you're thinking when you're thinking or doing something about the idea. Break down the idea into components/parts or sequential steps for better understanding. Determine the relationships among the parts and between the parts and the whole.[179] Identify the essential parts and interactions/relationships, and then classify and generalize them by extracting an insight, a conclusion, or an implication based on the relationships. Explain the reasons for the insight, the conclusion, or the implication.

(3) *Incrementally search and systematically evaluate an idea*, while recognizing illogical reasoning[180] and blocking distracting/irrelevant thoughts:[181] This maximizes resources and concentration.[182] Use negative emotions like anxiety, anger, or fear (not too much [leading to panicked and unclear thinking] and not too little [leading to anti-motivation]) to increase structure and focus for mental persistence.[183] They enhance calculations and logical thinking, and thus critical thinking by decreasing distractibility.[184] However, because negative emotions stimulate narrow or concreate thinking and persistence, rather than big-picture thinking,[185] they often decrease outbox thinking.[186] Also, as mental persistence increases, mental flexibility decreases,[187] so be aware that focus and persistence can reduce especially flexible thinking.

(4) *Deliberately amplify specific qualities to make a unique idea useful*: Instead of dwelling on qualities that make an idea *un*workable, ask "What could be added that would make it workable?" Debate, advocate, or write from a position that supports a quality you don't like. This is especially important for initially less-useful ideas that may be pruned too soon.[188]

(5) *Maintain objectivity and systematically evaluate the quality of selected ideas*:[189] Look closely at each branch of the tree (each quality of the idea) by developing and *applying* evaluation criteria such as *a rubric* or a SWOT (strengths, weaknesses, opportuni-

ties, and threats) for the ideas (or products, projects, or situations). To make a rubric, first make objectives based on the needs-identification stage. Second, list the criteria (like cost, time, quality, novelty, legality, safety, feasibility, ease of implementation, etc.). Third, develop a way to numerically value each idea against the criteria. Fourth, take *a break*, and then select the most useful ideas based on the total assigned values. Fifth, combine complimentary ideas into fewer, more comprehensive ideas.[190]

When ideas have been critically evaluated and selected in the idea-evaluation stage, innovators are ready to synthesize them in the next stage.

Summer ACP: Synthesis (Stage 6) and Transformation (Stage 7)

During the summer stages of an ACP, innovators use newbox thinking that consists of inbox and outbox thinking. For the synthesis stage, they use more outbox than inbox thinking, and for the transformation stage, they use more inbox than outbox thinking.

Stage 6 (Early Summer): Synthesis

Stage 7 (Long Summer): Transformation

Figure 9.4. Summer ACP (Apple-Tree Creative Process)

Stage 6 (Early Summer): Synthesis

Young fruits are uniquely formed *inside* the selected blossoms/fruits after blossom-pruning/fruit-pruning, as figure 9.4 shows. Likewise, innovators uniquely synthesize essential elements/attributes of the selected ideas.[191]

What Is Synthesis?

Synthesis is recombining things and information into a new coherent *whole* without losing the essence of each part. It's developing a comprehensive yet detailed view of the *forest* rather than individual trees. Innovators reorganize essential elements/attributes that emerge from the idea-evaluation stage and may connect the strengths of some ideas to the strengths of other ideas. Synthesis initially seems unproductive because it adds complexity. However, effective synthesis ultimately results in a unified creation.[192]

Connecting, combining, or copying existing ideas doesn't seem creative, but innovation starts by synthesizing elements of existing ideas (knowledge/skills),[193] which indicates that innovation is *not* a result of *a genius*, and that different innovators may simultaneously arrive at a similar innovation *without copying* each other. For example, several other physicists—including Hendrik Lorentz—were developing similar theories at the same time Einstein was.[194]

How to Synthesize?

Innovators use newbox thinking skills (highest-order skills) for synthesis—such as big-picture thinking, boundary crossing, pattern finding, and dot connecting—which use more outbox than inbox thinking for unique synthesis. Each synthesis skill is an opportunity to connect different aspects of unrelated ideas. This forces innovators to see different perspectives/opportunities that usual associations in their conscious mind prevent them from seeing. This results in unique synthesis of ideas (or elements/attributes of the ideas).

(1) *See the big picture*: Innovators use a big-picture thinking skill for synthesis, which is presenting information in a larger context/system rather than in the details.[195] It is enabled/enhanced by the big-picture-thinking/compassionate attitudes through thinking away from *me, here*, and *now*—abstract thinking instead of concrete thinking.[196] It is facilitated by the self-reflective/complexity-seeking attitudes, which reflect on the relationships of events, ideas, and attributes. It further enhances outbox and newbox thinking and creates a framework for unique synthesis to occur.[197]

Practice seeing the big picture: Enjoy abstract depictions and stories using objects that have interpretive meanings (like abstract art, sayings, or pictures), or create an abstract depiction of what's in front of you (like explaining where the place of *hope* is in the school/house and why). Move away from the me, the here, the now, and the reality; and change concrete mind-sets to abstract mind-sets, by first explaining something using graphics, then using outlines, and eventually using only abstract narratives.

(2) *Cross boundaries*: Most Big I Innovation involves synthesis from boundary crossing and connecting the most dramatically different/ irrelevant subjects/fields (like arts and sciences).[198] Innovators cross boundaries by developing diverse hobbies or passions (like earning degrees from very different fields or experiencing significant career changes).[199] Many artistic innovators have science or engineering backgrounds, whereas many scientific innovators have art backgrounds (including performing or creating art).[200] Boundary crossing distinguishes science Nobel laureates from others because of their artistic expertise.[201] Innovators' risk-taking/ defiant attitudes compel them to question norms/assumptions and cross boundaries between subjects/fields.[202] Their self-reflective/ complexity-seeking attitudes facilitate synthesis of the essential elements/attributes from crossing boundaries.[203] This results in unique synthesis of very different subjects.

Practice crossing boundaries: Redefine a problem by explaining it from an outsider's view or putting yourself in a situation where you feel uncomfortable and must learn something new to get through it. Work backward or start from a potential solution. Add unpredictability to your work, or showcase an obvious error in it. Learn about other fields or use cross-disciplinary approaches to learn new material (like using sports to learn physics or learning chemistry from mixing paint). Don't confine your work to one format (combine with writing, performing, or visual art; combine two approaches like visual arts with live band music; or combine different centuries' techniques like gothic art with steampunk). My daughter worried about wasting her previous years of developing expertise when she changed her CPI and major in medicine into brain research. But I assured her that her expertise in different subjects would eventually be combined by crossing the boundaries and facilitate her Big I.

(3) *Find patterns*: Innovators use a pattern-finding skill for synthesis, which is symbolizing complex ideas (or images/data) without losing the essence or distorting facts.[204] It finds patterns by disregarding irrelevant/superficial information and bringing essential elements/attributes forward. Innovators habitually look for patterns in data, ideas, images, sounds, math, history, language, music, and dance. This starts with their big-picture-thinking attitude that results in a wide field of view. It is often facilitated by their artistic training and nonverbal thinking.[205] They find patterns and trends in human behaviors, situations, and nature by recognizing similarities, differences, and relationships.[206] They seek repetition, meanings, or core principles even in chaos through their complexity-seeking/uncertainty-accepting attitudes. This helps extrapolate small ideas into Big I Innovation.

(4) *Connect dots*: Innovators use a dot-connecting skill for synthesis, which starts from seeing things as a connected *whole* instead of many unrelated pieces.[207] Their big-picture-thinking attitude enables them to recognize an entire tree (instead of separate branches) or a whole chain (instead of separate links). Their dot-connecting skill is enhanced by learning *general* principles and methods of subjects—rather than separate and particular bits of knowledge—which provides innovators with mental frameworks capable of connecting between the patterns/relationships and similarities/differences that they constantly find with their pattern-finding skill.[208]

Practice connecting dots: Be surrounded by people who are different or expound different ideas; and when working in a group, make your group as diverse as possible (like diverse characteristics, experiences, backgrounds, ways of thinking, or disciplines). Connect ideas through new experiences (like watching movies, reading, or looking at pieces of art in genres/styles that don't normally interest you); or using analogies (like asking and answering how is creativity like an oxymoron, such as cheerful pessimism, submissive independence, absent presence, lonely togetherness, or genuine imitation).

Nobel laureates' innovations are also unique syntheses of multiple existing ideas.[209] Connecting dots from very different sources (subjects/fields) of information takes time, which starts only in innovators' *imagination*.[210] Their imagination for synthesis is facilitated by their highest-order newbox thinking skills, such as the use of metaphor and nonverbal communication.[211]

Use metaphors. Innovators' metaphorical thoughts help form analogies and bridge conceptual gaps.[212] Metaphors are comparing two unlike objects by suggesting that one object is figuratively like another (like "time is money").[213] Thinking metaphorically enables seeing things from new perspectives, which leads to more unique synthesis.[214] It compels boundary-crossing comparisons and thinking outside existing boundaries of a subject, which further enhances outbox and newbox thinking, which also helps promote creations by grabbing the audience's attention.[215] Thus, using metaphors is an effective skill for the last stage of an ACP, the *promotion* stage.[216] Metaphors are easy to understand and create vivid images in the audience's mind. Therefore, they are persuasive and memorable especially when simple, catchy, informative, and surprising.[217] They are even more memorable when appealing to multiple senses.[218]

Practice using metaphors: Develop metaphors from your CPI that can hint at who you are or what you are passionate about (like my gardening metaphor for creativity development or cactus metaphor for creative attitudes). Use animals or symbols as metaphors to describe a story (like the journey of the pen that signed the Declaration of Independence—explaining how and what the pen did and how it changed many lives).

Communicate nonverbally. Innovators prefer nonverbal thinking/communication skills, such as visualizing, using the five senses, or using body movement, which are effective for unique synthesis.[219]

(1) *Visualize*: Innovators (and more males than females) often think in pictures than in words, and their self-reflective/daydreaming attitudes help them think in-depth through problems and develop a high capacity for visual imagery and fantasy.[220] Most Aha! moments arise from visualizing ideas (or objects, systems, processes, solutions, etc.).[221] Visualizing is essential for unique synthesis across mediums such as in visual/performance arts, writing, music, sports, inventions, and discoveries.[222] A picture is

worth a thousand words because the brain often thinks in images to subconsciously organize, understand, and remember ideas—faster than reading words. This is also effective for promoting their creation. (I use many illustrations in this book!)

Practice visualizing: Make drawing a habit by doodling and scribbling without worrying about drawing well; and draw in different ways (like rotating, mirroring, or drawing only with words). Visualize what's read in a story or a book and create drawings, flowcharts, and sequences of stories, sounds, or movements. Practice impossible perspectives (like impossible buildings/constructions, impossibly connected drawings, endless staircases down or in all directions forever, or impossible geometric planes or surfaces). Collect visual metaphors and images, and use them for presentations without words. Put pictures, objects, or visual reminders nearby that are related to a problem that you're trying to solve.

(2) *Think with the five senses*: Innovators use and/or combine sight, sound, touch, smell, and/or taste to illustrate their ideas or make new connections between irrelevant ideas, which results in unique synthesis.[223]

Practice thinking with the five senses: Pay attention to the senses, but focus on one sense at a time; or block out one of your senses and describe how different it feels. Write with your non-dominant hand, your mouth, or your toes. Touch, feel, smell, and manipulate a wide variety of materials for work or play. Imagine what the location in a story or a book smells or sounds like and what the characters smell or hear; or imagine what a song tastes or feels like. Visit ethnic sections of cities (like Chinatown, Greek Town, Little Italy, or Korea Town) and reflect on the smells and sights—every flavor, sound, and interaction. Use all five senses to describe a fruit or a vegetable to someone who's never tried it.

(3) *Think with the body*: Physically acting out abstract concepts makes them more concrete, which facilitates generating more and better ideas.[224] Practicing physical spontaneity stimulates mental spontaneity because gestures and body language spontaneously occur before conscious thought.[225] Innovators think and communicate ideas in physical, lively, and emotionally vivid ways.[226] This helps generate, expand, or mature ideas, and it facilitates unique

synthesis. It is also effective for promoting creations (in the pro-motion stage) because it can evoke strong physical/emotional responses from the audience.[227]

Practice thinking with the body: Act out metaphors that enhance outbox thinking (like turning on a light for an Aha! idea or stepping outside of a box for "outbox thinking"), which makes abstract ideas more concrete through the body movement. Work collaboratively and tell a story or describe situations/objects using only the body, without dialogue. Communicate concepts, ideas, poems, stories, and songs through movement. Interpret written words through movement, mime, and sound; and interpret the meaning of movement of others and animals. Put on concerts with homemade instruments, and make room for physical movement and spontaneity.

Stage 7 (Long Summer): Transformation

Apples slowly, gradually transform, becoming bigger and sweeter, changing color, and ripening until they become edible (useful). The long apple transformation is complete when an apple is ready to be picked and eaten, as figure 9.4 shows. Similarly, innovators transform their synthe-sized ideas into a *useful* creation by elaborating, refining, and simplifying them, which takes a long time.[228] Steve Jobs, for example, uniquely *syn-thesized* the mouse-driven graphical user interface (from Xerox) with his computer-as-an-appliance concept. Then through elaborating, refining, and, simplifying the functions for a long time, he *transformed* them into the useful Macintosh computer.[229]

To transform apples into the best quality (size, color, sweetness, etc.), gardeners provide the right amount of fertilizer and water while control-ling weeds and pests and culling damaged fruit. Too much fertilizer causes many leaves and shoots but fewer/smaller fruits. Similarly, when trans-forming ideas into their maximum usefulness, innovators must find the perfect balance between elaboration and simplicity.

How to Transform?

Transforming the idea into a creation is much more difficult than just *having* a great idea. It's similar to the difference between actually writing a story for a long time (to be useful) and just spontaneously *imagining* a story (to be unique). Innovators use newbox thinking skills (highest-order thinking)—such as elaboration, imaginative refinement, and pursuit of simplicity—to transform their synthesized ideas into a creation.[230] They persistently elaborate their creation while imaginatively refining through cross-pollination and pursuing simplicity, which uses more inbox than outbox thinking.

(1) *Persistently elaborate*: Innovators are newbox thinkers who switch from spontaneous/flexible outbox thinking to persistent/ systematic inbox thinking as necessary. This enables their laborious elaboration process and skill (working out the details, explaining, expanding, and enriching) and completion of the lengthy transformation stage. Persistence is one of the most important attitudes shared by all innovators,[231] and it is necessary for the transformation stage, especially for elaboration. Females are often good at inbox thinking and this elaboration skill of newbox thinking because of their persistence and attention to the details.[232] But their elaboration sacrifices their outbox thinking.[233] Inbox thinkers are persistent and use logical and systematic thoughts, which contribute to the usefulness of their creation.[234] Yet their persistent minds sacrifice flexible minds, and thus outbox thinking.[235] In contrast, outbox thinkers are spontaneous and use random and subconscious thoughts without giving much thought to practicality, which contributes to the uniqueness of their creation. Yet they may lack persistence because they're often distracted by other new ideas/opportunities.[236] Also, their flexible minds sacrifice persistent minds, and thus inbox thinking.[237] An inbox or an outbox thinker alone can't achieve innovation because both inbox and outbox thinking lead to innovation only through newbox thinking.[238] Consequently, cross-pollination between inbox and outbox thinkers increases a chance of innovation.

Practice elaborating: Elaborate on a recent journey or on what you'd do if you were in a different time/place, using as many credible details as possible. Explore, examine, and add relevant details to unsolved mysteries, or the deep meanings of stories, characters' behaviors, or poems. From a picture of a random page from a magazine, decorate, embellish, and add details about what's going on; what the people are doing or feeling; how they got there; and what their background story is.

(2) *Imaginatively refine*: After elaborating the synthesized ideas (or functions, or products) with details, innovators further refine them, which is a skill to improve something by small/subtle changes to bring out its uniqueness. Refinement can be either concrete or imaginative. Inbox thinkers prefer concrete refinement that uses incremental changes and repetitive testing to measure the impact of the new refinement on performance. Outbox thinkers make greater use of *imaginative* refinement. This refinement isn't repetitive, but it experiments with unexpected variations that magnify uniqueness of a creation.[239] Newbox innovators cross-pollinate with outbox thinkers to imaginatively refine their creation. For example, Jobs did so with Wozniak,[240] and Einstein did so with Besso.[241] Innovators' cross-pollination with others also unleashes new ideas, helping them further refine the creation.[242] They gain perspectives, incorporate brutally honest criticisms, persist through mistakes and failures, and make a *good* creation *better*.[243]

(3) *Pursue simplicity*: Too much elaboration and complexity reduces a creation's usefulness, and so does too little.[244] Basic concepts or technologies taken for granted today were once too complex for most people to comprehend. But innovators throughout history have transformed complexity into simplicity.[245] This isn't just filtering or down-selecting possible options. The opposite of complexity is minimalism, which results in limited usefulness. But a simplicity skill starts with a thorough understanding of a complex system (including functions and desired effects), and then it removes distracting or unessential elements to make the essence *useful* to others.[246] A simplicity skill uses more inbox than outbox thinking for useful transformation.

Practice simplicity: First, find simple joy in life despite its drama and complexity; life is too short to be cynical. Look for the essential elements of a complex situation that can be utilized and reused to describe and simplify future situations (like historical trends, descriptive data, and legal precedents). Remove obvious information to amplify critical functionality (like choosing only 10 percent of the data that makes the biggest difference). Find a balance between having too few or too many details by comparing how others respond to different levels of elaboration/simplicity.

For example, Jobs transformed the complexity of synthesizing a phone, a music player, and navigation into a simple, easy-to-use device—the iPhone.[247] O'Keeffe achieved simplicity by magnifying a flower's most unique essence in colorful and provocative composition instead of painting every petal and detail.[248] Mandela's long confinement helped him focus on his life's internal qualities instead of external accomplishments,[249] which helped him achieve simplicity within himself and compassion for others instead of personal gain.[250] Einstein was only a low-level patent examiner, but he learned to simplify when examining and rewriting confusing or complex patent applications. This enabled him to transform complex concepts into simple yet bold explanations that other physicists could understand and use.[251] Although they came up with similar ideas, only Einstein simplified, promoted, and gained credit for his innovative theory, which Hendrik Lorentz failed to do.[252]

Sometimes transforming others' creations into simple explanations that people can understand make the creations accessible to a broader audience. For example, Freeman Dyson, after thorough mastery of complex physics theories, wrote two powerful papers that combined the quantum electrodynamics' theories of Richard Feynman, Julian Schwinger, and Sin-Itiro Tomonaga.[253] Dyson's simple explanations transformed the *unique* complex theories in ways that were understandable and *useful* to other physicists. This simplification led the three physicists to win the Nobel Prize in Physics in 1965.

Autumn ACP: Promotion (Stage 8)

During the last stage of an ACP (short autumn), innovators depend primarily on outbox thinking to grab the audience's attention, then use inbox thinking to explain the features and benefits of the creation.

Stage 8 (Short Autumn): Promotion

Figure 9.5. Autumn ACP (Apple-Tree Creative Process)

Stage 8 (Short Autumn): Promotion

As figure 9.5 shows, gardeners know good timing is imperative when planning, harvesting, and selling the fruits of their labor; if picked too soon, the fruits' flavor won't be fully developed; but if left too late, the fruits storage quality will be poor, they may be rotten, or birds and insects may damage or destroy them. When gardeners sell fruits, they must sell as quickly as possible (during the *short* autumn) before they go bad. Also, location is critical because they might have to be transported a long distance.

Likewise, innovators promote their creation in the right place at the right time. They become the right person by completing all previous stages of an ACP *before* they are at either the right place or time.[254] The right place is one that is receptive to their creation—often a big multicultural city (Zurich for Einstein; Silicon Valley for Jobs; Johannesburg for Mandela; New York City for O'Keeffe; and Paris for Curie). Multicultural cities value nonconformity and accept outsiders from diverse nationalities, ethnicities, religions, and sexual orientations. Being in these cities increases the likelihood of successful cross-pollination and promotion.[255]

How to Promote?

Innovators use the highest-order newbox thinking skills for promotion—such as use of metaphor and nonverbal communication including visualizing and using the five senses and body movement. These skills are also used for the synthesis stage. Innovators also use other highest-order newbox thinking skills for promotion—such as articulation, naming, and storytelling.[256] An articulation skill uses more inbox than outbox thinking to explain features and benefits, whereas naming and storytelling skills use more outbox than inbox thinking to grab attention and persuade.

(1) *Articulate features and benefits*: Innovators develop a skill to articulate their own emotions and thoughts,[257] which is critical throughout the ACP. Their open-minded/resourceful/empathetic attitudes help them to learn from others and understand what their audiences want and need.[258] When they finish transforming their synthesized ideas into a creation, they cross-pollinate again and articulate the unique and useful features and benefits of their creation to others.[259] They articulate them in simple ways so that others can understand, accept, and desire the creation—not only to receptive audiences, but also to idea killers and critics.[260]

　　Practice articulating: Externalize your ideas with several key points and then communicate focusing on those points. When negotiating, shake hands; offer warm drinks or food; or mimic communication styles of the negotiating counterpart or the audience, which builds trust. Practice presentation in front of a mirror or trusted friends, or videotape yourself and observe your own body language. Speak firmly and avoid hesitant phrases (like "ummm" or "I mean") and negative gestures (like frowns, raised eyebrows, wandering eyes, fidgety hands, or constant sniffling).[161]

(2) *Uniquely name to grab attention*: Innovators use names or titles for their creation that grab others' attention: They make it short (accompanied by an informative subtitle) and specific (not generic

or common), which is easy for the audience to remember and convey to others.[262] (iPhone, for example.) Their names/titles include benefits for the audience and keywords, which tell what the creation is about, attract the intended audience, and optimize search engines for the media/information outlets; their names/titles are also exciting/provocative, which pique audiences' curiosity/emotional reaction.[263] For example, when the Curies isolated an additional radioactive element from pitchblende after removing uranium and thorium, Marie named the new element "polonium" after her motherland of Poland. Poland did not even exist as an independent country at that time, but she named it to promote recovering its independence, which was (unintentionally) provocative.

Practice naming: Think of titles for your own biography (or chapters of the biography) and select key phrases that fit your life experiences. Make titles cheerful, fun, and upbeat.

(3) *Use storytelling to persuade*: Storytelling is a skill to craft and share compelling and interesting stories[264] (which I use for this book). The brain remembers stories better and longer than other forms of communication because information is stored as a story and an experience—not long lists of facts.[265] Innovators use storytelling for promotion, which further enhances their outbox and newbox thinking.[266] Innovation depends more on emotional appeals of storytelling than on logical arguments or factual lists.[267] Storytelling communicates more simply and makes information memorable and more persuasive by appealing to emotions and creating mental images for the audience, which show, instead of just explain.[268] Storytelling communicates creations and also listens to the audience's own storytelling to arrive at a mutual understanding.[269] It also preempts others' negative or critical feedback; amplifies positive attributes of creations; encourages others' word-of-mouth transfer to a broader audience; and actually causes a sale.[270]

Practice storytelling: Start conversations with storytelling to build rapport or ease tense situations. Share story background knowledge with the audience to familiarize them with the topic and make it personally relevant to them. Provide a realistic plot and sequence of events; and when telling a secondhand story, be genuine about which details are absolute or inferred. Collaboratively seek goals with the audience and increase the knowledge of each other's needs and capabilities, instead of telling them what to buy.[271]

For example, when promoting new Apple products, Jobs was a skillful storyteller for his creation. As a shy and private boy, Jobs learned from his college friend Robert Friedland how to be persuasive and charismatic to convince others to share his vision.[272] Apple's famous sixty-second video in 1997 says,

> *Here's to the crazy ones. The misfits. The rebels. The trouble-makers. The round pegs in the square holes. The ones who see things differently. They're not fond of rules. And they have no respect for the status quo. You can quote them, disagree with them, glorify or vilify them. About the only thing you can't do is ignore them. Because they change things. They push the human race forward. And while some may see them as the crazy ones, we see genius. Because the people who are crazy enough to think they can change the world are the ones who do.*[273]

In this storytelling advertisement, Jobs visually refers to the lives of great innovators such as Albert Einstein, Bob Dylan (musician who showed how music and poetry can influence society), Martin Luther King Jr. (Baptist minister who lead a movement to overcome racism through nonviolent civil disobedience), Richard Branson (entrepreneur who started a small record company, which he eventually transitioned into a billion-dollar airline company), John Lennon (musician who used his celebrity to promote important causes like world peace), Thomas Edison (inventor who made life-changing technologies available to the world, such as light bulbs and the phonograph), Buckminster Fuller (architect and systems theorist who popularized the geodesic dome), Muhammad Ali (boxer who used his celebrity to fight racism and poverty), Ted Turner (media entrepreneur who created CNN, which revolutionized news media), Maria Callas (opera singer whose interpretations redefined the art form),

Mahatma Gandhi (leader of the Indian independence movement who codified and successfully demonstrated the application of civil disobedience to overcome tyranny), Amelia Earhart (early female pilot who overcame prejudice and stereotypes to pioneer and popularize aviation technology), Alfred Hitchcock (director and producer who elevated the genre of film as an art form), Martha Graham (dancer who revolutionized the art of choreography and dance), Jim Henson (puppeteer and producer who revolutionized the use of puppets in educational programs and film), Frank Lloyd Wright (architect who leveraged qualities of emerging technology and materials to radically change urban architecture and furniture), and Pablo Picasso (painter and fine artist who revealed the abstract foundation of human thought through visual art).

The stories in the ad celebrated these innovators and their energetic, big-picture-thinking, nonconforming, risk-taking, and defiant attitudes that changed the world for the better, despite the fact that many others saw their attitudes negatively. Jobs's storytelling created an image of Apple as an outsider who wants to use computers to help people change the world. This evoked Apple computer users' strong emotions, inspiration, desire, pride, and connection to Apple products. It helped save Apple from bankruptcy and led it to become one of the most valuable companies in the world.[274]

Storytelling was also important to the success of Mandela. He had initially committed to Mahatma Gandhi's nonviolent protest. But after police forces massacred sixty-nine unarmed black South Africans at Sharpeville in 1960 and subsequently banned the ANC, Mandela changed his commitment. In 1961, he co-founded a military wing of the ANC to use sabotage and guerilla-war tactics to end Apartheid. But this put him in prison and earned for him an accusation of inciting workers' strikes and leaving the country without the government's permission.[275] Facing a death sentence at the Rivonia trial in 1964, instead of testifying in his own defense, Mandela engaged his captive audience with four hours of *storytelling*; shared his life stories, including why he joined the struggle for racial equality and why he had to choose violent protest to achieve South Africa's multiracial democracy. He finally ended with,

During my lifetime I have dedicated myself to this struggle of the African people. I have fought against white domination, and I have fought against black domination. I have cherished the ideal of a democratic and free society in which all persons live together in harmony and with equal opportunities. It is an ideal which I hope to live for and to achieve. But if needs be, it is an ideal for which I am prepared to die.[276]

His stories stirred emotions in the minds of thousands of others, including his oppressors. He turned the trial from resistant argument of a lone defendant to something much bigger: an appeal from an ordinary man regarding injustice throughout the world and evoking compassion within humanity's deep conscience for those who live under oppression. His storytelling showed that he was indeed a courageous innovator who was willing to risk his life for a bigger purpose. The principles in his heart were the source of his courage.

His words made it clear to listeners that timidly denying his personal passion and goal was the biggest risk of all, and he was willing to face death to transform his big dream into reality. His final statement that he was "prepared to die" saved him from a death sentence.

EXAMPLES OF ION THINKING SKILLS WITHIN ACP

ION thinking and ACP are models for preparing and accomplishing innovation, as table 9.1 shows. They can be implemented by anyone and tailored according to one's own desired creation, regardless of how amateur or advanced.

When Jobs created the ability to display different fonts on the first Mac in 1984, his well-documented process can be described as ION thinking within the ACP.[277]

Stage 1 (expertise development): At age ten Jobs saw his first desktop computer, igniting his CPI. Immediately he began developing expertise in computers using *inbox* thinking through extensive experiences and reading.

Stage 2 (needs identification): While developing his expertise in computers, he used *outbox* thinking to identify user needs that became his computer-as-an-appliance concept.

Stage 3 (idea generation): He used *outbox* thinking with Wozniak when they considered many ideas for incorporating different materials, methods, devices, and technologies to improve personal computers. This included his idea for incorporating calligraphy, which started in a class that he audited right after dropping out college.

Stage 4 (subconscious processing): After generating those ideas, he took a break to see the big picture of all ideas that could meet the identified needs for personal computers, which helped him generate more unique ideas.

Stage 5 (idea evaluation): After a long break and distancing himself from the generated ideas, he used critical thinking to test and evaluate the generated ideas to see how useful they were or weren't.

Stage 6 (synthesis): One attribute that emerged by synthesizing technology and art/design, including calligraphy (using *newbox* thinking) was a selection of custom fonts instead of the primitive computer characters seen on most screens at that time. The custom fonts were a part of larger synthesis of technology and design to deliver a personalized user experience.

Stage 7 (transformation): He used *newbox* thinking to transform the unique synthesis into the useful Mac, including its refined font menus that added tremendous value to desktop digital publishing.

Stage 8 (promotion): Finally, he used *newbox* thinking to promote the creation to the audience in fun and unconventional ways. He created new, enthusiastic customers through unique storytelling and a likeable, easy-to-remember name for his creation. He became the right person at the right place at the right time for innovation.

Table 9.1. ION Thinking Skills (Inbox, Outbox, and Newbox)
within ACP (Apple-Tree Creative Process)

ACP			ION	
Season		Stage	Specific Skills	Main Skills
Winter	1. Long	Expertise Development	Memorization	Inbox (expertise)
			Comprehension	
			Application	
	2. Late	Needs Identification	Finding a hidden/underlying need	Outbox
Spring	3. Early	Idea Generation	Fluent thinking	
			Flexible thinking	
			Original thinking	
	4. Break	Subconscious Processing	Aha!	
	5. Late	Idea Evaluation	Analysis	Inbox (critical thinking)
			Evaluation	
Summer	6. Early	Synthesis	Big-picture thinking	Newbox
			Boundary crossing	
			Pattern finding	
			Dot connecting	
	7. Long	Transformation	Elaboration	
			Refinement	
			Simplicity	
Autumn	8. Short	Promotion	Articulation	
			Naming	
			Storytelling	

The Last Step: Apply ION Thinking Skills within the ACP to Achieve Innovation

Just like all apple seeds are capable of producing gloriously delicious apples, all babies are born with the potential to be creative geniuses. Yet only seeds planted in diverse soil, subjected to bright sun, fierce storms, and free space can produce the best apples. Gardeners understand that they must cultivate the 4S climates to bring out the best in seeds and not rely on the seeds' genetics. Likewise, parents and educators must cultivate the 4S climates for children, regardless of their gender, instead of relying on genetics or *waiting* for a sign of inborn gifts/talents—which may never come. Adults' belief in inborn ability negatively influences children's attitudes toward future endeavors. The biggest difference between my former students in Korea and my current American students is that American students believe in inborn ability (an "external locus of control") while Korean students believe in diligence and hard work ("internal locus of control"). More important, these beliefs and attitudes impact how they perceive and apply feedback to improve.[278] My American students are offended by my blunt, honest feedback and think that it is a personal attack, which is also because they have always received positive feedback. But my Korean students were motivated to work even harder in response to such feedback. Giving everybody trophies or constantly sugarcoating feedback for mediocre accomplishments will deprive children of reality and what it truly takes to accomplish a goal. Many believe that only praise/positive feedback is good and negative feedback is bad for children, but negative feedback is more effective than positive feedback when helping students achieve their goal.[279] Brutally honest feedback for children's improvement is critical for the storm climate.

Within the ACP (the Apple-tree Creative Process), applying all inbox, outbox, and newbox thinking at appropriate times facilitates innovation.[280] While cultivating all four of the climates (including the storm climate) parents and educators must help children independently find their curiosity, preference, or interest (CPI) as early as possible and develop ION (inbox, outbox, and newbox) thinking. Memorization and comprehension skills are necessary for developing initial expertise in their CPI, and further development requires application skills so they can use their learned material to apply to or solve new and real-world situations or problems. Unfortunately, these application skills are not measured by most standardized tests.[281] Along with inbox thinking, children must also develop outbox thinking to generate unique ideas. Most young children are capable of outbox thinking, but it progressively decreases if they're in anti-creative climates—especially test-centric climates—that foster anti-creative attitudes. The decrease occurs at home first, then in schools, and then it continues in large-scale social institutions.[282]

The negative impact of standardized testing on inbox and outbox thinking is one important reason that we must stop wasting resources supporting America's increasingly test-centric climates. Standardized tests—such as state-mandated tests (by the No Child Left Behind Act and recently by the Every Student Succeeds Act), gifted-identification measures, the SAT, and the ACT—are not always "standardized" (meaning that those tests are not always administered and scored in a consistent/standard manner). For example, when my son took his SAT on May 5, 2012, the proctors left the testing room and came back late, and then accommodated their error by shortening the testing time for some subjects, which panicked the examinees (including my son, who has difficulty focusing on tests) and influenced their scores. Immediately following that incident, I sent numerous e-mails, letters, and phone calls to the College Board. One of the administrators wrote back saying that the investigation was ongoing and that they would be able to provide additional information in the "near" future. However, I never received any result or update even four years after the incident. This one incident suggests a lack of commitment to the reliability and validity of the SAT as an assessment for students' academic potential, aptitude, or achievement. It further indicates that testing companies might be more focused on making money than on staying true to their mission. For example, the website of the College Board says, "The College Board is a mission-driven not-for-profit organization that connects students to college success and opportunity."[283] Its mission indicates that it does not have to pay federal taxes because it is a "not-for-profit organization." This fact forces me to call into question the extremely high salaries of its top executives. They make more money than the presidents of prestigious universities do.[284] Again, this is another small example of how America's test-centric climate is devolving into a Confucian exam hell that benefits testing companies (and the test-prep industry) far more than it does students.[285] Annually, American parents pay testing companies hundreds of millions of dollars for tests and test-prep materials.[286] But this money should be invested in developing students' CPIs.

The scores on the SAT or ACT have the biggest impact on students' college choice, including which college they go to or whether they go at all.[287] Some argue that students' GPA[288] and other experiences, including extracurricular activities, are more important than the test scores, but using a national longitudinal data set, my analysis shows that test scores are the most important to colleges.[289] Moreover, highly selective colleges weight test scores more heavily in the admission decision than less-selective colleges do.[290] SAT[291] and ACT[292] scores are highly correlated with students' IQ, which indicates that colleges are looking for only "smart" students. But these tests are supposed to measure students' "readiness" for college education.[293] Preparing for standardized tests that are designed to find who's smart, smarter, and smartest decreases creative-thinking skills in individuals. More important, these scores are correlated to students' family income, disfavoring disadvantaged students.[294] This is because students from high-income backgrounds have the money to take the tests multiple times and enroll expensive private college-prep high schools, test-prep classes, or test-prep tutoring, while disadvantaged students are not afforded these luxuries. For example, when my son wanted to attend a test-prep class in northern Virginia in June 2013, I visited the institution with him, but the tuition was shockingly expensive, and I could not afford it. Fortunately, we had already found a mentor for his CPI in computer programming, so he was focused on developing his expertise. He started working on his CPI even harder because he didn't spend time preparing for the tests. Now he is advancing his expertise at a university, pursuing degrees in nano-technology and computer science.

America's increasingly wasteful pursuit to identify who is smart, smarter, and smartest mutates into a contest to identify who is rich, richer, or richest, which is actually counterproductive to the goals of testing. In this climate, children's 4S attitudes are evidently discouraged and punished, and children become bonsaied trees or wing-clipped birds. Children who resist this climate are labeled as troublemakers, and if they don't find a different way to apply their ION thinking skills, they may actually become troublemakers outside of the classroom by participating in risky behaviors like joining a gang.[295] At the same time, American educators turn into teaching technicians or *cheaters* themselves to falsely boost their students' test scores.[296] How can America resist the counterproductive results of test-centric climates, and produce future innovators?

We must recognize the creative potential in every individual (children and adults) rather than stigmatizing them as troublemakers. My mentor Dr. Torrance (the Father of Creativity) discovered this when he took his first teaching position after graduating from college in 1937. He taught at Georgia Military College, a vocational high school for students who were labeled "troublemakers" and were unable to attend local schools. He found "a special spark" in these students, which spurred him to start pursuing a graduate degree in psychology. Thereafter, he returned to a career in teaching and counseling but was drafted in 1945 to serve as a psychologist for the US Air Force in WWII. He saw the same "spark" in the best jet aces during WWII and the Korean War, whom he trained for survival. He found that the spark was the creative attitudes that enabled their creative-thinking skills.[297] Like cacti's attitudes, Dr. Torrance's "troublemakers" displayed the 4S attitudes, which were instrumental to their survival and success, but when they were in anti-creative climates, they were viewed negatively by others.

Most of the greatest innovators in history, including Albert Einstein, Steve Jobs, Nelson Mandela, Georgia O'Keeffe, and Marie Curie, were never good at memorization or rote learning, and they were also labeled troublemakers due to their 4S attitudes when they were in anti-creative climates. We must learn from this, and instead of pushing children to perform well on tests or achieve academically, we must identify their CPI. We must look at the positive long-term aspects of their 4S attitudes, including personality traits and behaviors that seem prickly, so we can encourage the underlying 4S attitudes that enable their ION thinking skills, which are further enabled by prickly attitudes such as the daydreaming, resilient, nonconforming, and defiant attitudes.

Also, all individuals must view their 4S attitudes positively. Both as a student and as a teacher in Korea, I saw myself as a failure and a hopeless troublemaker. Later, in my married life, I felt the same failure until I experienced the 4S climates at the Torrance Center in America. Dr. Torrance had no children, but he considered his students to be his children. (He supported poor graduate students' tuition—they still think the support came from the university, not from him.) Dr. Torrance became my "grandfather" (he and I share the same birthday, October 8!), and he inspired me to become the "Granddaughter of Creativity." (I never met my own grandfather.) My frustrated dreams that I experienced in the Confucian anti-creative climates became my passion as I developed my expertise in creativity assessment and development in the over ten years I lived in the 4S climates of America. If I had not experienced the 4S climates and found mentors who recognized my creative potential and provided me with various academic resources and experiences (in the soil climate); inspired me to become an innovator by playfully introducing various theories and research results to me (in the sun climate); challenged me with extremely high expectations and brutally honest feedback (in the storm climate); and liberated me from the Confucian conformity and enabled me to discover and develop my individuality and uniqueness (in the space climate), I often wonder what kind of dissatisfied troublemaker would I have become. (Despite our difficult history, I still like my mother-in-law because she loves my son—and my daughter too, now—and when I became a professor at Eastern Michigan University in 2005, I thanked her for abusing me so thoroughly that I fled Korea to become successful in America!)

I fear that America is sharpening its tiger claws and slipping into an orange-and-black-striped costume to educate children. With an open-minded attitude, it's useful to learn from others, including tiger mothers and Confucian cultures. However, a complete adoption of tiger-mother parenting/teaching—and especially Confucian exam hell—will not lead to innovation. Parents and educators from America's past were comfortable with and understood that not all the answers could be found on standardized tests. They cultivated the 4S climates and nurtured the 4S attitudes. They produced children who were resourceful cross-pollinators, curious optimists, resilient hard workers, and defiant dreamers who applied ION thinking skills for innovation. The defiant spirit—not test-taking skill—resulted in generations of American innovators.

When we succeed in cultivating the 4S climates and nurturing individuals' 4S attitudes, we follow the footsteps of those who inspired, encouraged, taught, challenged, and mentored the greatest innovators in history. Only individuals who experience the diverse soil climate (diverse resources and experiences), the bright sun climate (inspiration and encouragement), the fierce storm climate (high expectations and challenges), and the free space climate (freedom to be alone and unique) can become the *innovative* light of the world!

NOTES

Chapter 1: The Creativity Crisis

1. Torrance Center, College of Education, University of Georgia, "2012 Torrance Lecture: The Creativity Crisis," *The Torrance Center for Creativity and Talent Development Spring 2012 Newsletter*, March 25, 2012, http://www.coe.uga.edu/torrance/news-events/.

2. Po Bronson and Ashley Merryman, "The Creativity Crisis," *Newsweek*, July 10, 2010. *Reporters originally sought my expertise on assessing creativity, not "Creativity Crisis" data.

3. Jonathan A. Plucker and Joseph S. Renzulli, "Psychometric Approaches to the Study of Human Creativity," in *Handbook of Creativity*, ed. Robert J. Sternberg (New York: Cambridge University Press, 1999), 35–61.

4. KH Kim, "The Creativity Crisis: The Decrease in Creative Thinking Score on the Torrance Tests of Creative Thinking," *Creativity Research Journal* 23, no. 4 (2011): 285–95.

5. Ibid.

6. Press Release, "MDC Partners and Allison and Partners Study Reveals Leading CEOs and CMOs View Creativity as a Critical Driver of the Global Economy," *Reuters*, October 4, 2011, http://www.reuters.com /article/2011/10/04/idUS123764+04-Oct-2011+BW20111004.

7. Kathryn A. Price and Anthea M. Tinker, "Creativity in Later Life," *Maturitas* 78, no. 4 (2014): 281–86; Carl R. Rogers, "Towards a Theory of Creativity," *ETC: A Review of General Semantics* 11, no. 4 (1954): 249–60; Mark A. Runco, "Creativity," *Annual Review of Psychology* 55 (2004): 657–87; Mark A. Runco and Ruth Richards, eds., *Eminent Creativity, Everyday Creativity, and Health* (Norwood, NJ: Ablex, 1997).

8. KH Kim, "Underachievement and Creativity: Are Gifted Underachievers Highly Creative?" *Creativity Research Journal* 20, no. 2 (2008): 234–42; KH Kim and Michael F. Hull, "Creative Personality and Anti-Creative Environment for High School Dropouts," *Creativity Research Journal* 24, no. 2–3 (2012): 169–76; KH Kim and Joyce VanTassel-Baska, "The Relationship between Creativity and Behavior Problems among Underachievers," *Creativity Research Journal* 22, no. 2 (2010): 185–93.

9. M. K. Raina, "Cross-Cultural Differences," in *Encyclopedia of Creativity*, eds. Mark A. Runco and Steven R. Pritzke (San Diego, CA: Academic, 1999), 453–64.

10. Richard Freeman, "Econocatastrophobia: Dissecting American Fears of Economic Decline in the New Global Economy," *Cornellcast*, Connell University, October 11, 2013, http://www.cornell.edu/video/harvard-professor-richard-freeman-on-american-fears-economic-decline; Matt Hourihan, "Federal R & D Budget Trends: A Short Summary," *American Association for the Advancement of Science*, January 15, 2015, http://www.aaas.org/news/primer-recent-trends-federal-rd-budgets.

11. David H. Cropley and Arthur J. Cropley, "Fostering Creativity in Engineering in Engineering Undergraduates," *High Ability Studies* 11, no. 2 (2000): 207–19.

12. Kim, "Creativity Crisis"; E. Paul Torrance and H. Tammy Safter, "Are Children Becoming More Creative?" *Journal of Creative Behavior* 20, no. 1 (1986): 1–13; E. Paul Torrance, "The Creative Personality and the Ideal Pupil," *Teachers College Record* 65, no. 3 (1963): 220–26; E. Paul Torrance, "Students of the Future: Their Abilities, Achievements, and Images of the Future," *Creative Child and Adult Quarterly* 1, no. 2 (1976): 76–90; E. Paul Torrance and Janet Ross, *Improving Social Studies in Minnesota* (Minneapolis: University of Minnesota, 1961).

13. Freeman, "Econocatastrophobia"; KH Kim, "Learning from Each Other: Creativity in East

Asian and American Education," *Creativity Research Journal* 17, no. 4 (2005): 337–47; Paul Krugman, "The Insecure American," *New York Times*, May 29, 2015, http://www.nytimes.com/2015/05/29/opinion/paul-krugman-the-insecure-american.html?_r=0; Adam Seth Levine, *American Insecurity: Why Our Economic Fears Lead to Political Inaction* (Princeton, NJ: Princeton University Press, 2015); Robert M. Morgan, "Educational Reform: Top-Down or Bottom-Up?" *Educational Technology* 32, no. 11 (1992): 47–51; Nel Noddings, "Thinking about Standards," *Phi Delta Kappan* 79, no. 3 (1997): 184–89; Gwen Ellyn Nordquist, "Japanese Education: No Recipe for Authentic Learning," *Educational Leadership* 50, no. 7 (1993): 64–67; NPR, "A Rhodes-Like Scholarship for Study in China," NPR, May 2, 2013, http://www.npr.org/2013/05/02/178783650/a-rhodes-like-scholarship-for-study-in-china; Jeanne Sahadi, "20% of Americans Hit by Major Economic Loss," CNN Money, July 22, 2010, http://money.cnn.com/2010/07/2 1/news/economy/economic_insecurity/; Robert J. Sternberg and James C. Kaufman, "Constraints on Creativity: Obvious and Not So Obvious," in *The Cambridge Handbook of Creativity*, eds. James C. Kaufman and Robert J. Sternberg (New York: Cambridge University Press, 2010), 467–82; E. Paul Torrance, "Lessons about Giftedness and Creativity from a Nation of 115 Million Overachievers," *Gifted Child Quarterly* 24, no. 1 (1980): 10–14; E. Paul Torrance, "What Might We Learn from the Japanese about Giftedness and Creativity?" *Gifted Child Today* 13 (1980): 2–9; E. Paul Torrance, "Education for 'Quality Circles' in Japanese Schools," *Journal of Research and Development in Education* 15, no. 2 (1982): 11–15.

14. For example, Levine, *American Insecurity*; Sternberg and Kaufman, "Constraints."

15. Bruce B. Henderson, Melvin H. Marx, and Yung Che Kim, "Academic Interests and Perceived Competence in American, Japanese and Korean Children," *Journal of Cross-Cultural Psychology* 30, no. 1 (1999): 32–50.

16. Pew Research Center, "A Portrait of 'Generation Next': How Young People View Their Lives, Futures and Politics," *Pew Research Center U.S. Politics and Policy*, January 9, 2007, http://www.people-press.org/2007/01/09/a-portrait-of-generation-next/.

17. Hourihan, "Federal."

18. Ibid; OECD (Organization for Economic Co-operation and Development), "China Headed to Overtake EU, US in Science and Technology Spending, OECD Says," *OECD Newsroom*, June 2014, http://www.oecd.org/newsroom/china-headed-to-overtake-eu-us-in-science-technology-spending.htm.

19. Lauren Morello, "More Cuts Loom for US Science: Stalemate in Congress Puts Spending Plans on Hold," *Nature*, September, 11, 2013, http://www.nature.com/news/more-cuts-loom-for-us-science-1.13720; National Science Board, "Research and Development: Essential Foundation for U.S. Competitiveness in a Global Economy," February 6, 2015, http://www.nsf.gov/statistics/nsb0803/start .htm?CFID=11916165and CFTOKEN=88593538and js essionid=f030c18b9118f2a515a9121639512 16703d6; US Patent and Trademark Office Patent Technology Monitoring Team (PYMT), "U.S. Patent Statistics Chart Calendar Years 1963–2014," US Patent and Trademark Office, March 18, 2015, http://www.uspto.gov/web/offices/ac/ido/oeip/taf/us_stat.htm.

20. Richard B. Freeman and Wei Huang, "China's 'Great Leap Forward' in Science and Engineering," in *Global Mobility of Research Scientists: The Economics of Who Goes Where and Why* (Elsevier, forthcoming).

21. Hourihan, "Primer"; Hourihan, "Federal."

22. Hourihan, "Federal."

23. Defense Advanced Research Projects Agency, "Where the Future Becomes Now," http://www.darpa.mil/about-us/darpa-history-and-timeline; Davey Winder, "10 Brilliant DADPA Inventions," alphr.com, March 16, 2012, http://www.alphr.com/features/373546/10-brilliant-darpa-inventions.

24. Morello, "Cuts"; National Science Board, "Research."

25. Liz Szabo, "NIH Director: Budget Cuts Put U.S. Science at Risk," *USA Today*, April 23, 2014, http://www.usatod ay.com/story/news/nation/2014/04/23/nih-budget-cuts/8056113/.

26. Sternberg and Kaufman, "Constraints."

27. Szabo, "NIH."

28. Boer Deng, "Congress Is Terrible at Science—and This Should Make Us Worried," *Weigel*,

May 7, 2014, http://www.slate.com/blogs/weigel/2014/05/07/the_first_bill_is_terrible_for_american_science_and_declining_research_funds.html.

29. William J. Clinton, "Remarks in a Roundtable Discussion on Education," *Weekly Compilation of President Documents* 33 (1997a): 443–47; William J. Clinton, "Remarks in a Roundtable Discussion on Education," *Weekly Compilation of President Documents* 33 (1997b): 848–50; Hy Kim, "A Comparative Study between an American and a Republic of Korean Textbook Series' Coverage of Measurement and Geometry Content in First through Eighth Grades," *School Science and Mathematics* 93 (1993): 123–26; Nordquist, "Japanese"; Scott D. Thomson, "How Much Do Americans Value Schooling?" *NASSP Bulletin* 73, no. 519 (1989): 51–67; Mortimer B. Zuckerman, "Why Schools Need Standards," *U. S. News & World Report* 121, no. 11 (1996): 128.

30. Morgan, "Educational"; Kim, "Learning"; Noddings, "Thinking"; Nordquist, "Japanese"; H. W. Stevenson and J. W. Stigler, *The Learning Gap: Why Our Schools Are Failing and What We Can Learn from Japanese and Chinese Education* (New York: Summit, 1992); Torrance, "Lessons"; Torrance, "What Might"; Torrance, "Education."

31. Kim, "Learning"; K. Cox, "Mathematics Performance Standards: Grades K–12," PowerPoint presentation, December 2003, http://wc.gpb.org/vs/binary_data/vs_webcasting/.

32. NPR, "Rhodes-Like."

33. Jihyun Lee, "Universals and Specifics of Math Self-Concept, Math Self-Efficacy, and Math Anxiety across 41 PISA 2003 Participating Countries," *Learning and Individual Differences* 19, no. 3 (2009): 355–65; Ina V. S. Mullis, Michael O. Martin, and Pierre Foy, *TIMSS 2007 International Mathematics Report: Findings from IEA's Trends in International Mathematics and Science Study at the Fourth and Eighth Grades* (Chestnut Hill, MA: TIMSS & PIRLS International Study Center, Boston College, 2008); National Center for Education Statistics, *Program for International Student Assessment (PISA): PISA 2009 Results*, April 10, 2016, http://nces.ed.gov/surveys/pisa/pisa2009highlights.asp.

34. So Yoon Yoon and Marcia Gentry, "Racial and Ethnic Representation in Gifted Programs: Current Status of and Implications for Gifted Asian American Students," *Gifted Child Quarterly* 53 (2009): 121–36.

35. US Census Bureau, "Educational Attainment by Race and Hispanic Origin: The 2012 Statistical Abstract," US Department of Commerce: Economics and Statistics Administration, http://www.ensus.gov/compendia/statabhttps.

36. Pew Research Center, "The Rise of Asian Americans," *Pew Research Center: Social and Demographic Trends*, April 4, 2013, http://www.pewsocialtrends.org/2012/06/19/the-rise-of-Asian Americans/2/.

37. Ibid.

38. Clinton, "Remarks," 443–47; Clinton, "Remarks," 848–50; Public Law No. 107–110, § 6301 (3), No Child Left Behind, 2002, http://www.ed.gov/policy/elsec/leg/esea02/index.html; US Department of Education, Race to the Top Fund, 2010, http://www2.ed.gov/programs/racetothetop/index.html.

39. Public Law No. 107–110.

40. US Department of Education, Race; Amy Stuart Wells, "'Our Children's Burden': A History of Federal Education Policies That Ask (Now Require) Our Public Schools to Solve Societal Inequality," in *NCLB at the Crossroads: Reexamining the Federal Effort to Close the Achievement Gap*, eds. Michael A. Rebell and Jessica R. Wolff (New York: Teachers College, 2009), 1–42.

41. Alison Dobrick, "Poverty and Pretense: Good Intentions and Misguided Educational Reform from No Child Left Behind through Race to the Top," in *The Obama Administration and Educational Reform: Advances in Education in Diverse Communities: Research, Policy and Praxis* vol.10 (Bingley, UK: Emerald Group, 2014), 27–44.

42. Ronald S. Anderson, "An American View of Japanese Education," *Phi Delta Kappan* 39 (1957): 99–103; Edward Foster, "'Exam Hell' in Japan," *Change* 5, no. 6 (1973): 16–19; Cheng-Hsien Li and Jing-Jyi Wu, "The Structural Relationships between Optimism and Innovative Behavior:

Understanding Potential Antecedents and Mediating Effects," *Creativity Research Journal* 23 (2011): 119–28; Kim, "Learning"; Ju-min Park and Jane Chung, "Military Discipline for 'Soldiers' on Korea Exam's Front Line," *Reuters*, November 5, 2012, http://www.reuters.com/article/2012/11/05/us-korea-exam-idUSBRE8A408Q20121105; Jean Wollam, "Equality versus Excellence: The South Korean Dilemma in Gifted Education," *Roeper Review* 14 (1992): 212–17.

43. Lisa M. Abrams, Joseph J. Pedulla, and George F. Madaus, "Views from the Classroom: Teachers' Opinions of Statewide Testing Programs," *Theory into Practice* 42, no. 1 (2003): 18–29.

44. Ibid; Mehmet Aydeniz and Sherry A. Southerland, "National Survey of Middle and High School Science Teachers' Responses to Standardized Testing: Is Science Being Devalued in Schools?" *Journal of Science Teacher Education* 23, no. 3 (2012): 233–57; Linda Darling-Hammond and Elle Rustique-Forrester, "The Consequences of Student Testing for Teaching and Teacher Quality," *Yearbook of the National Society for the Study of Education* 104, no. 2 (2005): 289–319; Tonya R. Moon, Catherine M. Brighton, and Carolyn M. Callahan, "State Standardized Testing Programs: Friend or Foe of Gifted Education," *Roeper Review* 25, no. 2 (2003): 49–60.

45. Arnold Aprill, "Toward a Finer Description of the Connection between Arts Education and Student Achievement," *Arts Education Policy Review* 102, no. 5 (2001): 25–26; Laura H. Chapman, "Status of Elementary Art Education: 1997–2004," *Studies in Art Education* (2005): 118–37; Thomas S. Dee, Brian Jacob, and Nathaniel L. Schwartz, "The Effects on NCLB on School Resources and Practices," *Educational Evaluation and Policy Analysis* 35, no. 2 (2013): 252–79; Brian A. Jacob and Thomas S. Dee, "The Impact of No Child Left Behind on Students, Teachers, and Schools," *Brookings Papers on Economy Activity* (Fall 2010), http://www.brookings.edu/ab out/projects/bpea/papers/2010/impact-of-no-child-left-behind-dee; Linda Darling-Hammond and Elle Rustique-Forrester, "The Consequences of Student Testing," 289–19; Gayle B. Roege and KH Kim, "Why We Need Art Education," *Empirical Studies of the Arts* 31, no. 2 (2013): 121–30.

46. Kathy Hirsh-Pasek et al., *A Mandate for Playful Learning* (Oxford: Oxford University Press, 2009); Robert Wood Johnson Foundation, *The State of Play: Gallup Survey of Principals on School Recess*, February 2010, http://www.rwjf.org/pr/p roduct.jsp?id=55249.

47. Patricia Lavon Hanna, "Gaining Global Perspective: Educational Language Policy and Planning," *International Journal of Bilingual Education and Bilingualism* 14, no. 6 (2011): 733–49; Kate Menken, *English Learners Left behind Standardized Testing as Language Policy* (New York: Multilingual Matters, 2008).

48. Abrams, Pedulla, and Madaus, "Views."

49. Michael Winerip, "Standardized Tests Face a Crisis over Standards," *New York Times*, March 22, 2006, http://www.nytimes.com/2006/03/22/education/22education.html?pagewanted=all.

50. Abrams, Pedulla, and Madaus, "Views"; Sam Dillon, "Schools Cut back Subjects to Push Reading and Math," *New York Times*, March 26, 2006, http://www.nytimes.com/2006/03/26/education/26child.html?pagewanted=alland _r=0; Dobrick, "Poverty"; Jamel K. Donner and Kmt G. Shockley, "'Leaving Us Behind': A Political Economic Interpretation of NCLB and the Miseducation of African American Males," *Educational Foundations* 24, no. 3/4 (2010): 43–54; Maureen Duffy et al., "No Child Left Behind: Values and Research Issues in High-Stakes Assessments," *Counseling and Values* 53, no. 1 (2008): 53–66; Kim and Hull, "Creative"; Kate McReynolds, "The No Child Left Behind Act Raises Growing Concerns," *Encounter: Education for Meaning and Social Justice* 19, no. 2 (2006): 33–36.

51. Howard Gardner, *Frames of Mind: The Theory of Multiple Intelligences* (New York: Basic Books, 1983); Allen Trent and Jorge-Ayn Riley, "Re-Placing the Arts in Elementary School Curricula: An Interdisciplinary, Collaborative Action Research Project," *Penn GSE Perspectives on Urban Education* 6, no. 2 (2009): 14–28.

52. Dee, Jacob, and Schwartz, "Effects"; Richard M. Haynes and Donald M. Chalker, "World-Class Schools," *American School Board Journal* 184, no. 5 (1997): 20–26; Richard M. Haynes and Donald M. Chalker, "The Making of a World-Class Elementary School," *Principal* 77, no. 3 (1998): 5–6, 8–9; Kim, "Learning"; Russell W. Rumberger, "Can NCLB Improve High School Graduation

Rates?" in *Holding NCLB Accountable: Achieving Accountability, Equity, and School Reform*, ed. Gail L. Sunderman (Thousand Oaks, CA: Corwin, 2008), 209–22; Andrew Trotter, "Korea Tops U.S. in Key Education Ratings," *Education Week* 23, no. 4 (2003): 3.

53. Haynes and Chalker, "World-Class"; Taipei National Tax Administration, "Scope of Exemption," Ministry of Finance, 2012, http://www.ntat.gov.tw/co unty/ntat_ch/ntat_en/en9-02-3-10 .jsp; Thomson, "How"; Esther Lee Yao and Fred D. Kierstead, "Can Asian Educational Systems Be Models for American Education? An Appraisal," *NASSP Bulletin* 68, no. 476 (1984): 82–89.

54. Kathryn A. McDermott and Laura S. Jensen, "Dubious Sovereignty: Federal Conditions of Aid and the No Child Left Behind Act," *Peabody Journal of Education* 80, no. 2 (2005): 39–56; Stephen R. Neely, "No Child Left Behind and Administrative Costs: A Resource Dependence Study of Local School Districts," *Education Policy Analysis Archives* 23, no. 26 (2015), http://dx.doi .org/10.14507/epaa.v23.1785.

55. Rumberger, "NCLB."

56. Dobrick, "Poverty"; Malkeet Singh, "A Longitudinal Study of a State-Wide Reading Assessment: The Importance of Early Achievement and Socio-Demographic Factors," *Educational Research and Evaluation* 19, no. 1 (2013): 4–18.

57. Betty Hart and Todd R. Risley, "The Early Catastrophe: The 30 Million Word Gap," *American Educator* 27, no. 1 (2003): 4–9.

58. Singh, "Longitudinal."

59. McDermott and Jensen, "Dubious"; Neely, "Child."

60. Bruce D. Baker, "State Policy Influences on the Internal Allocation of School District Resources: Evidence from the Common Core of Data," *Journal of Education Finance* 29, no. 2 (2003): 1–24; John Bohte, "School Bureaucracy and Student Performance at the Local Level," *Public Administration Review* 61, no. 1 (2001): 92–99; John E. Chubb and Terry M. Moe, *Politics, Markets, and America's Schools* (Washington, DC: Brookings Institution, 1990); McDermott and Jensen, "Dubious"; Neely, "Child"; Christopher A. Simon, "Public School Administration: Employing Thompson's Structural Contingency Theory to Explain Public School Administrative Expenditures in Washington State," *Administration and Society* 31, no. 4 (1999): 525–41; Pamela S. Tolbert, "Institutional Environments and Resource Dependence: Sources of Administrative Structure in Institutions of Higher Education," *Administrative Science Quarterly* 30, no. 1 (1985): 1–13.

61. Center for Education Policy, *From the Capital to the Classroom: Year 4 of the No Child Left Behind Act* (Washington: Canter on Education Policy, 2006).

62. Abrams, Pedulla, and Madaus, "Views."

63. Menken, *English.*

64. Duffy et al., "Child"; McReynolds, "Child."

65. Andrew Salute, Kristin M. Murphy, and Brittany Aronson, "What Can We Learn from the Atlanta Cheating Scandal?" *Phi Delta Kappan* 97, no. 6 (2016): 48–52.

66. G. Bohrnstedt, S. Kitmitto, B. Ogut, D. Sherman, and D. Chan, "School Composition and the Black–White Achievement Gap (NCES 2015-018)," US Department of Education, National Center for Education Statistics, June 2015, http://nces.ed.gov/nationsreportcard/subject/studies/pdf/school _composition_and_the_bw_achievement_gap_2015.pdf; Mary Byrne et al, "Top 12 Concerns about Every Student Succeeds Act, § 1177 & HR 5," December 2, 2015, http://truthinamericaneducation .com/elementary-and-secondary-education-act/top-12-concerns-about-every-studesnt-succeeds-act-s -1177-hr-5/; Jaekyung Lee, *Tracking Achievement Gaps and Assessing the Impact of NCLB on the Gaps: An In-Depth Look into Nation and State Reading and Math Outcome Trends* (Cambridge, MA: Harvard University, 2006); Jaekyung Lee, Hyejin Shin, and Laura Casey Amo, "Evaluating the Impact of NCLB School Interventions in New York State: Does One Size Fit All?" *Education Policy Analysis Archives* 21, no. 67 (2013), http://epaa.asu.edu/ojs/article/view/1122; Singh, "Longitudinal Study"; Manyee Wong, Thomas D. Cook, and Peter M. Steiner, "Adding Design Elements to Improve Time Series Designs: No Child Left Behind as an Example of Causal Pattern-Matching," *Journal of Research on Educational Effectiveness* 8, no. 2 (2015): 245–79.

67. McReynolds, "Child"; Sternberg and Kaufman, "Constraints."

68. Jennifer Medina, "On New York School Tests, Warning Signs Ignored," *New York Times*, October 10, 2010, http://www.nytimes.com/2010/10/11/education/11scores.html?pagewanted=all&_r=1.

69. Byrne et al, "Concerns"; Manny Otiko, "Critics Concerned Obama's Every Student Succeeds Act Won't Fix the Problems in American Schools," December 11, 2015, http://atlantablackstar .com/2015/12/11/critics-concerned-obamas-every-student-succeeds-act-wont-fix-problems-american -schools/; Alan Singer, "Will Every Student Succeed? Not with This New Law," December 6, 2015, http://www.huffingtonpost.com/alan-singer/will-every-student-succee_b_8730956.html; Mary Battenfeld, "Why Every Student Succeeds Act Still Leaves Most Vulnerable Kids Behind," *U.S. News & World Report*, December 14, 2015, http://www.usnews.com/news/articles/2015-12-14/why-every -student-succeeds-act-still-leaves-most-vulnerable-kids-behind; Alia Wong, "The Bloated Rhetoric of No Child Left Behind's Demise," December 9, 2015, http://www.theatlantic.com/education/ archive/2015/12/the-bloated-rhetoric-of-no-child-left-behinds-demise/419688/.

Chapter 2: The Creativity Solution

1. Frank Barron, "Creative Vision and Expression in Writing and Painting," in *The Creative Person*, ed. Donald W. MacKinnon (Berkeley: University of California, 1961), 237–51; David H. Feldman, "A Follow-Up of Subjects Scoring above 180 IQ in Terman's Genetic Studies of Genius," *Exceptional Children* 50 (1984): 518–23; J. P. Guilford, "Creativity," *American Psychologist* 5 (1950): 444–54; J. P. Guilford, *The Nature of Human Intelligence* (New York: McGraw-Hill, 1967); J. P. Guilford and Paul R. Christensen, "The One-Way Relation between Creative Potential and IQ," *Journal of Creative Behavior* 7, no. 4 (1973): 247–52; KH Kim, "Can Only Intelligent People Be Creative? A Meta-Analysis," *Journal of Secondary Gifted Education* 16 (2005): 57–66; KH Kim, "Meta-Analyses of the Relationship of Creative Achievement to Both IQ and Divergent Thinking Test Scores, *Journal of Creative Behavior* 42, no. 2 (2008): 106–30; Donald W. MacKinnon, "Creativity in Architects," in *The Creative Person*, ed. Donald W. MacKinnon (Berkeley, CA: University of California, 1961), 291–320; Donald W. MacKinnon, "Educating for Creativity: A Modern Myth?" in *Training Creative Thinking*, eds. Gary A. Davis and Joseph A. Scott (Melbourne, FL: Krieger, 1978), 194–207.

2. Robert McCrae, "Creativity, Divergent Thinking, and Openness to Experience," *Journal of Personality and Social Psychology* 52, no. 6 (1987): 1258–65; Mark A. Runco, "Interrater Agreement on a Socially Valid Measure of Students' Creativity," *Psychological Reports* 61 (1987): 1009–10; Mark A. Runco, "Creativity," *Annual Review of Psychology* 55 (2004): 657–87; Mark A. Runco, Diane Johnson, and Patricia K. Bear, "Parents' and Teachers' Implicit Theories of Children's Creativity," *Child Study Journal* 23, no. 2 (1993): 91–113; Robert J. Sternberg and James C. Kaufman, "Constraints on Creativity: Obvious and Not So Obvious," in *The Cambridge Handbook of Creativity*, eds. James C. Kaufman and Robert J. Sternberg (New York: Cambridge University Press, 2010), 467–82.

3. Elisabeth Rudowicz and Anna Hui, "The Creative Personality: Hong Kong Perspective," *Journal of Social Behavior and Personality* 12, no. 1 (1997): 139–57; Elisabeth Rudowicz, Anna Hui, and Helen Ku-Yu, "Implicit Theories of Creativity in Hong Kong Chinese Population," in *Proceedings of the Third Asia-Pacific Conference on Giftedness: Creativity for the 21st Century*, eds. S. Cho, J. O. Park, and J. W. Moon (Seoul, Korea, 1996), 197–206; Hae-Ae Seo, Eun Ah Lee, and KH Kim, "Korean Science Teachers' Understanding of Creativity in Gifted Education," *Journal of Secondary Gifted Education* 16, no. 2–3 (2005): 98–105.

4. Runco, "Creativity"; Dean Keith Simonton, *Greatness: Who Makes History and Why* (New York: Guilford, 1994); Dean Keith Simonton, "Political Pathology and Societal Creativity," *Creativity Research Journal* 3, no. 2 (1990): 85–99; Robert J. Sternberg, "Implicit Theories of Intelligence, Creativity and Wisdom," *Journal of Personality and Social Psychology* 49, no. 3 (1985): 607–27.

5. Robert S. Root-Bernstein and Michele M. Root-Bernstein, *Sparks of Genius: The Thirteen Thinking Tools of the World's Most Creative People* (Boston, MA: Houghton Mifflin, 1999); Albert

Rothenberg, "The Janusian Process in Scientific Creativity," *Creativity Research Journal* 9, no. 2–3 (1996): 207–31; Sternberg and Kaufman, "Constraints"; Thomas B. Ward, Steven M. Smith, and Ronald A. Finke, "Creative Cognition," in *Handbook of Creativity*, ed. Robert J. Sternberg (New York: Cambridge University Press, 1999), 189–212.

6. Dean Keith Simonton, *Genius 101*, The Psych 101 Series (New York: Springer, 2009).

7. Samuel D. Gosling, Carson J. Sandy, and Jeff Potter, "Personalities of Self-Identified 'Dog People' and 'Cat People,'" *Anthrozoos: A Multidisciplinary Journal of the Interactions of People and Animals* 23 (2010): 213–22; Charles E. Schaefer, "Imaginary Companions and Creative Adolescents," *Developmental Psychology* 1 (1969): 747–49; Charles E. Schaefer, *Biographical Inventory-Creativity* (San Diego, CA: Educational and Industrial Testing Service, 1970).

8. Jacob W. Getzels and Mihaly Csikszentmihalyi, *Creative Thinking in Art Students—An Exploratory Study* (Chicago: University of Chicago Press, 1964); Alfred Louis Kroeber, *Configuration of Culture Growth* (Berkeley: University of California Press, 1944); David Lamb and Susan M. Easton, *Multiple Discovery: The Pattern of Scientific Progress* (Trowbridge, UK: Avebury, 1984); Sternberg and Kaufman, "Constraints"; Leslie A. White, *The Science of Culture: A Study of Man and Civilization* (New York: Farrar, Straus, 1949).

9. Kathryn A. Price and Anthea M. Tinker, "Creativity in Later Life," *Maturitas* 78, no. 4 (2014): 281–86; Carl R. Rogers, "Towards a Theory of Creativity," *ETC: A Review of General Semantics* 11, no. 4 (1954): 249–60; Runco, "Creativity"; Mark A. Runco and Ruth Richards, eds., *Eminent Creativity, Everyday Creativity, and Health* (Norwood, NJ: Ablex, 1997).

10. Robert S. Albert, "Observations and Suggestions Regarding Giftedness, Familial Influence, and the Achievement of Eminence," *Gifted Child Quarterly* 22, no. 2 (1978): 201–11; Robert S. Albert, "The Contribution of Early Family History to the Achievement Eminence," in *Proceedings of the Wallace Symposium on Talent*, eds. Nicholas Colangelo, Susan G. Assouline, and DeAnn L. Ambroson (Iowa City: University of Iowa Press, 1993), 311–60; Anne Anastasi and Charles E. Schaefer, "Biographical Correlates of Artistic and Literary Creativity in Adolescent Girls," *Journal of Applied Psychology* 53, no. 4 (1969): 267–73; Benjamin S. Bloom, *Developing Talent in Young People* (New York: Ballantine Books, 1985); Arthur J. Cropley, *Creativity* (London: Longmans, 1967); Mihaly Csikszentmihalyi, "Implications of a Systems Perspective for the Study of Creativity," in *Handbook of Creativity*, ed. Robert J. Sternberg (New York: Cambridge University Press, 1999), 313–35; Kathleen Dewing and Ronald Taft, "Some Characteristics of the Parents of Creative Twelve-Year-Olds," *Journal of Personality* 41, no. 1 (1973): 71–85; George Domino, "Maternal Personality Correlates of Sons' Creativity," *Journal of Consulting and Clinical Psychology* 33, no. 2 (1969): 180–83; Albert S. Dreyer and Mary Beth Wells, "Parental Values, Parental Control, and Creativity in Young Children," *Journal of Marriage and the Family* 28, no. 1 (1966): 83–88; Danielle D. Fearon, Daelynn Copeland, and Terrill F. Saxon, "The Relationship between Parenting Styles and Creativity in a Sample of Jamaican Children," *Creativity Research Journal* 25, no. 1 (2013): 119–28; Jacob Getzels and Philip Jackson, *Creativity and Intelligence* (New York: Wiley, 1962); Caria Goble, James D. Moran III, and Anne K. Bomba, "Maternal Teaching Techniques and Preschool Children's Ideational Fluency," *Creativity Research Journal* 4, no. 3 (1991): 273–79; Kristen M. Kemple and Shari A. Nissengberg, "Nurturing Creativity in Early Childhood Education: Families Are Part of It," *Early Childhood Education* 28 (2000): 67–71; Barbara Kerr and Corissa Chopp, "Families and Creativity," in *Encyclopedia of Creativity*, eds. Mark A. Runco and Steven R. Pritzker (New York: Academic, 1999), 709–15; Robert J. Kirschenbaum, *Understanding the Creative Activity of Students* (St. Louis, MO: Creative Learning, 1989); Woong Lim and Jonathan A. Plucker, "Creativity through a Lens of Social Responsibility: Implicit Theories of Creativity with Korean Samples," *Journal of Creativity Behavior* 35 (2001) 115–30; Todd I. Lubart, "Creativity across Cultures," in *Handbook of Creativity*, ed. Robert J. Sternberg (Boston, MA: Cambridge University Press, 1999), 339–50; Todd I. Lubart, "Creativity and Cross-Cultural Variation," *International Journal of Psychology* 25 (1990): 39–59; Donald W. MacKinnon, "The Nature and Nurture of Creative Talent," *American Psychologist* 17, no. 7 (1962): 484–95; Angie L. Miller, Amber D. Lambert, and Kristie L. Speirs Neumeister, "Parenting

Style, Perfectionism, and Creativity in High-Ability and High-Achieving Young Adults," *Journal for the Education of the Gifted* 35 (2012): 344–65; Robert E. Myers and E. Paul Torrance, "Can Teachers Encourage Creative Thinking?" *Educational Leadership* 19, no. 3 (1961): 156–59; Leigh M. O'Brien and Sham'ah Md-Yunus, "For Parents Particularly: How Parents Can Encourage Creativity in Children," *Childhood Education* 83, no. 4 (2007): 236–37; James S. Raw and Kevin Marjoribanks, "Family and School Correlates of Adolescents' Creativity, Morality and Self Concept," *Educational Studies* 17, no. 2 (1991): 183–90; Rudowicz and Hui, "Personality"; Runco, "Creativity"; Charles E. Schaefer and Anne Anastasi, "A Biographical Inventory for Identifying Creativity in Adolescent Boys," *Journal of Applied Phycology* 52 no. 1 (1968): 42–48; Seo, Lee, and Kim, "Korean"; Morris I. Stein, *Stimulating Creativity: Individual Procedures* (New York: Academic, 1974); Sternberg and Kaufman, "Constraints"; Robert J. Sternberg and Todd I. Lubart, "The Concept of Creativity: Prospects and Paradigms," in *Handbook of Creativity*, ed. Robert J. Sternberg (Boston, MA: Cambridge University Press, 1999), 3–15; Paul S. Weisberg and Kayla J. Springer, "Environmental Factors in Creative Function: A Study of Gifted Children," *Archives of General Psychology* 5 (1961): 554–64; Xiao Dong Yue and Elisabeth Rudowicz, "Perception of the Most Creative Chinese by Undergraduates in Beijing, Guangzhou, Hong Kong, and Taipei," *Journal of Creative Behavior* 36, no. 2 (2002): 88–104.

11. Mihaly Csikszentmihalyi, "Society, Culture, and Person: A Systems View of Creativity," in *The Nature of Creativity: Contemporary Psychological Perspectives*, ed. Robert J. Sternberg (New York: Cambridge University Press, 1988), 325–39; Csikszentmihalyi, "Implications"; David J. Sill, "Integrative Thinking, Synthesis, and Creativity in Interdisciplinary Studies," *Journal of General Education* 50, no. 4 (2001): 288–311; Stein, *Stimulating*.

12. Gregory J. Feist, "A Meta-Analysis of Personality in Scientific and Artistic Creativity," *Personality and Social Psychology Review* 2, no. 4 (1998): 290–309; Harrison G. Gough, "A Creative Personality Scale for the Adjective Check List," *Journal of Personality and Social Psychology* 37, no. 8 (1979): 1398–1405; Ng Aik Kwang and Daphne Rodrigues, "A Big-Five Personality Profile of the Adapter and Innovator," *Journal of Creative Behavior* 36, no. 4 (2002): 254–68; Dean Keith Simonton, "Creativity: Cognitive, Developmental, Personal, and Social Aspects," *American Psychologist* 55, no. 1 (2000): 151–58.

13. Andrew M. Johnson and Phillip A. Vernon, "Behavioral Genetic Studies of Personality: An Introduction and Review of the Results of 50+ Years of Research," in *The SAGE Handbook of Personality Theory and Assessment, Personality Theories and Models*, eds. Gregory J. Boyle, Gerald Matthews, and Donald H. Saklofske (Thousand Oaks, CA: Sage, 2008), 145–73.

14. Frank Barron, *Creativity and Psychological Health Origins of Personal Vitality and Creative Freedom* (New York: Van Nostrand, 1963); Raymond Bernard Cattell, "The Personality and Motivation of the Researchers from Measurements of Contemporaries and from Biography," in *Scientific Creativity: Its Recognition and Development*, eds. Calvin W. Taylor and Frank Barron (New York: Wiley, 1963); Feist, "Meta-Analysis"; MacKinnon, "Nature"; Anne Roe, *The Making of a Scientist* (New York: Dodd, Mead, 1952); Morris I. Stein, "A Transactional Approach to Creativity," in *Scientific Creativity: Its Recognition and Development*, eds. Calvin W. Taylor and Frank Barron (New York: Wiley, 1963).

15. Abdullah Aljughaiman and Elizabeth Mowrer-Reynolds, "Teachers' Conceptions of Creativity and Creative Students," *Journal of Creative Behavior* 39, no. 1 (2005): 17–34; Teresa Amabile, *Growing up Creative: Nurturing a Lifetime of Creativity* (Williston, VT: Crown House, 1989); Bonnie Cramond, "Attention-Deficit Hyperactivity Disorder and Creativity—What Is the Connection?" *Journal of Creative Behavior* 28, no. 3 (1994): 193–210; Arthur J. Cropley, *More Ways Than One: Fostering Creativity in the Classroom* (Norwood, NJ: Ablex, 1992); Gary A. Davis and Sylvia B. Rimm, *Education of the Gifted and Talented*, 3rd ed. (Needham Heights, MA: Allyn and Bacon, 1994); Mildred G. Goertzel and Victor H. Goertzel, "Intellectual and Emotional Climate in Families Producing Eminence," *Gifted Child Quarterly* 4 (1960): 59–60; John Curtis Gowan, Joe Khatena, and E. Paul Torrance, *Educating the Ablest: A Book of Readings on the Education of Gifted Children* (Itasca: Peacock, 1979); Eleni Mellou, "Can Creativity Be Nurtured in Young Children?"

Early Child Development and Care 119 (1996): 119–30; M. K. Raina, "Parental Perception about Ideal Child: A Cross-Cultural Study," *Journal of Marriage and the Family* 37, no. 1 (1975): 229–32; M. K. Raina, Girijesh Kumar, and V. K. Raina, "A Cross-Cultural Study of Parental Perception of the Ideal Child," *Creative Child and Adult Quarterly* 5, no. 4 (1980): 234–41; T. N. Raina and M. K. Raina, "Perception of Teacher-Educators in India about the Ideal Pupil," *Journal of Educational Research* 64, no. 7 (1971): 303–06; Elisabeth Rudowicz, "Creativity and Culture: A Two-Way Interaction," *Scandinavian Journal of Educational Research* 47, no. 3 (2003): 273–90; Elisabeth Rudowicz and Xiao Dong Yue, "Compatibility of Chinese and Creative Personalities," *Creativity Research Journal* 14, no. 3–4 (2000): 387–94; Christina Lynn Scott, "Teachers' Biases toward Creative Children," *Creativity Research Journal* 12, no. 4 (1999): 321–28; Kenneth R. Seeley, "Perspectives on Adolescent Giftedness and Delinquency," *Journal for the Education of the Gifted* 8 (1984): 59–72; R. P. Singh, "Parental Perception about Creative Children," *Creative Child and Adult Quarterly* 12, no. 1 (1987): 39–42; Bruce Torff, "Encouraging the Creative Voice of the Child," *NAMTA Journal* 25, no. 1 (1999): 195–214; E. Paul Torrance, *Guiding Creative Talent* (Englewood Cliffs, NJ: Prentice-Hall, 1962); E. Paul Torrance, "The Creative Personality and the Ideal Pupil," *Teachers College Record* 65 (1963): 220–27; E. Paul Torrance, *Thinking Creatively in Action and Movement: Administration, Scoring, and Norms Manual* (Benseville, IL: Scholastic Testing Services, 1981).

16. K. Anders Ericsson, "Expertise," *Current Biology* 24, no. 11 (2014): 508–10; Howard E. Gruber, *Darwin on Man: A Psychological Study of Scientific Creativity* (Chicago: University of Chicago Press, 1981); John R. Hayes, *The Complete Problem Solver*, 2nd ed. (Hillsdale, NJ: Erlbaum, 1989); Michael D. Mumford et al., "Process-Based Measures of Creative Problem-Solving Skills: II. Information Encoding," *Creativity Research Journal* 9, no. 1 (1996): 77–88; Michael D. Mumford et al., "Process-Based Measures of Creative Problem-Solving Skills: III. Category Selection," *Creativity Research Journal* 9, no. 4 (1996): 395–406; Andrea S. Vincent, Brian P. Decker, and Michael D. Mumford, "Divergent Thinking, Intelligence, and Expertise: A Test of Alternative Models," *Creativity Research Journal* 14, no. 2 (2002): 163–78; Robert W. Weisberg, *Creativity: Beyond the Myth of Genius* (New York: W. H. Freeman, 1993); Robert W. Weisberg, "Prolegomena to Theories of Insight in Problem Solving: Definition of Terms and a Taxonomy of Problems," in *The Nature of Insight*, ed. Robert J. Sternberg and Janet E. Davidson (Cambridge, MA: MIT Press, 1995), 157–96.

17. Teresa Amabile, *The Social Psychology of Creativity* (New York: Springer-Verlag, 1983); Csikszentmihalyi, "Society"; Csikszentmihalyi, "Implications"; Tse-Yang Huang, "Fostering Creativity: A Meta-Analytic Inquiry into the Variability of Effects," *Dissertation Abstracts International* A66/04 (2005); Laura Hall Rose and Hsin-Tai Lin, "A Meta-Analysis of Long-Term Creativity Training Programs," *Journal of Creative Behavior* 18, no. 1 (1984): 11–22; Mellou, "Nurtured"; Ginamarie Scott, Lyle E. Leritz, and Michael D. Mumford, "The Effectiveness of Creativity Training: A Quantitative Review," *Creativity Research Journal* 16, no. 4 (2004): 361–88; Sill, "Integrative"; Stein, *Stimulating*; E. Paul Torrance, *The Search for Satori and Creativity* (Buffalo, NY: Bearly Limited Creative Education Foundation, 1979); E. Paul Torrance, *Creativity: Just Wanting to Know* (Republic of South Africa: Benedic Books, 1994); E. Paul Torrance, *Why Fly? A Philosophy of Creativity* (Norwoord, NJ: Ablex, 1995); E. Paul Torrance and Tammy Safter, *Making the Creative Leap Beyond* (Buffalo, NY: Creative Education Foundation, 1999); E. Paul Torrance and Pansy J. Torrance, *Is Creativity Teachable?* (Bloomington, IN: Phi Delta Kappa Educational Foundation, 1973).

18. Weihua Niu and Robert J. Sternburg, "The Philosophical Roots of Western and Eastern Conceptions of Creativity," *Journal of Theoretical and Philosophical Psychology* 26 (2006): 1001–21.

19. Amabile, *Social*; Csikszentmihalyi, "Society"; Csikszentmihalyi, "Implications"; Sill, "Integrative"; Stein, *Stimulating*.

20. Albert, "Observations"; Albert, "Contribution"; Anastasi and Schaefer, "Biographical"; Bloom, *Developing*; Cropley, *Creativity*; Csikszentmihalyi, "Implications"; Dewing and Taft, "Characteristics"; Domino, "Maternal"; Dreyer and Wells, "Parental"; Fearon, Copeland, and Saxon, "Relationship"; Getzels and Jackson, *Creativity*; Goble, Moran, and Bomba, "Maternal"; Kemple and Nissengberg, "Nurturing"; Kerr and Chopp, "Families"; Kirschenbaum, *Understanding*; Lim

and Plucker, "Creativity"; Lubart, "Creativity across"; Lubart, "Creativity"; MacKinnon, "Nature"; Miller, Lambert, and Speirs Neumeister, "Parenting"; Myers and Torrance, "Teachers"; O'Brien and Md-Yunus, "Parents"; Raw and Marjoribanks, "Family"; Rudowicz and Hui, "Personality"; Runco, "Creativity"; Schaefer and Anastasi, "Biographical"; Seo, Lee, and Kim, "Korean"; Stein, *Stimulating*; Sternberg and Kaufman, "Constraints"; Sternberg and Lubart, "Concept"; Weisberg and Springer, "Environmental"; Yue and Rudowicz, "Perception."

21. KH Kim, Jae-Young Shim, Sin-Gyu Park, and Michael F. Hull, "Killing the Creative Potential of a Korean Mathematical Prodigy: A Three-Year Case Study" (paper presented at the 2009 annual meeting of the American Educational Research Association, San Diego, CA, April 2009).

22. Albert, "Observations"; Albert, "Contribution"; Anastasi and Schaefer, "Biographical"; Bloom, *Developing*; Cropley, *Creativity*; Dewing and Taft, "Characteristics"; Domino, "Maternal"; Dreyer and Wells, "Parental"; Fearon, Copeland, and Saxon, "Relationship"; Getzels and Jackson, *Creativity*; Goble, Moran, and Bomba, "Maternal"; Kemple and Nissengberg, "Nurturing"; Kerr and Chopp, "Families"; MacKinnon, "Nature"; Miller, Lambert, and Speirs Neumeister, "Parenting"; O'Brien and Md-Yunus, "Parents"; Schaefer and Anastasi, "Biographical"; Weisberg and Springer, "Environmental."

23. Kirschenbaum, *Understanding*; Myers and Torrance, "Teachers"; Raw and Marjoribanks, "Family"; Sternberg and Kaufman, "Constraints."

24. Amabile, *Growing*; Goertzel and Goertzel, "Intellectual"; Gowan, Khatena, and Torrance, *Educating*.

25. Seeley, "Perspectives"; Torrance, *Guiding*; Torrance, *Thinking*.

26. Aljughaiman and Mowrer-Reynolds, "Teachers"; Cramond, "Attention-Deficit"; Cropley, *Ways*; Davis and Rimm, *Education*; Mellou, "Nurtured"; Raina, "Parental"; Raina, Kumar, and Raina, "Cross-Cultural"; Raina and Raina, "Perception"; Rudowicz, "Creativity"; Rudowicz and Yue, "Compatibility"; Scott, "Teachers"; Singh, "Parental"; Torff, "Encouraging"; Torrance, "Creative Personality."

27. V. L. Dawson et al., "Predicting Creative Behavior: A Reexamination of the Divergence between Traditional and Teacher-Defined Concepts of Creativity," *Creativity Research Journal* 12, no. 1 (1999): 57–66; Erik L. Westby and V. L. Dawson, "Creativity: Asset or Burden in the Classroom?" *Creativity Research Journal* 8, no. 1 (1995): 1–10.

28. Amabile, *Growing*; Dawson et al., "Predicting"; Goertzel and Goertzel, "Intellectual"; Mark A. Runco, "Parents' and Teachers' Ratings of the Creativity of Children," *Journal of Social Behavior and Personality* 4 (1989): 73–83; Westby and Dawson, "Creativity."

Chapter 3: The Soil Climate That Nurtures the Soil Attitudes

1. Walter Isaacson, *Einstein: His Life and Universe* (New York: Simon and Schuster, 2007).

2. Fiona MacDonald, *Albert Einstein: Genius behind the Theory of Relativity* (Woodbridge, CT: Blackbirth, 2000).

3. Marfe Ferguson Delano, *Genius: A Photobiography of Albert Einstein* (Washington, DC: National Geographic Society, 2005); MacDonald, *Einstein*.

4. Delano, *Genius*; MacDonald, *Einstein*.

5. Kathleen Krull, *Albert Einstein*, Giants of Science Series (New York: Viking, 2009); MacDonald, *Einstein*.

6. Krull, *Einstein*.

7. Delano, *Genius*; Marie Hammontree, *Albert Einstein: Young Thinker. Childhood of Famous Americans* (New York: Simon and Schuster, 1986); MacDonald, *Albert Einstein*.

8. Ibid.

9. Denis Brian, *Einstein: A Life* (New York: John Wiley and Sons, 1996).

10. Ibid.

11. Delano, *Genius*; Hammontree, *Einstein*; Isaacson, *Einstein*.

12. Isaacson, *Einstein*.

13. Delano, *Genius*; Isaacson, *Einstein*.

14. Andrea Gabor, "The Forgotten Wife," in *E = Einstein: His Life, His Thought and His Influence on Our Culture*, eds. Donald Goldsmith and Marcia Bartusiak (New York: Sterling, 2006), 39–65; Isaacson, *Einstein*.

15. Brian, *Einstein*; Krull, *Einstein*.

16. Hammontree, *Einstein*.

17. Delano, *Genius*; MacDonald, *Einstein*; Elizabeth MacLeod, *Albert Einstein: A Life of a Genius* (Toronto, Canada: Kids Can, 2003); Stephanie Sammartino McPherson, *Ordinary Genius: The Story of Albert Einstein* (Minneapolis, MN: Carolrhoda Books, 1995).

18. Brian, *Einstein*; Isaacson, *Einstein*.

19. Isaacson, *Einstein*; Krull, *Einstein*.

20. Brian, *Einstein*; Krull, *Einstein*; MacDonald, *Einstein*.

21. Krull, *Einstein*; MacDonald, *Einstein*.

22. Hammontree, *Einstein*.

23. Isaacson, *Einstein*; Krull, *Einstein*.

24. Ibid.; McPherson, *Ordinary*.

25. Hammontree, *Einstein*.

26. Delano, *Genius*; MacDonald, *Einstein*.

27. Hammontree, *Einstein*; Isaacson, *Einstein*; Krull, *Einstein*; Gary F. Moring, *The Complete Idiot's Guide to Understanding Einstein* (New York: Alpha Books, 2004).

28. Isaacson, *Einstein*.

29. Ibid.; Moring, *Complete*.

30. Krull, *Einstein*.

31. Brian, *Einstein*.

32. Krull, *Einstein*.

33. MacLeod, *Einstein*.

34. Brian, *Einstein*.

35. Ibid.; McPherson, *Ordinary*; Moring, *Complete*.

36. MacDonald, *Einstein*.

37. Isaacson, *Einstein*; Moring, *Complete*.

38. Isaacson, *Einstein*; McPherson, *Ordinary*.

39. Delano, *Genius*; Krull, *Einstein*; McPherson, *Ordinary*.

40. Brian, *Einstein*.

41. Ibid.; Hammontree, *Einstein*; Isaacson, *Einstein*; Krull, *Einstein*; Moring, *Complete*.

42. Hammontree, *Einstein*; Krull, *Einstein*.

43. Delano, *Genius*; Isaacson, *Einstein*.

44. Isaacson, *Einstein*; Krull, *Einstein*.

45. Brian, *Einstein*; Delano, *Genius*; Hammontree, *Einstein*; Krull, *Einstein*.

46. Isaacson, *Einstein*; Krull, *Einstein*.

47. Isaacson, *Einstein*.

48. Hammontree, *Einstein*; Isaacson, *Einstein*.

49. Brian, *Einstein*; Isaacson, *Einstein*.

50. Isaacson, *Einstein*; Krull, *Einstein*.

51. Isaacson, *Einstein*.

52. Hammontree, *Einstein*.

53. Krull, *Einstein*; MacDonald, *Einstein*.

54. Delano, *Genius*; Isaacson, *Einstein*; Krull, *Einstein*; McPherson, *Ordinary*.

55. Delano, *Genius*; McPherson, *Ordinary*.

56. Delano, *Genius*; Isaacson, *Einstein*; Krull, *Einstein*.

57. Isaacson, *Einstein*.

58. Krull, *Einstein*.

59. Isaacson, *Einstein*; Krull, *Einstein*.

60. Isaacson, *Einstein*.

61. Delano, *Genius*; Isaacson, *Einstein*.

62. Isaacson, *Einstein*.

63. Ibid.

64. Ibid.

65. Isaacson, *Einstein*; Krull, *Einstein*.

66. Ibid.

67. Isaacson, *Einstein*; Moring, *Complete*.

68. Delano, *Genius*; Isaacson, *Einstein*; Krull, *Einstein*.

69. Isaacson, *Einstein*; Krull, *Einstein*.

70. Isaacson, *Einstein*.

71. Krull, *Einstein*; MacDonald, *Einstein*.

72. Isaacson, *Einstein*; Krull, *Einstein*.

73. Isaacson, *Einstein*; MacDonald, *Einstein*.

74. Isaacson, *Einstein*; Krull, *Einstein*.

75. Delano, *Genius*; Isaacson, *Einstein*; Krull, *Einstein*.

76. Isaacson, *Einstein*.

77. Ibid.

78. K. Anders Ericsson, "The Acquisition of Expert Performance: An Introduction to Some of the Issues," in *The Road to Expert Performance: Empirical Evidence from the Arts and Sciences, Sports, and Games* (Mahwah, NJ: Erlbaum, 1996), 1–50; K. Anders Ericsson, Neil Charness, Paul J. Feltovich, and Robert R. Hoffman, eds, *The Cambridge Handbook of Expertise and Expert Performance* (New York: Cambridge University Press, 2006); Howard Gardner, *Creating Minds* (New York: NY: Basic Books, 1993); John R. Hayes, *The Complete Problem Solver* (Hillsdale, NJ: Erlbaum, 1989); Dean Keith Simonton, *Greatness: Who Makes History and Why* (New York, Guilford, 1994); Dean Keith Simonton, *Genius 101*, The Psych 101 Series (New York: Springer, 2009).

79. Isaacson, *Einstein*.

80. Anne Anastasi and Charles E. Schaefer, "Biographical Correlates of Artistic and Literary Creativity in Adolescent Girls," *Journal of Applied Phycology* 53, no. 4 (1969): 267–73; Kathleen Dewing and Ronald Taft, "Some Characteristics of the Parents of Creative Twelve-Year-Olds," *Journal of Personality* 41, no. 1 (1973): 71–85; Charles E. Schaefer and Anne Anastasi, "A Biographical Inventory for Identifying Creativity in Adolescent Boys," *Journal of Applied Psychology* 52, no. 1 (1968): 42–48; Herbert J. Walberg et al., "Childhood Traits and Experiences of Eminent Women," *Creativity Research Journal* 9, no. 1 (1996): 97–102.

81. Kay Slama, "Rural Culture Is a Diversity Issue," *Minnesota Psychologist* 1 (2004): 9–13; Philip E. Vernon, *Intelligence and Cultural Environment* (London, UK: Methuen, 1969).

82. Richard Florida, "Bohemia and Economic Geography," *Journal of Economic Geography* 2 (2002): 55–71; Richard Florida, "The Economic Geography of Talent," *Annals of the Association of American Geographers* 92, no. 4 (2002): 743–55; Richard Florida, *The Rise of the Creative Class: And How It's Transforming Work, Leisure, and Everyday Life* (New York: Basic Books, 2002); Gary Gates and Richard Florida, *Technology and Tolerance: The Importance of Diversity to High-Tech Growth* (Washington, DC: Brookings Institution, Center for Urban and Metropolitan Policy, 2001); AnnaLee Saxenian, *Silicon Valley's New Immigrant Entrepreneurs: Skills, Networks, and Careers* (University of California at Berkeley: Public Policy Institute of California, 1999); Pascal Zachary, *The Global Me: New Cosmopolitans and the Competitive Edge—Picking Globalism's Winners and Losers* (New York: Perseus Books, 2000).

83. Morten Berg Jensen et al., "Forms of Knowledge and Modes of Innovation," *Research Policy* 36, no. 5 (2007): 680–93; Brian Knudsen et al., "Density and Creativity in U.S. Regions," *Annals of the Association of American Geographers* 98, no. 2 (2008): 461–78; P. Cooke and G. Schienstock, "Structural Competitiveness and Learning Regions," *Enterprise and Innovation Management Studies*

1, no. 3 (2000): 265–80; AnnaLee Saxenian, *Regional Advantage: Culture and Competition in Silicon Valley and Route 128* (Boston: Harvard University Press, 1994); Scott Andrew Shane, *General Theory of Entrepreneurship: The Individual-Opportunity Nexus* (Northampton, NY: Elgar, 2003).

84. Roland Andersson, John Quigley, and Mats Wilhelmsson, "Agglomeration and the Spatial Distribution of Creativity," *Papers in Regional Science* 84 (2005): 445–64; Gerald Carlino, Satyajit Chaterjee, and Robert Hunt, "Urban Density and the Rate of Invention," *Journal of Urban Economics* 61 (2007): 389–419; A. Ciccone, and R. Hall, "Productivity and the Density of Economic," *American Economic Review* 86 (1996): 54–70; Florida, "Economic"; Florida, *Rise*; Gates and Florida, *Technology*; Norman Sedgely and Bruce Elmslie, "The Geographic Concentration of Knowledge: Scale, Agglomeration, and Congestion in Innovation Across U.S. States," *International Regional Science Review* 27 (2004): 111–37; Deborah Strumsky, Jose Lobo, and Lee Fleming, "Metropolitan Patenting, Inventor Agglomeration and Social Networks: A Tale of Two Effects" (Los Alamos, NM: Thompson, 2005).

85. Richard Florida, *The Great Reset: How New Ways of Living and Working Drive Post-Crash Prosperity* (New York: HarperCollins, 2010); Edward L. Glaeser, *The Triumph of the City: How Our Greatest Invention Makes Us Richer, Smarter, Greener, Healthier and Happier* (New York: Macmillan, 2011); Edward L. Glaeser, Stuart S. Rosenthal, and William C. Strange, "Urban Economics and Entrepreneurship," *Journal of Urban Economics* 67, no. 1 (2010): 1–14; Jane Jacobs, *The Economy of Cities* (New York: Vintage, 1969); Knudsen et al., "Density."

86. Ibid.

87. Santiago Ramon y Cajal, *Precepts and Counsels on Scientific Investigation: Stimulants of the Spirit*, trans. J. M. Sanchez-Perez (Mountain View, CA: Pacific, 1951); Ravenna Helson, "Childhood Interest Clusters Related to Creativity in Women," *Journal of Consulting Psychology* 29, no. 4 (1965): 352–61; Ravenna Helson, "Personality of Women with Artistic and Imaginative Interests: The Role of Masculinity, Originality, and Other Characteristics of Their Creativity," *Journal of Personality* 34, no. 1 (1966): 1–25; Ravenna Helson, "Personality Characteristics and Developmental History of Creative College Women," *Genetic Psychology Monographs* 76, no. 2 (1967): 205–56; Anne Roe, "A Psychological Study of Eminent Psychologists and Anthropologists and a Comparison with Biological and Physical Scientists," *Psychology Monographs* 67 (1953): 1; Dean Keith Simonton, "Creativity, Leadership, and Chance," in *The Nature of Creativity: Contemporary Psychological Perspectives*, ed. Robert J. Sternberg (New York: Cambridge University Press, 1988), 386–426; Simonton, *101*; Herbert J. Walberg, Sue Pinzur Rasher, and JoAnn Parkerson, "Childhood and Eminence," *Journal of Creative Behavior* 13, no. 4 (1979): 225–31.

88. Frank Barron and David M. Harrington, "Creativity, Intelligence, and Personality," *Annual Review of Psychology* 32, no. 1 (1981): 439–76; Benjamin S. Bloom, *Developing Talent in Young People* (New York: Ballantine Books, 1985); Paul T. Costa and Robert R. McCrae, *The NEO Personality Inventory Manual* (Odessa, FL: Psychological Assessment Resources, 1985); Gregory J. Feist, "A Meta-Analysis of Personality in Scientific and Artistic Creativity," *Personality and Social Psychology Review* 2, no. 4 (1998): 290–309; Gregory J. Feist, "The Influence of Personality on Artistic and Scientific Creativity," in *Handbook of Creativity*, ed. Robert J. Sternberg (Cambridge, UK: Cambridge University Press, 1999), 273–96; William Fleeson, "Toward a Structure-and-Process-Integrated View of Personality: Traits as Density Distributions of States," *Journal of Personality and Social Psychology* 80, no. 6 (2001): 1011–27; Robert R. McCrae and Paul T. Costa, "Validation of the Five-Factor Model of Personality across Instruments and Observers," *Journal of Personality and Social Psychology* 52, no. 1 (1987): 81–90.

89. Pasl A. Jalil and Mohammed Boujettif, "Some Characteristics of Nobel Laureates," *Creativity Research Journal* 17, no. 2/3 (2005): 265–72; Robert S. Root-Bernstein, Maurine Bernstein, and Helen Garnier, "Correlations between Avocations, Scientific Style, Work Habits, and Professional Impact of Scientists," *Creativity Research Journal* 8, no. 2 (1995): 115–37; Robert Root-Bernstein et al., "Arts Foster Scientific Success: Avocations of Nobel, National Academy, Royal Society, and Sigma Xi Members," *Journal of Psychology of Science and Technology* 1, no. 2 (2008): 51–63;

Schaefer and Anastasi, "Biographical"; Dean Keith Simonton, "Creativity and Genius," in *Handbook of Personality: Theory and Research*, eds. Oliver P. John Richard, W. Robins, and Lawrence A. Pervin, 3rd ed. (New York: Guilford, 2008), 679–98.

90. Timothy B. Smith and Lynda Silva, "Ethnic Identity and Personal Well-Being of People of Color: A Meta-Analysis," *Journal of Counseling Psychology* 58 (2011): 42–60; Jessie Wilson, Colleen Ward, and Ronald Fischer, "Beyond Culture Learning Theory: What Can Personality Tell Us about Cultural Competence?" *Journal of Cross-Cultural Psychology* 44, no. 6 (2013): 900–27; Eunju Yoon et al., "A Meta-Analysis of Acculturation/Enculturation and Mental Health," *Journal of Counseling Psychology* 60, no. 1 (2013): 15–30.

91. Jean S. Phinney, "Understanding Ethnic Diversity: The Role of Ethnic Identity," *American Behavioral Scientist* 40, no. 2 (1996): 143–52; Jean S. Phinney and D. A. Rosenthal, "Ethnic Identity in Adolescence: Process, Context, and Outcome," in *Adolescent Identity Formation*, ed. G. Adams, T. Gulotta, and K. Montemayor (Newbury Park, CA: Sage, 1992).

92. Mario Mikulincer, "Adult Attachment Style and Information Processing: Individual Differences in Curiosity and Cognitive Closure," *Journal of Personality and Social Psychology* 72, no. 5 (1997): 1217–30; Mario Mikulincer, Phillip R. Shaver, and Eldad Rom, "The Effects of Implicit and Explicit Security Priming on Creative Problem Solving," *Cognition and Emotion* 25, no. 3 (2011): 519–31.

93. Mikulincer, "Adult."

94. Ellen Bialystok, *Bilingualism in Development: Language, Literacy, and Cognition* (New York: Cambridge University Press, 2001); Jen Ho Chang et al., "Multicultural Families and Creative Children," *Journal of Cross-Cultural Psychology* 45, no. 8 (2014): 1288–96; Jen-Ho Chang, Jenny C. Su, and Hsueh-Chih Chen, "Cultural Distance between Parents' and Children's Creativity: A Within-Country Approach in Taiwan," *Cultural Diversity and Ethnic Minority Psychology* 21, no. 3 (2015): 477–85; Anthony Fee and Sidney J. Gray, "The Expatriate-Creativity Hypothesis: A Longitudinal Field Test," *Human Relations* 65, no. 12 (2012): 1515–38; Howard Gardner, *Frames of Mind: The Theory of Multiple Intelligences* (New York: Basic Books, 1983); Gardner, *Creating*; Christine S. Lee, David J. Therriault, and Tracy Linderholm, "On the Cognitive Benefits of Cultural Experience: Exploring the Relationship between Studying Abroad and Creative Thinking," *Applied Cognitive Psychology* 26, no. 5 (2012): 768–78; Hangeun Lee and KH Kim, "Can Speaking More Languages Enhance Your Creativity? Relationship between Bilingualism and Creative Potential among Korean American Students with Multicultural Link," *Personality and Individual Differences* 50, no. 8 (2011): 1186–90; Angela Ka-yee Leung et al., "Multicultural Experience Enhances Creativity: The When and How," *American Psychologist* 63, no. 3 (2008): 169; William W. Maddux, Hajo Adam, and Adam D. Galinsky, "When in Rome . . . Learn Why the Romans Do What They Do: How Multicultural Learning Experiences Facilitate Creativity," *Personality and Social Psychology Bulletin* (2010): 731–41; Simonton, *Greatness*; Smith and Silva, "Ethnic"; Carmit T. Tadmor, Adam D. Galinsky, and William W. Maddux, "Getting the Most out of Living Abroad: Biculturalism and Integrative Complexity as Key Drivers of Creative and Professional Success," *Journal of Personality and Social Psychology* 103, no. 3 (2012): 520–42; Wilson, Ward, and Fischer, "Beyond Culture"; Yoon et al., "Meta-Analysis."

95. Verónica Benet-Martinez, Fiona Lee, and Janxin Leu, "Biculturalism and Cognitive Complexity: Expertise in Cultural Representations," *Journal of Cross-Cultural Psychology* 37, no. 4 (2006): 386–407; Richard J. Crisp and Rhiannon N. Turner, "Cognitive Adaptation to the Experience of Social and Cultural Diversity," *Psychological Bulletin* 137, no. 2 (2011): 242–66; Maddux, Adam, and Galinsky, "Rome."

96. Bryan S. K. Kim et al., "Cultural Value Similarities and Differences among Asian American Ethnic Groups," *Cultural Diversity and Ethnic Minority Psychology* 7, no. 4 (2001): 343–61; Maddux, Adam, and Galinsky, "Rome."

97. Patricia Lavon Hanna, "Gaining Global Perspective: Educational Language Policy and Planning," *International Journal of Bilingual Education and Bilingualism* 14, no. 6 (2011): 733–49; Kate Menken, *English Learners Left behind Standardized Testing as Language Policy* (New York: Multilingual Matters, 2008).

98. Robert A. Pierce and KH Kim, "Third Culture Kids," in *Encyclopedia of Diversity and Social Justice*, ed. Sherwood Thompson (Lanham, MD: Rowman and Littlefield, 2014).

99. Joe Greenholtz and Jean Kim, "The Cultural Hybridity of Lena: A Multi-Method Case Study of a Third-Culture Kid," *International Journal of Intercultural Relations* 33 (2009): 391–98.

100. Emily Hearn, "Setting the Stage for Creativity," *Education Canada* 43, no. 4 (2004): 20–23; Beth A. Hennessey and Teresa M. Amabile, *Creativity and Learning* (Washington, DC: National Education Association, 1987); Zach Kelehear and Karen A. Heid, "Mentoring in the Art Classroom," *Studies in Art Education* 44, no. 1 (2002): 67–78; Larisa Shavinina, "Explaining High Abilities of Nobel Laureates," *High Ability Studies* 15, no. 2 (2004): 243–54; Dean Keith Simonton, "Creativity from a Historiometric Perspective," in *Handbook of Creativity*, ed. Robert J. Sternberg (New York: Cambridge University Press, 1999), 116–33; E. Paul Torrance, *Guiding Creative Talent* (Englewood Cliffs, NJ: Prentice-Hall, 1962); E. Paul Torrance, *The Manifesto: A Guide to Developing a Creative Career* (West Westport, CT: Ablex, 2002); Harriet Zuckerman, "The Scientific Elite: Nobel Laureates' Mutual Influences," in *Genius and Eminence*, ed. Robert S. Albert (Oxford, UK: Pergamon, 1983).

101. KH Kim and Darya Zabelina, "Mentors," in *Encyclopedia of Creativity*, eds. Mark. A. Runco and Steven R. Pritzker, 2nd ed. (Oxford: Elsevier, 2010).

102. Gloria Crisp and Irene Cruz, "Mentoring College Students: A Critical Review of the Literature between 1990 and 2007," *Research in Higher Education* 50, no. 6 (2009): 525–45.

103. Crisp and Cruz, "Mentoring"; Robyn Ewing et al., "Building Community in Academic Settings: The Importance of Flexibility in a Structured Mentoring Program," *Mentoring and Tutoring: Partnership in Learning* 16, no. 3 (2008): 294–310; Karen A. Randolph and Jeannette L. Johnson, "School-Based Mentoring Programs: A Review of the Research," *Children and Schools* 30, no. 3 (2008): 177–85.

104. Hennessey and Amabile, *Creativity*; Kelehear and Heid, "Mentoring"; Shavinina, "Explaining"; Simonton, "Historiometric"; Torrance, *Guiding*; Torrance, *Manifesto*; Zuckerman, "Scientific."

105. Bloom, *Developing*; Torrance, *Guiding*; Zuckerman, "Scientific."

106. Bloom, *Developing*; Torrance, *Guiding*.

107. Bloom, *Developing*.

108. Richard S. Mansfield and Thomas V. Busse, *The Psychology of Creativity and Discovery: Scientists and Their Work* (Chicago: Nelson-Hall, 1981).

109. Shavinina, "Explaining"; Zuckerman, "Scientific."

110. Robert S. Albert, "Family Positions and the Attainment of Eminence: A Study of Special Family Positions and Special Family Experiences," in *Genius and Eminence: The Social Psychology of Creativity and Exceptional Achievement*, ed. Robert S. Albert (Oxford: Pergamon, 1983), 141–54; Dewing and Taft, "Characteristics"; Schaefer and Anastasi, "Biographical"; Rodney W. Skager, Charles B. Schultz, and Stephen Klein, "Quality and Quantity of Accomplishments as Measures of Creativity," *Journal of Educational Psychology* 56, no. 1 (1965): 31–39; Simonton, *Greatness*; Dean Keith Simonton, "Significant Samples: The Psychological Study of Eminent Individuals," *Psychological Methods* 4, no. 4 (1999): 425–51.

111. Albert S. Dreyer and Mary Beth Wells, "Parental Values, Parental Control, and Creativity in Young Children," *Journal of Marriage and the Family* 28, no. 1 (1966): 83–88; Richard Koestner, Marie Walker and Laura Fichman, "Childhood Parenting Experiences and Adult Creativity," *Journal of Research in Personality* 33, no. 1 (1999): 92–107.

112. Koestner, Walker, and Fichman, "Childhood"; Simonton, *Greatness*; Simonton, "Samples."

113. Jacob Getzels and Philip W. Jackson, "Family Environment and Cognitive Style: A Study of the Sources of Highly Intelligent and of Highly Creative Adolescents," *American Sociological Review* 26, no. 3 (1961): 351–59; Carmen Hudson and Nick Stinnett, "The Relationship of Family Type to Aspects of Wellness of Young Children," *Creativity and Wellness Perspectives* 6, no. 3 (1990): 31–41.

114. Albert, "Family"; Dewing and Taft, "Characteristics"; Schaefer and Anastasi, "Biographical"; Skager, Schultz, and Klein, "Quality"; Simonton, *Greatness*; Simonton, "Samples."

115. Leung et al., "Multicultural"; Tadmor, Galinsky, and Maddux, "Getting."

116. Skager, Schultz, and Klein, "Quality."

117. Anastasi and Schaefer, "Biographical"; Catharine M. Cox, *Genetic Studies of Genius: Aol.2. The Early Mental Traits of Three Hundred Geniuses* (Stanford, CA: Stanford University Press, 1926); Havelock Ellis, *A Study of a British Genius*, rev. ed. (Boston: Houghton Mifflin, 1926); Francis Galton, *English Men of Science: Their Nature and Nurture* (London, UK: Macmillan, 1874); Roe, "Psychological"; Schaefer and Anastasi, "Biographical"; Simonton, *Greatness*; Simonton, *101*.

118. Markus Baer et al., "Win or Lose the Battle for Creativity: The Power and Perils of Intergroup Competition," *Academy of Management Journal* 53, no. 4 (2010): 827–45; Julian Birkinshaw, "Strategies for Managing Internal Competition," *California Management Review* 44, no. 1 (2001): 21–38; Cooke and Schienstock, "Structural"; Florida, "Economic"; Lucy L. Gilson and Christina E. Shalley, "A Little Creativity Goes a Long Way: An Examination of Teams' Engagement in the Creative Process," *Journal of Management* 30, no. 4 (2004): 453–70; Jensen et al., "Forms"; Szabolcs Kéri, "Solitary Minds and Social Capital: Latent Inhibition, General Intellectual Functions and Social Network Size Predict Creative Achievements," *Psychology of Aesthetics, Creativity, and the Arts* 5, no. 3 (2011): 215–21; Knudsen et al., "Density"; Saxenian, *Regional*; Shane, *General*.

119. Simonton, *Greatness*; Simonton, *101*.

120. Feist, "Meta-Analysis"; Fleeson, "Structure"; Wenfu Li et al., "Brain Structure Links Trait Creativity to Openness to Experience," *Social Cognitive and Affective Neuroscience* 10, no. 2 (2015): 191–98.

121. Feist, "Meta-Analysis"; Costa and McCrae, *NEO*; Robert R. McCrae, "Creativity, Divergent Thinking, and Openness to Experience," *Journal of Personality and Social Psychology* 52, no. 6 (1987): 1258–65; Sandra Walker Russ, *Affect and Creativity: The Role of Affect and Play in the Creative Process* (Hillsdale, NJ: Erlbaum, 1993).

122. Feist, "Influence"; McCrae, "Creativity"; John M. Mezias and William H. Starbuck, "What Do Managers Know, Anyway? A Lot Less Than They Think. But Now, the Good News," *Harvard Business Review* 81, no. 5 (2003): 16–17; Twila Z. Tardif and Robert J. Sternberg, "What Do We Know about Creativity?" in *The Nature of Creativity*, ed. Robert J. Sternberg (New York: Cambridge University Press, 1999), 429–40.

123. Walberg et al., "Childhood."

124. Barron and Harrington, "Creativity"; Christine Charyton and Glenn E. Snelbecker, "Engineers' and Musicians' Choices of Self-Descriptive Adjectives as Potential Indicators of Creativity by Gender and Domain," *Psychology of Aesthetics, Creativity, and the Arts* 1, no. 2 (2007): 91–99; McCrae, "Creativity"; Feist, "Influence"; Tardif and Sternberg, "Know."

125. Costa and McCrae, *NEO*; Feist, "Influence."

126. Bo Burlingham and George Gendron, "The Entrepreneur of the Decade: An Interview with Steven Jobs, Inc.'s Entrepreneur of the Decade," *Inc.*, April 1, 1989, http://www.inc.com/magazine/19890401/5602.html.

127. Paul R. Christensen, Joy Paul Guilford, and R. C. Wilson, "Relations of Creative Responses to Working Time and Instructions," *Journal of Experimental Psychology* 53, no. 2 (1957): 82–88; Carsten KW De Dreu et al., "Working Memory Benefits Creative Insight, Musical Improvisation, and Original Ideation through Maintained Task-Focused Attention," *Personality and Social Psychology Bulletin* 38, no. 5 (2012): 656–69; Paul B. Paulus, Nicholas W. Kohn, and Lauren E. Arditti, "Effects of Quantity and Quality Instructions on Brainstorming," *Journal of Creative Behavior* 45, no. 1 (2011): 38–46; Paul B. Paulus et al., "Effects of Task Instructions and Brief Breaks on Brainstorming," *Group Dynamics: Theory, Research, and Practice* 10, no. 3 (2006): 206; Vicky L. Putman and Paul B. Paulus, "Brainstorming, Brainstorming Rules and Decision Making," *Journal of Creative Behavior* 43, no. 1 (2009): 29–40.

128. * It is also called "perceiving": Dale Richard Buchanan and Carole Bandy, "Jungian Typology of Prospective Psychodramatists: Myers-Briggs Type Indicator Analysis of Applicants for Psychodrama Training," *Psychological Reports* 55, no. 2 (1984): 599–606; Dale Richard Buchanan and Jane A. Taylor, "Jungian Typology of Professional Psychodramatists: Myers-Briggs Type Indicator Analysis of

Certified Psychodramatists," *Psychological Reports* 58, no. 2 (1986): 391–400; G. C. Carne and Michael J. Kirton, "Styles of Creativity: Test-Score Correlations between Kirton Adaption-Innovation Inventory and Myers-Briggs Type Indicator," *Psychological Reports* 50, no. 1 (1982): 31–36; Barbara A. Carter, David L. Nelson, and Linda W. Duncombe, "The Effect of Psychological Type on the Mood and Meaning of Two Collage Activities," *American Journal of Occupational Therapy* 37, no. 10 (1983): 688–93; Yiling Cheng, KH Kim, and Michael F. Hull, "Comparisons of Creative Styles and Personality Types between American and Taiwanese College Students and the Relationship between Creative Potential and Personality Types," *Psychology of Aesthetics, Creativity, and the Arts* 4, no. 2 (2010): 103–12; Ronald Fisher and James Scheib, "Creative Performance and the Hallucinogenic Drug-Induced Creative Experience or One Man's Brain-Damage Is Another's Creativity," *Confinia Psychiatrica* 14, no. 3/4 (1971): 174–202; Nur Gryskiewicz and W. L. Tullar, "The Relationship between Personality Type and Creativity Style among Managers," *Journal of Psychological Type* 32 (1995): 30–35; Wallace B. Hall and Donald W. MacKinnon, "Personality Inventory Correlates of Creativity among Architects," *Journal of Applied Psychology* 53, no. 4 (1969): 322–26; Helson, "Childhood"; Scott G. Isaksen, Kenneth J. Lauer, and Glenn V. Wilson, "An Examination of the Relationship between Personality Type and Cognitive Style," *Creativity Research Journal* 15, no. 4 (2003): 343–54; Carolyn McKinnell Jacobson, "Cognitive Styles of Creativity: Relations of Scores on the Kirton Adaption-Innovation Inventory and the Myers-Briggs Type Indicator among Managers in USA," *Psychological Reports* 72 (1993): 1131–38; Ronald C. Johnson, "Study of the Relationship between Cognitive Styles of Creativity and Personality Types of Military Leaders," *Dissertation Abstracts International* 64, no. 10-A (2004): 3859; Isabel Briggs Myers and Mary H. McCaulley, *Manual: A Guide to the Development and Use of the Myers-Briggs Type Indicator* (Palo Alto, CA: Consulting Psychological, 1985); Robert H. Richter and William D. Winter, "Holtzman Inkblot Correlates of Creative Potential," *Journal of Projective Techniques & Personality Assessment* 30, no. 1 (1966): 62–67.

129. Roshan Cools, "Role of Dopamine in the Motivational and Cognitive Control of Behavior," *Neuroscientist* 4 (2008): 381–95; Gesine Dreisbach and Thomas Goschke, "How Positive Affect Modulates Cognitive Control: Reduced Perseveration at the Cost of Increased Distractibility," *Journal of Experimental Psychology: Learning, Memory, and Cognition* 30, no. 2 (2004): 343–53; Gesine Dreisbach et al., "Dopamine and Cognitive Control: The Influence of Spontaneous Eyeblink Rate and Dopamine Gene Polymorphisms on Perseveration and Distractibility," *Behavioral Neuroscience* 119 (2005): 483–90; Severine Koch, Rob W. Holland, and Ad van Knippenberg, "Regulating Cognitive Control through Approach-Avoidance Motor Actions," *Cognition* 109, no. 1 (2008): 133–42; McCrae, "Creativity"; Johannes Muller et al., "Dopamine and Cognitive Control: The Prospect of Monetary Gains Influences the Balance between Flexibility and Stability in a Set-Shifting Paradigm," *European Journal of Neuroscience* 26 (2007): 3661–68; Bernard A. Nijstad et al., "The Dual Pathway to Creativity Model: Creative Ideation as a Function of Flexibility and Persistence," *European Review of Social Psychology* 21 (2010): 34–77; Richter and Winter, "Holtzman."

130. Cools, "Role"; McCrae, "Creativity"; Dreisbach and Goschke, "Positive"; Dreisbach et al., "Dopamine"; Koch, Holland, and Knippenberg, "Regulating"; Muller et al., "Dopamine"; Nijstad et al., "Dual"; Richter and Winter, "Holtzman."

131. Benet-Martinez, Lee, and Leu, "Biculturalism"; Gardner, *Frames*; Gardner, *Creating*; K.-Y. Leung and Chi-yue Chiu, "Interactive Effects of Multicultural Experiences and Openness to Experience on Creative Potential," *Creativity Research Journal* 20, no. 4 (2008): 376–82; William W. Maddux and Adam D. Galinsky, "Cultural Borders and Mental Barriers: The Relationship between Living Abroad and Creativity," *Journal of Personality and Social Psychology* 96, no. 5 (2009): 1047–61; Simonton, *Greatness*; Tadmor, Galinsky, and Maddux, "Getting."

132. Leung and Chiu, "Interactive"; Angela K.-Y. Leung and Chi-yue Chiu, "Multicultural Experience, Idea Receptiveness, and Creativity," *Journal of Cross-Cultural Psychology* 41, no. 5/6 (2010): 723–41; Maddux, Adam, Galinsky, "Rome"; Maddux and Galinsky, "Cultural"; Robert W. Weisberg, "Creativity and Knowledge: A Challenge to Theories," in *Handbook of Creativity*, ed. Robert J. Sternberg (Cambridge, MA: Cambridge University Press, 1999).

133. Benet-Martinez, Lee, and Leu, "Biculturalism"; Maddux, Adam, Galinsky, "Rome"; Smith and Silva, "Ethnic"; Tadmor, Galinsky, and Maddux, "Getting"; Weisberg, "Creativity"; Wilson, Ward, and Fischer, "Beyond Culture"; Yoon et al., "Meta-Analysis."

134. Leung et al., "Multicultural"; Charlan Jeanne Nemeth and Julianne L. Kwan, "Minority Influence, Divergent Thinking and Detection of Correct Solutions," *Journal of Applied Social Psychology* 17, no. 9 (1987): 788–99; Simonton, *Greatness*; Simonton, "Samples"; Tadmor, Galinsky, and Maddux, "Getting."

135. Chang, Su, and Chen, "Cultural."

136. Anders Hallengren, "Nelson Mandela and the Rainbow of Culture," Nobelprize.org, last modified September 11, 2001, http://www.nobelprize.org/nobel_prizes/peace/laureates/1993/mandela -article.html.

137. Walter Isaacson, *Steve Jobs* (New York: Simon and Schuster, 2011).

138. Jan Garden Castro, *The Art and Life of Georgia O'Keeffe* (New York: Crown, 1985).

139. Garnet W. Millar, *The Torrance Kids At Mid-life: Selected Case Studies of Creative Behavior* (Westport, CT: Ablex, 2002); Mark Runco et al., "Torrance Tests of Creative Thinking as Predictors of Personal and Public Achievement: A Fifty-Year Follow-Up," *Creativity Research Journal* 22 (2010): 361–68; Dean Keith Simonton, *Scientific Genius: A Psychology of Science* (Cambridge, UK: Cambridge University Press, 1988); Simonton, *Greatness*; E. Paul Torrance, *Why Fly? A Philosophy of Creativity* (Norwoord, NJ: Ablex, 1995); Torrance, *Manifesto*.

140. K. Anders Ericsson, "Expertise," *Current Biology* 24, no. 11 (2014): 508–10; K. Anders Ericsson, Ralf Th. Krampe, and Clemens Tesch-Romer, "The Role of Deliberate Practice in the Acquisition of Expert Performance," *Psychological Review* 100 (1993): 363–406; K. Anders Ericsson, Kiruthiga Nandagopal, and Roy W. Roring, "Giftedness Viewed from the Expert-Performance Perspective," *Journal for the Education of the Gifted* 28, no. 3/4 (2005): 287–311; Ralf Th. Krampe and K. Anders Ericsson, "Maintaining Excellence: Deliberate Practice and Elite Performance in Young and Older Pianists," *Journal of Experimental Psychology: General* 125 (1996): 331–59.

141. Arthur Cropley, "Dimensions of Creativity: Creativity, a Social Approach," *Roeper Review* 28 (2006): 125–30; Millar, *Torrance*; Simonton, *Scientific*; Simonton, *Greatness*; Torrance, *Manifesto*; Herbert J. Walberg, "Creativity and Talent as Learning," in *The Nature of Creativity: Contemporary Psychological Perspectives*, ed. Robert J. Sternberg (New York: Cambridge University Press, 1988), 340–61; Echo H. Wu, "Cultural Perspectives on Talent Development and Parenting," *Dissertation Abstracts International Section A: Humanities and Social Sciences* 68, no. 11-A (2008): 4610; Zuckerman, *Scientific*.

142. Cropley, "Dimensions"; Zuckerman, *Scientific*.

143. Adrian Cho, "Skewed Symmetries Net Honors for Particle Theorists," *Science* 322, no. 5900 (2008): 360–61; Simonton, *Greatness*; Walberg, "Creativity"; Steven Weinberg, "To the Postdocs," *Physics Today* 60, no. 3 (2007): 58; Wu, "Cultural"; Zuckerman, "Scientific."

144. Simonton, *Greatness*.

145. Mihaly Csikszentmihalyi, *Flow: The Psychology of Optimal Experience* (New York: Harper and Row, 1990); Ravenna Helson, "Women in Creativity," in *The Creativity Question*, eds. Albert Rothenberg and Carl Hausman (Durham: Duke University Press, 1976), 242–49; Arthur Koestler, *The Act of Creation* (New York: Macmillan, 1964).

146. Tadmor, Galinsky, and Maddux, "Getting"; Gary M. Wederspahn, "Costing Failures in Expatriate Human Resources Management," *Human Resource Planning* 15 (1992): 27.

147. Siegfried Streufert and Robert W. Swezey, *Complexity, Managers, and Organizations* (Orlando, FL: Academic, 1986).

148. Barron and Harrington, "Creativity"; Frank Farley, "The Type-T Personality," in *Self-Regulatory Behavior and Risk Taking: Causes and Consequences*, eds. Lewis P. Lipsitt and Leonard L. Mitnick (Norwood, NJ: Ablex, 1991), 371–82; Mihaly Csikszentmihalyi, *Creativity: Flow and the Psychology of Discovery and Invention* (New York: Harper Perennial, 1996); Feist, "Meta-Analysis"; Chiara Simone Haller and Delphine Sophie Courvoisier, "Personality and Thinking Style in Different Creative Domains," *Psychology of Aesthetics, Creativity, and the Arts* 4, no. 3 (2010): 149–60;

149. Frank Barron, "The Needs for Order and for Disorder as Motives in Creative Activity," in *Scientific Creativity: Its Recognition and Development*, eds. Calvin W. Taylor and Frank Barron (New York: Wiley, 1963), 153–60; Donald W. MacKinnon, *In Search of Human Effectiveness* (Buffalo, NY: Creative Education Foundation, 1978).

150. Barron and Harrington, "Creativity"; Csikszentmihalyi, *Creativity*; Haller and Courvoisier, "Personality"; Leung and Chiu, "Multicultural"; Tadmor, Galinsky, and Maddux, "Getting."

151. Arthur J. Cropley, "Creativity: A Bundle of Paradoxes," *Gifted and Talented International* 12, no. 1 (1997): 8–14; Csikszentmihalyi, *Creativity*; Haller and Courvoisier, "Personality"; W. E. McMullan, "Creative Individuals: Paradoxical Personages," *Journal of Creative Behavior* 10, no. 4 (1976): 265–75; Tardif and Sternberg, "Know."

152. Robert J. Sternberg and James C. Kaufman, "Constraints on Creativity: Obvious and Not So Obvious," in *The Cambridge Handbook of Creativity*, eds. James C. Kaufman and Robert J. Sternberg (New York: Cambridge University Press, 2010), 467–82.

153. Charyton and Snelbecker, "Engineers"; Feist, "Meta-Analysis."

154. David H. Feldman, "Creativity: Dreams, Insights, and Transformations," in *The Nature of Creativity: Contemporary Psychological Perspectives*, ed. Robert J. Sternberg (New York: Cambridge University Press, 1988), 271–97; Simonton, "Creativity"; Zuckerman, *Scientific*.

155. Isaacson, *Jobs*.

156. Baer et al., "Win"; Birkinshaw, "Strategies"; Gilson and Shalley, "Little."

157. Feldman, "Creativity"; Knudsen et al., "Density"; Simonton, "Creativity"; Zuckerman, *Scientific*.

158. Birkinshaw, "Strategies."

159. Baer et al., "Win"; Birkinshaw, "Strategies"; Hoon-Seok Choi and Leigh Thompson, "Old Wine in a New Bottle: Impact of Membership Change on Group Creativity," *Organizational Behavior and Human Decision Processes* 98, no. 2 (2005): 121–32; Gilson and Shalley, "Little."

160. Florida, "Economic"; Kéri, "Solitary."

161. Ronald S. Burt, "Structural Holes and Good Ideas," *American Journal of Sociology* 110, no. 2 (2004): 349–99; Cooke and Schienstock, "Structural"; Lee Fleming, Santiago Mingo, and David Chen, "Collaborative Brokerage, Generative Creativity, and Creative Success," *Administrative Science Quarterly* 52, no. 3 (2007): 443–75; Jensen et al., "Forms"; Kéri, "Solitary"; Knudsen et al., "Density"; Saxenian, *Regional*; Shane, *General*; Simon Rodan and Charles Galunic, "More Than Network Structure: How Knowledge Heterogeneity Influences Managerial Performance and Innovativeness," *Strategic Management Journal* 25, no. 6 (2004): 541–62; Manuel E. Sosa, "Where Do Creative Interactions Come From? The Role of Tie Content and Social Networks," *Organization Science* 22, no. 1 (2011): 1–21; Brian Uzzi and Jarrett Spiro, "Collaboration and Creativity: The Small World Problem," *American Journal of Sociology* 111, no. 2 (2005): 447–504.

162. Paul B. Paulus and Huei-Chuan Yang, "Idea Generation in Groups: A Basis for Creativity in Organizations," *Organizational Behavior and Human Decision Processes* 82, no. 1 (2000): 76–87.

163. Hans J. Eysenck, *Genius: The Natural History of Creativity* (Cambridge, UK: Cambridge University Press, 1995); Feist, "Meta-Analysis"; Anne Roe, *The Making of a Scientist* (New York: John Wiley and Sons, 1953); Simonton, *Greatness*.

164. Isaacson, *Jobs*.

165. Isaacson, *Einstein*.

166. Castro, *Art*; Danielle Peltakian, "Georgia O'Keeffe (1887–1986): American Modernist," *Sullivan Goss: An American Gallery*, December 2, 2015, http://www.sullivangoss.com/georgia_OKeeffe/.

167. Isaacson, *Einstein*; Krull, *Einstein*.

168. Ibid.

Chapter 4: The Sun Climate That Nurtures the Sun Attitudes

1. Walter Isaacson, *Steve Jobs* (New York: Simon and Schuster, 2011).

2. Ibid.

3. Barbara Sheen, *Steve Jobs*, People in the News (Farmington Hills, MI: Gale, Cengage Learning, 2010).

4. Isaacson, *Jobs.*

5. Isaacson, *Jobs*; "Steve Jobs," interview by Daniel Morrow, *The Computerworld Information Technology Awards Foundation*, April 1995, http://www.computerworld.com/s/.

6. Ibid.

7. Isaacson, *Jobs.*

8. Karen Blumenthal, *Steve Jobs: The Man Who Thought Different* (New York: Feiwel, 2012).

9. Isaacson, *Jobs*; Susan Wilson, *Steve Jobs: A Wizard of Apple Computer* (Springfield, NJ: Enslow, 2001).

10. Jim Corrigan, *Business Leaders: Steve Jobs* (Greensboro, NC: Reynolds, 2009).

11. Isaacson, *Jobs.*

12. Ibid.

13. Isaacson, *Jobs*; Wilson, *Jobs.*

14. Isaacson, *Jobs.*

15. Ibid.

16. "Jobs," interview by Morrow.

17. Isaacson, *Jobs*; "Jobs," interview by Morrow.

18. Isaacson, *Jobs.*

19. Wilson, *Jobs.*

20. Isaacson, *Jobs*; Sheen, *Jobs*; "Jobs," interview by Morrow; Wilson, *Jobs.*

21. Isaacson, *Jobs*; "Jobs," interview by Morrow.

22. Isaacson, *Jobs.*

23. Corrigan, *Business.*

24. Corrigan, *Business*; Isaacson, *Jobs.*

25. Sheen, *Jobs.*

26. Isaacson, *Jobs.*

27. United States Securities and Exchange Commission, "Apple Inc. Form 10-K for the Fiscal Year Ended September 27, 2014," http://investor.apple.com/ssecfiling.cfm?filingid=1193125-14-383437and cik=.

28. Isaacson, *Jobs.*

29. Steve Jobs, interview by Walter Isaacson, "The Impatience (and Genius) of Jobs," Acceler8or.com, November 29, 2011, http://www.acceler8or.com/2011/11/the-impatience-and-genius-of-jobs-an-interview-with-walter-isaacson/.

30. "Steve Jobs," interview by David Sheff, *Playboy*, February 8, 1985, http://www.scribd.com/fullscreen/ 43945579.

31. Trevor Timm, "Reform the CFAA: Don't Let It Stop the Next Steve Jobs, Bill Gates, Mark Zuckerberg, or Steve Wozniak," *Electronic Frontier Foundation: Defending Your Rights in the Digital World*, March 7, 2013, https://www.eff.org/deeplinks/2013/03/innovators.

32. Wilson, *Jobs.*

33. John Arlidge, "Jonathan Ive Designs Tomorrow," *Time*, March 17, 2014, http://time.com/jonathan-ive-apple-interview/; Isaacson, *Steve Jobs.*

34. Arlidge, "Ive."

35. "Jobs," interview by Morrow.

36. Isaacson, *Jobs.*

37. Sheen, *Jobs.*

38. Ibid.

39. Isaacson, *Jobs*.

40. Nick Wingfield, "Steve Jobs's Search for His Father," *New York Times*, October 23, 2011, http://bits.blogs.nytimes.com/2011/10/23/steve-jobss-search-for-his-father/?_r=0.

41. E. Paul Torrance, "Predicting the Creativity of Elementary School Children (1958–80)—and the Teacher Who Made a Difference," *Gifted Child Quarterly* 25, no. 2 (1981): 55–62; E. Paul Torrance, "Understanding Creativity: Where to Start?" *Psychological Inquiry* 4, no. 3 (1993): 232–34; E. Paul Torrance, *Creativity: Just Wanting to Know* (Republic of South Africa: Benedic Books, 1994); E. Paul Torrance, *Why Fly? A Philosophy of Creativity* (Norwood, NJ: Ablex, 1995); E. Paul Torrance, *The Manifesto: A Guide to Developing a Creative Career* (West Westport, CT: Ablex, 2002).

42. Xinyin Chen, Qi Dong, and Hong Zhou, "Authoritative and Authoritarian Parenting Practices and Social and School Performance in Chinese Children," *International Journal of Behavioral Development* 21, no. 4 (1997): 855–73; Christina M. Rinaldi and Nina Howe, "Mothers' and Fathers' Parenting Styles and Associations with Toddlers' Externalizing, Internalizing, and Adaptive Behaviors," *Early Childhood Research Quarterly* 27, no. 2 (2012): 266–73.

43. Brooke C. Feeney and Meredith Van Vleet, "Growing through Attachment: The Interplay of Attachment and Exploration in Adulthood," *Journal of Social and Personal Relationships* 27, no. 2 (2010): 226–34; Mario Mikulincer, "Adult Attachment Style and Information Processing: Individual Differences in Curiosity and Cognitive Closure," *Journal of Personality and Social Psychology* 72, no. 5 (1997): 1217–30; Mario Mikulincer and Phillip R. Shaver, *Attachment in Adulthood: Structure, Dynamics, and Change* (New York: Guilford, 2007); Mario Mikulincer, Phillip R. Shaver, and Eldad Rom, "The Effects of Implicit and Explicit Security Priming on Creative Problem Solving," *Cognition and Emotion* 25, no. 3 (2011): 519–31.

44. "Nobel Prize Awarded Women," Nobelprize.org, April, 20, 2016, http://www.nobelprize.org/nobel_prizes/lists/women.html; Dean Keith Simonton, *Greatness: Who Makes History and Why* (New York: Guilford, 1994); E. Paul Torrance, *The Search for Satori and Creativity* (Buffalo, NY: Bearly Limited Creative Education Foundation, 1979); E. Paul Torrance and H. Tammy Safter, *Making the Creative Leap Beyond* (Buffalo, NY: Creative Education Foundation, 1999).

45. Anne Anastasi and Charles E. Schaefer, "Biographical Correlates of Artistic and Literary Creativity in Adolescent Girls," *Journal of Applied Phycology* 53 no. 4 (1969): 267–73; Charles E. Schaefer and Anne Anastasi, "A Biographical Inventory for Identifying Creativity in Adolescent Boys," *Journal of Applied Phycology* 52, no. 1 (1968): 42–48;

46. John E. Drevdahl, "Some Developmental and Environmental Factors in Creativity," in *Widening Horizons in Creativity*, ed. Calvin W. Taylor (New York: Wiley, 1964), 170–85; Donald W. MacKinnon, "The Nature and Nurture of Creative Talent," *American Psychologist* 17, no. 7 (1962): 484–95; Robert C. Nichols, "Parental Attitudes of Mothers of Intelligent Adolescents and Creativity of Their Children," *Child Development* 35, no. 4 (1964): 1041–49.

47. Ronald A. Finke, "Creative Insight and Preinventive Forms," in *The Nature of Insight*, eds. Robert J. Sternberg and Janet E. Davidson (Cambridge, MA: MIT Press, 1995), 225–80; Kentaro Fujita et al., "Spatial Distance and Mental Construal of Social Events," *Psychological Science* 17, no. 4 (2006): 278–82; Lile Jia, Edward R. Hirt, and Samuel C. Karpen, "Lessons from a Faraway Land: The Effect of Spatial Distance on Creative Cognition," *Journal of Experimental Social Psychology* 45, no. 5 (2009): 1127–31; Nira Liberman, Yaacov Trope, and Cheryl Wakslak, "Construal Level Theory and Consumer Behavior," *Journal of Consumer Psychology* 17, no. 2 (2007): 113–17; Ido Liviatan, Yaacov Trope, and Nira Liberman, "Interpersonal Similarity as a Social Distance Dimension: Implications for Perception of Others' Actions," *Journal of Experimental Social Psychology* 44, no. 5 (2008): 1256–69; Evan Polman and Kyle J. Emich, "Decisions for Others Are More Creative Than Decisions for the Self," *Personality and Social Psychology Bulletin* 37 (2001): 492–501; Emily Pronin and Lee Ross, "Temporal Differences in Trait Self-Ascription: When the Self Is Seen as an Other," *Journal of Personality and Social Psychology* 90, no. 2 (2006): 197–209; Cheryl J. Wakslak et al., "Representations of the Self in the Near and Distant Future," *Journal of Personality and Social Psychology 95, no. 4 (2008)*: 757–73; Thomas B. Ward, "What's Old about New Ideas?" in

The Creative Cognition Approach, eds. Steven M. Smith, Thomas B. Ward, and Ronald A. Finke (Cambridge, MA: MIT Press, 1995), 157–78.

48. Adam D. Galinsky et al., "Power and Perspectives Not Taken," *Psychological Science* 17, no. 12 (2006): 1068–74; Adam M. Grant, "Relational Job Design and the Motivation to Make a Prosocial Difference," *Academy of Management Review* 32, no. 2 (2007): 393–417; Polman and Emich, "Decisions."

49. Mikulincer, Shaver, and Rom, "Effects."

50. Rosa Aurora Chávez-Eakle, Ma del Carmen Lara, and Carlos Cruz-Fuentes, "Personality: A Possible Bridge between Creativity and Psychopathology?" *Creativity Research Journal* 18, no. 1 (2006): 27–38; Mikulincer, Shaver, and Rom, "Effects"; Eric Rayner et al., *Human Development: An Introduction to the Psychodynamics of Growth, Maturity and Ageing* (Sussex, UK: Routledge, 2005).

51. David M. Harrington, Jeanne H. Block, and Jack Block, "Testing Aspects of Carl Rogers's Theory of Creative Environments: Child-Reading Antecedents of Creative Potential in Young Adolescents," *Journal of Personality and Social Psychology* 52, no. 4 (1987): 851–56; Carl R. Rogers, "Towards a Theory of Creativity," *ETC: A Review of General Semantics* 11, no. 4 (1954): 249–60; E. Paul Torrance, *Guiding Creative Talent* (Englewood Cliffs, NJ: Prentice-Hall, 1962).

52. Colin Berry, "The Nobel Scientists and the Origins of Scientific Achievement," *British Journal of Sociology* 32 (1981): 381–91; Benjamin S. Bloom, *Developing Talent in Young People* (New York: Ballantine Books, 1985); Kathleen Dewing and Ronald Taft, "Some Characteristics of the Parents of Creative Twelve-Year-Olds," *Journal of Personality* 41, no. 1 (1973): 71–85; Robert Root-Bernstein et al., "Arts Foster Scientific Success: Avocations of Nobel, National Academy, Royal Society, and Sigma Xi Members," *Journal of Psychology of Science and Technology* 1 (2008): 51–63; Echo H. Wu, "Cultural Perspectives on Talent Development and Parenting," *Dissertation Abstracts International Section A: Humanities and Social Sciences* 68, no. 11-A (2008): 4610.

53. Twila Z. Tardif and Robert J. Sternberg, "What Do We Know about Creativity?" in *The Nature of Creativity*, ed. Robert J. Sternberg (New York: Cambridge University Press, 1999), 429–40; Todd M. Thrash et al., "Mediating between the Muse and the Masses: Inspiration and the Actualization of Creative Ideas," *Journal of Personality and Social Psychology* 98, no. 3 (2010): 469–87.

54. Howard Gardner, "Giftedness: Speculations from a Biological Perspective," *New Directions for Child and Adolescent Development* 17 (1982): 47–60; Ellen J. Langer, *Mindfulness* (Reading, MA: Addison-Wesley, 1989); Robert R. McCrae and Paul T. Costa, "The NEO Personality Inventory: Using the Five-Factor Model in Counseling," *Journal of Counseling & Development* 69, no. 4 (1991): 367–72; Jonathan A. Plucker, Ronald A. Beghetto, and Gayle T. Dow, "Why Isn't Creativity More Important to Educational Psychologists? Potentials, Pitfalls, and Future Directions in Creativity Research," *Educational Psychologist* 39, no. 2 (2004): 83–96; Elizabeth Rosenblatt and Ellen Winner, "The Art of Children's Drawing," *Journal of Aesthetic Education* 22 (1988): 3–15; Mary Rothbart and John Bates, "Temperament," in *Handbook of Child Psychology*, eds. Nancy Eisenberg, William Damon, and Richard M. Lerner (New York: Wiley, 2006); M. Rosario Rueda, Michael I. Posner, and Mary Rothbart, "The Development of Executive Attention: Contributions to the Emergence of Self-Regulation," *Developmental Neuropsychology* 28, no. 2 (2005): 573–94; Irving A. Taylor and Jacob W. Getzels, eds. *Perspectives in Creativity* (Chicago, IL: Aldine, 1975).

55. "Albert Einstein Quotes," Brainyquote.com, http://www.brainyquote. com/quotes/quotes/a/alberteins174001.html.

56. Schaefer and Anastasi, "Biographical."

57. Bloom, *Developing*.

58. Bloom, *Developing*; David H. Feldman and Lynn T. Goldsmith, *Nature's Gambit: Child Prodigies and the Development of Human Potential* (New York: Basic Books, 1986); Harold G. McCurdy, "The Childhood Pattern of Genius," *Horizon* 2, no. 5 (1960): 32–38; Anne Roe, *The Making of a Scientist* (New York: Dodd Mead, 1953); Herbert J. Walberg, Sue Pinzur Rasher, and JoAnn Parkerson, "Childhood and Eminence," *Journal of Creative Behavior* 13, no. 4 (1979): 225–31.

59. Dean Keith Simonton, *Genius 101*, The Psych 101 Series (New York: Springer, 2009).

60. James Mackay, *Sounds Out of Silence: A Life of Alexander Graham Bell* (Edinburgh, EH: Mainstream, 1997).

61. Matthew Josephson, *Edison* (New York: McGraw Hill, 1959).

62. David Herbert Donald, *Lincoln* (New York: Simon and Schuster, 1996).

63. Benjamin Franklin, *Autobiography of Benjamin Franklin with Introduction and Notes* (New York: Macmillan, 1913).

64. Simonton, *Greatness*; Walberg et al., "Childhood Traits and Experiences of Eminent Women," *Creativity Research Journal* 9, no. 1 (1996): 97–102.

65. Jaak Panksepp, "Can Play Diminish ADHD and Facilitate the Construction of the Social Brain?" *Journal of the Canadian Academy of Child and Adolescent Psychiatry* 16, no. 2 (2007): 57–66; Darya L. Zabelina and Michael D. Robinson, "Child's Play: Facilitating the Originality of Creative Output by a Priming Manipulation," *Psychology of Aesthetics, Creativity, and the Arts* 4, no. 1 (2010): 57–65.

66. Torrance, *Guiding*; E. Paul Torrance, *Education and the Creative Potential* (Minneapolis: University of Minnesota, 1963).

67. Bloom, *Developing*.

68. Amabile, *Creativity*; James A. Middleton, Joan Littlefield, and Richard Lehrer, "Gifted Students' Conceptions of Academic Fun: An Examination of a Critical Construct for Gifted Education," *Gifted Child Quarterly* 36, no. 1 (1992): 38–44; E. Paul Torrance, "Prediction of Adult Creative Achievement among High School Seniors," *Gifted Child Quarterly* 13 (1969): 223–29.

69. Rob M. Fielding, "Creativity Revisited: Strategies for Developing Creative Potential," *Journal of the Institute of Art Education* 7, no. 2 (1983): 51–60; E. Paul Torrance, *Creativity in the Classroom* (Washington, DC: National Education Association, 1977); Ved P. Varma, *How and Why Children Fail* (UK: Kingsley, 1993).

70. Kathy Hirsh-Pasek and Roberta Michnick Golinkoff, *Einstein Never Used Flash Cards: How Our Children Really Learn—and Why They Need to Play More and Memorize Less* (Pennsylvania: Rodale, 2003); Kathy Hirsh-Pasek et al., *A Mandate for Playful Learning* (Oxford: Oxford University Press, 2009); H. L. Kaila, "Democratizing Schools across the World to Stop Killing Creativity in Children: An Indian Perspective," *Counseling Psychology Quarterly* 18 (2005): 1–6; Sandra W. Russ and Julia A. Fiorelli, "Developmental Approaches to Creativity," in *The Cambridge Handbook of Creativity*, eds. James C. Kaufman and Robert J. Sternberg (New York: Cambridge University Press, 2010), 233–49; Robert Wood Johnson Foundation, "The State of Play: Gallup Survey of Principals on School Recess," February 2010, http://www.rwjf.org/pr/product.jsp?id=55249.

71. Beth A. Hennessey and Teresa Amabile, *Creativity and Learning* (Washington, DC: National Education Association of the United States, 1987).

72. Simonton, *Greatness*; Walberg et al., "Childhood."

73. Hennessey and Amabile, *Creativity*; Anastasi and Schaefer, "Biographical"; Roe, *Making*; Schaefer and Anastasi, "Biographical"; Torrance, *Fly*; Torrance, *Manifesto*.

74. Torrance, "Predicting"; Torrance, *Classroom*; Torrance, "Understanding; Torrance, *Fly*.

75. Dewing and Taft, "Characteristics."

76. Torrance, "Predicting"; Torrance, *Classroom*; Torrance, "Understanding"; Torrance, *Fly*.

77. Bonnie Cramond, *The Coincidence of Attention Deficit Hyperactivity Disorder and Creativity* (Storrs, CT: National Research Center of Gifted and Talented, 1995).

78. Bonnie Cramond, "Attention-Deficit Hyperactivity Disorder and Creativity—What Is the Connection?" *Journal of Creative Behavior* 28 (1994): 193–210; Dione Healey and Julia J. Rucklidge, "An Investigation into the Psychosocial Functioning of Creative Children: The Impact of ADHD Symptomatology," *Journal of Creative Behavior* 40, no. 4 (2006): 243–64;

79. *Niall Hartnett,* Jason M. Nelson, and Anne N. Rinn, "Gifted or ADHD? The Possibilities of Misdiagnosis," *Roeper Review* 26, no. 2 (2004): 73–76; Healey and Rucklidge, "Investigation"; D. Lara Honos-Webb, *The Gift of ADHD: How to Transform Your Child's Problems into Strengths* (Oakland, CA: New Harbinger, 2010); Jason M. Nelson, Anne N. Rinn, and D. Niall Hartnett, "The

Possibility of Misdiagnosis of Giftedness and ADHD Still Exists: A Response to Mika," *Roeper Review* 28, no. 4 (2006): 243–48; Christian J. Krautkramer, "Beyond Creativity: ADHD Drug Therapy as a Moral Damper on a Child's Future Success," *American Journal of Bioethics* 5, no. 3 (2005): 52–53.

80. From the Print Edition, "Exams in South Korea: The One-Shot Society," *Economist*, December 17, 2011, http://www.economist.com/node/21541713; Jiyeon Lee, "South Korean Students' 'Year of Hell' Culminates with Exams Day," CNN, November 13, 2011, http://www.cnn.com/2011/11/10/world/asia/south-korea-exams/.

81. Richard M. Haynes and Donald M. Chalker, "The Making of a World-Class Elementary School," *Principal* 77, no. 3 (1998): 5–6, 8–9.

82. Geir Grundvåg Ottesen and Kjell Grønhaug, "Positive Illusions and New Venture Creation: Conceptual Issues and an Empirical Illustration," *Creativity and Innovation Management* 14, no. 4 (2005): 405–12; Feirong R. Yuan and Richard W. Woodman, "Innovative Behavior in the Workplace: The Role of Performance and Image Outcome Expectations," *Academy of Management Journal* 53 (2010): 323–42.

83. Cheng-Hsien Li and Jing-Jyi Wu, "The Structural Relationships between Optimism and Innovative Behavior: Understanding Potential Antecedents and Mediating Effects," *Creativity Research Journal* 23, no. 2 (2011): 119–28.

84. Edward C. Chang, "Dispositional Optimism and Primary and Secondary Appraisal of a Stressor: Controlling for Confounding Influences and Relations to Coping and Psychological and Physical Adjustment," *Journal of Personality and Social Psychology* 74, no. 4 (1998): 1109–20; Heidi Grant and E. Tory Higgins, "Optimism, Promotion Pride, and Prevention Pride as Predictors of Quality of Life," *Personality and Social Psychology Bulletin* 29, no. 12 (2003): 1521–32; Michael La Hsu, Sheng-Tsung Hou, and Hsueh-Liang Fan, "Creative Self-Efficacy and Innovative Behavior in a Service Setting: Optimism as a Moderator," *Journal of Creative Behavior* 45, no. 4 (2011): 258–72; Alice M. Isen, "Missing in Action in the AIM: Positive Affect's Facilitation of Cognitive Flexibility, Innovation, and Problem Solving," *Psychological Inquiry* 13, no. 1 (2002): 57–65; Heather N. Rasmussen et al., "Self-Regulation Processes and Health: The Importance of Optimism and Goal Adjustment," *Journal of Personality* 74, no. 6 (2006): 1721–48; Michael F. Scheier and Charles S. Carver, "Optimism, Coping, and Health: Assessment and Implications of Generalized Outcome Expectancies," *Health Psychology* 4, no. 3 (1985): 219–47; Michael F. Scheier, Charles S. Carver, and Michael W. Bridges, "Optimism, Pessimism, and Psychological Well-Being," in *Optimism and Pessimism: Implications for Theory, Research, and Practice*, ed. Edward C. Chang (Washington, DC: American Psychological Association, 2002), 189–216.

85. Polman and Emich, "Decisions"; Pronin and Ross, "Temporal."

86. Liviatan, Trope, and Liberman, "Interpersonal"; Polman and Emich, "Decisions."

87. Fujita et al., "Spatial."

88. Fujita et al., "Spatial"; Pronin and Ross, "Temporal"; Wakslak et al., "Representations."

89. Jia, Hirt, and Karpen, "Lessons."

90. Finke, "Insight"; Jia, Hirt, and Karpen, "Lessons"; Liberman, Trope, and Wakslak, "Construal"; Liviatan, Trope, and Liberman, "Interpersonal"; Wakslak et al., "Representations"; Polman and Emich, "Decisions"; Pronin and Ross, "Temporal"; Ward, "What's Old." *It is also called "abstract" or "intuitive (type)": Weston H. Agor, "How Intuition Can Be Used to Enhance Creativity in Organizations," *Journal of Creative Behavior* 25, no. 1 (1991): 11–19; Dale Richard Buchanan and Carole Bandy, "Jungian Typology of Prospective Psychodramatists: Myers-Briggs Type Indicator Analysis of Applicants for Psychodrama Training," *Psychological Reports* 55, no. 2 (1984): 599–606; Dale Richard Buchanan and Jane A. Taylor, "Jungian Typology of Professional Psychodramatists: Myers-Briggs Type Indicator Analysis of Certified Psychodramatists," *Psychological Reports* 58, no. 2 (1986): 391–400; Todd Burley and Leonard Handler, "Personality Factors in the Accurate Interpretation of Projective Tests," in *Advances in Projective Drawing Interpretation*, ed. Emanuel Frederick Hammer (Springfield, IL: Thomas, 1997), 359 –77; Barbara A. Carter, David L. Nelson, and Linda W. Duncombe, "The Effect of Psychological Type on the Mood and Meaning of Two Collage

Activities," *American Journal of Occupational Therapy* 37, no. 10 (1983): 688–693; Yiling Cheng, KH Kim, and Michael F. Hull, "Comparisons of Creative Styles and Personality Types between American and Taiwanese College Students and the Relationship between Creative Potential and Personality Types," *Psychology of Aesthetics, Creativity, and the Arts* 4, no. 2 (2010): 103–12; Ronald Fisher and James Scheib, "Creative Performance and the Hallucinogenic Drug-Induced Creative Experience or One Man's Brain-Damage Is Another's Creativity," *Confinia Psychiatrica* 14, no. 3 (1971): 174–202; Nur Gryskiewicz and W. L. Tullar, "The Relationship between Personality Type and Creativity Style among Managers," *Journal of Psychological Type* 32 (1995): 30–35; Wallace B. Hall and Donald W. MacKinnon, "Personality Inventory Correlates of Creativity among Architects," *Journal of Applied Psychology* 53, no. 4 (1969): 322–26; Oliver W. Hill, "Intuition: Inferential Heuristic or Epistemic Mode?" *Imagination, Cognition and Personality* 7, no. 2 (1987): 137–54; Isabel Briggs Myers and Mary H. McCaulley, *Manual: A Guide to the Development and Use of the Myers-Briggs Type Indicator* (Palo Alto, CA: Consulting Psychological, 1985); Mariko Ruth Pope, "Creativity and the Computer Professional: The Impact of Personality Perception on Innovation Approach Preferences in Terms of Creative Thinking and Behavior," *Dissertation Abstracts International* 58, no. 4-A (1997): 1366; Robert H. Richter and William D. Winter, "Holtzman Inkblot Correlates of Creative Potential," *Journal of Projective Techniques & Personality Assessment* 30, no. 1 (1966): 62–67.

91. Jens Förster, Ronald S. Friedman, and Nira Liberman, "Temporal Construal Effects on Abstract and Concrete Thinking: Consequences for Insight and Creative Cognition," *Journal of Personality and Social Psychology* 87, no. 2 (2004): 177–89; Jens Förster, Kal Epstude, and Amina Özelsel, "Why Love Has Wings and Sex Not: How Reminders of Love and Sex Influence Creative and Analytic Thinking," *Personality and Social Psychology Bulletin* 35, no. 11 (2009): 1479–91; Faby M. Gagné and John E. Lydon, "Bias and Accuracy in Close Relationships: An Integrative Review," *Personality and Social Psychology Review* 8, no. 4 (2004): 322–38; Cindy Hazan and Phillip Shaver, "Romantic Love Conceptualized as an Attachment Process," *Journal of Personality and Social Psychology* 52, no. 3 (1987): 511–24; Nira Liberman and Oren Shapira, "Does Falling in Love Make Us More Creative?" *Scientific American*, last modified September 29, 2009, http://www.scientificamerican.com/article/does-falling-in-love-make/; Sandra L. Murray, "The Quest for Conviction: Motivated Cognition in Romantic Relationships," *Psychological Inquiry* 10, no. 1 (1999): 23–34; Sandra L. Murray and John G. Holmes, "A Leap of Faith? Positive Illusions in Romantic Relationships," *Personality and Social Psychology Bulletin* 23, no. 6 (1997): 586–604.

92. Hennessey and Amabile, *Creativity*; Thrash et al., "Mediating"; Torrance, *Search*; Torrance and Safter, *Making*.

93. Marina A. Kholodnaya, "Psychological Mechanisms of Intellectual Giftedness," *Voprosy Psichologii* 1 (1991): 32–39; Larisa Shavinina, "Explaining High Abilities of Nobel Laureates," *High Ability Studies* 15, no. 2 (2004): 243–54.

94. Galinsky et al., "Power"; Grant, "Relational"; Polman and Emich, "Decisions."

95. Colleen Walsh, "Jobs, Einstein, and Franklin: Isaacson Deconstructs Their Genius and Dedication to Larger Goals," *Harvard Gazette*, April 9, 2013, http://news.harvard.edu/gazette/stroy/2013/ 04/jobs-einstein-and-franklin/.

96. Howard Gardner, *Creating Minds* (New York: Basic Books, 1993).

97. Bloom, *Developing*; Robert S. Root-Bernstein and Michele M. Root-Bernstein, *Sparks of Genius: The Thirteen Thinking Tools of the World's Most Creative People* (Boston: Houghton Mifflin, 1999); Oya Gürdal Tamdogon, "Creativity in Education: Clearness in Perception, Vigorousness in Curiosity," *Education for Information* 24, no. 2 (2006): 139–51.

98. Dean Keith Simonton, "Creativity and Genius," in *Handbook of Personality: Theory and Research*, eds. Oliver P. John and Richard W. Robins (New York: Guilford, 2008), 679–98.

99. Russell A. Barkley, "Behavioral Inhibition, Sustained Attention, and Executive Functions: Constructing a Unifying Theory of ADHD," *Psychological Bulletin* 121, no. 1 (1997): 65–94; Gardner, "Giftedness"; Gardner, *Creating*; McCrae and Costa, "NEO"; Plucker, Beghetto, and Dow, "Why Isn't"; Rosenblatt and Winner, "Art"; Rothbart and Bates, "Temperament"; Rueda, Posner, and

Rothbart, "Development"; Simonton, *Greatness*; Taylor and Getzels, *Perspectives*; Walberg et al., "Childhood."

100. *It is also called "perceiving (type)": Buchanan and Bandy, "Jungian"; Buchanan and Taylor, "Jungian"; Burley and Handler, "Personality"; Carter, Nelson, and Duncombe, "Effect"; Cheng, Kim, and Hull, "Comparisons"; Fisher and Scheib, "Creative"; Gryskiewicz and Tullar, "Relationship"; Hall and MacKinnon, "Personality"; Ravenna Helson, "Childhood Interest Clusters Related to Creativity in Women," *Journal of Consulting Psychology* 29, no. 4 (1965): 352–61; Hill, "Intuition"; Isaksen, Lauer, and Wilson, "Examination"; Ronald C. Johnson, "Study of the Relationship between Cognitive Styles of Creativity and Personality Types of Military Leaders," *Dissertation Abstracts International* 64, no. 10-A (2004): 3859; Jacobson, "Cognitive"; Myers and McCaulley, *Manual*; Pope, "Creativity"; Richter and Winter, "Holtzman."

101. Barkley, "Behavioral"; Gary A. Davis, "Barriers to Creativity and Creative Attitudes," in *Encyclopedia of Creativity*, vol. 2, eds. Mark A. Runco and Steven R. Pritzker (Boston: Academic, 1999), 165–74; Rothbart and Bates, "Temperament"; Rueda, Posner, and Rothbart, "Development."

102. Gardner, "Giftedness"; McCrae and Costa, "NEO"; Plucker, Beghetto, and Dow, "Why Isn't"; Taylor and Getzels, *Perspectives*.

103. Arne Dietrich, "The Cognitive Neuroscience of Creativity," *Psychonomic Bulletin and Review* 11, no. 6 (2004): 1011–26.

104. Ibid.

105. Torrance, *Search*; Torrance, *Wanting*; Torrance, *Fly*; Torrance and Safter, *Making*.

106. Elisabeth Rudowicz and Anna Hui, "The Creative Personality: Hong Kong Perspective," *Journal of Social Behavior and Personality* 12, no. 1 (1997): 139–57; Hae-Ae Seo, Eun Ah Lee, and KH Kim, "Korean Science Teachers' Understanding of Creativity in Gifted Education," *Journal of Secondary Gifted Education* 16, no. 2–3 (2005): 98–105.

107. Guo-Ming Chen and Jensen Chung, "The Impact of Confucianism on Organizational Communication," *Communication Quarterly* 42, no. 2 (1994): 93–105; Ruiping Fan, "Reconsidering Surrogate Decision Making: Aristotelianism and Confucianism on Ideal Human Relations," *Philosophy East and West* 52, no. 3 (2002): 346–72; Ranjoo Seodu Herr, "Is Confucianism Compatible with Care Ethics? A Critique," *Philosophy East and West* 53, no. 4 (2003): 471–89; Geert Hofstede and Michael Harris Bond, "The Confucius Connection: From Cultural Roots to Economic Growth," *Organizational Dynamics* 16 (1988): 5–21; Kwang-Kuo Hwang, "Filial Piety and Loyalty: Two Types of Social Identification in Confucianism," *Asian Journal of Social Psychology* 2, no. 1 (1999): 163–83; Kwang-Kuo Hwang, "The Deep Structure of Confucianism: A Social Psychological Approach," *Asian Philosophy* 11, no. 3 (2001): 179–204; Josephine Chinying Lang and Chay Hoon Lee, "Workplace Humor and Organizational Creativity," *International Journal of Human Resource Management* 21, no. 1 (2010): 46–60; Long-Chuan Lu, Ya-Wen Huang, and Hsiu-Hua Chang, "Confucian Dynamism, the Role of Money and Consumer Ethical Beliefs: An Exploratory Study in Taiwan," *Ethics and Behavior* 24, no. 1 (2014): 34–52; Zhenzhong Ma et al., "Confucian Ideal Personality and Chinese Business Negotiation Styles: An Indigenous Perspective," *Group Decis Negot* 24 (2015): 383–400.

108. Hennessey and Amabile, *Creativity*; Saba Ghayas and Farah Malik, "Sense of Humor as Predictor of Creativity Level in University Undergraduates," *Journal of Behavioural Sciences* 23, no. 2 (2013): 49–61; Graeme Galloway, "Psychological Studies of Relationship of Sense of Humor to Creativity and Intelligence: A Review," *European Journal of High Ability* 5, no. 2 (1994): 133–44; Mary C. Murdock and Rita M. Ganim, "Creativity and Humor: Integration and Incongruity," *Journal of Creative Behavior* 27, no. 1 (1993): 57–70; Lynne Rouff, "Creativity and Sense of Humor," *Psychological Reports* 37 (1975): 1022.

109. Christine Charyton and Glenn E. Snelbecker, "Engineers' and Musicians' Choices of Self-Descriptive Adjectives as Potential Indicators of Creativity by Gender and Domain," *Psychology of Aesthetics, Creativity, and the Arts* 1, no. 2 (2007): 91–99; Gregory J. Feist, "The Influence of Personality on Artistic and Scientific Creativity," in *Handbook of Creativity*, ed. Robert J. Sternberg (Cambridge, UK: Cambridge University Press, 1999), 273–96; Bonnie C. Graham, Janet K. Sawyers,

and Karen B. DeBord, "Teachers' Creativity, Playfulness, and Style of Interaction with Children," *Creativity Research Journal* 2, no. 1–2 (1989): 41–50; Deborah W. Tegano, "Relationship of Tolerance of Ambiguity and Playfulness to Creativity," *Psychological Reports* 66, no. 3 (1990): 1047–56.

110. Teresa Amabile, "Effects of External Evaluation on Artistic Creativity," *Journal of Personality and Social Psychology* 37, no. 2 (1979): 221–33; Doyle W. Bishop and Charles A. Chace, "Parental Conceptual Systems, Home Play Environment, and Potential Creativity in Children," *Journal of Experimental Child Psychology* 12 (1971): 318–38; Charyton and Snelbecker, "Engineers"; Mihaly Csikszentmihalyi and Isabella Selega Csikszentmihalyi, *Optimal Experience: Psychological Studies of Flow in Consciousness* (New York: Cambridge University Press, 1988); Feist, "Influence"; Fielding, "Creativity"; Gardner, "Giftedness"; Graham, Sawyers, and DeBord, "Teachers"; Tegano, "Relationship"; Torrance, *Guiding*; Torrance, *Education*; Samuel West, Eva Hoff, and Ingegerd Carlsson, "Playing at Work: Professionals' Conceptions of the Functions of Play on Organizational Creativity," *International Journal of Creativity and Problem Solving* 23, no. 2 (2013): 5–23.

111. Charyton and Snelbecker, "Engineers"; Csikszentmihalyi and Csikszentmihalyi, *Optimal*; Torrance, *Search*; Torrance, *Manifesto*; Torrance and Safter, *Making*.

112. David McClelland and Adam Cheriff, "The Immunoehancing Effects of Humor on Secretory IgA and Resistance to Respiratory Infections," *Psychology and Health* 12 (1997): 329–44; Norbert Schwarz, "Feelings as Information: Informational and Motivational Functions of Affective States in *Handbook of Motivational Cognition*, vol. 2, eds. E. Tory Higgins and Richard M. Sorrentino (New York: Guildford, 1996); Norbert Schwarz and Gerd Bohner, "Feelings and Their Motivational Implications: Moods and the Action Sequence," in *The Psychology of Action: Linking Cognition and Motivation to Behavior*, eds. Peter M. Gollwitzer and John A. Bargh (New York: Guildford, 1996), 119–45.

113. Teresa Amabile, "Effects of External Evaluation on Artistic Creativity," *Journal of Personality and Social Psychology* 37, no. 2 (1979): 221–33; Bishop and Chace, "Parental"; Fielding, "Creativity"; Gardner, "Giftedness"; Torrance, *Guiding*; Torrance, *Education*; Torrance, *Search*; Torrance and Safter, *Making*; Samuel West, Eva Hoff, and Ingegerd Carlsson, "Playing at Work: Professionals' Conceptions of the Functions of Play on Organizational Creativity," *International Journal of Creativity and Problem Solving* 23, no. 2 (2013): 5–23; Robert S. Wyer Jr. and James E. Collins II, "A Theory of Humor Elicitation," *Psychological Review* 99 (1992): 663–88; Avner Ziv, "The Influence of Humorous Atmosphere on Divergent Thinking," *Contemporary Educational Psychology* 8 (1983): 68–75.

114. Michael K. Cundall Jr., "Humor and the Limits of Incongruity," *Creativity Research Journal* 19, no. 2–3 (2007): 203–11; Allan Filipowicz, "From Positive Affect to Creativity: The Surprising Role of Surprise," *Creativity Research Journal* 18 (2006): 141–52.

115. Bloom, *Developing*; Torrance, *Search*; Torrance and Safter, *Making*.

116. Ted Cohen, *Jokes: Philosophical Thoughts on Joking Matters* (Chicago: University of Chicago Press, 1999); Michael K. Cundall Jr., "Humor and the Limits of Incongruity," *Creativity Research Journal* 19, no. 2–3 (2007): 203–11; Elizabeth E. Graham, "The Involvement of Sense of Humor in the Development of Social Relationships," *Communication Reports* 8, no. 2 (1995): 158–69; Josephine Chinying Lang and Chay Hoon Lee, "Workplace Humor and Organizational Creativity," *The International Journal of Human Resource Management* 21, no. 1 (2010): 46–60; Herbert M. Lefcourt, *Humor: The Psychology of Living Buoyantly* (New York: Kluwer Academic, 2001); John B. Nezlek and Peter Derks, "Use of Humor as a Coping Mechanism, Psychological Adjustment, and Social Interaction," *Humor* 14, no. 4 (2001): 395–413; Torrance, *Search*; Torrance and Safter, *Making*.

117. Teresa Amabile, "The Motivation to Be Creative," in *Frontiers of Creativity Research: Beyond the Basics*, ed. Scott G. Isaksen (Buffalo, NY: Bearly Limited, 1987), 223–54; Judith B. Alter, "Creativity Profile of University and Conservatory Dance Students," *Journal of Personality Assessment* 48, no. 2 (1984): 153–58; Judith B. Alter, "Creativity Profile of University and Conservatory Music Students," *Creativity Research Journal* 2, no. 3 (1989): 184–95; Frank Barron and David M. Harrington, "Creativity, Intelligence, and Personality," *Annual Review of Psychology* 32, no. 1 (1981):

439–76; Jack A. Chambers, "Relating Personality and Biographical Factors to Scientific Creativity," *Psychological Monographs: General and Applied* 78, no. 7 (1964): 1–20; Gary A. Davis, *Creativity Is Forever* (Dubuque, IA: Kendall/Hunt, 2004); Feist, "Influence"; Arthur Koestler, *The Act of Creation* (New York: Macmillan, 1964).

118. Robert L. Helmreich, Janet T. Spence, and Robert S. Pred, "Making It without Losing It: Type A, Achievement Motivation, and Scientific Attainment Revisited," *Personality and Social Psychology Bulletin* 14 (1987): 495–504; Ding-Bang Luh and Chia-Chen Lu, "From Cognitive Style to Creativity Achievement: The Mediating Role of Passion," *Psychology of Aesthetics, Creativity, and the Arts* 6, no. 3 (2012): 282–88; K. A. Matthews et al., "Pattern A, Achievement Striving, and Scientific Merit: Does Pattern A Help or Hinder?" *Journal of Personality and Social Psychology* 39 (1980): 962–67; Roe, *Making*; Simonton, "Creativity and Genius"; Tardif and Sternberg, "Know"; Ellen Winner, "Creativity and Talent," in *Well-Being: Positive Development across the Life Course*, eds. Marc H. Bornstein, Lucy Davidson, Corey L. M. Keyes, and Kristin A. Moore (Mahwah, NJ: Erlbaum, 2003), 371–80; Robert J. Vallerand et al., "Les Passions de L'ame: On Obsessive and Harmonious Passion," *Journal of Personality and Social Psychology* 85, no. 4 (2003): 756–67; Robert J. Vallerand et al., "Passion in Sport: A Look at Determinants and Affective Experiences," *Journal of Sport and Exercise Psychology* 28, no. 4 (2006): 454–78.

119. J. A. Horne, "Sleep Loss and 'Divergent' Thinking Ability," *Sleep: Journal of Sleep Research and Sleep Medicine* 11, no. 6 (1988): 528–36.

120. Ap Dijksterhuis and Teun Meurs, "Where Creativity Resides: The Generative Power of Unconscious Thought," *Consciousness and Cognition* 15, no. 1 (2006): 135–46; Ap Dijksterhuis and Loran F. Nordgren, "A Theory of Unconscious Thought," *Perspectives on Psychological Science* 1, no. 2 (2006): 95–109; Koestler, *Act*; Laura J. Kray, Adam D. Galinsky, and Elaine M. Wong, "Thinking within the Box: The Relational Processing Style Elicited by Counterfactual Mind-Sets," *Journal of Personality and Social Psychology* 91, no. 1 (2006): 33–48; Colin Martindale, "Biological Bases of Creativity," in *Handbook of Creativity*, ed. Robert J. Sternberg (New York: Cambridge University Press, 1999), 137–52; Jonathan W. Schooler and Joseph Melcher, "The Ineffability of Insight," in *The Creative Cognition Approach*, eds. Steven M. Smith, Thomas B. Ward, and Ronald A. Finke (Cambridge: MIT Press, 1995), 97–134; Steven M. Smith and Steven E. Blankenship, "Incubation Effects," *Bulletin of the Psychonomic Society* 27, no. 4 (1989): 311–14; Thomas B. Ward, "Structured Imagination: The Role of Category Structure in Exemplar Generation," *Cognitive Psychology* 27, no. 1 (1994): 1–40.

121. Dean Keith Simonton, "Creative Productivity and Age: A Mathematical Model Based on a Two-Step Cognitive Process," *Developmental Review* 4, no. 1 (1984): 77–111; Simonton, *Greatness*; Dean Keith Simonton, "Film Music: Are Award-Winning Scores and Songs Heard in Successful Motion Pictures?" *Psychology of Aesthetics, Creativity, and the Arts* 1 (2007): 53–60.

122. Simonton, *Greatness*.

123. Ibid.

124. Lauren D. Baker et al., "Effects of Aerobic Exercise on Mile Cognitive Impairment: A Controlled Trial," *Archives of Neurology* 67 (2010): 71–79; C. B. Hall et al., "Cognitive Activities Delay Onset of Memory Decline in Persons Who Develop Dementia," *Neurology* 73 (2009): 356–61; Nikolaos Scarmeas and Yaakov Stern, "Cognitive Reserve and Lifestyle," *Journal of Clinical and Experimental Neuropsychology* 25 (2003): 625–33.

125. Laurie Lisle, *Portrait of an Artist: A Biography of O'Keeffe* (Albuquerque: University of New Mexico Press, 1986).

126. Nelson Mandela, *Long Walk to Freedom: The Autobiography of Nelson Mandela* (New York: Little, Brown, 1994).

127. Sheen, *Jobs*.

128. "About Georgia O'Keeffe," Georgia O'Keeffe Museum, April, 20, 2016, http://www.okeeffemuseum.org/about-georgia-okeeffe.html.

Chapter 5: The Storm Climate That Nurtures the Storm Attitudes

1. Anthony Sampson, *Mandela: The Authorized Biography* (New York: Vintage Books, 1999).

2. Laaren Brown and Lenny Hort, *DK Biography: Nelson Mandela: A Photographic Story of a Life* (New York: DK, 2006).

3. Nelson Mandela Foundation, "Names," 2015, https://www.nelsonmandela.org/content/page/names.

4. Sampson, *Mandela*.

5. Nelson Mandela, *Long Walk to Freedom: The Autobiography of Nelson Mandela* (New York: Little, Brown, 1994).

6. Ibid.

7. Mandela, *Freedom*.

8. Brown and Hort, *DK*.

9. Sampson, *Mandela*.

10. Ibid.

11. Ibid.

12. Ibid.

13. Mandela, *Freedom*; Sampson, *Mandela*.

14. Anders Hallengren, "Nelson Mandela and the Rainbow of Culture," Nobelprize.org, September 11, 2001, http://www.nobelprize.org/nobel_prizes/peace/laureates/1993/mandela-article.html; Sampson, *Mandela*.

15. Nelson Mandela Foundation, "Timeline," 2015, https://www.nelsonmandela.org/content/page/timeline.

16. Mandela, *Freedom*.

17. Ibid.

18. Ibid.

19. Ibid.

20. Ibid.

21. Ibid.

22. Mandela, *Freedom*; Sampson, *Mandela*.

23. Mandela, *Freedom*.

24. Brown and Hort, *DK*.

25. Mandela, *Freedom*.

26. Ibid.; Sampson, *Mandela*.

27. Sampson, *Mandela*.

28. Mandela, *Freedom*.

29. Brown and Hort, *DK*.

30. Sampson, *Mandela*.

31. Mandela, *Freedom*.

32. Ibid.

33. Ibid.

34. Ibid.

35. John Battersby, "What Made Nelson Mandela Great," CNN, December 5, 2013, http://www.cnn.com/2013/12/05/opinion/battersby-nelson-mandela/.

36. Mandela, *Freedom*.

37. Battersby, "Nelson."

38. Mandela, *Freedom*.

39. Sampson, *Mandela*.

40. Mandela, *Freedom*.

41. Brown and Hort, *DK*.

42. Hallengren, "Mandela."

43. Ibid.
44. Sampson, *Mandela*.
45. Ibid.
46. Hallengren, "Mandela."
47. Walter G. Bowerman, *Studies in Genius* (New York: Philosophical Library, 1947); Havelock Ellis, *A Study of a British Genius*, rev. ed. (Boston, MA: Houghton Mifflin, 1926); Francis Galton, *English Men of Science: Their Nature and Nurture* (UK: Macmillan, 1874); Evelyn Raskin, "Comparison of Scientific and Literary Ability: A Biographical Study of Eminent Scientists and Men of Letters of the Nineteenth Century," *Journal of Abnormal and Social Psychology* 31, no. 1 (1936): 20–35; Anne Roe, *The Making of a Scientist* (New York: Dodd, Mead, 1953); Dean Keith Simonton, "Creativity and Genius," in *Handbook of Personality: Theory and Research*, eds. Oliver P. John, Richard W. Roberts, and Lawrence A. Pervin (New York: Gilford, 2008), 679–98.
48. Trinidad Maniquis Balagtas, "The Relationship between Parental Attitudes and Children's Creativity in Rhythmic Movements," *Dissertation Abstracts* 29, no. 12-A (1969): 4304–4305; Rosa Aurora Chávez-Eakle, "Creativity and Personality," in *Measuring Creativity: Proceedings for the Conference: Can Creativity Be Measured?* ed. Ernesto Villalba (Luxembourg: Office of the European Union, 2009), 245–55; Lois E. Datta and Morris B. Parloff, "On the Relevance of Autonomy: Parent-Child Relationships and Early Scientific Creativity," *Proceedings of the 75th Annual Convention of the American Psychological Association* 2 (1967): 149–50; George Domino, "Maternal Personality Correlates of Sons' Creativity," *Journal of Consulting and Clinical Psychology* 33, no. 2 (1969): 180–83; Bernice T. Eiduson, "Artist and Non-Artist: A Comparative Study," *Journal of Personality* 26, no. 1 (1958): 13–28; Gregory J. Feist, "A Meta-Analysis of Personality in Scientific and Artistic Creativity," *Personality and Social Psychology Review* 2, no. 4 (1998): 290–309; Jacob W. Getzels and Philip W. Jackson, "Family Environment and Cognitive Style: A Study of the Sources of Highly Intelligent and of Highly Creative Adolescents," *American Sociological Review* 26 (1961): 351–59; Donald W. MacKinnon, "The Nature and Nurture of Creative Talent," *American Psychologist* 17, no. 7 (1962): 484–95; Richard S. Mansfield and Thomas V. Busse, *The Psychology of Creativity and Discovery: Scientists and Their Work* (Chicago: Nelson-Hall, 1981); Paula Olszewski-Kubilius, *The Social and Emotional Development of Gifted Children: What Do We Know?* (Waco, TX: Prufrock, 2001); Roe, *Making of Scientist*; Rodney Julian Shapiro, "Creative Research Scientists," *Psychologica Africana Monograph Supplement* no. 4 (1968); Morris Isaac Stein, "A Transactional Approach to Creativity," in *Scientific Creativity: Its Recognition and Development*, eds. Calvin Taylor and Frank Barron (New York: Wiley, 1963), 217–27; Pamela Tierney and Steven M. Farmer, "Creative Self-Efficacy: Its Potential Antecedents and Relationship to Creative Performance," *Academy of Management Journal* 45, no. 6 (2002): 1137–48; Donald Woods Winnicott, *Playing and Reality* (London, UK: Tavistock, 1971).
49. Robert S. Albert, "Family Positions and the Attainment of Eminence: A Study of Special Family Positions and Special Family Experiences," in *Genius and Eminence: The Social Psychology of Creativity and Exceptional Achievement*, ed. Robert S. Albert (Oxford: Pergamon, 1983), 141–54; Teresa Amabile, *Creativity in Context* (Boulder, CO: Westview, 1996); Kathleen Dewing, "Family Influences on Creativity: A Review and Discussion," *Journal of Special Education* 4, no. 4 (1970): 399–404; John E. Drevdahl, "Some Developmental and Environmental Factors in Creativity," in *Widening Horizons in Creativity*, ed. Calvin W. Taylor (New York: Wiley, 1964), 170–85; Carman Hudson and Nick Stinnett, "The Relationship of Family Type to Aspects of Wellness of Young Children: Creativity and Self-Perceived Competence," *Wellness Perspectives* 6, no. 3 (1990): 31–41; Saroj Saxena and Rakesh Kumar, "Study of Creativity in Relation to Anxiety," *Indian Psychological Review* 28 (1985): 5–8; Marvin Siegelman, "Parent Behavior Correlates of Personality Traits Related to Creativity in Sons and Daughters," *Journal of Consulting and Clinical Psychology* 40, no. 1 (1973): 43–47; Paul S. Weisberg and Kayla J. Springer, "Environmental Factors in Creative Function: A Study of Gifted Children," *Archives of General Psychiatry* 5, no. 6 (1961): 554–64.
50. Brooke C. Feeney and Meredith Van Vleet, "Growing through Attachment: The Interplay of

Attachment and Exploration in Adulthood," *Journal of Social and Personal Relationships* 27, no. 2 (2010): 226–34; Mario Mikulincer, "Adult Attachment Style and Information Processing: Individual Differences in Curiosity and Cognitive Closure," *Journal of Personality and Social Psychology* 72, no. 5 (1997): 1217–30; Mario Mikulincer and Phillip R. Shaver, *Attachment in Adulthood: Structure, Dynamics, and Change* (New York: Guilford, 2007); Mario Mikulincer, Phillip R. Shaver, and Eldad Rom, "The Effects of Implicit and Explicit Security Priming on Creative Problem Solving," *Cognition and Emotion* 25, no. 3 (2011): 519–31; Rhona A. Ochse, *Before the Gates of Excellence: The Determinants of Creative Genius* (Cambridge, UK: Cambridge University Press, 1990).

51. Rob M. Fielding, "A Socio-Cognitive Perspective on Cross-Cultural Attitudes and Practices in Creativity Development," *Australian Art Education* 20 (1997): 27–33; Leslie Kathleen Williams and Stephen J. J. McGuire, "Effects of National Culture on Economic Creativity and Innovation Implementation," *Institutions of Market Exchange* (2005): 31–40.

52. Diana Baumrind, "Current Patterns of Parental Authority," *Developmental Psychology Monograph* 4, no. 12 (1971): 1–103; Danielle D. Fearon, Daelynn Copeland, and Terrill F. Saxon, "The Relationship between Parenting Styles and Creativity in a Sample of Jamaican Children," *Creativity Research Journal* 25, no. 1 (2013): 119–28; Zahari Ishak, Suet Fin Low, and Poh Li Lau, "Parenting Style as a Moderator for Students' Academic Achievement," *Journal of Science Education and Technology* 21, no. 4 (2012): 487–93; Angie L. Miller, Amber D. Lambert, and Kristie L. Speirs Neumeister, "Parenting Style, Perfectionism, and Creativity in High-Ability and High-Achieving Young Adults," *Journal for the Education of the Gifted* 35 (2012): 344–65; Brent C. Miller and Diana Gerard, "Family Influences on the Development of Creativity in Children: An Integrative Review," *Family Coordinator* 28, no. 3 (1979): 295–312.

53. Mojdeh Bayat, "Clarifying Issues Regarding the Use of Praise with Young Children," *Topics in Early Childhood Special Education* 31, no. 2 (2011): 121–28; David J. Sill, "Integrative Thinking, Synthesis, and Creativity in Interdisciplinary Studies," *Journal of General Education* 50, no. 4 (2001): 288–311.

54. Edwin A. Locke and Gary P. Latham, "Building a Practically Useful Theory of Goal Setting and Task Motivation: A 35-Year Odyssey," *American Psychologist* 57, no. 9 (2002): 705–17; Edwin A. Locke and Gary P. Latham, *A Theory of Goal Setting and Task Performance* (Englewood Cliffs, NJ: Prentice Hall, 1990).

55. Sarah Sayeed et al., "Adolescent Marijuana Use Intentions: Using Theory to Plan an Intervention," *Drugs: Education, Prevention, and Policy* 12, no. 1 (2005): 19–34; Ben Sessa, "Is It Time to Revisit the Role of Psychedelic Drugs in Enhancing Human Creativity?" *Journal of Psychopharmacology* 22, no. 8 (2008): 821–27; Substance Abuse and Mental Health Services Administration [SAMHSA], *Results from the 2009 National Survey on Drug Use and Health*, vol. 1, *Summary of National Findings* (DHHS No. SMA 10-4586 Findings) (Rockville, MD: SAMHSA, 2010).

56. Allan Beveridge and Graeme Yorston, "I Drink, Therefore I Am: Alcohol and Creativity," *Journal of the Royal Society of Medicine* 92 (1999): 646–48; Roland Gustafson and Håkan Källmén, "The Effect of Alcohol Intoxication on Primary and Secondary Processes in Male Social Drinkers," *British Journal of Addiction* 84, no. 12 (1989): 1507–13; Joshua A. Hicks et al., "Expecting Innovation: Psychoactive Drug Primes and the Generation of Creative Solutions," *Experimental and Clinical Psychopharmacology* 19, no. 4 (2011): 314–20; Ryan E. Holt and James C. Kaufman, "Marijuana and Creativity," in *Cannabis-Philosophy for Everyone: What Were We Just Talking About?* ed. Dale Jacquette (New York: Wiley-Blackwell, 2010), 114–20; Arnold M. Ludwig, *The Price of Greatness: Resolving the Creativity and Madness Controversy* (New York: Guilford, 1995); Jonathan A. Plucker, Andrea McNeely, and Carla Morgan, "Controlled Substance-Related Beliefs and Use: Relationships to Undergraduates' Creative Personality Traits," *Journal of Creative Behavior* 43, no. 2 (2009): 94–101.

57. Nora D. Volkow, Joanna S. Fowler, and Gene-Jack Wang, "The Addicted Human Brain Viewed in Light of Imaging Studies: Brain Circuits and Treatment Strategies," *Neuropharmacology* 47 (2004): 3–13.

58. K. F. Haven *Marvels of Science: 50 Fascinating 5-Minute Reads* (Westport, CT: Libraries

Unlimited, 1994); J. S. Smith, *Patenting the Sun: Polio and the Salk Vaccine* (New York: William Morrow, 1990).

59. Robyn Beaman and Kevin Wheldall, "Teachers' Use of Approval and Disapproval in the Classroom," *Educational Psychology* 20, no. 4 (2000): 431–46.

60. Jacinta Bronte-Tinkew, Kristin A. Moore, and Jennifer Carrano, "Father-Child Relationship, Parenting Styles, and Adolescent Risk Behaviors in Intact Families," *Journal of Family Issues* 27, no. 6 (2006): 850–81; Dean C. Dauw, "Life Experiences of Original Thinkers and Good Elaborators," *Exceptional Children* 32, no. 7 (1966): 433–40; Domino, "Maternal"; Fearon, Copeland, and Saxon, "Relationship"; Machteld Hoeve, Arjan Blokland, Judith Semon Dubas, Rolf Loeber, Jan R. M. Gerris, and P. H. van der Laan, "Trajectories of Delinquency and Parenting Styles," *Journal of Abnormal Child Psychology* 36, no. 2 (2008): 223–35; Miller, Lambert, and Speirs Neumeister, "Parenting"; Miller and Gerard, "Family"; Christian L. Porter et al., "A Comparative Study of Child Temperament and Parenting in Beijing, China and the Western United States," *International Journal of Behavioral Development* 29, no. 6 (2005): 541–51.

61. Alfred L. Baldwin, "The Effect of Home Environment on Nursery School Behavior," *Child Development* 20 (1949): 49–61; Bronte-Tinkew, Moore, and Carrano, "Father-Child"; Dauw, "Life"; John S. Dacey, "Discriminating Characteristics of the Families of Highly Creative Adolescents," *Journal of Creative Behavior* 23, no. 4 (1989): 263–71; Domino, "Maternal"; Hoeve et al., "Trajectories"; Donald W. MacKinnon, "Creativity in Architects," in *The Creative Person*, ed. Donald W. MacKinnon (Berkeley: Institute of Personality Assessment Research, University of California, 1961), 291–320; Porter et al., "Comparative"; Mark A. Runco and Jill Nemiro, "Problem Finding, Creativity, and Giftedness," *Roeper Review* 16, no. 4 (1994): 235–41; Deborah W. Tegano, Janet K. Sawyers, and James D. Moran III, "Problem-Finding and Solving in Play: The Teacher's Role," *Childhood Education* 66, no. 2 (1989): 92–97; K. E. Williams, J. Ciarrochi, and P. C. L. Heaven, "Inflexible Parents, Inflexible Kids: A 6-Year Longitudinal Study of Parenting Style and the Development of Psychological Flexibility in Adolescents," *Journal of Youth & Adolescence* 41 (2012): 1053–66.

62. Baldwin, "Effect"; Bronte-Tinkew, Moore, and Carrano, "Father-Child"; Dauw, "Life"; Dacey, "Discriminating"; Domino, "Maternal"; Hoeve et al., "Trajectories"; MacKinnon, "Architects"; Porter et al., "Comparative"; Runco and Nemiro, "Problem"; Tegano, Sawyers, and Moran, "Problem-Finding"; Williams, Ciarrochi, and Heaven, "Inflexible."

63. Bronte-Tinkew, Moore, and Carrano, "Father-Child"; Dauw, "Life"; Domino, "Maternal"; Hoeve et al., "Trajectories"; Porter et al., "Comparative."

64. Robert S. Albert, "The Contribution of Early Family History to the Achievement of Eminence," in *Talent Development*, eds. Nicholas Colangelo, Susan Assouline and D. L. Ambroson (Dayton, OH: Psychology, 1994), 311–60; Robert S. Albert, "Some Reasons Why Childhood Creativity Often Fails to Make It Past Puberty into the Real World," *New Directions for Child Development* 72 (1996): 43–56; Caria Goble, James D. Moran III, and Anne K. Bomba, "Maternal Teaching Techniques and Preschool Children's Ideational Fluency," *Creativity Research Journal* 4, no. 3 (1991): 273–79.

65. Bronte-Tinkew, Moore, and Carrano, "Father-Child"; Dauw, "Life"; Domino, "Maternal"; Fearon, Copeland, and Saxon, "Relationship"; Hoeve et al., "Trajectories"; Porter et al., "Comparative"; Miller, Lambert, and Speirs Neumeister, "Parenting"; Miller and Gerard, "Family."

66. Fearon, Copeland, and Saxon, "Relationship"; Miller, Lambert, and Speirs Neumeister, "Parenting"; Miller and Gerard, "Family."

67. Amabile, *Creativity*; Balagtas, "Relationship"; K. Chan and S. Chan, "Perceived Parenting Styles and Goal Orientations: A Study of Teacher Education Students in Hong Kong," *Research in Education* 74 (2005): 9–21; Datta and Parloff, "Relevance"; Dewing, "Family"; Getzels and Jackson, "Family"; Ishak, Low, and Lau, "Parenting"; MacKinnon, "Nature"; Miller, Lambert, and Speirs Neumeister, "Parenting"; Shapiro, "Scientists"; Woodwin Watson, "Some Personality Differences in Children Related to Strict or Permissive Parental Discipline, *Journal of Psychology* 44, no. 1 (1957): 227–49.

68. Pew Research Center, "The Rise of Asian Americans," *Pew Research Center: Social and*

Demographic Trends, April 4, 2013, http://www.pewsocialtrends.org/2012/06/19/the-rise-of-Asian Americans/2/.

69. Ibid.

70. Albert Bandura et al., "Multifaceted Impact of Self-Efficacy Beliefs on Academic Functioning," *Child Development* 67 (1996): 1206–22; Albert Bandura et al., "Self-Efficacy Beliefs as Shapers of Children's Aspirations and Career Trajectories, *Child Development* 72 (2001): 187–206; Jacquelynne S. Eccles, Mina N. Vida, and Bonnie Barber, "The Relation of Early Adolescents' College Plans and Both Academic Ability and Task-Value Beliefs to Subsequent College Enrollment," *Journal of Early Adolescence* 24, no. 1 (2004): 63–77; Levon T. Esters, "Factors Influencing Postsecondary Education Enrollment Behaviors of Urban Agricultural Education Students," *Career and Technical Education Research* 32, no. 2 (2007): 79–98; John Mark Froiland, Aubrey Peterson, and Mark L. Davison, "The Long-Term Effects of Early Parent Involvement and Parent Expectation in the USA," *School Psychology International* 34 (2013): 33–50; Timothy Z. Keith et al., "Does Parental Involvement Affect Eighth-Grade Student Achievement? Structural Analysis of National Data," *School Psychology Review* 22 (1993): 474–96; Chris Michael Kirk et al., "The Role of Parent Expectations on Adolescent Educational Aspirations," *Educational Studies* 37 (2011): 89–99; Kun-Shia Liu et al., "Longitudinal Effects of Educational Expectations and Achievement Attributions on Adolescents' Academic Achievements," *Adolescence* 44, no. 176 (2009): 911–24; Laura W. Perna, "Differences in the Decision to Attend College among African Americans, Hispanics, and Whites," *Journal of Higher Education* 7 (2000): 117–42; Hannu Raty and Kati Kasanen, "A Seven-Year Follow-Up Study on Parents' Expectations of Their Children's Further Education," *Journal of Applied Social Psychology* 40 (2010): 2711–35; Abraham M. Rutchick et al., "Great Expectations: The Biasing Effects of Reported Child Behavior Problems on Educational Expectancies and Subsequent Academic Achievement," *Journal of Social and Clinical Psychology* 28 (2009): 39–413; Maxine Seaborn Thompson, Karl L. Alexander, and Doris R. Entwisle, "Household Composition, Parental Expectations, and School Achievement," *Social Forces* 67 (1988): 424–51; Dan Wood, Rachel Kaplan, and Vonnie C. McLoyd, "Gender Differences in the Educational Expectations of Urban, Low-Income African American Youth: The Role of Parents and the School," *Journal of Youth and Adolescence* 36 (2007): 417–27; Min Zhan, "Assets, Parental Expectations and Involvement, and Children's Educational Performance," *Children and Youth Services Review* 28 (2006): 961–75.

71. Drevdahl, "Developmental."

72. Bayat, "Clarifying"; Sill, "Integrative."

73. Locke and Latham, "Building"; Locke and Latham, *Theory.*

74. Howard E. Gruber, *Darwin on Man: A Psychological Study of Scientific Creativity* (Chicago: University of Chicago Press, 1981); John R. Hayes, *The Complete Problem Solver*, 2nd ed. (Hillsdale, NJ: Erlbaum, 1989); Ann McGreevy, "All in the Golden Afternoon: The Early Life of Charles L. Dodgson (Lewis Carroll)," *Gifted Child Quarterly* 36, no. 1 (1992): 6–10; Michael D. Mumford et al., "Process-Based Measures of Creative Problem-Solving Skills: II. Information Encoding," *Creativity Research Journal* 9, no. 1 (1996): 77–88; Michael D. Mumford et al., "Process-Based Measures of Creative Problem-Solving Skills: III. Category Selection," *Creativity Research Journal* 9, no. 4 (1996): 395–406; Andrea S. Vincent, Brian P. Decker, and Michael D. Mumford, "Divergent Thinking, Intelligence, and Expertise: A Test of Alternative Models," *Creativity Research Journal* 14, no. 2 (2002): 163–78; Robert W. Weisberg, *Creativity: Beyond the Myth of Genius* (New York: W. H. Freeman, 1993); Robert W. Weisberg, "Prolegomena to Theories of Insight in Problem Solving: Definition of Terms and a Taxonomy of Problems," in *The Nature of Insight*, ed. Robert J. Sternberg and Janet E. Davidson (Cambridge, MA: MIT Press, 1995), 157–96.

75. Arthur J. Cropley, *More Ways Than One: Fostering Creativity in the Classroom* (Norwood, NJ: Ablex, 1992); J. McV. Hunt and John Paraskevopoulos, "Children's Psychological Development as a Function of the Inaccuracy of Their Mothers' Knowledge of Their Abilities," *Journal of Genetic Psychology* 136, no. 2 (1980): 285–98; Mark A. Runco and Joni Radio Gaynor, "Creativity as Optimal Development," in *Creativity and Consciousness: Philosophical and Psychological Dimensions*, eds.

Jerry Brzezinski, Sanot Di Nuovo, Tadeusz Marek, and Tomasz Maruszewski (Amsterdam/Atlanta: Rodopi, 1993), 395–412; Raj Pal Singh, "Parental Perception about Creative Children," *Creative Child and Adult Quarterly* 12, no. 1 (1987): 39–42; E. Paul Torrance, *Guiding Creative Talent* (Englewood Cliffs, NJ: Prentice-Hall, 1962).

76. Albert Bandura, *Self-Efficacy: The Exercise of Control* (New York: Freeman, 1997); Bandura, *Foundations*; Ronald A. Beghetto, "Creative Self-Efficacy: Correlates in Middle and Secondary Students," *Creativity Research Journal* 18, no. 4 (2006): 447–57; Locke and Latham, "Building."

77. Getzels and Jackson, "Family"; Twila Z. Tardif and Robert J. Sternberg, "What Do We Know about Creativity?" in *The Nature of Creativity*, ed. Robert J. Sternberg (New York: Cambridge University Press, 1999), 429–40; E. Paul Torrance, "Prediction of Adult Creative Achievement among High School Seniors," *Gifted Child Quarterly* 13 (1969): 223–29.

78. Locke and Latham, "Building"; Locke and Latham, *Theory*.

79. Albert Bandura, "Self-Efficacy: Toward a Unifying Theory of Behavioral Change," *Psychological Review* 84, no. 2 (1977): 191–215; Tierney and Farmer, "Creative."

80. Bandura, "Determinants"; Bandura, *Foundations*; Bandura, "Human"; Bandura, "Conception"; Bandura, "Social"; Mimi Bong, "Role of Self-Efficacy and Task-Value in Predicting College Students' Course Performance and Future Enrollment Intentions," *Contemporary Educational Psychology* 26 (2001): 553–70; Lane, Lane, and Kyprianou, "Self-Efficacy"; Locke and Latham, "Building"; Prat-Sala and Redford, "Interplay; Richardson, "Motives."

81. Roy F. Baumeister, Jennifer D. Campbell, Joachim I. Krueger, and Kathleen D. Vohs, "Does High Self-Esteem Cause Better Performance, Interpersonal Success, Happiness, or Healthier Lifestyles?" *Psychological Science in the Public Interest* 4, no. 1 (2003): 1–44; Michael La Hsu, Sheng-Tsung Hou, and Hsueh-Liang Fan, "Creative Self-Efficacy and Innovative Behavior in a Service Setting: Optimism as a Moderator," *Journal of Creative Behavior* 45, no. 4 (2011): 258–72.

82. Baumeister et al., "Self-Esteem"; Roy F. Baumeister, Dianne M. Tice, and Debra G. Hutton, "Self-Presentational Motivations and Personality Differences in Self-Esteem," *Journal of Personality* 57, no. 3 (1989): 547–79.

83. Steven J. Heine and Darrin R. Lehman, "Cultural Variation in Unrealistic Optimism: Does the West Feel More Invulnerable Than the East? *Journal of Personality and Social Psychology* 68 (1995): 595–607; Steven J. Heine and Darrin R. Lehman, "Culture, Dissonance, and Self-Affirmation," *Personality and Social Psychology Bulletin* 23 (1997): 389–400; Steven J. Heine and Darrin R. Lehman, "The Cultural Construction of Self-Enhancement: An Examination of Group-Serving Biases," *Journal of Personality and Social Psychology* 72 (1997): 1268–83; Steven J. Heine, Toshitake Takata, and Darrin R. Lehman, "Beyond Self-Presentation: Evidence for Self-Criticism among Japanese," *Personality and Social Psychology Bulletin* 26 (2000): 71–78; Y. Kashima and H. C. Triandis, "The Self-Serving Bias in Attributions as a Coping Strategy: A Cross-Cultural Study," *Journal of Cross-Cultural Psychology* 17 (1986): 83–97; Shinobu Kitayama et al., "Individual and Collective Processes in the Construction of the Self: Self-Enhancement in the United States and Self-Criticism in Japan," *Journal of Personality and Social Psychology* 72 (1997): 1245–67; Shinobu Kitayama, H. Takagi, and Hisaya Matsumoto, "Causal Attribution of Success and Failure: Cultural Psychology of the Japanese Self [in Japanese]," *Japanese Psychological Review* 38 (1995): 247–80; Hazel Rose Markus and Shinobu Kitayama, "Culture and the Self: Implications for Cognition, Emotion, and Motivation," *Psychological Review* 98, no. 2 (1991): 224–53.

84. McKinney et al., "Parenting"; Miller, Lambert, and Speirs Neumeister, "Parenting."

85. Baumeister et al., "Self-Esteem."

86. Ibid.

87. Beghetto, "Self-Efficacy."

88. Bandura, *Self-Efficacy*; Bandura, *Foundations*; Beghetto, "Self-Efficacy"; Locke and Latham, "Building."

89. Linda M. Anderson, Carolyn M. Evertson, and Jere E. Brophy, "An Experimental Study of Effective Teaching in First-Grade Reading Groups," *Elementary School Journal* 79 (1979): 193–223;

Jere Brophy, "Teacher Praise: A Functional Analysis," *Review of Educational Research* 51, no. 1 (1981): 5–32; Paul C. Burnett and Valerie Mandel, "Praise and Feedback in the Primary Classroom: Teachers' and Students' Perspectives," *Australian Journal of Educational and Developmental Psychology* 10 (2010): 145–54; Carol S. Dweck, "Caution—Praise Can Be Dangerous," *American Educator* 23 (1999): 4–9; Shannon M. Hawkins and L. Juane Heflin, "Increasing Secondary Teachers' Behavior-Specific Praise Using a Video Self-Modeling and Visual Performance Feedback Intervention," *Journal of Positive Behavior Interventions* 13 (2011): 97–108; Jennifer Henderlong and Mark R. Lepper, "The Effects of Praise on Children's Intrinsic Motivation: A Review and Synthesis," *Psychological Bulletin* 128, no. 5 (2002): 774–95; Lyndsay N. Jenkins and Margaret T. Floress, "A Preliminary Investigation of Kindergarten Teachers' Use of Praise in General Education," *Preventing School Failure: Alternative Education for Children and Youth* 59, no. 4 (2015): 253–62; Lyndsay N. Jenkins, Margaret T. Floress, and Wendy Reinke, "Rates and Types of Teacher Praise: A Review and Future Directions," *Psychology in the Schools* 52, no. 5 (2015): 463–76; Tara M. Kalis, Kimberly J. Vannest, and Rich Parker, "Praise Counts: Using Self-Monitoring to Increase Effective Teaching Practices," *Preventing School Failure* 51, no. 3 (2007): 20–27; Melissa L. Kamins and Carol S. Dweck, "Person versus Process Praise and Criticism: Implications for Contingent Self-Worth and Coping," *Developmental Psychology* 35, no. 3 (1999): 835–47; Claudia M. Mueller and Carol S. Dweck, "Praise for Intelligence Can Undermine Children's Motivation and Performance," *Journal of Personality and Social Psychology* 75 (1998): 33–52; Wendy Reinke, Keith C. Herman, and Melissa Stormont, "Classroom-Level Positive Behavior Supports in Schools Implementing SW-PBIS: Identifying Areas for Enhancement," *Journal of Positive Behavior Interventions* 5 (2013): 39–50; Wendy M. Reinke, Teri Lewis-Palmer, and Emma Martin, "The Effect of Visual Performance Feedback on Teacher Use of Behavior-Specific Praise," *Behavior Modification* 31 (2007): 247–63; Wendy M. Reinke, Teri Lewis-Palmer, and Kenneth Merrell, "The Classroom Check-Up: A Classwide Teacher Consultation Model for Increasing Praise and Decreasing Disruptive Behavior," *School Psychology Review* 37 (2008): 315–32; Kevin S. Sutherland, Joseph H. Wehby, and Susan R. Copeland, "Effect of Varying Rates of Behavior-Specific Praise on the On-Task Behavior of Students with EBD," *Journal of Emotional and Behavioral Disorders* 8 (2000): 2–8.

90. McKinney et al., "Parenting"; Miller, Lambert, and Speirs Neumeister, "Parenting."

91. Anderson, Evertson, and Brophy, "Experimental"; Brophy, "Teacher"; Burnett and Mandel, "Praise"; Dweck, "Caution"; Hawkins and Heflin, "Behavior-Specific"; Henderlong and Lepper, "Effects"; Jenkins and Floress, "Preliminary"; Jenkins, Floress, and Reinke, "Rates"; Kalis, Vannest, and Parker, "Praise"; Kamins and Dweck, "Person"; Mueller and Dweck, "Praise"; Reinke, Herman, and Stormont, "Classroom-Level"; Reinke, Lewis-Palmer, and Martin, "Visual"; Reinke, Lewis-Palmer, and Merrell, "Classroom"; Sutherland, Wehby, and Copeland, "Behavior-Specific."

92. Baumeister et al., "Self-Esteem"; Daniela J. Owen, Amy M. S. Slep, and Richard E. Heyman, "The Effect of Praise, Positive Nonverbal Response, Reprimand, and Negative Nonverbal Response on Child Compliance: A Systematic Review," *Clinical Child and Family Psychology Review* 15, no. 4 (2012): 364–85; Wietske M. W. J. van Oorsouw, Petri J. C. M. Embregts, Anna M. T. Bosman, and Andrew Jahoda, "Training Staff Serving Clients with Intellectual Disabilities: A Meta-Analysis of Aspects Determining Effectiveness," *Research in Developmental Disabilities* 30, no. 3 (2009): 503–11.

93. Dweck, "Caution"; Mueller and Dweck, "Praise."

94. Baumeister et al., "Self-Esteem"; Hsu, Hou, and Fan, "Self-Efficacy."

95. Bandura, "Determinants"; Bandura, *Foundations*; Bandura, "Human"; Albert Bandura, "Self-Efficacy Conception of Anxiety," in *Anxiety and Self-Focused Attention*, eds. Ralf Schwarzer and Robert A. Wicklund (New York: Harwood Academic, 1991), 89–110; Bandura, "Social"; Beghetto, "Self-Efficacy"; Bong, "Role"; Hsu, Hou, and Fan, "Self-Efficacy"; John Lane, Andrew M. Lane, and Anna Kyprianou, "Self-Efficacy, Self-Esteem and Their Impact on Academic Performance," *Social Behavior and Personality* 32 (2004): 247–56; Locke and Latham, "Building"; Merce Prat-Sala and Paul Redford, "The Interplay between Motivation, Self-Efficacy, and Approaches to Studying," *British Journal of Educational Psychology* 80, no. 2 (2010): 83–305; John T. E. Richardson, "Motives, Attitudes and Approaches to Studying in Distance Education," *Higher Education* 54 (2007): 385–416.

96. David H. Feldman, "Creativity: Dreams, Insights, and Transformations," in *Changing the World: A Framework for the Study of Creativity*, eds. Mihaly Csikszentmihalyi, David H. Feldman, and Howard Gardner (Westport, CT: Praeger, 1994), 85–102.

97. Bandura, *Foundations*; Bandura, *Self-Efficacy*.

98. Ayelet Fishbach, Tal Eyal, and Stacey R. Finkelstein, "How Positive and Negative Feedback Motivate Goal Pursuit," *Social and Personality Psychology Compass* 4, no. 8 (2010): 517–30; Maria J. Louro, Rik Pieters, and Marcel Zeelenberg, "Dynamics of Multiple Goal Pursuit," *Journal of Personality and Social Psychology* 93 (2007): 174–93.

99. Fishbach, Eyal, and Finkelstein, "Positive"; Maria J. Louro, Rik Pieters, and Marcel Zeelenberg, "Dynamics of Multiple Goal Pursuit," *Journal of Personality and Social Psychology* 93 (2007): 174–93.

100. Baumeister et al., "Self-Esteem"; Charles S. Carver and Michael F. Scheier, *On the Self-Regulation of Behavior* (New York: Cambridge University Press, 1987); Stacey R. Finkelstein and Ayelet Fishbach, "Tell Me What I Did Wrong: Experts Seek and Respond to Negative Feedback," *Journal of Consumer Research* 39, no. 1 (2012): 22–38; Geir Grundvåg Ottesen and Kjell Grønhaug, "Positive Illusions and New Venture Creation: Conceptual Issues and an Empirical Illustration," *Creativity and Innovation Management* 14, no. 4 (2005): 405–12; E. Tory Higgins, "Self-Discrepancy: A Theory Relating Self and Affect," *Psychological Review* 94 (1998): 319–40; Avraham N. Kluger and Angelo DeNisi, "The Effects of Feedback Interventions on Performance: A Historical Review, a Meta-Analysis, and a Preliminary Feedback Intervention Theory," *Psychological Bulletin* 119 (1996): 254–84; Tracy Kwang and William B. Swann Jr., "Do People Embrace Praise Even When They Feel Unworthy? A Review of Critical Tests of Self-Enhancement versus Self-Verification," *Personality and Social Psychology Review* 14, no. 3 (2010): 263–80; Kevin Marjoribanks, "Teacher Perceptions of Student Behavior, Social Environment, and Cognitive Performance," *Journal of Genetic Psychology* 133, no. 2 (1978): 217–28; Robert Rosenthal, "Teacher Expectancy Effects: A Brief Update 25 Years after the Pygmalion Experiment," *Journal of Research in Education* 1, no. 3 (1991): 3–12; Owen, Slep, and Heyman, "Effect"; Yaacov Trope and Efrat Neter, "Reconciling Competing Motives in Self-Evaluation: The Role of Self-Control in Feedback Seeking," *Journal of Personality and Social Psychology* 66 (1994): 646–57; Van Oorsouw et al., "Training Staff Serving Clients with Intellectual Disabilities: A Meta-Analysis of Aspects Determining Effectiveness," *Research in Developmental Disabilities* 30, no. 3 (2009): 503–11; Joanne Rand Whitmore, *Giftedness, Conflict, and Underachievement* (Boston: Allyn and Bacon, 1980).

101. Mansfield and Busse, *Psychology of Creativity*; Felix Post, "Creativity and Psychopathology: A Study of 291 World-Famous Men," *British Journal of Psychiatry* 165 (1994): 22–34; Mikulincer and Shaver, *Attachment*.

102. Michael Jordan, "Michael Jordan Quotes," Brainy Quote, June 2016, http://www .brainyquote.com/quotes/quotes/m/michaeljor127660.html.

103. Colin Berry, "The Nobel Scientists and the Origins of Scientific Achievement," *British Journal of Sociology* 32 (1981): 381–91; Mihaly Csikszentmihalyi, *Flow: The Psychology of Optimal Experience* (New York: Harper and Row, 1990); Ellis, *Study*; Daniel Lim and David DeSteno, "Suffering and Compassion: The Links among Adverse Life Experiences, Empathy, Compassion, and Prosocial Behavior," *Emotion* 16, no. 2 (2016): 175–82; Ludwig, *Price*; Mansfield and Busse, *Psychology*; Felix Post, "Creativity and Psychopathology: A Study of 291 World-Famous Men," *British Journal of Psychiatry* 165 (1994): 22–34; Raskin, "Comparison"; Roe, *Making*; Dean Keith Simonton, "Biographical Typicality, Eminence, and Achievement Style," *Journal of Creative Behavior* 20 (1986): 14–22; Dean Keith Simonton, *Greatness: Who Makes History and Why* (New York: Gilford, 1994); Dean Keith Simonton, *Creativity in Science: Chance, Logic, Genius, and Zeitgeist* (Cambridge, UK: Cambridge University Press, 2004); Simonton, "Creativity and Genius"; Dean Keith Simonton, *Genius 101*, The Psych 101 Series (New York: Springer, 2009); Carolin J. Showers and Kristen C. Kling, "Organization of Self-Knowledge: Implications for Recovery from Sad Mood," *Journal of Personality and Social Psychology* 70 (1996): 578–90; E. Paul Torrance, *The Manifesto: A Guide to Developing a Creative Career* (West Westport, CT: Ablex, 2002).

104. Datta and Parloff, "Relevance"; Dewing, "Family"; Kathleen Dewing and Ronald Taft, "Some Characteristics of the Parents of Creative Twelve-Year-Olds," *Journal of Personality* 41, no. 1 (1973): 71–85; Feist, "Meta-Analysis"; Florence P. Foster, "The Human Relationships of Creative Individuals," *Journal of Creative Behavior* 2 (1968): 111–18; Jacob Getzels and Philip W. Jackson, *Creativity and Intelligence: Explorations with the Gifted Child* (New York: Wiley, 1962); Kathleen Green Gardner and J. D. Moran III, "Family Adaptability, Cohesion, and Creativity," *Creativity Research Journal* 3 (1990): 281–86; Robert C. Nichols, "Parental Attitudes of Mothers of Intelligent Adolescents and Creativity of Their Children," *Child Development* 35, no. 4 (1964): 1041–49.

105. Frank Barron and David M. Harrington, "Creativity, Intelligence, and Personality," *Annual Review of Psychology* 32, no. 1 (1981): 439–76; Ronald A. Beghetto, "Correlates of Intellectual Risk Taking in Elementary School Science," *Journal of Research in Science Teaching* 46, no. 2 (2009): 210–23; Feist, "Meta-Analysis"; Fielding, "Socio-Cognitive"; Joan Freeman, "The Early Years: Preparation for Creative Thinking," *Gifted Education International* 3, no. 2 (1985): 100–104; Nicholas T. Gallucci, George Middleton, and Adam Kline, "Perfectionism and Creative Strivings," *Journal of Creative Behavior* 34, no. 2 (2000): 135–41; Getzels and Jackson, "Family"; Marilyn E. Gist and Terrence R. Mitchell, "Self-Efficacy: A Theoretical Analysis of Its Determinants and Malleability," *Academy of Management Review* 17 (1992): 183–211; John Curtis Gowan, George D. Demos, and E. Paul Torrance, *Creativity: Its Educational Implications* (New York: Wiley, 1967); Leilani Greening, Laura Stoppelbein, and Aaron Luebbe, "The Moderating Effects of Parenting Styles on African-American and Caucasian Children's Suicidal Behaviors," *Journal of Youth and Adolescence* 39 (2010): 357–69; David M. Harrington, Jeanne H. Block, and Jack Block, "Testing Aspects of Carl Rogers's Theory of Creative Environments: Child-Rearing Antecedents of Creative Potential in Young Adolescents," *Journal of Personality and Social Psychology* 52, no. 4 (1987): 851–56; Hsu, Hou, and Fan, "Self-Efficacy"; Ishak, Low, and Lau, "Parenting"; Yanrong Kang and Joyce Moore, "Parenting Style and Adolescents' School Performance in Mainland China," *US-China Education Review* 1 (2011): 132–37; Cheng-Hsien Li and Jing-Jyi Wu, "The Structural Relationships between Optimism and Innovative Behavior: Understanding Potential Antecedents and Mediating Effects," *Creativity Research Journal* 23, no. 2 (2011): 119–28; MacKinnon, "Architects"; Muriel Michel and Stephanie Z. Dudek, "Mother-Child Relationships and Creativity," *Creativity Research Journal* 4, no. 3 (1991): 281–86; Robert E. Myers and E. Paul Torrance, "Can Teachers Encourage Creative Thinking?" *Educational Leadership* 19, no. 3 (1961): 156–59; Mauree Neihart, "Systematic Risk-Taking," *Roeper Review* 21, no. 4 (1999): 289–92; George Szekely, "The Artist and the Child—A Model Program for the Artistically Gifted," *Gifted Child Quarterly* 25, no. 2 (1981): 67–72; Torrance, "Prediction"; Rick Trinkner et al., "Don't Trust Anyone over 30: Parental Legitimacy as a Mediator between Parenting Style and Changes in Delinquent Behavior over Time," *Journal of Adolescence* 35, no. 1 (2012): 119–32; Leslie Kathleen Williams and Stephen J. J. McGuire, "Effects of National Culture on Economic Creativity and Innovation Implementation," *Institutions of Market Exchange* (2005): 31–40.

106. Randy O. Frost et al., "The Dimensions of Perfectionism," *Cognitive Therapy and Research* 14, no. 5 (1990): 449–68; Miller, Lambert, and Speirs Neumeister, "Parenting"; Cheryl Nakata and Kumar Sivakumar, "National Culture and New Product Development: An Integrative Review," *Journal of Marketing* 60 (1996): 61–72; Milton Schwebel, "Jack London: A Case Study of Moral Creativity," *Creativity Research Journal* 21, no. 4 (2009): 319–25.

107. Frank H. Farley, "Psychobiology and Cognition: An Individual-Differences Model," in *The Biological Bases of Personality and Behavior*, vol. 1, eds. Jan Strelau, Frank H. Farley, and Anthony Gale (Washington, DC: Hemisphere, 1985), 61–74; Frank H. Farley, "The Big T in Personality," *Psychology Today* 20 (1986): 44–52; Frank H. Farley, "The Type-T Personality," in *Self-Regulatory Behavior and Risk Taking: Causes and Consequences*, eds. Lewis Paeff Lipsitt and Leonard L. Mitnick (Norwood, NJ: Ablex, 1991), 371–82; Frank H. Farley and Sonja V. Farley, "Extraversion and Stimulus-Seeking Motivation," *Journal of Consulting Psychology* 31, no. 2 (1967): 215–16; Richard E. Morehouse, Frank H. Farley, and James V. Youngquist, "Type T Personality and the Jungian Classification System," *Journal of Personality Assessment* 54, no. 1–2 (1990): 231–35.

108. K. Anders Ericsson, "Basic Capacities Can Be Modified or Circumvented by Deliberate Practice: A Rejection of Talent Accounts of Expert Performance. A Commentary on Michael J. A. Howe, Jane W. Davidson, and John A. Sloboda, 'Innate Talents: Reality or Myth?'" *Behavioral and Brain Sciences* 21 (1998): 413–14; K. Anders Ericsson, Ralf Th. Krampe, and Clemens Tesch-Romer, "The Role of Deliberate Practice in the Acquisition of Expert Performance," *Psychological Review* 100 (1993): 363–406; Michael J. A. Howe, "Prodigies and Creativity," in *Handbook of Creativity*, ed. Robert J. Sternberg (New York: Cambridge University Press, 1999), 116–33; Ralf Th. Krampe and K. Anders Ericsson, "Maintaining Excellence: Deliberate Practice and Elite Performance in Young and Older Pianists," *Journal of Experimental Psychology: General* 125 (1996): 331–59; Mark A. Runco, "The Creativity of Children's Art," *Child Study Journal* 19 (1989): 177–89; Simonton, *Greatness*; Simonton, "Creativity and Genius," 679–98; Ellen Winner, *Gifted Children: Myths and Realities* (New York: Basic Books, 1996).

109. Ibid.

110. Simonton, *Greatness*.

111. Bandura, *Self-Efficacy*; Locke and Latham, "Building"; Locke and Latham, *Theory*.

112. Ibid.

113. Bandura, *Self-Efficacy*; Bandura, *Foundations*; Beghetto, "Self-Efficacy"; Hsu, Hou, and Fan, "Self-Efficacy"; Locke and Latham, "Building"; Locke and Latham, *Theory*.

114. I. Holme, "Sir William Henry Perkin: A Review of His Life, Work and Legacy," *Coloration Technology* 122 (2006): 235–51; Msn.com, "Bubble Wrap Celebrating Its 50th Birthday: Product People Love to Pop Was Originally Envisioned as Type of Wallpaper," 2010, http://www.msnbc.msn.com/id/35046691; NNDB.com, "Spencer Silver," Notable Names Database Tracking the Entire World (NNDB), 2012, http://www.nndb.com/people/758/000173239/; M. Pendergrast, *For God, Country, and Coca-Cola: The Definitive History of the Great American Soft Drink and the Company That Makes It* (New York: Basic Books, 2000).

115. Ochse, *Excellence*; Celeste Rhodes, "Growth from Deficiency Creativity to Being Creativity," in *Eminent Creativity, Everyday Creativity, and Health*, eds. Mark A. Runco and Ruth Richards (Greenwich, CT: Ablex, 1997), 247–64; Simonton, "Biographical"; Simonton, *Greatness*; Simonton, "Creativity and Genius"; Simonton, *101*.

116. Allison Canty, "The Early Failures of Famous Entrepreneurs (And What They Learned)," November, 17, 2011, http://grasshopper.com/blog/the-early-failures-of-famous-entrepreneurs-and-what-they-learned-3/; Harry R. Silver, "Scientific Achievement and the Concept of Risk," *British Journal of Sociology* 34 (1983): 39–43; Simonton, *Greatness*.

117. Lim and DeSteno, "Suffering."

118. Barron and Harrington, "Creativity"; J. Chan and Y. Chen, "Processes and Outcomes of Encouraging Universities to Implement Creative Studies Colleges," in *Creative Education Programs in Taiwan: Development and Implementation*, ed. J. Chan (Taipei, Taiwan: Ministry of Education, 2008), 244–57; Hans J. Eysenck, *Genius: The Natural History of Creativity* (Cambridge, UK: Cambridge University Press, 1995); Feist, "Meta-Analysis"; Li and Wu, "Structural"; Meihua Qian, Jonathan A. Plucker, and Jiliang Shen, "A Model of Chinese Adolescents' Creative Personality," *Creativity Research Journal* 22, no. 1 (2010): 62–67; Roe, *Making*; Kennon M. Sheldon, "Creativity and Self-Determination in Personality," *Creativity Research Journal* 8, no. 1 (1995): 25–36; Simonton, *Greatness*; E. Paul Torrance, *Why Fly? A Philosophy of Creativity* (Norwood, NJ: Ablex, 1995); Donald J. Treffinger et al., *Assessing Creativity: A Guide for Educators* (Storrs, CT: National Research Center on the Gifted and Talented, 2002); Rick B. Van Baaren et al., "The Forest, the Trees, and the Chameleon: Context Dependence and Mimicry," *Journal of Personality and Social Psychology* 86, no. 3 (2004): 453–59.

119. Van Baaren et al., "Forest."

120. Barron and Harrington, "Creativity"; Feist, "Meta-Analysis"; Li and Wu, "Structural"; Qian, Plucker, and Shen, "Model"; Sheldon, "Creativity"; Treffinger et al., "Assessing."

121. Eysenck, *Genius*; Feist, "Meta-Analysis"; Roe, *Making*; Sheldon, "Creativity"; Simonton, *Greatness*; Torrance, *Fly*.

122. K. Anders Ericsson, "The Acquisition of Expert Performance: An Introduction to Some of the Issues," in *The Road to Expert Performance: Empirical Evidence from the Arts and Sciences, Sports, and Games*, ed. K. Anders Ericsson (Mahwah, NJ: Erlbaum, 1996), 1–50; Mihaly Csikszentmihalyi, *Creativity: Flow and the Psychology of Discovery and Intervention* (New York: Harper Perennial, 1996); Locke and Latham, "Building"; Locke and Latham, *Theory*; Simonton, *101*; Robert J. Sternberg and James C. Kaufman, "Constraints on Creativity: Obvious and Not So Obvious," in *The Cambridge Handbook of Creativity*, eds. James C. Kaufman and Robert J. Sternberg (New York: Cambridge University Press, 2010), 467–82; Treffinger et al., "Assessing"; Tardif and Sternberg, "Know."

123. Locke and Latham, "Building"; Locke and Latham, *Theory*; Simonton, *Greatness*.

124. Ericsson, "Acquisition"; K. Anders Ericsson, Neil Charness, Paul J. Feltovich, and Robert R. Hoffman, eds, *The Cambridge Handbook of Expertise and Expert Performance* (New York: Cambridge University Press, 2006); Howard Gardner, *Creating Minds* (New York: Basic Books, 1993); Hayes, *Complete*; Locke and Latham, "Building"; Locke and Latham, *Theory*; McGreevy, "All"; Simonton, *Greatness*; Dean Keith Simonton, "Totally Made, Not at All Born: Review of the Book, *The Psychology of High Abilities*," *Contemporary Psychology* 46 (2001): 176–79; Simonton, *101*.

125. Csikszentmihalyi, *Creativity*.

126. Sternberg and Kaufman, "Constraints"; Treffinger et al., "Assessing."

127. Ibid.

128. Ericsson et al., *Handbook*.

129. Ericsson, "Acquisition"; Ericsson et al., *Handbook*; Gardner, *Creating*; Haven, *Marvels*; Hayes, *Complete*; Locke and Latham, "Building"; Locke and Latham, *Theory*; McGreevy, "All"; Simonton, *Greatness*; Simonton, "Totally"; Simonton, *101*; Sternberg and Kaufman, "Constraints"; Treffinger et al., "Assessing."

130. Simonton, *Greatness*; Simonton, "Totally."

131. Haven, *Marvels*; Simonton, *101*; Sternberg and Kaufman, "Constraints."

132. Steven J. Heine and Darrin R. Lehman, "Culture, Self-Discrepancies, and Self-Satisfaction," *Personality and Social Psychology Bulletin* 25 (1999): 915–25; Steven J. Heine et al., "Is There a Universal Need for Positive Self-Regard?" *Psychological Review* 106 (1999): 766–94; Steven J. Heine, Shinobu Kitayama, and Darrin R. Lehman, "Cultural Differences in Self-Evaluation: Japanese Readily Accept Negative Self-Relevant Information," *Journal of Cross-Cultural Psychology* 32, no. 4 (2001): 434–43; Shinobu Kitayama et al., "Individual and Collective Processes in the Construction of the Self: Self-Enhancement in the United States and Self-Criticism in Japan," *Journal of Personality and Social Psychology*, 72 (1997): 1245–67; Hazel Rose Markus and Shinobu Kitayama, "Culture and the Self: Implications for Cognition, Emotion, and Motivation," *Psychological Review* 98, no. 2 (1991): 224–53.

133. Bruce B. Henderson, Melvin H. Marx, and Yung Che Kim, "Academic Interests and Perceived Competence in American, Japanese, and Korean Children," *Journal of Cross-Cultural Psychology* 30, no. 1 (1999): 32–50; David Y. F. Ho, "Cognitive Socialization in Confucian Heritage Cultures," in *Cross-Cultural Roots of Minority Child Development*, eds. Patricia M. Greenfield and Rodney R. Cocking (Hillsdale, NJ: Erlbaum, 1994), 285–313; Jihyun Lee, "Universals and Specifics of Math Self-Concept, Math Self-Efficacy, and Math Anxiety across 41 PISA 2003 Participating Countries," *Learning and Individual Differences* 19, no. 3 (2009): 355–65; Li-Rong Lilly Cheng, Kenji Ima, and Gene Labovitz, "Assessment of Asian and Pacific Islander Students for Gifted Programs," in *Addressing Cultural and Linguistic Diversity in Special Education*, ed. Shernaz B. García (Reston, VA: Council for Exceptional Children, 1994), 30–45; Lazar Stankov, "Unforgiving Confucian Culture: A Breeding Ground for High Academic Achievement, Test Anxiety and Self-Doubt?" *Learning and Individual Differences* 20, no. 6 (2010): 555–63; Harold W. Stevenson and James W. Stigler, *The Learning Gap: Why Our Schools Are Failing and What We Can Learn from Japanese and Chinese Education* (New York: Summit, 1992); Jesse L. M. Wilkins, "Mathematics and Science Self-Concept: An International Investigation," *Journal of Experimental Education* 72, no. 4 (2004): 331–46.

134. Bandura, *Foundations*; Bandura, *Self-Efficacy*; Barron and Harrington, "Creativity"; Beghetto, "Self-Efficacy"; Jin Nam Choi, "Individual and Contextual Predictors of Creative

Performance: The Mediating Role of Psychological Processes," *Creativity Research Journal* 16, no. 2/3 (2004): 187–99; Csikszentmihalyi, *Creativity*; Feist, "Meta-Analysis"; Yaping P. Gong, Jia-Chi Huang, and Jing-Lih Farh, "Employee Learning Orientation, Transformational Leadership, and Employee Creativity: The Mediating Role of Employee Creative Self-Efficacy," *Academy of Management Journal* 52 (2009): 765–78; Hsu, Hou, and Fan, "Self-Efficacy"; Li and Wu, "Structural"; Edwin A. Locke et al., "Effect of Self-Efficacy, Goals, and Task Strategies on Task Performance," *Journal of Applied Psychology* 69, no. 2 (1984): 241–51; Robert R. McCrae, "Creativity, Divergent Thinking, and Openness to Experience," *Journal of Personality and Social Psychology* 52, no. 6 (1987): 1258–65; Qian, Plucker, and Shen, "Model; D. N. Sansanwal and Deepika Sharma, "Scientific Creativity as a Function of Intelligence, Self-Confidence, Sex and Standard," *Indian Journal of Psychometry and Education* 24 (1993): 37–44; Gina D. Schack, "Self-Efficacy as a Mediator in the Creative Productivity of Gifted Children," *Journal of the Education of the Gifted* 12, no. 3 (1989): 231–49; Larisa V. Shavinina, "Explaining High Abilities of Nobel Laureates," *High Ability Studies* 15, no. 2 (2004): 243–54; Robert Solomon, "Creativity and Normal Narcissism," *Journal of Creative Behavior* 19, no. 1 (1985): 47–55; Tardif and Sternberg, "Know"; Tierney and Farmer, "Self-Efficacy"; Pamela Tierney and Steven M. Farmer, "The Pygmalion Process and Employee Creativity," *Journal of Management* 30 (2004): 413–32; Treffinger et al., "Assessing"; Li and Wu, "Structural."

135. Bandura, *Foundations*; Bandura, *Self-Efficacy*; Barron and Harrington, "Creativity"; Feist, "Meta-Analysis"; Hsu, Hou, and Fan, "Self-Efficacy"; Tardif and Sternberg, "Know"; Tierney and Farmer, "Self-Efficacy."

136. Bandura, *Foundations*; Bandura, *Self-Efficacy*; Li and Wu, "Structural"; Tierney and Farmer, "Pygmalion."

137. James B. Avey, Fred Luthans, and Susan M. Jensen, "Psychological Capital: A Positive Resource for Combating Employee Stress and Turnover," *Human Resource Management* 48 (2009): 677–93; James B. Avey, Fred Luthans, and Carolyn M. Youssef, "The Additive Value of Positive Psychological Capital in Predicting Work Attitudes and Behaviors," *Journal of Management* 36 (2010): 430–52.

138. Shavinina, "Explaining"; Solomon, "Creativity."

139. Csikszentmihalyi, *Creativity*.

140. Christopher G. Davis and Ersin Asliturk, "Toward a Positive Psychology of Coping with Anticipated Events," *Canadian Psychology/Psychologie Canadienne* 52, no. 2 (2011): 101–10; Chun Bun Lam and Catherine A. McBride-Chang, "Resilience in Young Adulthood: The Moderating Influences of Gender-Related Personality Traits and Coping Flexibility," *Sex Roles* 56, no. 3–4 (2007): 159–72; Li and Wu, "Structural."

141. Jacob Lomranz, "Endurance and Living: Long-Term Effects of the Holocaust," in *Extreme Stress and Communities: Impact and Intervention*, eds. Stevan E. Hobfoll and Marten W. de Vries (Dordrecht, the Netherlands: Kluwer, 1995), 325–52.

142. Efrat Barel et al., "Surviving the Holocaust: A Meta-Analysis of the Long-Term Sequelae of a Genocide," *Psychological Bulletin* 136 (2010): 677–98; Leo Eitinger and Ellinor F. Major, "Stress of the Holocaust," in *Handbook of Stress: Theoretical and Clinical Aspects*, eds. Leo Goldberger and Shlomo Breznitz, 2nd ed. (New York: Free Press, 1993), 617–40.

143. Kevin J. Eschleman, Nathan A. Bowling, and Gene M. Alarcon, "A Meta-Analytic Examination of Hardiness," *International Journal of Stress Management* 17 (2010): 277–307; William Helmreich, *Against All Odds: Holocaust Survivors and the Successful Lives They Made in America* (New York: Simon and Schuster, 1992).

144. Davis and Asliturk, "Positive"; Eschleman, Bowling, and Alarcon, "Meta-Analytic"; Heidi Grant and E. Tory Higgins, "Optimism, Promotion Pride, and Prevention Pride as Predictors of Quality of Life," *Personality and Social Psychology Bulletin* 29, no. 12 (2003): 1521–32; Helmreich, *Holocaust*; Hsu, Hou, and Fan, "Self-Efficacy"; Lam and McBride-Chang, "Resilience"; Li and Wu, "Structural"; Ottesen and Grønhaug, "Illusions"; Heather N. Rasmussen et al., "Self-Regulation Processes and Health: The Importance of Optimism and Goal Adjustment," *Journal of Personality*

74, no. 6 (2006): 1721–48; Simonton, *Greatness*; Simonton, *101*; Feirong R. Yuan and Rirchard W. Woodman, "Innovative Behavior in the Workplace: The Role of Performance and Image Outcome Expectations," *Academy of Management Journal* 53 (2010): 323–42.

145. Christine Charyton and Glenn E. Snelbecker, "Engineers' and Musicians' Choices of Self-Descriptive Adjectives as Potential Indicators of Creativity by Gender and Domain," *Psychology of Aesthetics, Creativity, and the Arts* 1, no. 2 (2007): 91–99; Feist, "Meta-Analysis"; Feldman, "Creativity"; Albert Rothenberg, "Bipolar Illness, Creativity, and Treatment," *Psychiatric Quarterly* 72, no. 2 (2001): 131–47; Dean Keith Simonton, "Creativity, Leadership, and Chance," in *The Nature of Creativity: Contemporary Psychological Perspectives*, ed. Robert J. Sternberg (New York: Cambridge University Press, 1988), 386–426; Simonton, *101*; Sternberg and Kaufman, "Constraints"; Zuckerman, *Scientific*.

146. Ottesen and Grønhaug, "Illusions."

147. Finkelstein and Fishbach, "Tell Me"; Ottesen and Grønhaug, "Illusions."

148. Ibid.

149. Karen A. Jehn and Elizabeth A. Mannix, "The Dynamic Nature of Conflict: A Longitudinal Study of Intragroup Conflict and Group Performance," *Academy of Management Journal* 44, no. 2 (2001): 238–51; Charlan J. Nemeth et al., "The Liberating Role of Conflict in Group Creativity: A Study in Two Countries," *European Journal of Social Psychology* 34, no. 4 (2004): 365–74.

150. Jehn and Mannix, "Conflict"; Nemeth et al. , "Conflict"; Karen Leggett Dugosh et al., "Cognitive Stimulation in Brainstorming," *Journal of Personality and Social Psychology* 79, no. 5 (2000): 722–35.

151. Hsu, Hou, and Fan, "Self-Efficacy"; Yuan and Woodman, "Innovative."

152. Simonton, *Greatness*.

153. Ibid.

154. Hsu, Hou, and Fan, "Self-Efficacy"; Li and Wu, "Structural"; Ottesen and Grønhaug, "Illusions."

155. Amabile, *Creativity*; Todd Dewett, "Exploring the Role of Risk in Employee Creativity," *Journal of Creative Behavior* 40, no. 1 (2006): 27–45; Russell Eisenman, "Creativity, Birth Order, and Risk Taking," *Bulletin of the Psychonomic Society* 25 (1987): 87–88; Hans J. Eysenck, "Creativity and Personality: Suggestions for a Theory," *Psychological Inquiry* 4 (1993): 147–78; Onne Janssen, "How Fairness Perceptions Make Innovative Behavior More or Less Stressful," *Journal of Organizational Behavior* 25, no. 2 (2004): 201–15; Farley, "Big T in Personality"; Grant and Higgins, "Optimism," 1521–32; John T. Lanzetta and Vera T. Kanareff, "Information Cost, Amount of Payoff, and Level of Aspiration as Determinants of Information Seeking in Decision Making," *Behavioral Science* 7, no. 4 (1962): 459–73; Li and Wu, "Structural"; Hsu, Hou, and Fan, "Self-Efficacy"; Angelo A. Marade, Jeffrey A. Gibbons, and Thomas M. Brinthaupt, "The Role of Risk-Taking in Songwriting Success," *Journal of Creative Behavior* 41, no. 2 (2007): 125–49; Rollo May, *The Courage to Create* (New York: Bantam, 1985); McCrae, "Creativity"; Neihart, "Systematic"; Ottesen and Grønhaug, "Illusions"; Qian, Plucker, and Shen, "Model"; Rasmussen et al., "Self-Regulation"; Betty B. Rossman and John L. Horn, "Cognitive, Motivational and Temperamental Indicants of Creativity and Intelligence," *Journal of Educational Measurement* 9 (1972): 265–86; Silver, "Risk"; Tardif and Sternberg, "Know"; E. Paul Torrance, *The Search for Satori and Creativity* (Buffalo, NY: Bearly Limited Creative Education Foundation, 1979); Torrance, *Fly*; E. Paul Torrance and H. Tammy Safter, *Making the Creative Leap Beyond* (Buffalo, NY: Creative Education Foundation, 1999); Treffinger et al., "Assessing"; David Viscott, *Risking* (New York: Pocket Books, 1977).

156. Janssen, "Fairness"; Torrance, *Search*; Torrance and Safter, *Making*.

157. Lanzetta and Kanareff, "Information."

158. Grant and Higgins, "Optimism," 1521–32; Hsu, Hou, and Fan, "Self-Efficacy"; Rasmussen et al., "Self-Regulation."

159. Ottesen and Grønhaug, "Illusions."

160. Qian, Plucker, and Shen, "Model"; Rasmussen et al., "Self-Regulation"; Silver, "Scientific";

Torrance, *Search*; Torrance and Safter, *Making the Creative Leap*; Treffinger et al., "Assessing Creativity"; Viscott, *Risking*.

161. Neihart, "Systematic."

162. Angelo A. Marade, Jeffrey A. Gibbons, and Thomas M. Brinthaupt, "The Role of Risk-Taking in Songwriting Success," *Journal of Creative Behavior* 41, no. 2 (2007): 125–49.

163. Janssen, "Fairness"; Rollo May, *The Courage to Create* (New York: Bantam, 1985); Tardif and Sternberg, "Know"; Paul Tillich, *The Courage to Be* (New Haven, CT: Yale University Press, 1952); Torrance, *Fly*; Viscott, *Risking*.

164. Tardif and Sternberg, "Know."

165. Torrance, *Fly*; Viscott, *Risking*.

166. May, *Courage*.

167. Viscott, *Risking*.

168. Janssen, "Fairness"; Tillich, *Courage*; Torrance, *Fly*.

169. Steve Amireault, Gaston Godin, and Lydi-Anne Vézina-Im, "Determinants of Physical Activity Maintenance: A Systematic Review and Meta-Analyses," *Health Psychology Review* 7, no. 1 (2013): 55–91; Tierney and Farmer, "Self-Efficacy."

170. Ericsson et al., *Handbook*; Hayes, *Complete*; Simonton, *Greatness*; Simonton, *101*.

171. Ronald A. Finke, "Imagery, Creativity, and Emergent Structure," *Consciousness and Cognition* 5 (1996): 381–93; Andrew B. Leber, Nicholas B. Turk-Browne, and Marvin M. Chun, "Neural Predictor of Moment-to-Moment Fluctuations in Cognitive Flexibility," *Proceedings of the National Academy of Sciences* 105 (2008): 13592–97; Bernard A. Nijstad et al., "The Dual Pathway to Creativity Model: Creative Ideation as a Function of Flexibility and Persistence," *European Review of Social Psychology* 21, no. 1 (2010): 34–77.

172. Roshan Cools, "Role of Dopamine in the Motivational and Cognitive Control of Behavior," *Neuroscientist* 4 (2008): 381–95; Dreisbach and Goschke, "Positive"; Gesine Dreisbach et al., "Dopamine and Cognitive Control: The Influence of Spontaneous Eyeblink Rate and Dopamine Gene Polymorphisms on Perseveration and Distractibility," *Behavioral Neuroscience* 119 (2005): 483–90; Johannes Muller et al., "Dopamine and Cognitive Control: The Prospect of Monetary Gains Influences the Balance between Flexibility and Stability in a Set-Shifting Paradigm," *European Journal of Neuroscience* 26 (2007): 3661–68; Nijstad et al., "Dual."

173. Andrea Abele-Brehm, "Positive and Negative Mood Influences on Creativity: Evidence for Asymmetrical Effects," *Polish Psychological Bulletin* 23 (1992): 203–21; Dreu, Baas, and Nijstad, "Hedonic"; Jens Förster, Kal Epstude, and Amina Özelsel, "Why Love Has Wings and Sex Not: How Reminders of Love and Sex Influence Creative and Analytic Thinking," *Personality and Social Psychology Bulletin* 35, no. 11 (2009): 1479–91; Alice M. Isen, Kimberly A. Daubman, and Gary P. Nowicki, "Positive Affect Facilitates Creative Problem Solving," *Journal of Personality and Social Psychology* 52, no. 6 (1987): 1122–31; Alice M. Isen, Mitzi M. Johnson, Elizabeth Mertz, and Gregory F. Robinson, "The Influence of Positive Affect on the Unusualness of Word Associations," *Journal of Personality and Social Psychology* 48, no. 6 (1985): 1413–26; Geir Kaufmann and Suzanne K. Vosburg, "'Paradoxical' Mood Effects on Creative Problem-Solving," *Cognition and Emotion* 11, no. 2 (1997): 151–70; Kray, Galinsky, and Wong, "Thinking"; Suzanne K. Vosburg, "The Effects of Positive and Negative Mood on Divergent-Thinking Performance," *Creativity Research Journal* 11, no. 2 (1998): 165–72; Zhong, Dijksterhuis, and Galinsky, "Merits."

174. Ap Dijksterhuis and Teun Meurs, "Where Creativity Resides: The Generative Power of Unconscious Thought," *Consciousness and Cognition* 15, no. 1 (2006): 135–46; Ap Dijksterhuis and Loran F. Nordgren, "A Theory of Unconscious Thought," *Perspectives on Psychological Science* 1, no. 2 (2006): 95–109; Carsten KW De Dreu, Matthijs Baas, and Bernard A. Nijstad, "Hedonic Tone and Activation Level in the Mood-Creativity Link: Toward a Dual Pathway to Creativity Model," *Journal of Personality and Social Psychology* 94, no. 5 (2008): 739–56; Finke, "Imagery"; Klinger, "Thought"; Arthur Koestler, *The Act of Creation* (New York: Macmillan, 1964); Kounios and Beeman, "Aha!"; Kray, Galinsky, and Wong, "Thinking"; Leber, Turk-Browne, and Chun, "Neural"; Colin

Martindale, "Biological Based of Creativity," in *Handbook of Creativity*, ed. Robert J. Sternberg (New York: Cambridge University Press, 1999), 137–52; Nijstad et al., "Dual"; Jonathan W. Schooler and Joseph Melcher, "The Ineffability of Insight," in *The Creative Cognition Approach*, eds. Steven M. Smith, Thomas B. Ward, and Ronald A. Finke (Cambridge, MA: MIT Press, 1995), 97–134; Simonton, "Creativity and Genius"; Dorothy G. Singer and Jerome L. Singer, *The House of Make-Believe: Children's Play and the Developing Imagination* (Cambridge, MA: Harvard University Press, 1990); Dorothy G. Singer and Jerome L. Singer, *Imagination and Play in the Electronic Age* (Cambridge, MA: Harvard University Press, 2005); Jerome L. Singer, "Researching Imaginative Play and Adult Consciousness: Implications for Daily and Literary Creativity," *Psychology of Aesthetics, Creativity, and the Arts* 3, no. 4 (2009): 190–99; Jerome L. Singer and Vivian G. McCraven, "Some Characteristics of Adult Daydreaming," *Journal of Psychology* 51, no. 1 (1961): 151–64; Jonathan Smallwood and Jonathan W. Schooler, "The Restless Mind," *Psychological Bulletin* 132, no. 6 (2006): 946–58; Steven M. Smith and Steven E. Blankenship, "Incubation Effects," *Bulletin of the Psychonomic Society* 27, no. 4 (1989): 311–14; Aaron J. Ungersma, "Fantasy, Creativity, Conformity," *Humanitas* 12 (1976): 73–88; Thomas B. Ward, "Structured Imagination: The Role of Category Structure in Exemplar Generation," *Cognitive Psychology* 27, no. 1 (1994): 1–40; Zhong, Dijksterhuis, and Galinsky, "Merits."

175. Teresa Amabile, "The Motivation to Be Creative," in *Frontiers of Creativity Research: Beyond the Basics*, ed. Scott G. Isaksen (Buffalo, NY: Bearly Limited, 1987), 223–54.

176. Amabile, "Motivation"; Steve Amireault, Gaston Godin, and Lydi-Anne Vézina-Im, "Determinants of Physical Activity Maintenance: A Systematic Review and Meta-Analyses," *Health Psychology Review* 7, no. 1 (2013): 55–91; Jack A. Chambers, "Relating Personality and Biographical Factors to Scientific Creativity," *Psychological Monographs: General and Applied* 78, no. 7 (1964): 1–20; Gary A. Davis, *Creativity Is Forever* (Dubuque, IA: Kendall/Hunt, 2004); Ericsson et al., *Handbook*; Hayes, *Complete*; Qian, Plucker, and Shen, "Model;" Simonton, *Greatness*; Simonton, *101*; Simonton, "Creativity and Genius"; Tierney and Farmer, "Self-Efficacy"; Treffinger et al., "Assessing."

177. Dean Keith Simonton, "Creative Productivity and Age: A Mathematical Model Based on a Two-Step Cognitive Process," *Developmental Review* 4, no. 1 (1984): 77–111; Simonton, *Greatness*; Dean Keith Simonton, "Film Music: Are Award-Winning Scores and Songs Heard in Successful Motion Pictures?" *Psychology of Aesthetics, Creativity, and the Arts* 1 (2007): 53–60.

178. K. Anders Ericsson, Kiruthiga Nandagopal, and Roy W. Roring, "Giftedness Viewed from the Expert-Performance Perspective," *Journal for the Education of the Gifted* 28, no. 3/4 (2005): 287–311.

179. O. E. Ball, and E. Paul Torrance, "Streamlines Scoring Workbook: Figural A (Bensenville, IL: Scholastic Testing Service, 1984); KH Kim, "Can We Trust Creativity Tests? A Review of the Torrance Tests of Creative Thinking (TTCT)," *Creativity Research Journal* 18, no. 1 (2006): 3–14; KH Kim, "Is Creativity Unidimensional or Multidimensional? Analyses of the Torrance Tests of Creative Thinking," *Creativity Research Journal* 18, no. 3 (2006): 251–59; KH Kim, Bonnie Cramond, and Deborah L. Bandalos, "The Latent Structure and Measurement Invariance of Scores on the Torrance Tests of Creative Thinking–Figural," *Educational and Psychological Measurement* 66, no. 3 (2006): 459–77; Nijstad et al., "Dual; Paul B. Paulus, Nicholas W. Kohn, and Lauren E. Arditti, "Effects of Quantity and Quality Instructions on Brainstorming," *Journal of Creative Behavior* 45, no. 1 (2011): 38–46; Paul B. Paulus et al., "Effects of Task Instructions and Brief Breaks on Brainstorming," *Group Dynamics: Theory, Research, and Practice* 10, no. 3 (2006): 206–19; Vicky L. Putman and Paul B. Paulus, "Brainstorming, Brainstorming Rules and Decision Making," *Journal of Creative Behavior* 43, no. 1 (2009): 29–40; Eric F. Rietzschel, Bernard Nijstad, and Wolfgang Stroebe, "Relative Accessibility of Domain Knowledge and Creativity: The Effects of Knowledge Activation on the Quantity and Originality of Generated Ideas," *Journal of Experimental Social Psychology* 43, no. 6 (2007): 933–46; Dean Keith Simonton, "Creativity and Wisdom in Aging," in *Handbook of the Psychology of Aging*, eds. James E. Birren and Klaus Warner Schaie (San Diego, CA: Academic, 1990), 320–29; Torrance, *Search*; E. Paul Torrance, *Guidelines for Administration and Scoring/Comments on Using the Torrance Tests of Creative Thinking* (Bensenville, IL: Scholastic Testing Services, 1987); E. Paul Torrance,

Creativity: Just Wanting to Know (Republic of South Africa: Benedic Books, 1994); Torrance, *Fly*; E. Paul Torrance, *Research Review for the Torrance Tests of Creative Thinking Figural and Verbal Forms A and B* (Bensenville, IL: Scholastic Testing Services, 2000); Torrance and Safter, *Making*.

180. Adrian Furnham, "The Relationship of Personality and Intelligence to Cognitive Learning Style and Achievement," in *International Handbook of Personality and Intelligence*, ed. Donald H. Saklofske and Moshe Zeidner (New York: Plenum, 1995), 397–413.

181. Jennifer S. Mueller, Shimul Melwani, and Jack A. Goncalo, "The Bias against Creativity: Why People Desire but Reject Creative Ideas," *Psychological Science* 23, no. 1 (2012): 13–17.

182. Eric F. Rietzschel, Bernard A. Nijstad, and Wolfgang Stroebe, "The Selection of Creative Ideas after Individual Idea Generation: Choosing between Creativity and Impact," *British Journal of Psychology* 101, no. 1 (2010): 47–68.

183. Jennifer A. Whitson and Adam D. Galinsky, "Lacking Control Increases Illusory Pattern Perception," *Science* 322, no. 5898 (2008): 115–17.

184. Julie Aitken Harris, "Measured Intelligence, Achievement, Openness to Experience, and Creativity, *Personality and Individual Differences* 36 (2004): 913–29; McCrae, "Creativity"; Jordan B. Peterson and Shelly Carson, "Latent Inhibition and Openness to Experience in a High-Achieving Student Population," *Personality and Individual Differences* 28 (2000): 323–32; Simonton, "Creativity and Genius."

185. Adrian Furnham, "A Content, Correlational and Factor Analytic Study of Four Tolerance of Ambiguity Questionnaires," *Personality and Individual Differences* 16, no. 3 (1994): 403–10; Bonnie C. Graham, Janet K. Sawyers, and Karen B. DeBord, "Teachers' Creativity, Playfulness, and Style of Interaction with Children," *Creativity Research Journal* 2, no. 1–2 (1989): 41–50; Tardif and Sternberg, "Know"; Shuhong Wang, Xiaomeng Zhang, and Joseph Martocchio, "Thinking outside of the Box When the Box Is Missing: Role Ambiguity and Its Linkage to Creativity," *Creativity Research Journal* 23, no. 3 (2011): 211–21.

186. Barron and Harrington, "Creativity"; Stanley Budner, "Intolerance of Ambiguity as a Personality Variable," *Journal of Personality* 30 (1962): 29–50; Mark E. Comadena, "Brainstorming Groups: Ambiguity Tolerance, Communication Apprehension, Task Attraction, and Individual Productivity," *Small Group Research* 15, no. 2 (1984): 251–64; Furnham, "Content"; Furnham, "Relationship"; Adrian Furnham and Margaret Avison, "Personality and Preference for Surreal Paintings," *Personality and Individual Differences* 23, no. 6 (1997): 923–35; Stuart E. Golann, "Psychological Study of Creativity," *Psychological Bulletin* 60, no. 6 (1963): 548–65; Julie Aitken Harris, "Measured Intelligence, Achievement, Openness to Experience, and Creativity," *Personality and Individual Differences* 36 (2004): 913–29; McCrae, "Creativity"; Simonton, "Creativity and Genius"; Robert J. Sternberg and Todd I. Lubart, *Defying the Crowd: Cultivating Creativity in a Culture of Conformity* (New York: Free Press, 1995); Katya Stoycheva, "Ambiguity Tolerance: Adolescents' Responses to Uncertainty in Life," Research Report (ERIC Document Reproduction Service No. ED 422 547, 1998); Tardif and Sternberg, "Know"; Deborah W. Tegano, "Relationship of Tolerance of Ambiguity and Playfulness to Creativity," *Psychological Reports* 66, no. 3 (1990): 1047–56; Klaus K. Urban, "Toward a Componential Model of Creativity," in *Creative Intelligence: Toward Theoretic Integration*, eds. Don Ambrose, Leonora M. Cohen, and Abraham J. Tannenbaum (Cresskill, NJ: Hampton, 2003), 81–112; Wang, Zhang, and Martocchio, "Thinking"; Franck Zenasni, Maud Besançon, and Todd Lubart, "Creativity and Tolerance of Ambiguity: An Empirical Study," *Journal of Creative Behavior* 42, no. 1 (2008): 61–73.

187. Barron and Harrington, "Creativity"; Golann, "Psychological"; Sternberg and Lubart, *Defying*; Urban, "Componential"; Zenasni, Besançon, and Lubart, "Creativity."

188. Walter Isaacson, *Steve Jobs* (New York: Simon and Schuster, 2011).

189. Ibid.

190. Ibid.

191. "Steve Jobs," interview by Daniel Morrow, Computerworld Information Technology Awards Foundation, April 1995, http://www.computerworld.com/s/ article/9220609/Steve_Jobs _interview_One_on_one_in_1995?taxonomyId=214and pageNumber=.

192. Isaacson, *Jobs*; Susan Wilson, *Steve Jobs: Wizard of Apple Computer* (Berkeley Heights, NJ: Enslow, 2001).

193. Isaacson, *Jobs*.

194. Mandela, *Freedom*.

195. Susan Adams, "Nelson Mandela: A Great Leader Dies," *Forbes*, December 5, 2013, http://www.forbes.com/sites/susanadams/2013/12/05/nelson-mandela-a-great-leader-dies.

196. Roxana Robinson, *Georgia O'Keeffe: A Life* (New York: Burlingame/Harper and Row, 1989).

197. Barbara Sheen, *Steve Jobs*, People in the News (Farmington Hills, MI: Gale, Cengage Learning, 2010).

198. "Jobs," interview by Morrow.

199. Bo Burlingham and George Gendron, "The Entrepreneur of the Decade: An Interview with Steven Jobs, *Inc.*'s Entrepreneur of the Decade," *Inc.*, April 1, 1989, http://www.inc.com/magazine/19890401/5602.html; Isaacson, *Jobs*.

200. Eve Curie, *Madame Curie: A Biography* (Garden City, NY: Doubleday, Doran, 1937).

Chapter 6: The Space Climate That Nurtures the Space Attitudes

1. Roxana Robinson, *Georgia O'Keeffe: A Life* (New York: Burlingame/Harper and Row, 1989).

2. Laurie Lisle, *Portrait of an Artist: A Biography of O'Keeffe* (Albuquerque: University of New Mexico Press, 1986).

3. Robinson, *O'Keeffe*.

4. Lisle, *Portrait*.

5. Robinson, *O'Keeffe*.

6. Ibid.

7. Lisle, *Portrait*.

8. Robinson, *O'Keeffe*.

9. Lisle, *Portrait*; Robinson, *O'Keeffe*.

10. Lisle, *Portrait*.

11. Ibid.

12. Jan Garden Castro, *The Art and Life of Georgia O'Keeffe* (New York: Crown, 1985); Lisle, *Portrait*.

13. Robinson, *O'Keeffe*.

14. Ibid.

15. Lisle, *Portrait*; Robinson, *O'Keeffe*.

16. Lisle, *Portrait*.

17. Robinson, *O'Keeffe*.

18. Ibid.

19. Ibid.

20. Lisle, *Portrait*.

21. Georgia O'Keeffe, *Georgia O'Keeffe* (New York: Viking, 1976).

22. Lisle, *Portrait*.

23. Ibid.

24. Ibid.; O'Keeffe, *O'Keeffe*.

25. O'Keeffe, *O'Keeffe*.

26. Ibid.

27. Lisle, *Portrait*.

28. Ibid.; Robinson, *O'Keeffe*.

29. Robinson, *O'Keeffe*.

30. Lisle, *Portrait*.

31. Robinson, *O'Keeffe*.

32. Lisle, *Portrait*; Robinson, *O'Keeffe*.

33. Lisle, *Portrait*.

34. Ibid.

35. Ibid.; O'Keeffe, *O'Keeffe*; Robinson, *O'Keeffe*.

36. Edith Evans Asbury, "Obituary: Georgia O'Keeffe Dead at 98, Shaper of Modern Art in U.S.," *On This Day*, March 7, 1986, http://www.nytimes.com/learning/general/onthisday/bday/1115 .html; Castro, *Art*; O'Keeffe, *O'Keeffe*.

37. Ibid.

38. Castro, *Art*.

39. Ibid.

40. Asbury, "Obituary."

41. Danielle Peltakian, "Georgia O'Keeffe (1887–1986): American Modernist," Sullivan Goss: An American Gallery, 2015, http://www.sullivangoss.com/georgia_OKeeffe/.

42. Castro, *Art*; Lisle, *Portrait*.

43. Castro, *Art*; O'Keeffe, *O'Keeffe*.

44. Asbury, "Obituary"; Robinson, *O'Keeffe*.

45. James R. Averill, Kyum Koo Chon, and Doug Woong Hahn, "Emotions and Creativity, East and West," *Asian Journal of Social Psychology* 4, no. 3 (2001): 165–83.

46. Rob M. Fielding, "A Socio-Cognitive Perspective on Cross-Cultural Attitudes and Practices in Creativity Development," *Australian Art Education* 20 (1997): 27–33; Donald W. MacKinnon, *In Search of Human Effectiveness* (Buffalo, NY: Creative Education Foundation, 1978); Gudmund J. W. Smith and Ingegerd M. Carlsson, *The Creative Process: A Functional Model Based on Empirical Studies from Early Childhood to Middle Age* (Madison, CT: International Universities Press, 1990).

47. Kathleen Dewing, "Family Influence on Creativity: A Review and Discussion," *Journal of Special Education* 4, no. 4 (1970): 399–404; Kathleen Dewing and Ronald Taft, "Some Characteristics of the Parents of Creative Twelve-Year-Olds," *Journal of Personality* 41, no. 1 (1973): 71–85; Albert S. Dreyer and Mary Beth Wells, "Parental Values, Parental Control, and Creativity in Young Children," *Journal of Marriage and the Family* 28, no. 1 (1966): 83–88; Fielding, "Socio-Cognitive"; Jacob W. Getzels and Philip W. Jackson, "Family Environment and Cognitive Style: A Study of the Sources of Highly Intelligent and of Highly Creative Adolescents," *American Sociological Review* 26 (1961): 351–59; MacKinnon, *Search*; Eric Rayner et al., *Human Development: An Introduction to the Psychodynamics of Growth, Maturity and Ageing* (Sussex, UK: Routledge, 2005); Carl R. Rogers, "Towards a Theory of Creativity," *ETC: A Review of General Semantics* 11, no. 4 (1954): 249–60; Gudmund J. W. Smith and Ingegerd M. Carlsson, *The Creative Process: A Functional Model Based on Empirical Studies from Early Childhood to Middle Age* (Madison, CT: International Universities Press, 1990); Paul S. Weisberg and Kayla J. Springer, "Environmental Factors in Creative Function: A Study of Gifted Children," *Archives of General Psychology* 5 (1961): 554–64;

48. Getzels and Jackson, "Family"; Rogers, "Theory."

49. Winfred R. Bion, *Second Thoughts: Selected Papers on Psychoanalysis* (New York: Aronson, 1967); Rosa Aurora Chávez-Eakle, "Creativity and Personality," in *Measuring Creativity: Proceedings for the Conference, "Can Creativity Be Measured?"* ed. Ernesto Villalba (Luxembourg: Publications Office of the European Union, 2009), 245–55; Donald Woods Winnicott, *Playing and Reality* (London, UK: Tavistock, 1971).

50. KH Kim and Sharon Kim, "Empathy," in Sherwood Thompson, ed., *Encyclopedia of Diversity and Social Justice* (Lanham, MD: Rowman and Littlefield, 2014); Heinz Kohut, *How Does Analysis Cure?* eds. Arnold Goldberg and Paul E. Stepansky, vol. 52 (Chicago: University of Chicago Press, 1984).

51. Dreyer and Wells, "Parental"; Weisberg and Springer, "Environmental."

52. Adam D. Galinsky et al., "Why It Pays to Get inside the Head of Your Opponent: The Differential Effects of Perspective Taking and Empathy in Negotiations," *Psychological Science* 19, no. 4 (2008): 378–84.

53. Sandra W. Russ, *Play in Child Development and Psychotherapy: Toward Empirically Supported Practice* (Mahwah, NJ: Erlbaum, 2004); Dorothy G. Singer and Jerome L. Singer, *The House of Make-Believe: Children's Play and the Developing Imagination* (Cambridge, MA: Harvard University Press, 1990); Dorothy G. Singer and Jerome L. Singer, *Imagination and Play in the Electronic Age* (Cambridge, MA: Harvard University Press, 2005); Jerome L. Singer, "Researching Imaginative Play and Adult Consciousness: Implications for Daily and Literary Creativity," *Psychology of Aesthetics, Creativity, and the Arts* 3, no. 4 (2009): 190–99.

54. BT Ayele, I. Lipkovich G. Molenberghs, CH. Mallinckrodt, "A Multiple-Imputation-Based Approach to Sensitivity Analyses and Effectiveness Assessments in Longitudinal Clinical Trials," *Journal of Biomedical Statistics* 24, no. 2 (2014): 211–28; Hannah Bayne, Ed Neukrug, Danica Hays, and Bruce Britton, "A Comprehensive Model for Optimizing Empathy in Person-Centered Care," *Patient Education and Counseling* 93, no. 2 (2013): 209–15; John M. Gottman, "Psychology and the Study of Marital Processes," *Annual Review of Psychology* 49 no. 1 (1998): 169–97; Tess B. O'Brien, Anita DeLongis, Georgia Pomaki, Eli Puterman, and Amy Zwicker, "Couples Coping with Stress: The Role of Empathic Responding," *European Psychologist* 14, no. 1 (2009): 18–28; David D Vachon, Donald R Lynam, and Jarrod A Johnson, "The (Non)relation between Empathy and Aggression: Surprising Results from a Meta-Analysis," *Psychological Bulletin 140*, no. 3 (2014): 751–73.

55. Sara H. Konrath, Edward H. O'Brien, and Courtney Hsing, "Changes in Dispositional Empathy in American College Students over Time: A Meta-Analysis," *Personality and Social Psychology Review* 15 (2011): 180–98; Jean M. Twenge et al., "Egos Inflating over Time: A Cross-Temporal Meta-Analysis of the Narcissistic Personality Inventory," *Journal of Personality* 76, no. 4 (2008): 875–902.

56. Konrath, O'Brien, and Hsing, "Changes."

57. Pew Research Center, "A Portrait of 'Generation Next': How Young People View Their Lives, Futures and Politics, 2007, http://www.people-press.org/2007/01/09/a-portrait-of-generation-next/.

58. Kathy Hirsh-Pasek and Roberta Michnick Golinkoff, *Einstein Never Used Flash Cards: How Our Children Really Learn—and Why They Need to Play More and Memorize Less* (Pennsylvania: Rodale, 2003); Roberta Michnick Golinkoff, Laura E. Berk, and Dorothy Singer, *A Mandate for Playful Learning* (Oxford: Oxford University Press, 2009).

59. Dewing, "Family"; Dewing and Taft, "Characteristics"; Jacob Getzels and Philip W. Jackson, *Creativity and Intelligence: Explorations with the Gifted Child* (New York: Wiley, 1962); Hans J. Eysenck, *Genius: The Natural History of Creativity*, vol. 12 (Cambridge, UK: Cambridge University Press, 1995); Gregory J. Feist, "A Meta-Analysis of Personality in Scientific and Artistic Creativity," *Personality and Social Psychology Review* 2, no. 4 (1998): 290–309; Donald W. MacKinnon, "The Nature and Nurture of Creative Talent," *American Psychologist* 17, no. 7 (1962): 484–95; Anne Roe, *The Making of a Scientist* (New York: Dodd, Mead, 1953); Dean Keith Simonton, *Greatness: Who Makes History and Why* (New York: Gilford, 1994).

60. Eysenck, *Genius*; Feist, "Meta-Analysis"; Roe, *Making*; Simonton, *Greatness*.

61. Eysenck, *Genius*; Feist, "Meta-Analysis"; Roe, *Making*; Simonton, *Greatness*

62. Echo H. Wu, "Cultural Perspectives on Talent Development and Parenting," *Dissertation Abstracts International Section A: Humanities and Social Sciences* 68 no. 11–A (2008): 4610.

63. Gary A. Davis and Michael J. Subkoviak, "Multidimensional Analysis of a Personality-Based Test of Creative Potential," *Journal of Educational Measurement* 12 (1978): 37–43; Dewing, "Family"; Dewing and Taft, "Characteristics"; John E. Drevdahl, "Some Developmental and Environmental Factors in Creativity," in *Widening Horizons in Creativity*, ed. Calvin W. Taylor (New York: Wiley, 1964), 170–85; Getzels and Jackson, *Creativity*; MacKinnon, "Nature"; Richard S. Mansfield and Thomas V. Busse, *The Psychology of Creativity and Discovery: Scientists and Their Work* (Chicago: Nelson-Hall, 1981); Rhona A. Ochse, *Before the Gates of Excellence: The Determinants of Creative Genius* (Cambridge, UK: Cambridge University Press, 1990); Saroj Saxena and Rakesh Kumar, "Study of Creativity in Relation to Anxiety," *Indian Psychological Review* 28 (1985): 5–8; Weisberg and Springer, "Environmental."

64. Dewing and Taft, "Characteristics"; Getzels and Jackson, *Creativity*; MacKinnon, "Nature."

65. Lois E. Datta and Morris B. Parloff, "On the Relevance of Autonomy: Parent-Child Relationships and Early Scientific Creativity," *Proceedings of the Annual Convention of the American Psychological Association* 2 (1967): 149–50; Dewing, "Family"; Caria Goble, James D. Moran III, and Anne K. Bomba, "Maternal Teaching Techniques and Preschool Children's Ideational Fluency," *Creativity Research Journal* 4, no. 3 (1991): 273–79; Zahari Ishak, Suet Fin Low, and Poh Li Lau, "Parenting Style as a Moderator for Students' Academic Achievement," *Journal of Science Education and Technology* 21, no. 4 (2012): 487–93; Robert J. Kirschenbaum, *Understanding the Creative Activity of Students* (St. Louis, MO: Creative Learning, 1989); James D. Moran III, Janet K. Sawyers, and Amy J. Moore, "The Effects of Structure in Instructions and Materials on Preschoolers' Creativity," *Home Economic Research Journal* 17, no. 2 (1988): 148–52.

66. Drevdahl, "Developmental."

67. Datta and Parloff, "Relevance"; Dewing, "Family"; John Marshall Reeve, "Why Teachers Adopt a Controlling Motivating Style Toward Students and How They Can Become More Autonomy Supportive," *Educational Psychologist* 44, no. 3 (2009): 159–75; George Domino, "Maternal Personality Correlates of Sons' Creativity," *Journal of Consulting and Clinical Psychology* 33, no. 2 (1969): 180–83; Maarten Vansteenkiste et al., "Motivating Learning, Performance, and Persistence: The Synergistic Effects of Intrinsic Goal Contents and Autonomy-Supportive Contexts," *Journal of Personality and Social Psychology* 87, no. 2 (2004): 246–60.

68. Ishak, Low, and Lau, "Parenting"; Kirschenbaum, *Understanding*.

69. Datta and Parloff, "Relevance"; Dewing, "Family"; Goble, Moran, and Bomba, "Maternal"; Moran, Sawyers, and Moore, "Effects."

70. Marjory Roberts Gray and Laurence Steinberg, "Unpacking Authoritative Parenting: Reassessing a Multidimensional Construct," *Journal of Marriage and Family* 61 (1999): 574–87.

71. Diana Baumrind, "Current Patterns of Parental Authority," *Developmental Psychology Monograph* 4, no. 12 (1971): 1–103; Datta and Parloff, "Relevance; Dewing, "Family"; Dewing and Taft, "Characteristics"; Domino, "Maternal"; Drevdahl, "Developmental"; Goble, Moran, and Bomba, "Maternal"; Gray and Steinberg, "Unpacking"; Kirschenbaum, *Understanding*; MacKinnon, "Nature"; Moran, Sawyers, and Moore, "Effects"; Reeve, "Teachers"; E. Paul Torrance, *The Search for Satori and Creativity* (Buffalo, NY: Bearly Limited, 1979); E. Paul Torrance and H. Tammy Safter, *Making the Creative Leap Beyond* (Buffalo, NY: Creative Education Foundation, 1999); Rick Trinkner et al., "Don't Trust Anyone over 30: Parental Legitimacy as a Mediator between Parenting Style and Changes in Delinquent Behavior over Time," *Journal of Adolescence* 35, no. 1 (2012): 119–32; Weisberg and Springer, "Environmental."

72. Thomas J. Bouchard, "Genes, Environment, and Personality," *Science—New York Then Washington* (1994): 1700–1701; Robert Plomin, "Commentary: Why Are Children in the Same Family So Different? Non-Shared Environment Three Decades Later," *International Journal of Epidemiology* 40, no. 3 (2011): 582–92; Dean Keith Simonton, *Genius 101*, The Psych 101 Series (New York: Springer, 2009).

73. Matthijs Baas, Carsten KW De Dreu, and Bernard A. Nijstad, "A Meta-Analysis of 25 Years of Mood-Creativity Research: Hedonic Tone, Activation, or Regulatory Focus?" *Psychological Bulletin* 134, no. 6 (2008): 779–806; Valeria Drago et al., "Cyclic Alternating Pattern in Sleep and Its Relationship to Creativity," *Sleep Medicine* 12, no. 4 (2011): 361–66; Michael D. Mumford et al., "Process-Based Measures of Creative Problem-Solving Skills: II. Information Encoding," *Creativity Research Journal* 9, no. 1 (1996): 77–88; Dean Keith Simonton, "The Genetics of Giftedness: What Does It Mean to Have Creative Talent?" in *Creatively Gifted Students Are Not Like Other Gifted Students: Research, Theory, and Practice*, eds. KH Kim, James C. Kaufman, John Baer, and Bharath Sriraman (The Netherlands: Sense, 2013), 167–79.

74. Baas, Dreu, and Nijstad, "Meta-Analysis"; Drago et al., "Cyclic"; Simonton, "Genetics."

75. Simonton, "Genetics."

76. Doyle W. Bishop and Charles A. Chace, "Parental Conceptual Systems, Home Play Environment,

and Potential Creativity in Children," *Journal of Experimental Child Psychology* 12, no. 3 (1971): 318–38; Hazel Feldhusen, "Teaching Gifted, Creative, and Talented Students in an Individualized Classroom," *Gifted Child Quarterly* 25, no. 3 (1981): 108–11; Rob M. Fielding, "Creativity Revisited: Strategies for Developing Creative Potential," *Journal of the Institute of Art Education* 7, no. 2 (1983): 51–60; Beth A. Hennessey and Teresa M. Amabile, *Creativity and Learning* (Washington, DC: National Education Association, 1987); Ochse, *Excellence*; Ruth Richards, "Beyond Piaget: Accepting Divergent, Chaotic, and Creative Thought," *New Directions for Child and Adolescent Development* 72 (1996): 67–86; Dean Keith Simonton, "Leaders of American Psychology, 1879–1967: Career Development, Creative Output, and Professional Achievement," *Journal of Personality and Social Psychology* 62 (1992): 5–17; Dean Keith Simonton, "The Social Context of Career Success and Course for 2,026 Scientists and Inventors," *Personality and Social Psychology Bulletin* 18 (1992): 452–63; E. Paul Torrance, *Guiding Creative Talent* (Englewood Cliffs, NJ: Prentice-Hall, 1962); E. Paul Torrance, *Education and the Creative Potential* (Minneapolis, MN: University of Minnesota, 1963); E. Paul Torrance, "Education and Creativity," in *Creativity Progress and Potential*, ed. Calvin Walker Taylor (New York: McGraw-Hill, 1964).

77. Hennessey and Amabile, *Creativity*; Ochse, *Excellence*; Jean Piaget, *Play, Dreams and Imitation in Childhood* (New York: Norton, 1962); Simonton, "Leaders"; Simonton, "Social Context"; Torrance, "Education"; Serena E. Wade, "Adolescents, Creativity, and Media: An Exploratory Study," *American Behavioral Scientist* 14 (1971): 341–49.

78. Feldhusen, "Teaching"; Joseph S. Renzulli, "A General Theory for the Development of Creative Productivity through the Pursuit of Ideal Acts of Learning," *Gifted Child Quarterly* 36, no. 4 (1992): 170–82.

79. Sigmund Freud, "Creative Writers and Daydreaming," in *Standard Edition of the Complete Psychological Works of Sigmund Freud*, vol. 9, ed. and trans. James Strachey (London, UK: Hogarth, 1959), 141–53; Piaget, *Play*; Singer and Singer, *House*; Singer and Singer, *Imagination*; Jerome L. Singer, *The Child's World of Make-Believe* (New York: Academic, 1973); Singer, "Researching"; Lev S. Vygotsky, "The Development of Imagination in Childhood," in *The Collected Works of L. S. Vygotsky*, vol. 2, eds. Robert W. Rieber and Aaron S. Carton (New York: N. Minick, Tranc., 1987); Lev S. Vygotsky, "Imagination and Creativity in Childhood," *Soviet Psychology* 28, no. 1 (1990): 84–96; Lev S. Vygotsky, "Imagination and Creativity of the Adolescent," in *The Vygotsky Reader*, eds. R. Van Der Veer and Jaan Valsiner (Cambridge: Blackwell, 1994), 266–88.

80. Singer and Singer, *House*; Torrance, *Search*; Torrance and Safter, *Making*.

81. Hirsh-Pasek and Golinkoff, *Einstein Never Used*; "The State of Play: Gallup Survey of Principals on School Recess," *Robert Wood Johnson Foundation*, February 2010, http://www.rwjf.org/pr/product .jsp?id=55249; Golinkoff, Berk, and Singer, *A Mandate*;

82. Bishop and Chace, "Parental Conceptual Systems," 318–38; Fielding, "Creativity"; H. L. Kaila, "Democratizing Schools across the World to Stop Killing Creativity in Children: An Indian Perspective," *Counseling Psychology Quarterly* 18 (2005): 1–6; Kirschenbaum, *Understanding*; Golinkoff, Berk, and Singer, *A Mandate*; Torrance, *Guiding*; Torrance, *Education*; Torrance, "Education."

83. Dewing and Taft, "Characteristics"; Getzels and Jackson, *Creativity*; Jacob Getzels and Philip W. Jackson, "The Meaning of Giftedness—An Examination of an Expanding Concept," *Phi Delta Kappan* 40, no. 2 (1958): 75–77; MacKinnon, "Nature"; Robert C. Nichols, "Parental Attitudes of Mothers of Intelligent Adolescents and Creativity of Their Children," *Child Development* 35, no. 4 (1964): 1041–49; Ann McGreevy, "All in the Golden Afternoon: The Early Life of Charles L. Dodgson (Lewis Carroll)," *Gifted Child Quarterly* 36, no. 1 (1992): 6–10.

84. Dewing, "Family"; Dewing and Taft, "Characteristics."

85. Anne Anastasi and Charles E. Schaefer, "Biographical Correlates of Artistic and Literary Creativity in Adolescent Girls," *Journal of Applied Phycology* 53 no. 4 (1969): 267–73.

86. Bonnie Cramond, "Attention-Deficit Hyperactivity Disorder and Creativity—What Is the Connection?" *Journal of Creative Behavior* 28, no. 3 (1994): 193–210; Christina Lynn Scott, "Teachers' Biases toward Creative Children," *Creativity Research Journal* 12, no. 4 (1999): 321–28; Torrance, *Guiding*.

87. Abdullah Aljughaiman and Elizabeth Mowrer-Reynolds, "Teachers' Conceptions of Creativity and Creative Students," *Journal of Creative Behavior* 39, no. 1 (2005): 17–34; Kenneth E. Anderson, *Research on the Academically Talented Student* (Washington, DC: National Education Association, 1961); Louise M. Bachtold, "The Creative Personality and the Ideal Pupil Revisited," *Journal of Creative Behavior* 8, no. 1 (1974): 47–54; Cramond, "Attention-Deficit"; Arthur J. Cropley, *More Ways Than One: Fostering Creativity in the Classroom* (Norwood, NJ: Ablex, 1992); Gary A. Davis and Sylvia B. Rimm, *Education of the Gifted and Talented*, 3rd ed. (Needham Heights, MA: Allyn and Bacon, 1994); V. L. Dawson et al., "Predicting Creative Behavior: A Reexamination of the Divergence between Traditional and Teacher-Defined Concepts of Creativity," *Creativity Research Journal* 12, no. 1 (1999): 57–66; Elizabeth Monroe Drews, *Creative Intellectual Style in Gifted Adolescents* (East Lansing: Michigan State University, 1961); Mark A. Kunkel et al., "The Experience of Giftedness: A Concept Map," *Gifted Child Quarterly* 39, no. 3 (1995): 126–34; Catherine C. Oliphant, "Descriptive Study of Factors Associated with Teacher Identification of Gifted Students" (PhD diss., Temple University, 1986), 1691; Catherine Patrick, *What Is Creative Thinking?* (New York: Philosophical Library, 1955); T. N. Raina and M. K. Raina, "Perception of Teacher-Educators in India about the Ideal Pupil," *Journal of Educational Research* 64, no. 7 (1971): 303–306; Shirley P. Ritchie, "Creativity and Risk-Taking in Young Children" (PhD diss., University of North Carolina at Greensboro, 1980), 539; Elisabeth Rudowicz, "Creativity and Culture: A Two-Way Interaction," *Scandinavian Journal of Educational Research* 47, no. 3 (2003): 273–90; Elisabeth Rudowicz and Xiao Dong Yue, "Compatibility of Chinese and Creative Personalities," *Creativity Research Journal* 14, no. 3–4 (2000): 387–94; Mark A. Runco and Sakamoto S. Okuda, "Reaching Creatively Gifted Children through Their Learning Styles," in *Teaching and Counseling Gifted and Talented Adolescents: An International Learning Style Perspective*, eds. Roberta M. Milgram, Rita Dunn, and Gary E. Price (New York: Praeger, 1993), 103–15; Scott, "Biases"; Kenneth R. Seeley, "Perspectives on Adolescent Giftedness and Delinquency," *Journal for the Education of the Gifted* 8, no. 1 (1984): 59–72; E. Paul Torrance, "The Creative Personality and the Ideal Pupil," *Teachers College Record* 65 (1963): 220–27; E. Paul Torrance, *Why Fly? A Philosophy of Creativity* (Norwood, NJ: Ablex, 1995); E. Paul Torrance, "Reflections on a Career in Creative Teaching," in *On the Edge and Keeping on the Edge*, ed. E. Paul Torrance (Westport, CT: Greenwood, 2000), 2–11; Ved Varma, *How and Why Children Fail* (UK: Kingsley, 1993); Erik L. Westby and V. L. Dawson, "Creativity: Asset or Burden in the Classroom?" *Creativity Research Journal* 8, no. 1 (1995): 1–10.

88. Getzels and Jackson, "Meaning"; Kunkel et al., "Experience"; Patrick, *What Is*; Seeley, "Perspectives"; Torrance, *Fly*; Torrance, "Reflections."

89. Joan Axtell, "Discontinuities in the Perception of Curiosity in Gifted Preadolescents," *Gifted Child Quarterly* 10, no. 2. (1966): 78–82; E. Paul Torrance, "A Longitudinal Examination of the Fourth Grade Slump in Creativity," *Gifted Child Quarterly* 12, no. 4 (1968): 195–99.

90. KH Kim, "The Creativity Crisis: The Decrease in Creative Thinking Score on the Torrance Tests of Creative Thinking," *Creativity Research Journal* 23, no. 4 (2011): 285–95.

91. John W. Alspaugh, "The Effect of Transition Grade to High School, Gender, and Grade Level upon Dropout Rates," *American Secondary Education* 29, no. 1 (2000): 2–9; KH Kim and Michael F. Hull, "Creative Personality and Anti-Creative Environment for High School Dropouts," *Creativity Research Journal* 24, no. 2–3 (2012): 169–76; Susanne P. Lajoie and Bruce M. Shore, "Three Myths? The Over-Representation of the Gifted among Dropouts, Delinquents, and Suicides," *Gifted Child Quarterly* 25, no. 3 (1981): 138–43.

92. Deborah Denno, "The Elementary School Teacher: Conformity and Maladjustment in a Prefabricated Role," *Adolescence* 12, no. 46 (1977): 247–59; Douglas Murphy, Reva Jenkins Friedman, and Nona Tollefson, "A New Criterion for the Ideal Child?" *Gifted Child Quarterly* 28, no. 1 (1984): 31–36; Robert D. Storm and Paris S. Storm, "Changing the Rules: Education for Creative Thinking," *Journal of Creative Behavior* 36, no. 3 (2002): 183–200.

93. David M. Harrington and Susan M. Anderson, "Creativity, Masculinity, Femininity and Three Models of Psychological Androgyny," *Journal of Personality and Social Psychology* 41 (1981):

744–57; D. Niall Hartnett, Jason M. Nelson, and Ann N. Rinn, "Gifted or ADHD? The Possibilities of Misdiagnosis," *Roeper Review* 26 (2004): 73–77; Torsten Norlander, Anna Erixon, and Trevor Archer, "Psychological Androgyny and Creativity: Dynamics of Gender-Role and Personality Trait," *Social Behavior and Personality* 28, no. 5 (2000): 423–35; Torrance, *Guiding*.

94. Anastasi and Schaefer, "Biographical"; Dean C. Dauw, "Life Experiences of Original Thinkers and Good Elaborators," *Exceptional Children* 32, no. 7 (1966): 433–40; Dewing, "Family"; Dewing and Taft, "Characteristics"; Fielding, "Creativity"; Thomas N. Grant, "A Study of Masculinity-Femininity in Creative Male Adolescents and Their Parents" (PhD diss., ProQuest Information and Learning, 1973); Ravenna Helson, "Childhood Interest Clusters Related to Creativity in Women," *Journal of Consulting Psychology* 29, no. 4 (1965): 352–61; Ravenna Helson, "Personality of Women with Artistic and Imaginative Interests: The Role of Masculinity, Originality, and Other Characteristics of Their Creativity," *Journal of Personality* 34, no. 1 (1966): 1–25; Ravenna Helson, "Personality Characteristics and Developmental History of Creative College Women," *Genetic Psychology Monographs* 76, no. 2 (1967): 205–56; MacKinnon, "Nature"; Charles E. Schaefer and Anne Anastasi, "A Biographical Inventory for Identifying Creativity in Adolescent Boys," *Journal of Applied Psychology* 52 no. 1 (1968): 42–48; Torrance, *Guiding*.

95. Anastasi and Schaefer, "Biographical"; Dauw, "Life"; Helson, "Childhood"; Helson, "Personality"; Helson, "Personality Characteristics"; MacKinnon, "Nature"; Schaefer and Anastasi, "Biographical."

96. Dewing, "Family"; Torrance, *Guiding*.

97. Harrington and Anderson, "Creativity"; Hartnett, Nelson, and Rinn, "Gifted"; Norlander, Erixon, and Archer, "Psychological"; Torrance, *Guiding*.

98. Robert S. Root-Bernstein, "Music, Creativity and Scientific Thinking," *Leonardo* 34, no. 1 (2001): 63–68; Robert S. Root-Bernstein, "Multiple Giftedness, Polymathy, and the Bases of Creativity," in *The Handbook on Giftedness*, ed. Larisa Shavinina (New York: Springer Science, 2008).

99. Simonton, "Genetics."

100. Teresa M. Amabile, *Growing up Creative: Nurturing a Lifetime of Creativity* (Williston, VT: Crown House, 1989); Anastasi and Schaefer, "Biographical"; Richard S. Crutchfield, "Conformity and Character," *American Psychologist* 10, no. 5 (1955): 191–98; Richard S. Crutchfield, "Conformity and Creative Thinking," in *Contemporary Approaches to Creative Thinking: A Symposium Held at the University of Colorado*, eds. Howard E. Gruber, Glenn Terrell, and Michael Wertheimer (New York: Athgerton, 1962); Getzels and Jackson, *Creativity*; McGreevy, "All"; Nichols, "Parental"; Torrance, *Guiding*; E. Paul Torrance, "Predicting the Creativity of Elementary School Children (1958–80)— and the Teacher Who Made a Difference," *Gifted Child Quarterly* 25, no. 2 (1981): 55–62; E. Paul Torrance, "Understanding Creativity: Where to Start?" *Psychological Inquiry* 4, no. 3 (1993): 232–34; E. Paul Torrance, *The Manifesto: A Guide to Developing a Creative Career* (West Westport, CT: Ablex, 2002); Cheryl W. Van Hook and Deborah W. Tegano, "The Relationship between Creativity and Conformity among Preschool Children," *Journal of Creative Behavior* 36, no. 1 (2002): 1–16; William J. Walker, "Creativity and High School Climate," *Gifted Child Quarterly* 10 (1966): 164–69.

101. Amabile, *Growing*; Crutchfield, "Conformity"; Torrance, *Guiding*; Torrance, "Predicting"; Torrance, "Understanding"; Van Hook and Tegano, "Relationship."

102. Averill, Chon, and Hahn, "Emotions"; Baas, De Dreu, and Nijstad, "Meta-Analysis"; Jessie Ee and Tan Oon Seng, "Cultural Influences of the East and West: Implications on the Educational Reforms in the Singapore Context," *KEDI Journal of Educational Policy* 5, no. 1 (2008): 49–62; KH Kim et al., "Creativity and Confucianism among American and Korean Educators," *Creativity Research Journal* 23, no. 4 (2011): 357–71.

103. Cortney A. Evans et al., "Understanding Relations among Children's Shy and Antisocial/ Aggressive Behaviors and Mothers' Parenting: The Role of Maternal Beliefs," *Merrill-Palmer Quarterly* 58 (2012): 341–74; Cliff McKinney, Mary Catherine Milone, and Kimberly Renk, "Parenting and Late Adolescent Emotional Adjustment: Mediating Effects of Discipline and Gender," *Child Psychiatry and Human Development* 42 (2011): 463–81; Christian L. Porter et al., "A Comparative Study of Child

Temperament and Parenting in Beijing, China and the Western United States," *International Journal of Behavioral Development* 29, no. 5 (2005): 541–51.

104. Robert J. Englehart and David B. Hale, "Punishment, Nail-Biting, and Nightmares: A Cross-Cultural Study," *Journal of Multicultural Counseling and Development* 18, no. 3 (1990): 126–32.

105. Jacinta Bronte-Tinkew, Kristin A. Moore, and Jennifer Carrano, "Father-Child Relationship, Parenting Styles, and Adolescent Risk Behaviors in Intact Families," *Journal of Family Issues* 27 (2006): 850–81; Machteld Hoeve et al., "Trajectories of Delinquency and Parenting Styles," *Journal of Abnormal Child Psychology* 36, no. 2 (2008): 223–35; Porter et al., "Comparative."

106. Eysenck, *Genius*; Twila Z. Tardif and Robert J. Sternberg, "What Do We Know about Creativity?" in *The Nature of Creativity*, ed. Robert J. Sternberg (New York: Cambridge University Press, 1999), 429–40. *It is also called "feeling (type)": Weston H. Agor, "How Intuition Can Be Used to Enhance Creativity in Organizations," *Journal of Creative Behavior* 25, no. 1 (1991): 11–19; Dale Richard Buchanan and Jane A. Taylor, "Jungian Typology of Professional Psychodramatists: Myers-Briggs Type Indicator Analysis of Certified Psychodramatists," *Psychological Reports* 58, no. 2 (1986): 391–400; Stephen J. Dollinger, Dimitra G. Palaskonis, and Jodi L. Pearson, "Creativity and Intuition Revisited," *Journal of Creative Behavior* 38, no. 4 (2004): 244–59; Carolyn McKinnell Jacobson, "Cognitive Styles of Creativity: Relations of Scores on the Kirton Adaption-Innovation Inventory and the Myers-Briggs Type Indicator among Managers in USA," *Psychological Reports* 72 (1993): 1131–38; Shu Ching Yang and Wen Chaun Lin, "The Relationship among Creative, Critical Thinking and Thinking Styles in Taiwan High School Students," *Journal of Instructional Psychology* 31, no. 1 (2004): 33–45.

107. Rosa Aurora Chávez-Eakle, "On the Neurobiology of the Creative Process," *Bulletin of Psychology and the Arts* 5, no. 1 (2004): 29–35; Kazimierz Dabrowski, Andrzej Kawczak, and Michael M. Piechowski, *Mental Growth through Positive Disintegration* (London, UK: Gryf, 1970); Eysenck, *Genius*; Colin Martindale et al., "Creativity, Oversensitivity, and Rate of Habituation," *Personality and Individual Differences* 20, no. 4 (1996): 423–27.

108. Yiling Cheng, KH Kim, and Michael F. Hull, "Comparisons of Creative Styles and Personality Types between American and Taiwanese College Students and the Relationship between Creative Potential and Personality Types," *Psychology of Aesthetics, Creativity, and the Arts* 4, no. 2 (2010): 103–12; Feist, "Meta-Analysis"; Colin Robert R. McCrae, "Creativity, Divergent Thinking, and Openness to Experience," *Journal of Personality and Social Psychology* 52, no. 6 (1987): 1258–65; Sandra W. Russ, *Affect and Creativity: The Role of Affect and Play in the Creative Process* (Hillsdale, NJ: Erlbaum, 1993); Torrance, *Search*; Torrance and Safter, *Making*.

109. Averill, Chon, and Hahn, "Emotions"; Baas, De Dreu, and Nijstad, "Meta-Analysis"; Abraham H. Maslow, *The Farther Reaches of Human Nature* (New York: Viking, 1971).

110. Feist, "Meta-Analysis."

111. Larisa Shavinina, "Explaining High Abilities of Nobel Laureates," *High Ability Studies* 15, no. 2 (2004): 243–54.

112. Jens Förster, Kal Epstude, and Amina Özelsel, "Why Love Has Wings and Sex Not: How Reminders of Love and Sex Influence Creative and Analytic Thinking," *Personality and Social Psychology Bulletin* 35, no. 11 (2009): 1479–91; Geir Kaufmann and Suzanne K. Vosburg, "'Paradoxical' Mood Effects on Creative Problem-Solving," *Cognition and Emotion* 11, no. 2 (1997): 151–70.

113. Peter Heehs, "Genius, Mysticism, and Madness," *Psychohistory Review* 26 (1997): 45–75; James C. Kaufman, "Genius, Lunatics, and Poets: Mental Illness in Prize-Winning Authors," *Imagination, Cognition and Personality* 20, no. 4 (2001): 305–14.

114. Mark A. Runco, "Creativity," *Annual Review of Psychology* 55 (2004): 657–87; Mark A. Runco and Ruth Richards, eds., *Eminent Creativity, Everyday Creativity, and Health* (Norwood, NJ: Ablex, 1997).

115. Kaufman, "Genius"; Albert Rothenberg, *Creativity and Madness: New Findings and Old Stereotypes* (Baltimore, MD: Johns Hopkins University Press, 1990).

116. Benjamin Baird, Jonathan Smallwood, and Jonathan W. Schooler, "Back to the Future: Autobiographical Planning and the Functionality of Mind-Wandering," *Consciousness and Cognition* 20, no. 4 (2011): 1604–11; Kaufman, "Genius"; Jennifer C. McVay and Michael J. Kane, "Does Mind Wandering Reflect Executive Function or Executive Failure? Comment on Smallwood and Schooler (2006) and Watkins (2008)," *Psychological Bulletin* 136, no. 2 (2010): 188–97; Benjamin W. Mooneyham and Jonathan W. Schooler, "The Costs and Benefits of Mind-Wandering: A Review," *Canadian Journal of Experimental Psychology/Revue canadienne de psychologie expérimentale* 67, no. 1 (2013): 11–18; Rothenberg, *Creativity*; Jerome L. Singer and John S. Antrobus, "A Factor-Analytic Study of Daydreaming and Conceptually-Related Cognitive and Personality Variables (Monograph Supplement 3–V17)," *Perceptual and Motor Skills* 17, no. 1 (1963): 187–209.

117. Frank Barron, "The Needs for Order and for Disorder as Motives in Creative Activity," in *Scientific Creativity: Its Recognition and Development*, eds. Calvin W. Taylor and Barron (New York: Wiley, 1963), 153–60; Eysenck, *Genius*; Feist, "Meta-Analysis"; Ruth Richards et al., "Creativity in Manic-Depressives, Cyclothymes, Their Normal Relatives, and Control Subjects," *Journal of Abnormal Psychology* 97, no. 3 (1988): 281–88; Russ, *Affect*.

118. Frank Barron, *Creative Person and Creative Process* (New York: Holt, Rinehart and Winston, 1969); Carson, Peterson, and Higgins, "Decreased."

119. Runco and Richards, *Eminent*; Daniel SP Schubert and Angelo M. Biondi, "Creativity and Madness: Part I—The Image of the Creative Person as Mentally Ill," *Journal of Creative Behavior* 9 (1975): 223–27.

120. Albert Rothenberg, "Bipolar Illness, Creativity, and Treatment," *Psychiatric Quarterly* 72, no. 2 (2001): 131–47; Schubert and Biondi, "Creativity"; Simonton, *101*.

121. Simonton, *101*.

122. James C. Kaufman and Janel D. Sexton, "Why Doesn't the Writing Cure Help Poets?" *Review of General Psychology* 10, no. 3 (2006): 268–82; Runco, "Creativity."

123. Mihaly Csikszentmihalyi, *Flow: The Psychology of Optimal Experience* (New York: Harper and Row, 1990); Mihaly Csikszentmihalyi, *Creativity: Flow and the Psychology of Discovery and Invention* (New York: Harper Perennial, 1996); Karuna Subramaniam et al., "A Brain Mechanism for Facilitation of Insight by Positive Affect," *Journal of Cognitive Neuroscience* 21, no. 3 (2009): 415–32; Todd M. Thrash et al., "Mediating between the Muse and the Masses: Inspiration and the Actualization of Creative Ideas," *Journal of Personality and Social Psychology* 98, no. 3 (2010): 469–87.

124. Carsten KW De Dreu, Matthijs Baas, and Bernard A. Nijstad, "Hedonic Tone and Activation Level in the Mood-Creativity Link: Toward a Dual Pathway to Creativity Model," *Journal of Personality and Social Psychology* 94, no. 5 (2008): 739–56; Förster, Epstude, and Özelsel, "Love"; Alice M. Isen, Kimberly A. Daubman, and Gary P. Nowicki, "Positive Affect Facilitates Creative Problem Solving," *Journal of Personality and Social Psychology* 52, no. 6 (1987): 1122–31; Alice M. Isen et al., "The Influence of Positive Affect on the Unusualness of Word Associations," *Journal of Personality and Social Psychology* 48, no. 6 (1985): 1413–26.

125. Baas, De Dreu, and Nijstad, "Meta-Analysis"; Dreu, Baas, and Nijstad, "Hedonic"; Isen, Daubman, and Nowicki, "Positive"; Isen et al., "Influence."

126. F. Gregory Ashby, Alice M. Isen, and A. U. Turken, "A Neuropsychological Theory of Positive Affect and Its Influence on Cognition," *Psychological Review* 106 (1999): 529–50; Dreu, Baas, and Nijstad, "Hedonic"; Isen, Daubman, and Nowicki, "Positive"; Isen et al., "Influence"; Russ, *Affect*.

127. Förster, Epstude, and Özelsel, "Love"; Kaufmann and Vosburg, "'Paradoxical."

128. Andrea Abele-Brehm, "Positive and Negative Mood Influences on Creativity: Evidence for Asymmetrical Effects," *Polish Psychological Bulletin* 23 (1992): 203–21; Kaufmann and Vosburg, "'Paradoxical"; Suzanne K. Vosburg, "The Effects of Positive and Negative Mood on Divergent-Thinking Performance," *Creativity Research Journal* 11, no. 2 (1998): 165–72.

129. Abele-Brehm, "Positive"; Albert Bandura, *Social Foundations of Thought and Action: A*

Social Cognitive Theory (Englewood Cliffs, NJ: Prentice-Hall, 1986); Albert Bandura, *Self-Efficacy: The Exercise of Control* (New York: Freeman, 1997); Michael La Hsu, Sheng-Tsung Hou, and Hsueh-Liang Fan, "Creative Self-Efficacy and Innovative Behavior in a Service Setting: Optimism as a Moderator," *Journal of Creative Behavior* 45, no. 4 (2011): 258–72; Kaufmann and Vosburg, "'Paradoxical'"; Cheng-Hsien Li and Jing-Jyi Wu, "The Structural Relationships between Optimism and Innovative Behavior: Understanding Potential Antecedents and Mediating Effects," *Creativity Research Journal* 23, no. 2 (2011): 119–28; Pamela Tierney and Steven M. Farmer, "The Pygmalion Process and Employee Creativity," *Journal of Management* 30 (2004): 413–32; Torrance, *Fly*; Torrance, *Manifesto*; Vosburg, "Effects"; Frank Zenasni and Todd I. Lubart, "Pleasantness of Creative Tasks and Creative Performance," *Thinking Skills and Creativity* 6 (2011): 49–56.

130. Baas, De Dreu, and Nijstad, "Meta-Analysis."

131. Feist, "Meta-Analysis."

132. Eysenck, *Genius*; Feist, "Meta-Analysis"; Meihua Qian, Jonathan A. Plucker, and Jiliang Shen, "A Model of Chinese Adolescents' Creative Personality," *Creativity Research Journal* 22, no. 1 (2010): 62–67; Tardif and Sternberg, "Know"; Torrance, *Search*; Torrance and Safter, *Making*.

133. Feist, "Meta-Analysis"; Tardif and Sternberg, "Know"; Torrance, *Search*; Torrance and Safter, *Making*.

134. Daniel C. Batson et al., "Immorality from Empathy-Induced Altruism: When Compassion and Justice Conflict," *Journal of Personality and Social Psychology* 68, no. 6 (1995): 1042–54; Galinsky et al., "Why It."

135. Galinsky et al., "Why It"; Don A. Moore, "Myopic Biases in Strategic Social Prediction: Why Deadlines Put Everyone under More Pressure Than Everyone Else," *Personality and Social Psychology Bulletin* 31 (2005): 668–79.

136. Nicholas Epley, Eugene Caruso, and Max H. Bazerman, "When Perspective Taking Increases Taking: Reactive Egoism in Social Interaction," *Journal of Personality and Social Psychology* 91, no. 5 (2006): 872–89; Kohut, *Analysis*; William W. Maddux, Elizabeth Mullen, and Adam D. Galinsky, "Chameleons Bake Bigger Pies and Take Bigger Pieces: Strategic Behavioral Mimicry Facilitates Negotiation Outcomes," *Journal of Experimental Social Psychology* 44, no. 2 (2008): 461–68.

137. Adam M. Grant, "Does Intrinsic Motivation Fuel the Prosocial Fire? Motivational Synergy in Predicting Persistence, Performance, and Productivity," *Journal of Applied Psychology* 93, no. 1 (2008): 48–58.

138. Teresa Amabile, *Creativity in Context* (Boulder, CO: Westview, 1996); Evan Polman and Kyle J. Emich, "Decisions for Others Are More Creative Than Decisions for the Self," *Personality and Social Psychology Bulletin* 37, no. 4 (2011): 492–501; Torrance, *Search*; Torrance and Safter, *Making*.

139. Marina A. Kholodnaya, "Psychological Mechanisms of Intellectual Giftedness," *Voprosy Psichologii* 1 (1991): 32–39; Shavinina, "Explaining"; Thrash et al., "Mediating."

140. Galinsky et al., "Power"; Grant, "Relational"; Polman and Emich, "Decisions."

141. Dale Richard Buchanan and Carole Bandy, "Jungian Typology of Prospective Psychodramatists: Myers-Briggs Type Indicator Analysis of Applicants for Psychodrama Training," *Psychological Reports* 55, no. 2 (1984): 599–606; Buchanan and Taylor, "Jungian Typology," 391–400; Jack A. Chambers, "Relating Personality and Biographical Factors to Scientific Creativity," *Psychological Monographs: General and Applied* 78, no. 7 (1964): 1–20; Cheng, Kim, and Hull, "Comparisons," 103–12; Hans J. Eysenck, *Psychology of People* (London: Penguin Books, 1977); Feist, "Meta-Analysis"; Andreas Fink and Aljoscha C. Neubauer, "Eysenck Meets Martindale: The Relationship between Extraversion and Originality from the Neuroscientific Perspective," *Personality and Individual Differences* 44, no. 1 (2008): 299–310; Dibakar Kundu, "Creativity and Its Relation to Some Personality Variables in High School Students: An Empirical Investigation," *Journal of Psychology Research* 31, no. 2 (1987): 55–63; Debdulal Dutta Roy, "Personality Model of Fine Artists," *Creativity Research Journal* 9, no. 4 (1996): 391–94; Darya L. Zabelina and Michael D. Robinson, "Child's Play: Facilitating the Originality of Creative Output by a Priming Manipulation," *Psychology of Aesthetics, Creativity, and the Arts* 4, no. 1 (2010): 57–65.

142. Eysenck, *Genius*; Feist, "Meta-Analysis"; Roe, *Making*; Simonton, *Greatness*; Anthony Storr, *Solitude: A Return to the Self* (New York: Free Press, 1988).

143. Eysenck, *Psychology*; Eysenck, *Genius*; Feist, "Meta-Analysis"; Carl Gustav Jung, *Psychological Types* (Princeton, NJ: Princeton University Press, 1971); John M. Mezias and William H. Starbuck, "What Do Managers Know, Anyway? A Lot Less Than They Think. But Now, the Good News," *Harvard Business Review* 81, no. 5 (2003): 16–17; Roe, *Making*; Simonton, *Greatness*; Sternberg and Kaufman, "Constraints"; Storr, *Solitude*; Tardif and Sternberg, "Know."

144. Chambers, "Relating"; Csikszentmihalyi, *Flow*; Hans J. Eysenck, "Creativity and Personality: Suggestions for a Theory," *Psychological Inquiry* 4 (1993): 147–78.

145. Feist, "Meta-Analysis."

146. Csikszentmihalyi, *Creativity*.

147. Mary Ann Collins and Teresa M. Amabile, "Motivation and Creativity," in *Handbook of Creativity*, ed. Robert J. Sternberg (New York: Cambridge University Press, 1999), 297–312; Edward L. Deci and Richard M. Ryan, "The 'What' and 'Why' of Goal Pursuits: Human Needs and the Self-Determination of Behavior," *Psychological Inquiry* 11, no. 4 (2000): 227–68.

148. Vansteenkiste et al., "Motivating Learning," 246–60.

149. Ding-Bang Luh and Chia-Chen Lu, "From Cognitive Style to Creativity Achievement: The Mediating Role of Passion," *Psychology of Aesthetics, Creativity, and the Arts* 6, no. 3 (2012): 282–88; Richard M. Ryan and Edward L. Deci, "Overview of Self-Determination Theory: An Organismic Dialectical Perspective," in *Handbook of Self-Determination Research*, eds. Edward L. Deci and Richard M. Ryan (Rochester, NY: University of Rochester Press, 2002), 3–33.

150. Deci and Ryan, "What"; Robert L. Helmreich, Janet T. Spence, and Robert S. Pred, "Making It without Losing It: Type A, Achievement Motivation, and Scientific Attainment Revisited," *Personality and Social Psychology Bulletin* 14 (1987): 495–504; Luh and Lu, "Cognitive"; Karen A. Matthews et al., "Pattern A, Achievement Striving, and Scientific Merit: Does Pattern A Help or Hinder?" *Journal of Personality and Social Psychology* 39 (1980): 962–67; Roe, *Making*; Ryan and Deci, "Overview"; Dean Keith Simonton, "Creativity and Genius," in *Handbook of Personality: Theory and Research*, eds. Oliver P. John, Richard W. Roberts, and Lawrence A. Pervin (New York: Gilford, 2008), 679–98; Tardif and Sternberg, "Know"; Robert J. Vallerand et al., "Les Passions de L'ame: On Obsessive and Harmonious Passion," *Journal of Personality and Social Psychology* 85, no. 4 (2003): 756–67; Robert J. Vallerand et al., "Passion in Sport: A Look at Determinants and Affective Experiences," *Journal of Sport and Exercise Psychology* 28, no. 4 (2006): 454–78; Ellen Winner, "Creativity and Talent," in *Well-Being: Positive Development across the Life Course*, eds. Marc H. Bornstein, Lucy Davidson, Corey L. M. Keyes, and Kristin A. Moore (Mahwah, NJ: Erlbaum, 2003), 371–80.

151. Sternberg and Kaufman, "Constraints."

152. Frank Barron and David M. Harrington, "Creativity, Intelligence, and Personality," *Annual Review of Psychology* 32, no. 1 (1981): 439–76; Kennon M. Sheldon, "Creativity and Self-Determination in Personality," *Creativity Research Journal* 8, no. 1 (1995): 25–36; Simonton, *Greatness*; Donald J. Treffinger et al., *Assessing Creativity: A Guide for Educators* (Storrs, CT: National Research Center on the Gifted and Talented, 2002); Herbert J. Walberg and Winifred E. Stariha, "Productive Human Capital: Learning, Creativity, and Eminence," *Creativity Research Journal* 5 (1992): 323–40.

153. Deci and Ryan, "What'"; Helmreich, Spence, and Pred, "Making"; Luh and Lu, "Cognitive"; Matthews et al., "Pattern"; Roe, *Making*; Ryan and Deci, "Overview"; Simonton, "Creativity and Genius"; Tardif and Sternberg, "Know"; Vallerand et al., "Passions"; Vallerand et al., "Passion"; Winner, "Creativity."

154. Jonathan W. Schooler, Erik D. Reichle, and David V. Halpern, "Zoning out While Reading: Evidence for Dissociations between Experience and Metaconsciousness," in *Thinking and Seeing: Visual Metacognition in Adults and Children*, ed. Daniel T. Levin (Cambridge: MIT Press, 2004), 203–26; Jonathan Smallwood and Jonathan W. Schooler, "The Restless Mind," *Psychological Bulletin* 132, no. 6 (2006): 946–58; Jonathan Smallwood and Jonathan W. Schooler, "The Restless Mind," *Psychology of Consciousness: Theory, Research, and Practice* 1 (2013): 130–49; Matthew R. Yanko

and Thomas M. Spalek, "Driving with the Wandering Mind: The Effect That Mind-Wandering Has on Driving Performance," *Human Factors* 56, no. 2 (2014): 260–69.

155. Mooneyham and Schooler, "Costs"; Smallwood and Schooler, "Restless," 946–58.

156. Schooler, Reichle, and Halpern, "Zoning."

157. Jonathan Smallwood and Jonathan W. Schooler, "The Science of Mind Wandering: Empirically Navigating the Stream of Consciousness," *Annual Review of Psychology* 66 (2015): 487–518.

158. Baird, Smallwood, and Schooler, "Back"; Benjamin Baird et al., "Inspired by Distraction: Mind Wandering Facilitates Creative Incubation," *Psychological Science* 23, no. 10 (2012): 1117–22; Eric Klinger, "Thought Flow: Properties and Mechanisms Underlying Shifts in Content," in *At Play in the Fields of Consciousness: Essays in the Honour of Jerome L. Singer*, eds. Jefferson A. Singer and Peter Salovey (Mahwah, NJ: Erlbaum, 1999), 29–50; Singer and Singer,; Singer and Singer, *Imagination*; Singer, "Researching"; Smallwood and Schooler, "Restless," 946–58; Smallwood and Schooler, "Science."

159. Smallwood and Schooler, "Science."

160. Baird et al., "Inspired"; Carson, Peterson, and Higgins, "Decreased"; Carsten KW De Dreu et al., "Working Memory Benefits Creative Insight, Musical Improvisation, and Original Ideation through Maintained Task-Focused Attention," *Personality and Social Psychology Bulletin* 38, no. 5 (2012): 656–69; Ap Dijksterhuis and Teun Meurs, "Where Creativity Resides: The Generative Power of Unconscious Thought," *Consciousness and Cognition* 15, no. 1 (2006): 135–46; Ap Dijksterhuis and Loran F. Nordgren, "A Theory of Unconscious Thought," *Perspectives on Psychological Science* 1, no. 2 (2006): 95–109; Arthur Koestler, *The Act of Creation* (New York: Macmillan, 1964); Jordan B. Peterson, Kathleen W. Smith, and Shelley Carson, "Openness and Extraversion Are Associated with Reduced Latent Inhibition: Replication and Commentary," *Personality and Individual Differences* 33 (2002): 1137–47; Dean Keith Simonton, "Significant Samples: The Psychological Study of Eminent Individuals," *Psychological Methods* 4, no. 4 (1999): 425–45; Jerome L. Singer and Vivian G. McCraven, "Some Characteristics of Adult Daydreaming," *Journal of Psychology* 51, no. 1 (1961): 151–64; Ut Na Sio and Thomas C. Ormerod, "Does Incubation Enhance Problem Solving? A Meta-Analytic Review," *Psychological Bulletin* 135, no. 1 (2009): 94–120; Jonathan Smallwood, "Mind-Wandering while Reading: Attentional Decoupling, Mindless Reading and the Cascade Model of Inattention," *Language and Linguistics Compass* 5, no. 2 (2011): 63–77; Smallwood and Schooler, "Restless," 946–58.

161. Baird, Smallwood, and Schooler, "Back"; McVay and Kane, "Wandering"; Mooneyham and Schooler, "Costs"; Singer and Antrobus, "Factor-Analytic."

162. Csikszentmihalyi, *Creativity*; Arne Dietrich, "The Cognitive Neuroscience of Creativity," *Psychonomic Bulletin and Review* 11, no. 6 (2004): 1011–26; Michael D. Mrazek et al., "Mindfulness Training Improves Working Memory Capacity and GRE Performance while Reducing Mind Wandering," *Psychological Science* 24, no. 5 (2013): 776–81; Torrance, *Search*; Torrance and Safter, *Making*.

163. Ochse, *Excellence*; Shavinina, "Explaining"; Dean Keith Simonton, "Intuition and Analysis: A Predictive and Explanatory Model," *Genetic Psychology Monographs* 102 (1980): 3–60; Singer and Singer, *Imagination*; Singer, "Researching"; Aaron J. Ungersma, "Fantasy, Creativity, Conformity," *Humanitas* 12 (1976): 73–88.

164. Kim et al., "Creativity."

165. Koestler, *Act*; Torrance, *Search*; Torrance and Safter, *Making*.

166. Chambers, "Relating."

167. Koestler, *Act*; Tardif and Sternberg, "Know"; Torrance, *Search*; Torrance and Safter, *Making*.

168. Barron and Harrington, "Creativity"; Christine Charyton and Glenn E. Snelbecker, "Engineers' and Musicians' Choices of Self-Descriptive Adjectives as Potential Indicators of Creativity by Gender and Domain," *Psychology of Aesthetics, Creativity, and the Arts* 1, no. 2 (2007): 91–99; Csikszentmihalyi, *Flow*; Eysenck, *Genius*; Feist, "Meta-Analysis"; Ravenna Helson, "Women in Creativity," in *The Creativity Question*, eds. Albert Rothenberg and Carl Hausman (Durham, NC: Duke University Press, 1976), 242–49; Qian, Plucker, and Shen, "Model"; Roe, *Making*; Dean

Keith Simonton, "Creativity: Cognitive, Developmental, Personal, and Social Aspects," *American Psychologist* 55 (2000): 151–58; Treffinger et al., "Assessing"; Rick B. Van Baaren et al., "The Forest, the Trees, and the Chameleon: Context Dependence and Mimicry," *Journal of Personality and Social Psychology* 86, no. 3 (2004): 453–59.

169. Wendi L. Gardner, Shira Gabriel, and Angela Y. Lee, "'I' Value Freedom, But 'We' Value Relationships: Self-Construal Priming Mirrors Cultural Differences in Judgment," *Psychological Science* 10 (1999): 321–26; Kim et al., "Creativity"; Scott A. Shane, "Why Do Some Societies Invent More Than Others?" *Journal of Business Venturing* 7, no. 1 (1992): 29–46; Scott A. Shane, "Cultural Influences on National Rates of Innovation," *Journal of Business Venturing* 8, no. 1 (1993): 59–73.

170. Gardner, Gabriel, and Lee, "I"; Angela Y. Lee, Jennifer L. Aaker, and Wendi L. Gardner, "The Pleasures and Pains of Distinct Self-Construals: The Role of Interdependence in Regulatory Focus," *Journal of Personality and Social Psychology* 78 (2000): 1122–34; Hazel Rose Markus and Shinobu Kitayama, "Culture, Self, and the Reality of the Social," *Psychological Inquiry* 14 (2003): 277–83; Diederik A. Stapel and Willem Koomen, "I, We, and the Effects of Others on Me: How Self-Construal Level Moderates Social Comparison Effects," *Journal of Personality and Social Psychology* 80, no. 5 (2001): 766–81; Baaren et al., "Forest"; Carina J. Wiekens and Diederik A. Stapel, "I versus We: The Effects of Self-Construal Level on Diversity," *Social Cognition* 26, no. 3 (2008): 368–77.

171. Stapel and Koomen, "I"; Van Baaren et al., "Forest"; Wiekens and Stapel, "I"; Leslie Kathleen Williams and Stephen JJ McGuire, "Effects of National Culture on Economic Creativity and Innovation Implementation," *Institutions of Market Exchange* (2005): 31–40.

172. Wiekens and Stapel, "I."

173. Howard Gardner, *Frames of Mind: The Theory of Multiple Intelligences* (New York: Basic Books, 1983); Liam Hudson and Bernadine Jacot, "The Outsider in Science: A Selective Review of Evidence with Special Reference to the Nobel Prize," in *Personality, Cognition, and Values*, eds. Christopher Bagley and Gajendra K. Verma (Calgary, AB: University of Calgary, 1986); Simonton, *Greatness*; Dean Keith Simonton, "Creativity from a Historiometric Perspective," in *Handbook of Creativity*, ed. Robert J. Sternberg (New York: Cambridge University Press, 1999), 116–33.

174. Dijksterhuis and Meurs, "Creativity"; Dijksterhuis and Nordgren, "Unconscious"; Koestler, *Act*; Kray, Galinsky, and Wong, "Thinking"; Schooler and Melcher, "Ineffability"; Smith and Blankenship, "Incubation"; Thrash et al., "Mediating."

175. Donald T. Campbell, "Blind Variation and Selective Retentions in Creative Thought as in Other Knowledge Processes," *Psychological Review* 67, no. 6 (1960): 380–400; Hudson and Jacot, "Outsider"; Simonton, *Greatness*.

176. John P. Aggleton, Robert W. Kentridge, and James MM Good, "Handedness and Musical Ability: A Study of Professional Orchestral Players, Composers, and Choir Members," *Psychology of Music* 22, no. 2 (1994): 148–56; Nicolas Cherbuin and Cobie Brinkman, "Hemispheric Interactions Are Different in Left-Handed Individuals," *Neuropsychology* 20, no. 6 (2006): 700–707; Stanley Coren, "Differences in Divergent Thinking as a Function of Handedness and Sex," *American Journal of Psychology* 108 (1995): 311–25; David W. Johnston et al., "Nature's Experiment? Handedness and Early Childhood Development," *Demography* 46, no. 2 (2009): 281–301; John M. Peterson and Leonard M. Lansky, "Left-Handedness among Architects: Partial Replication and Some New Data," *Perceptual and Motor Skills* 45, no. 3f (1977): 1216–18; Antonio Preti and Marcello Vellante, "Creativity and Psychopathology: Higher Rates of Psychosis Proneness and Nonright-Handedness among Creative Artists Compared to Same Age and Gender Peers," *Journal of Nervous and Mental Disease* 195, no. 10 (2007): 837–45; Cynthia Stewart and Dennis Clayson, "A Note on Change in Creativity by Handedness over a Maturational Time Period," *Journal of Psychology* 104 (1980): 39–42.

177. Silvano Arieti, *Creativity: The Magic Synthesis* (Oxford, England: Basic, 1976); Gjurgjica Badzakova-Trajkov, Isabelle S. Häberling, and Michael C. Corballis, "Magical Ideation, Creativity, Handedness, and Cerebral Asymmetries: A Combined Behavioural and fMRI Study," *Neuropsychologia* 49, no. 10 (2011): 2896–2903; Rosa Aurora Chávez-Eakle et al., "Cerebral Blood Flow Associated with Creative Performance: A Comparative Study," *Neuroimage* 38, no. 3 (2007): 519–28; Norbert

Jaušovec, "Differences in Cognitive Processes between Gifted, Intelligent, Creative, and Average Individuals while Solving Complex Problems: An EEG Study," *Intelligence* 28, no. 3 (2000): 213–37; Yasuyuki Kowatari et al., "Neural Networks Involved in Artistic Creativity," *Human Brain Mapping* 30, no. 5 (2009): 1678–90; Annukka K. Lindell, "Lateral Thinkers Are Not So Laterally Minded: Hemispheric Asymmetry, Interaction, and Creativity," *Laterality: Asymmetries of Body, Brain and Cognition* 16, no. 4 (2011): 479–98.

178. Lindell, "Lateral"; Elizabeth R. Shobe, Nicholas M. Ross, and Jessica I. Fleck, "Influence of Handedness and Bilateral Eye Movements on Creativity," *Brain and Cognition* 71, no. 3 (2009): 204–14.

179. Ching-Chang Hung, Yong-Kwang Tu, Sing Hong Chen, and Rong-Chi Chen, "A Study on Handedness and Cerebral Speech Dominance in Right-Handed Chinese," *Journal of Neurolinguistics* 1 (1985): 143–63; Michael Peters, Stian Reimers, and John T. Manning, "Hand Preference for Writing and Associations with Selected Demographic and Behavioral Variables in 255,100 Subjects: The BBC Internet Study," *Brain and Cognition* 62 (2006): 177–89; Akinori Shimizu and Masaomi Endo, "Handedness and Familial Sinistrality in a Japanese Student Population," *Cortex: A Journal Devoted to the Study of the Nervous System and Behavior* 19 (1983): 265–72.

180. Ji-Sun Chung, "Women's Unequal Access to Education in South Korea," *Comparative Education Review* (1994): 487–505; KH Kim, "Cultural Influence on Creativity: The Relationship between Creativity and Confucianism" (PhD diss., University of Georgia, 2004).

181. Ibid.

182. Linda K. Johnsrud, "Korean Academic Women: Multiple Roles, Multiple Challenges," *Higher Education* 30, no. 1 (1995): 17–35.

183. Martin Kaste, "Korean Families Chase Their Dreams in the U.S.," *NPR*, July 11, 2012, http://www.npr.org/2012/07/11/156377938/korean-families-chase-their-dreams-in-the-u-s; K. Lee, "Korean Goose Families Migrate for Education," *New America Media*, October 26, 2004.

184. Eun-Gyong Kim, "History of English Education in Korea," *Korea Times*, April 2, 2008, http://www.koreatimes.co.kr/www/news/special/2008/04/181_21843.html.

185. Csikszentmihalyi, *Creativity*; Harrington and Anderson, "Creativity"; James B. Hittner and Jennifer R. Daniels, "Gender-Role Orientation, Creative Accomplishments and Cognitive Styles," *Journal of Creative Behavior* 36 (2002): 62–75; Norlander, Erixon, and Archer, "Psychological."

186. Csikszentmihalyi, *Flow*; Csikszentmihalyi, *Creativity*; Hittner and Daniels, "Gender-Role"; Chad J. Keller, Lea A. Lavish, and Chris Brown, "Creative Styles and Gender Roles in Undergraduates Students," *Creativity Research Journal* 19, no. 2–3 (2007): 273–80; Norlander, Erixon, and Archer, "Psychological"; Rhona A. Ochse, "Why There Were Relatively Few Eminent Women Creators," *Journal of Creative Behavior* 25, no. 4 (1991): 334–43; Olga M. Razumnikova, "Role, Sex and Professional Orientation of Students as Creativity Factors," *Voprosy Psikhologii* 1 (2002): 111–25; Anne Roe, "Personal Problems and Science," in *The Third (1959) University of Utah Research Conference on the Identification of Creative Scientific Talent*, ed. Calvin Walker Taylor (Salt Lake City: University of Utah Press, 1959), 202–12; Dean Keith Simonton, "Gender Differences in Birth Order and Family Size among 186 Eminent Psychologists," *Journal of Psychology of Science and Technology* 1 (2008), 15–22; Torrance, *Manifesto*.

187. Sarah White Bender et al., "Defining Characteristics of Creative Women," *Creativity Research Journal* 25, no. 1 (2013): 38–47; Ellen Piel Cook, *Psychological Androgyny* (New York: Pergamon, 1985); Chad J. Keller, Lea A. Lavish, and Chris Brown, "Creative Styles and Gender Roles in Undergraduates Students," *Creativity Research Journal* 19, no. 2–3 (2007): 273–80; Deborah S. Lyons and Samuel B. Green, "Sex Role Development as a Function of College Experiences," *Sex Roles* 18, no. 1–2 (1988): 31–40; Norlander, Erixon, and Archer, "Psychological Androgyny," 423–35; Razumnikova, "Role"; Geniffer Stoltzfus et al., "Gender, Gender Role, and Creativity," *Social Behavior and Personality: An International Journal* 39, no. 3 (2011): 425–32.

188. Cook, *Psychological*; Keller, Lavish, and Brown, "Gender"; Chun Bun Lam and Catherine A. McBride-Chang, "Resilience in Young Adulthood: The Moderating Influences of Gender-Related Personality Traits and Coping Flexibility," *Sex Roles* 56, no. 3–4 (2007): 159–72; Lyons and Green, "Sex."

189. Robert W. Weisberg, "Creativity and Knowledge: A Challenge to Theories," in *Handbook of Creativity*, eds. Robert J. Sternberg (Cambridge: Cambridge University Press, 1999), 226–50.

190. J. P. Guilford, "Creativity," *American Psychologist* 5 (1950): 444–54; Koestler, *Act*; Jonathan W. Schooler and Joseph Melcher, "The Ineffability of Insight," in *The Creative Cognition Approach*, eds. Steven M. Smith, Thomas B. Ward, and Ronald A. Finke (Cambridge: MIT Press, 1995), 97–134.

191. Sternberg and Kaufman, "Constraints."

192. Ibid.

193. Koestler, *Act*.

194. Charyton and Snelbecker, "Engineers"; Eysenck, *Genius*; Feist, "Meta-Analysis"; Jacob W. Getzels and Mihaly Csikszentmihalyi, "Scientific Creativity," *Science Journal* 3 (1967): 80–84; Ravenna Helson, Brent Roberts, and Gail Agronick, "Enduringness and Change in Creative Personality and the Prediction of Occupational Creativity," *Journal of Personality and Social Psychology* 69, no. 6 (1995): 1173–83; Roe, *Making*.

195. Barron and Harrington, "Creativity"; Csikszentmihalyi, *Flow*; Csikszentmihalyi, *Creativity*; Eysenck, *Genius*; Helson, "Women"; Koestler, *Act*; Qian, Plucker, and Shen, "Model; Roe, *Making*; Simonton, "Creativity"; Treffinger et al., "Assessing."

196. Trevor Timm, "Reform the CFAA: Don't Let It Stop the Next Steve Jobs, Bill Gates, Mark Zuckerberg, or Steve Wozniak," March 7, 2013, https://www.eff.org/deeplinks/ 2013/03/innovators.

197. William D. Altus, "Birth Order and Its Sequelae," *Science* 151 (1966): 44–48; Stanley Schachter, "Birth Order, Eminence, and Higher Education," *American Sociological Review* 28 (1966): 757–68; Simonton, "Gender Differences"; Simonton, *101*; Frank J. Sulloway, *Born to Rebel: Birth Order, Family Dynamics, and Creative Lives* (New York: Vintage Books, 1996).

198. Simonton, "Gender Differences."

199. Ibid.

200. Sternberg and Kaufman, "Constraints."

201. Walter Isaacson, *Steve Jobs* (New York: Simon and Schuster, 2011).

202. Ibid.

203. Anders Hallengren, "Nelson Mandela and the Rainbow of Culture," Nobelprize.org, September 11, 2001, http://www.nobelprize.org/nobel_prizes/peace/laureates/1993/mandela-article.html.

204. Zelda La Grange, *Good Morning, Mr. Mandela: A Memoir* (New York: Viking, 2014).

205. Walter Isaacson, *Einstein: His Life and Universe* (New York: Simon and Schuster, 2007).

206. Kathleen Krull, *Albert Einstein*, Giants of Science Series (New York: Viking, 2009);

207. Elizabeth MacLeod, *Albert Einstein: A Life of a Genius* (Toronto, Canada: Kids Can, 2003).

208. Gary F. Moring, *The Complete Idiot's Guide to Understanding Einstein* (New York: Alpha Books, 2004); Marie Hammontree, *Albert Einstein: Young Thinker*, Childhood of Famous Americans (New York: Simon and Schuster, 1986).

209. Marfe Ferguson Delano, *Genius: A Photobiography of Albert Einstein* (Washington, DC: National Geographic Society, 2005); Stephanie Sammartino McPherson, *Ordinary Genius: The Story of Albert Einstein* (Minneapolis, MN: Carolrhoda Books, 1995).

210. Delano, *Genius*; Krull, *Einstein*.

211. Ibid.

212. Castro, *Art*; Robinson, *O'Keeffe*.

213. Peltakian, "O'Keeffe."

214. Krull, *Einstein*.

Chapter 7: Are Men Really More Creative Than Women Are?

1. Mihaly Csikszentmihalyi, "Implications of a Systems Perspective for the Study of Creativity," in *Handbook of Creativity*, ed. Robert J. Sternberg (New York: Cambridge University Press, 1999), 313–35; Kirby Deater-Deckard et al., "The Association between Parental Warmth and

Control in Thirteen Cultural Groups," *Journal of Family Psychology* 25 (2011): 790–94; Marwan Dwairy and Mustafa Achoui, "Introduction to Three Cross-Regional Research Studies on Parenting Styles, Individuation, and Mental Health in Arab Societies," *Journal of Cross-Cultural Psychology* 37 (2006): 221–29; Marwan Dwairy and Mustafa Achoui, "Parental Control: A Second Cross-Cultural Research on Parenting and Psychological Adjustment of Children," *Journal of Child and Family Studies* 19 (2010): 16–22; Cynthia T. Garcia Coll, Elaine C. Meyer, and Lisa Brillon, "Ethnic and Minority Parenting," in *Handbook of Parenting*, vol. 2, *Biology and Ecology of Parenting*, ed. Marc H. Bornstein (Hillsdale, NJ: Erlbaum, 1995), 189–209; Sara Harkness and Charles M. Super, "Parental Ethnotheories," in *Parental Belief Systems: The Psychological Consequences for Children*, eds. Irving Sigel, Ann McGillicuddy-DeLisi, and Jacqueline Goodnow, 2nd ed. (Mahwah, NJ: Erlbaum, 1992), 373–92; Sara Harkness and Charles M. Super, "Themes and Variations: Parental Ethnotheories in Western Cultures," in *Parental Beliefs, Parenting, and Child Development in Cross-Cultural Perspective*, eds. Kenneth H. Rubin and O. Boon Chung (New York: Psychology, 2006), 61–80; Mally Shechory-Bitton, Sarah Ben David, and Eliane Sommerfeld, "Effect of Ethnicity on Parenting Styles and Attitudes toward Violence among Jewish and Arab Muslim Israeli Mothers: An Intergenerational Approach," *Journal of Cross-Cultural Psychology* 46, no. 4 (2015): 508–24.

2. Yiling Cheng, KH Kim, and Michael F. Hull, "Comparisons of Creative Styles and Personality Types between American and Taiwanese College Students and the Relationship between Creative Potential and Personality Types," *Psychology of Aesthetics, Creativity, and the Arts* 4, no. 2 (2010): 103; KH Kim, "Is Creativity Unidimensional or Multidimensional? Analyses of the Torrance Tests of Creative Thinking," *Creativity Research Journal* 18, no. 3 (2006): 251–59; KH Kim, "Developing Creativity in Gifted and Talented Students," in *Leading Change in Gifted Education: The Festschrift of Dr. Joyce VanTassel-Baska*, ed. Bronwyn MacFarlane and Tamra Stambaugh (Waco, TX: Prufrock, 2009), 37–48; KH Kim, "Which Creativity Tests Can We Use?" *Creativity Research Journal* (in press); KH Kim, Bonnie Cramond, and Deborah L. Bandalos, "The Latent Structure and Measurement Invariance of Scores on the Torrance Tests of Creative Thinking–Figural," *Educational and Psychological Measurement* 66, no. 3 (2006): 459–77; KH Kim et al., "Creativity and Confucianism among American and Korean Educators," *Creativity Research Journal* 23, no. 4 (2011): 357–71; Hangeun Lee and KH Kim, "Can Speaking More Languages Enhance Your Creativity? Relationship between Bilingualism and Creative Potential among Korean American Students with Multicultural Link," *Personality and Individual Differences* 50, no. 8 (2011): 1186–90; Olga M. Razumnikova, Nina Volf, and Irina Tarasova, "Strategy and Results: Sex Differences in Electrographic Correlates of Verbal and Figural Creativity," *Human Physiology* 35, no. 3 (2009): 285–94; E. Paul Torrance, *The Search for Satori and Creativity* (Buffalo, NY: Bearly Limited, 1979); E. Paul Torrance and Tammy Safter, *Making the Creative Leap Beyond* (Buffalo, NY: Creative Education Foundation Press, 1999). *Also, my analyses of the data sets from KH Kim, "Can Only Intelligent People Be Creative? A Meta-Analysis," *Journal of Secondary Gifted Education* 16 (2005): 57–66; KH Kim, "Meta-Analyses of the Relationship of Creative Achievement to Both IQ and Divergent Thinking Test Scores," *Journal of Creative Behavior* 42, no. 2 (2008): 106–30; KH Kim, "The Creativity Crisis: The Decrease in Creative Thinking Scores on the Torrance Tests of Creative Thinking," *Creative Research Journal* 23 (2011): 285–95.

3. Teresa Amabile, "The 'Atmosphere of Pure Work': Creativity in Research and Development," in *The Social Psychology of Science*, eds. William R. Shadish and Steve Fuller (New York: Guilford, 1994), 316–28; Sarah White Bender, BradyLeigh Nibbelink, Elizabeth Towner-Thyrum, and Debra Vredenburg, "Defining Characteristics of Creative Women," *Creativity Research Journal* 25, no. 1 (2013): 38–47; Christine Charyton et al., "Gender and Science: Women Nobel Laureates," *Journal of Creative Behavior* 45, no. 3 (2011): 203–14; Nicaise Geneviève Cogérino, Julien Bois, and Anthony J. Amorose, "Students' Perceptions of Teacher Feedback and Physical Competence in Physical Education Classes: Gender Effects," *Journal of Teaching in Physical Education* 25, no. 1 (2006): 36–57; Ravenna Helson, "Women, Mathematicians, and Creative Personality," *Journal of Consulting and Clinical Psychology* 36, no. 2 (1971): 210–20; Ravenna Helson, "Women in Creativity," in *The Creativity*

Question, eds. Albert Rothenberg and Carl Hausman (Durham, NC: Duke University Press, 1976), 242–49; Olga M. Razumnikova, "Role, Sex and Professional Orientation of Students as Creativity Factors," *Voprosy Psikhologii* 1 (2002): 111–25; Geniffer Stoltzfus et al., "Gender, Gender Role, and Creativity," *Social Behavior and Personality* 39, no. 3 (2011): 425–32.

4. John Baer and James C. Kaufman, "Gender Differences in Creativity," *Journal of Creative Behavior* 42, no. 2 (2008): 75–105; Kim, "Can Only"; Andre P. Walton and Markus Kemmelmeier, "Creativity in Its Social Context: The Interplay of Organizational Norms, Situational Threat, and Gender," *Creativity Research Journal* 24, no. 2–3 (2012): 208–19.

5. Baer and Kaufman, "Gender"; Mihaly Csikszentmihalyi, *Creativity: Flow and the Psychology of Discovery and Invention* (New York: Harper Perennial, 1996); Rhona A. Ochse, "Why There Were Relatively Few Eminent Women Creators," *Journal of Creative Behavior* 25, no. 4 (1991): 334–43; Anne Roe, "Personal Problems and Science," in *The Third (1959) University of Utah Research Conference on the Identification of Creative Scientific Talent*, ed. Calvin Walker Taylor (Salt Lake City: University of Utah Press, 1959), 202–12; Dean Keith Simonton, "Gender Differences in Birth Order and Family Size among 186 Eminent Psychologists," *Journal of Psychology of Science and Technology* 1, no. 1 (2008): 15–22; E. Paul Torrance, *The Manifesto: A Guide to Developing a Creative Career* (West Westport, CT: Ablex, 2002).

6. Baer and Kaufman, "Gender"; Charyton et al., "Gender"; Dean Keith Simonton, *Greatness: Who Makes History and Why* (New York: Guilford, 1994).

7. Dean Keith Simonton, "Creativity and Genius," in *Handbook of Personality: Theory and Research*, eds. Oliver P. John, Richard W. Roberts, and Lawrence A. Pervin (New York: Gilford, 2008), 679–98.

8. Denis Brian, *The Curies: A Biography of the Most Controversial Family in Science* (Hoboken, NJ: John Wiley and Sons, 2005); Barbara Goldsmith, *Obsessive Genius: The Inner World of Marie Curie* (New York: Norton, 2005); Della Yannuzzi, *New Elements: The Story of Marie Curie* (Greensboro, NC: Reynolds, 2006.)

9. Rachel A. Koestler-Grack, *Marie Curie: Scientist*, Women of Achievement (New York: Chelsea House, 2009).

10. Brian, *Curies*; Goldsmith, *Obsessive*; Koestler-Grack, *Curie*; Naomi Pasachoff, *Marie Madame Curie and the Science of Radioactivity* (New York: Oxford University Press, 1996); Margaret Poynter, *Marie Curie: Discoverer of Radium* (Hillside, NJ: Enslow, 1994); Yannuzzi, *New Elements*.

11. Goldsmith, *Obsessive*; Yannuzzi, *New*.

12. Goldsmith, *Obsessive*.

13. Brian, *Curies*; Yannuzzi, *New*.

14. Brian, *Curies*; Goldsmith, *Obsessive*.

15. Brian, *Curies*; Poynter, *Curie*.

16. Brian, *Curies*; Goldsmith, *Obsessive*.

17. Ibid; Yannuzzi, *New*.

18. Andrea Gabor, "The Forgotten Wife," in *E = Einstein: His Life, His Thought and His Influence on Our Culture*, eds. Donald Goldsmith and Marcia Bartusiak (New York: Sterling, 2006), 39–65.

19. Ibid; Walter Isaacson, *Einstein: His Life and Universe* (New York: Simon and Schuster, 2007).

20. Marfe Ferguson Delano, *Genius: A Photobiography of Albert Einstein* (Washington, DC: National Geographic Society, 2005); Gabor, "Forgotten"; Fiona MacDonald, *Albert Einstein: Genius behind the Theory of Relativity* (Woodbridge, CT: Blackbirth, 2000); Gary F. Moring, *The Complete Idiot's Guide to Understanding Einstein* (New York: Alpha Books, 2004).

21. Gabor, "Forgotten."

22. Brian, *Curies*; Gabor, "Forgotten."

23. Delano, *Genius*; Gabor, "Forgotten."

24. Ibid.; Kathleen Krull, *Albert Einstein*, Giants of Science Series (New York: Viking, 2009).

25. Isaacson, *Einstein*.

26. Gabor, "Forgotten"; Krull, *Einstein*; Elizabeth MacLeod, *Albert Einstein: A Life of Genius* (Toronto, Canada: Kids Can, 2003).

27. Gabor, "Forgotten."

28. Delano, *Genius*; Gabor, "Forgotten"; Krull, *Einstein*.

29. Linda K. Silverman, "Why Are There So Few Eminent Women?" *Roeper Review* 18, no. 1 (1995): 5–13; Tama Starr, *The "Natural Inferiority" of Women: Outrageous Pronouncements by Misguided Males* (New York: Poseidon, 1991).

30. Silverman, "Women"; Starr, *Inferiority*.

31. Confucius, *Confucius Analects: With Selections from Traditional Commentaries*, trans. Edward Slingerland (Indianapolis, IN: Hackett, 2003); Confucius. *The Analects of Confucius*, trans. Simon Leys (New York: W. W. Norton, 1997); Ranjoo Seodu Herr, "Is Confucianism Compatible with Care Ethics? A Critique," *Philosophy East and West* 53, no. 4 (2003): 471–89.

32. Starr, *Inferiority*.

33. Silverman, "Women."

34. Baer and Kaufman, "Gender"; Dean Keith Simonton, *Genius 101*, The Psych 101 Series (New York: Springer, 2009).

35. Baer and Kaufman, "Gender"; Mihaly Csikszentmihalyi, "Motivation and Creativity: Toward a Synthesis of Structural and Energistic Approaches to Cognition," *New Ideas in Psychology* 6, no. 2 (1988): 159–76.

36. Jacquelynne S. Eccles, "Why Doesn't Jane Run? Sex Differences in Educational and Occupational Patterns," in *The Gifted and Talented: Developmental Perspectives*, eds. Frances Degen Horowitz and Marion O'Brien (Washington, DC: American Psychological Association, 1985), 251–95; Ochse, "Women"; Simonton, "Gender."

37. Helson, "Mathematicians"; Ravenna Helson, "Creativity in Women: Outer and Inner Views over Time," in *Theories of Creativity*, eds. Mark A. Runco and Robert S. Albert (Newbury Park, CA: Sage, 1990); Margaret Hennig and Anne Jardim, *The Managerial Woman* (Garden City, NY: Anchor, 1977).

38. Ochse, "Women Creators"; Simonton, *Greatness*; Simonton, "Gender."

39. "Carol W. Greider—Biographical," Nobelprize.org, Nobel Media AB 2014, May 30, 2016, https://www.nobelprize.org/nobel_prizes/medicine/laureates/2009/greider-bio.html.

40. "Christiane Nüsslein-Volhard—Biographical," Nobelprize.org, Nobel Media AB 2014, May 30, 2016, https://www.nobelprize.org/nobel_prizes/medicine/laureates/1995/nusslein-volhard-bio.html.

41. "Linda B. Buck—Biographical," Nobelprize.org, Nobel Media AB 2014, May 30, 2016, https://www.nobelprize.org/nobel_prizes/medicine/laureates/2004/buck-bio.html.

42. Daphna Oyserman and Hazel R. Markus, "Possible Selves and Delinquency," *Journal of Personality and Social Psychology* 59, no. 1 (1990): 112–25; Simonton, *Greatness*.

43. Nancy E. Betz and Louise F. Fitzgerald, *The Career Psychology of Women* (San Diego: Academic, 1987).

44. Betz and Fitzgerald, *Career*.

45. C. R. Harris, "The Fruits of Early Intervention: The Hollingworth Group Today," *Advanced Development* 4 (1992): 91–104; Willard L. White, "Interviews with Child I, Child J, and Child L," *Roeper Review* 12 (1990): 222–27.

46. Anne Anastasi and Charles E. Schaefer, "Biographical Correlates of Artistic and Literary Creativity in Adolescent Girls," *Journal of Applied Phycology* 53 no. 4 (1969): 267–73; Dean C. Dauw, "Life Experiences of Original Thinkers and Good Elaborators," *Exceptional Children* 32, no. 7 (1966): 433–40; David M. Harrington and Susan M. Anderson, "Creativity, Masculinity, Femininity and Three Models of Psychological Androgyny," *Journal of Personality and Social Psychology* 41 (1981): 744–57; D. Niall Hartnett, Jason M. Nelson, and Ann N. Rinn, "Gifted or ADHD? The Possibilities of Misdiagnosis," *Roeper Review* 26 (2004): 73–77; Ravenna Helson, "Childhood Interest Clusters Related to Creativity in Women," *Journal of Consulting Psychology* 29, no. 4 (1965): 352–61; Ravenna Helson, "Personality of Women with Artistic and Imaginative Interests: The Role of Masculinity, Originality, and Other Characteristics of Their Creativity," *Journal of Personality* 34, no. 1 (1966): 1–25; Ravenna

Helson, "Personality Characteristics and Developmental History of Creative College Women," *Genetic Psychology Monographs* 76, no. 2 (1967): 205–56; Helson, "Mathematicians"; Helson, "Women"; MacKinnon, "Nature"; Charles E. Schaefer and Anne Anastasi, "A Biographical Inventory for Identifying Creativity in Adolescent Boys," *Journal of Applied Phycology* 52 no. 1 (1968): 42–48; Torsten Norlander, Anna Erixon, and Trevor Archer, "Psychological Androgyny and Creativity: Dynamics of Gender-Role and Personality Trait," *Social Behavior and Personality* 28, no. 5 (2000): 423–35.

47. Bender, Nibbelink, Towner-Thyrum, and Vredenburg, "Characteristics"; Jack A. Chambers, "Relating Personality and Biographical Factors to Scientific Creativity," *Psychological Monographs: General and Applied* 78, no. 7 (1964): 1–20; Christine Charyton and Glenn E. Snelbecker, "Engineers' and Musicians' Choices of Self-Descriptive Adjectives as Potential Indicators of Creativity by Gender and Domain," *Psychology of Aesthetics, Creativity, and the Arts* 1, no. 2 (2007): 91–99; Csikszentmihalyi, *Flow*; Hans J. Eysenck, *Genius: The Natural History of Creativity*, vol. 12 (Cambridge, UK: Cambridge University Press, 1995); Gregory J. Feist, "A Meta-Analysis of Personality in Scientific and Artistic Creativity," *Personality and Social Psychology Review* 2, no. 4 (1998): 290–309; Jacob Getzels and Mihaly Csikszentmihalyi, "Scientific Creativity," *Science Journal* 3 (1967): 80–84; David M. Harrington and Susan M. Anderson, "Creativity, Masculinity, Femininity and Three Models of Psychological Androgyny," *Journal of Personality and Social Psychology* 41 (1981): 744–57; Helson, "Women"; Arthur Koestler, *The Act of Creation* (New York: Macmillan, 1964); Meihua Qian, Jonathan A. Plucker, and Jiliang Shen, "A Model of Chinese Adolescents' Creative Personality," *Creativity Research Journal* 22, no. 1 (2010): 62–67; Razumnikova, "Role"; Stoltzfus et al., "Gender"; Anne Roe, *The Making of a Scientist* (New York: Dodd, Mead, 1953); Silverman, "Women"; Dean Keith Simonton, "Creativity: Cognitive, Developmental, Personal, and Social Aspects," *American Psychologist* 55 (2000): 151–58; Twila Z. Tardif and Robert J. Sternberg, "What Do We Know about Creativity?" in *The Nature of Creativity*, ed. Robert J. Sternberg (New York: Cambridge University Press, 1999), 429–40; E. Paul Torrance, *The Search for Satori and Creativity* (Buffalo, NY: Bearly Limited, 1979); E. Paul Torrance and Tammy Safter, *Making the Creative Leap Beyond* (Buffalo, NY: Creative Education Foundation, 1999); Donald J. Treffinger et al., *Assessing Creativity: A Guide for Educators* (Storrs, CT: National Research Center on the Gifted and Talented, 2002); Rick B. Van Baaren et al., "The Forest, the Trees, and the Chameleon: Context Dependence and Mimicry," *Journal of Personality and Social Psychology* 86, no. 3 (2004): 453–59.

48. Amabile, "Atmosphere"; Bender, Nibbelink, Towner-Thyrum, and Vredenburg, "Characteristics"; Charyton et al., "Gender"; Cogérino, Bois, and Amorose, "Perceptions"; Helson, "Women."

49. Bonnie Cramond et al., "A Report on the 40-Year Follow-Up of the Torrance Tests of Creative Thinking: Alive and Well in the New Millennium," *Gifted Child Quarterly* 49, no. 4 (2005): 283–91; Mark Runco et al., "Torrance Tests of Creative Thinking as Predictors of Personal and Public Achievement: A Fifty-Year Follow-Up," *Creativity Research Journal* 22 (2010): 361–68; Simonton, *Greatness*; Torrance, *Manifesto*.

50. Simonton, *Greatness*.

51. Charyton et al., "Gender."

52. Jonathan R. Cole and Harriet Zuckerman, "Marriage, Motherhood, and Research Performance in Science," in *The Outer Circle: Women in the Scientific Community*, eds. John T. Bruer, Jonathan R. Cole, and Harriet Zuckerman (New Haven: Yale University Press, 1992), 157–70; Bernice T. Eiduson, *Scientists: Their Psychological World* (New York: Basic Books, 1962); John R. Hayes, *The Complete Problem Solver*, 2nd ed. (Hillsdale, NJ: Erlbaum, 1989); S. Jean Emans et al., "Improving Adolescent and Young Adult Health—Training the Next Generation of Physician Scientists in Transdisciplinary Research," *Journal of Adolescent Health* 46, no. 2 (2010): 100–109; Sharon Bertsch McGrayne, *Nobel Prize Women in Science: Their Lives, Struggles, and Momentous Discoveries* (Secaucus, NJ: Carol Group, 1998); Roe, *Making*; Silverman, "Women"; Yue Xie and Kimberlee A. Shauman, *Women in Science: Career Processes and Outcomes* (Cambridge, MA: Harvard University Press, 2003); Scott T. Yabiku and Sarah Schlabach, "Social Change and the Relationships between Education and Employment," *Population Research and Policy Review* 28, no. 4 (2009): 533–49.

53. Gabor, "Forgotten"; Walter Isaacson, *Einstein: His Life and Universe* (New York: Simon and Schuster, 2007).

54. Brian, *Curies*; Goldsmith, *Obsessive.*

55. Betz and Fitzgerald, *Career.*

56. Colin Berry, "The Nobel Scientists and the Origins of Scientific Achievement," *British Journal of Sociology* (1981): 381–91; Harry R. Silver, "Scientific Achievement and the Concept of Risk," *British Journal of Sociology* (1983): 39–43; Harriet Zuckerman, "Nobel Laureates in Science: Patterns of Productivity, Collaboration, and Authorship," *American Sociological Review* (1967): 391–403; Harriet Zuckerman, *Scientific Elite: Nobel Laureates in the United States* (New York: Free Press, 1977).

57. Cramond et al., "40-Year"; Anne Roe, "Women in Science," *Personnel and Guidance Journal* 44 (1966): 784–87; Runco et al., "Fifty-Year"; Simonton, *Greatness*; E. Paul Torrance, *Why Fly? A Philosophy of Creativity* (Norwoord, NJ: Ablex, 1995); Torrance, *Manifesto.*

58. Dean Keith Simonton, "Leaders, 1979–1967: Career Development, Creative Output, and Professional Achievement," *Journal of Personality and Social Psychology* 62 (1992): 5–17.

59. Silverman, "Women."

60. Nicole B. Koppel et al., "Single Gender Programs: Do They Make a Difference?" (ASEE/IEE Frontiers in Education Conference, Boulder, CO, 2003).

61. Silverman, "Women"; Simonton, *Greatness.*

62. Brian, *Curies.*

63. Goldsmith, *Obsessive*; Krull, *Curie.*

64. Brian, *Curies.*

65. Ibid.

66. "Rosalyn Yalow—Biographical," Nobelprize.org, Nobel Media AB 2014, May 30, 2016, https://www.nobelprize.org/nobel_prizes/medicine/laureates/1977/yalow-bio.html.

67. "Elizabeth H. Blackburn—Biographical," Nobelprize.org, Nobel Media AB 2014, May 30, 2016, http://www.nobelprize.org/nobel_prizes/medicine/laureates/2009/blackburn-bio.html.

68. Ada E. Yonath , lecture given at Moriah College, February 18, 2010, https://en.wikipedia.org/wiki/Ada_Yonath.

Chapter 8: Are Jews Really More Creative Than Asians Are?

1. Dean Keith Simonton, "Creativity and Genius," in *Handbook of Personality: Theory and Research*, eds. Oliver P. John, Richard W. Roberts, and Lawrence A. Pervin (New York: Gilford, 2008), 679–98.

2. "The World Total Jewish Population Is 14,212,800 as of 2014 (Berman Jewish DataBank)," World Jewish Population, 2014, http://www.jewishdatabank.org/Studies/details.cfm?StudyID=776.

3. *My statistical analyses of the Jewish culture are based on the number of Jewish Nobel laureates from JINFO.org, "Jewish Nobel Prize Winners," 2015, http://jinfo.org/Nobel_Prizes.html.

4. James R. Averill, Kyum Koo Chon, and Doug Woong Hahn, "Emotions and Creativity, East and West," *Asian Journal of Social Psychology* 4, no. 3 (2001): 165–83.

5. *The total population for all Confucian countries (China [1,367,485,388], Japan [126,919,659], Vietnam [94,348,835], South Korea [49,115,196], North Korea [24,983,205], Taiwan [23,415,126], Hong Kong [7,141,106], Singapore [5,674,472], and Macau [592,731]) was 1,699,675,718, which was calculated based on the United States Census Bureau, "International Programs: Countries and Areas Ranked by Population: 2015," http://www.census.gov/population/international/ data/countryrank/rank.php.

6. *My statistical analyses of Confucian culture are based on the number of Nobel laureates from the Confucian countries (i.e., China, Japan, Vietnam, South Korea, North Korea, Taiwan, Hong Kong, Singapore, and Macau) from Nobelprize.org, "Nobel Laureates and Country of Birth," Nobel Media AB 2014, August 7, 2015, http://www.nobelprize.org/nobel_prizes/ lists/countries.html.

7. Sarah Breger et al., "A Moment Symposium: The Origins of Jewish Creativity," *Moment*

(November/December 2011), 32–37; Richard Lynn and Satoshi Kanazawa, "How to Explain High Jewish Achievement: The Role of Intelligence and Values," *Personality and Individual Differences* 44, no. 4 (2008): 801–808; Richard Lynn and David Longley, "On the High Intelligence and Cognitive Achievements of Jews in Britain," *Intelligence* 34, no. 6 (2006): 541–47; Kevin MacDonald, *A People That Shall Dwell Alone* (Westport, CT: Praeger, 1994); Hank Pellissier, "Why Is the IQ of Ashkenazi Jews so High?" *Institute for Emerging Ethics and Technologies*, July 19, 2011, http://ieet.org/index. php/IEET/more/pellissier20110719; Lewis Regenstein, "Why Are Jews So Smart?" *Jewish Magazine*, July 2007, http://www.jewishmag.com/115m ag/smartjews/smartjews.htm; Nathaniel Weyl and Stefan T. Possony Weyl, *The Geography of Intellect* (Chicago: Henry Regnery, 1963).

    8. Margaret E. Backman, "Patterns of Mental Abilities: Ethnic, Socioeconomic, and Sex Differences," *American Educational Research Journal* (1972): 1–12; Richard Lynn, "The Intelligence of American Jews," *Personality and Individual Differences* 36, no. 1 (2004): 201–206; Lynn and Longley, "High"; Richard Lynn and Gerhard Meisenberg, "National IQs Calculated and Validated for 108 Nations," *Intelligence* 38, no. 4 (2010): 353–60.

    9. Lynn and Meisenberg, "National"; Richard Lynn and Tatu Vanhanen, "National IQs: A Review of Their Educational, Cognitive, Economic, Political, Demographic, Sociological, Epidemiological, Geographic and Climatic Correlates," *Intelligence* 40, no. 2 (2012): 226–34.

    10. K. Anders Ericsson, "The Acquisition of Expert Performance: An Introduction to Some of the Issues," in *The Road to Expert Performance: Empirical Evidence from the Arts and Sciences, Sports, and Games* (Mahwah, NJ: Erlbaum, 1996), 1–50; K. Anders Ericsson, Ralf Th. Krampe, and Clemens Tesch-Romer, "The Role of Deliberate Practice in the Acquisition of Expert Performance," *Psychological Review* 100 (1993): 363–406; John R. Hayes, *The Complete Problem Solver* (Hillsdale, NJ: Erlbaum, 1989); Janet L. Starkes et al., "Deliberate Practice in Sports: What Is It Anyway?" in *The Road to Expert Performance: Empirical Evidence from the Arts and Sciences, Sports, and Games*, ed. K. Anders Ericsson (Mahwah, NJ: Erlbaum, 1996), 81–106.

    11. Hans J. Eysenck, *Genius: The Natural History of Creativity* (Cambridge, UK: Cambridge University Press, 1995); Donald W. MacKinnon, "The Nature and Nurture of Creative Talent," *American Psychologist* 17 (1962): 482; Anne Roe, "A Psychological Study of Eminent Psychologists and Anthropologists and a Comparison with Biological and Physical Scientists," *Psychology Monographs* 67 (1953): 1; Simonton, "Creativity and Genius"; Dean Keith Simonton, *Genius 101*, The Psych 101 Series (New York: Springer, 2009).

    12. Richard T. Schaefer, *Racial and Ethnic Groups*, 13th ed. (New York: Pearson, 2013).

    13. Regenstein, "Jews."

    14. Dean Keith Simonton, *Greatness: Who Makes History and Why* (New York: Guilford, 1994).

    15. Allan Mohl, "The Evolution of Anti-Semitism: Historical and Psychological Roots," *Journal of Psychohistory* 39, no. 2 (2011): 115–28.

    16. Efrat Barel et al., "Surviving the Holocaust: A Meta-Analysis of the Long-Term Sequelae of a Genocide," *Psychological Bulletin* 136 (2010): 677–98; Lazar Berman, "The 2011 Nobel Prize and the Debate over Jewish IQ," American Enterprise Institute, October 19, 2011, http://www.american.com/ archive/2011/october/the-2011-nobel-prize-and-the-debate-over-jewish-iq; Kevin J. Eschleman, Nathan A. Bowling, and Gene M. Alarcon, "A Meta-Analytic Examination of Hardiness," *International Journal of Stress Management* 17 (2010): 277–307; Leo Eitinger and Ellinor F. Major, "Stress of the Holocaust," in *Handbook of Stress: Theoretical and Clinical Aspects*, eds. Leo Goldberger and Shlomo Breznitz, 2nd ed. (New York: Free Press, 1993), 617–40; William Helmreich, *Against All Odds: Holocaust Survivors and the Successful Lives They Made in America* (New York: Simon and Schuster, 1992); Robert Kaplan, "Soaring on the Wings of the Wind: Freud, Jews and Judaism," *Australasian Psychiatry* 17, no. 4 (2009): 318–25.

    17. Herbert J. Gans, "Symbolic Ethnicity and Symbolic Religiosity: Towards a Comparison of Ethnic and Religious Acculturation," *Ethnic and Racial Studies* 17 (1994): 577–92; Richard Alba, "On the Sociological Significance of the American Jewish Experience: Boundary Blurring, Assimilation, and Pluralism," *Sociology of Religion* 67 (2006): 347–58; Myrna L. Friedlander et al., "Introducing

a Brief Measure of Cultural and Religious Identification in American Jewish Identity," *Journal of Counseling Psychology* 57, no. 3 (2010): 345–60; Harriet Hartman and Debra Kaufman, "Decentering the Study of Jewish Identity," *Sociology of Religion* 67 (2006): 365–85; Susan Martha Kahn, "The Multiple Meanings of Jewish Genes," *Culture, Medicine and Psychiatry* 29 (2005): 179–92; Vivian Klaff, "Defining American Jewry from Religious and Ethnic Perspectives: The Transitions to Greater Heterogeneity," *Sociology of Religion* 67 (2006): 415–38; Jack Kugelmass, ed., *Between Two Worlds: Ethnographic Essays on American Jewry* (Ithaca, NY: Cornell University Press, 1988).

18. Gans, "Symbolic"; Alba, "Sociological"; Friedlander et al., "Introducing"; Hartman and Kaufman, "Jewish"; Klaff, "Jewry"; Kugelmass, *Two*.

19. Breger et al., "Moment."

20. Harriet Hartman and Moshe Hartman, "Jewish Identity: Denomination and Denominational Mobility," *Social Identities* 5 (1999): 279–312.

21. Erik H. Cohen, "Symbols of Diaspora Jewish Identity: An International Survey and Multi-Dimensional Analysis," *Religion* 38 (2008): 293–304.

22. Kerri Steinberg, "The Ties That Bind: Americans, Ethiopians, and the Extended Jewish Family," *Race, Gender and Class: American Jewish Perspectives* 6, no. 4 (1999): 136–51.

23. Maureen Davey et al., "Ethnic Identity Development in Jewish Families," *Journal of Marital and Family Therapy* 29, no. 2 (2003): 195–208; Maureen Davey, Linda Stone Fish, and Mihaela Robila, "Parenting Practices and the Transmission of Ethnic Identity Development in Jewish Families," *Contemporary Family Therapy* 23 (2001): 323–42; Maureen P. Semans and Linda Stone Fish, "Dissecting Life with a Jewish Scalpel: A Qualitative Analysis of Jewish-Centered Family Life," *Family Process* 39 (2000): 121–39.

24. Schaefer, *Racial*.

25. Sylvia Barack Fishman, "American Jewishness Today: Identity and Transmissibility in an Open World," Marshall Sklare Award Lecture, *Contemporary Jewry* 35, no. 2 (2015): 109–28; Eric L. Goldstein, *The Price of Whiteness: Jews, Race, and American Identity* (Princeton, NJ: Princeton University Press, 2006); Shaul Magid, "The Holocaust and Jewish Identity in America: Memory, the Unique, and the Universal," *Jewish Social Studies* 18, no. 2 (2012): 100–35; Cokie Roberts and Steven V. Roberts, *Our Haggadah: Uniting Traditions for Interfaith Families* (New York: Harper, 2011).

26. S. Luis Lugo et al., *A Portrait of Jewish Americans: Findings from a Pew Research Center Survey of U.S. Jews* (Washington, DC: Pew Research Center, 2013).

27. Davey et al., "Identity."

28. David J. Graham, "The Impact of Communal Intervention Programs on Jewish Identity: An Analysis of Jewish Students in Britain," *Contemporary Jewry* 34 (2014): 31–57.

29. Magid, "Holocaust."

30. Breger et al., "Moment"; Pellissier, "IQ."

31. Schaefer, *Racial*.

32. Ibid.

33. Esta Miran, "Judaism: An Incubator of Creativity," *Journal of the Institute for Jewish Ideas and Ideals*, December 11, 2011, http://www.jewishideas.org/articles/judaism-incubator-creativity.

34. Rabbi Jeffrey K. Salkin, *Putting God on the Guest List: How to Reclaim the Spiritual Meaning of Your Child's Bar or Bat Mitzvah* (Woodstock, VT: Jewish Lights, 1996).

35. Harriet Zuckerman, "Nobel Laureates in Science: Patterns of Productivity, Collaboration, and Authorship," *American Sociological Review* 32, no. 3 (1967): 391–403.

36. Mihaly Csikszentmihalyi, *Flow: The Psychology of Optimal Experience* (New York: Harper and Row, 1990); Ravenna Helson, "Women in Creativity," in *The Creativity Question*, eds. Albert Rothenberg and Carl Hausman (Durham, NC: Duke University Press, 1976), 242–49; Arthur Koestler, *The Act of Creation* (New York: Macmillan, 1964).

37. Christine Charyton et al., "What Are Significant Predictors of Age for Receiving the Nobel Prize in Science?" *International Journal of Creativity and Problem Solving* 20, no.2 (2010): 73–83.

38. William G. Bowen and Derek Bok, *The Shape of the River: Long-Term Consequences of*

Considering Race in College and University Admissions (Princeton, NJ: Princeton University Press, 1998); Thomas J. Espenshade and Alexandria Walton Radford, *No Longer Separate, Not Yet Equal: Race and Class in Elite College Admission and Campus Life* (Princeton, NJ: Princeton University Press, 2009).

39. Abby N. Altman et al., "An Exploration of Jewish Ethnic Identity," *Journal of Counseling and Development* 88 (2010): 163–73; Lewis Z. Schlosser, "Affirmative Psychotherapy for American Jews," *Psychotherapy: Theory, Research, Practice, Training* 43 (2006): 424–35.

40. Bowen and Bok, *Shape*; Espenshade and Radford, *Separate*.

41. Isidore Singer and Cyrus Adler, *The Jewish Encyclopedia: A Descriptive Record of the History, Religion, Literature, and Customs of the Jewish People from the Earliest Times Complete*, 12 vols. (New York: KTAV, 1901).

42. Elliot N. Dorff, *The Way into Tikkun Olam (Repairing the World)* (Woodstock, VT: Jewish Lights, 2005); Jacob Neusner, *Tzedakah: Can Jewish Philanthropy Buy Jewish Survival?* (Chappaqua, NY: Rossel, 1982); Paul Ritterband, "The Determinants of Jewish Charitable Giving in the Last Part of the Twentieth Century," in *Contemporary Jewish Philanthropy in America*, eds. Barry A. Kosmin and Paul Ritterband (Savage, MD: Rowman and Littlefield, 1991), 57–72; Schaefer, *Racial*; Ira Silverman, "The New Jewish Philanthropies," in *Contemporary Jewish Philanthropy in America*, eds. Barry A. Kosmin and Paul Ritterband (Savage, MD: Rowman and Littlefield, 1991), 205–16; Gary A. Tobin, *The Transition of Communal Values and Behavior in Jewish Philanthropy* (San Francisco, CA: Institute for Jewish and Community Research, 2001); Jonathan Woocher, *Sacred Survival: The Civil Religion of American Jews* (Bloomington: Indiana University Press, 1986).

43. Alexander H. Joffe, "American Jews beyond Judaism," *Society* 48, no. 4 (2011): 323–29; Joseph Isaac Lifshitz, "Welfare, Property, and Charity in Jewish Thought," *Transaction Social Science and Modern Society* 44, no. 2 (2007): 71–78.

44. Tracey R. Rich, "Tzedakah: Charity," Judaism 101, 2011, http://www.jewfaq.org/tzedakah.htm.

45. René Bekkers, "Measuring Altruistic Behavior in Surveys: The All-or-Nothing Dictator Game," *Survey Research Methods* 1, no. 3 (2007): 139–44; René Bekkers and Theo Schuyt, "And Who Is Your Neighbor? Explaining Denominational Differences in Charitable Giving and Volunteering in the Netherlands," *Review of Religious Research* 50, no. 1 (2008): 74–96; Catherine C. Eckel and Philip J. Grossman, "Giving to Secular Causes by the Religious and Nonreligious: An Experimental Test of the Responsiveness of Giving to Subsidies," *Nonprofit and Voluntary Sector Quarterly* 33, no. 2 (2004): 271–89; Mark Ottoni-Wilhelm, "Giving to Organizations That Help People in Need: Differences across Denominational Identities," *Journal for the Scientific Study of Religion* 49, no. 3 (2010): 389–412; Mark D. Regnerus, Christian Smith, and David Sikkink, "Who Gives to the Poor? The Influence of Religious Tradition and Political Location on the Personal Generosity of Americans toward the Poor," *Journal for the Scientific Study of Religion* 37, no. 3 (1998): 481–93.

46. Ottoni-Wilhelm, "Giving."

47. Ibid.

48. Fishman, "Jewishness."

49. Joffe, "Jews"; Schaefer, *Racial*.

50. Tom Tugend, "Why Aren't Jews Giving to Jews? Jewish Philanthropic Donations to the Secular Community Are Outweighing Those Going to the Jewish Community," *Jewish Journal*, June 26, 2003, http://www.jewishjournal.com/los_angeles/article/why_arent_jews_giving_to_jews_20030627/.

51. Samuel Kurinsky, "Artisanship, and Literacy; The Salvation of the Jews," Hebrew History Federation, 2012, http://www.hebrewhistory.info/factpapers/fp012_creativity.htm.

52. Pellissier, "IQ."

53. "Classic CD-100 Greatest Conductors of the Century," Muzieklijstjes.nl, http://www.muzieklijstjes.nl/100cond uctors.htm.

54. Muzieklijstjes.nl, "Classic CD-100 Greatest Players of the Century," http://www.muzieklijstjes.nl/100players.htm.

55. Crystal Gibson, Bradley S. Folley, and Sohee Park, "Enhanced Divergent Thinking and

Creativity in Musicians: A Behavioral and Near-Infrared Spectroscopy Study," *Brain and Cognition* 69, no. 1 (2009): 162–69; Jay Woodward and Paul L. Sikes, "The Creative Thinking Ability of Musicians and Nonmusicians," *Psychology of Aesthetics, Creativity, and the Arts* 9, no. 1 (2015): 75–80.

56. William Novak and Moshe Waldoks, *The Big Book of Jewish Humor* (New York: Harper and Row, 1981).

57. Ibid.

58. Ibid.

59. Ibid.

60. Breger et al., "Moment."

61. Ibid.

62. David Berman et al., "A Moment Symposium: Can There Be Judaism without Belief in God?" *Moment* (September/October 2011), 34–39; Amy E. Schwartz, "A Moment Symposium: Is There Life after Death?" *Moment* (July/August 2011), 34–41.

63. Salo Wittmayer Baron, *A Social and Religious History of the Jews* (New York: Columbia University Press, 1952).

64. Breger et al., "Moment."

65. Nathan Glazer and Daniel P. Moynihan, *Beyond the Melting Pot* (New York: Random House, 1970); Lynn and Longley, "High"; Schaefer, *Racial.*

66. Cohen, "Symbols"; Michelle L. Friedman, Myrna L. Friedlander, and David L. Blustein, "Toward an Understanding of Jewish Identity: A Phenomenological Study," *Journal of Counseling Psychology* 52 (2005): 77–83; Schlosser, "Affirmative"; Lewis Z. Schlosser, "Introduction," in *The Lost Tribe: American Jews and Multicultural Psychology*, ed. Lewis Z. Schlosser (Symposium Presented at the American Psychological Association Annual Convention, San Francisco, CA, 2007).

67. Lynn, "Intelligence"; Pellissier, "IQ."

68. Magid, "Holocaust."

69. Cohen, "Symbols"; Adam M. Weisberger, *The Jewish Ethic and the Spirit of Socialism* (New York: Peter Lang, 1997).

70. Breger et al., "Moment."

71. Joan Joesting and Robert Joesting, "Correlations of Scores on Full-Range Picture Vocabulary Test, Three Measures of Creativity, SAT Scores, and Age," *Psychological Reports* 33, no. 3 (1973): 981–82.

72. Cohen, "Symbols"; Raymond-Jean Frontain and Jan Wojcik, *The David Myth in Western Literature* (West Lafayette, IN: Purdue University Press, 1980); Stanley Jeroe Isser, *The Sword of Goliath: David in Heroic Literature* (Philadelphia, PA: Society of Biblical Literature, 2003).

73. Cohen, "Symbols"; Anita Shapira, *Israeli Identity in Transition* (Westport, CT: Greenwood, 2004).

74. Ibid.

75. Cohen, "Symbols"; Mona Sue Weissmark, *Justice Matters: Legacies of the Holocaust and World War II* (New York: Oxford University Press, 2004).

76. Cohen, "Symbols."

77. Weinberg, "Secrets."

78. Salkin, *God.*

79. Miran, "Judaism"; Cheryl Nakata and Kumar Sivakumar, "National Culture and New Product Development: An Integrative Review," *Journal of Marketing* 60 (1996): 61–72.

80. Salkin, *God.*

81. Davey et al., "Identity"; Shechory-Bitton, David, and Sommerfeld, "Effect."

82. Davey et al., "Identity."

83. Ibid.

84. Shechory-Bitton, David, and Sommerfeld, "Effect."

85. Dwairy and Achoui, "Introduction"; Lynn and Kanazawa, "Explain"; Larissa Remennick, "Exploring Intercultural Relationships: A Study of Russian Immigrants Married to Native Israelis," *Journal of Comparative Family Studies* 40 (2009): 719–38.

86. Lynn and Kanazawa, "Explain."

87. Ibid.

88. Baron, *Jews*.

89. Ibid.

90. Michael C. Reichert and Sharon M. Ravitch, "Defying Normative Male Identities: The Transgressive Possibilities of Jewish Boyhood," *Youth and Society* 42, no. 1 (2010): 104–31.

91. Ibid.

92. Susan Martha Kahn, *Reproducing Jews: A Cultural Account of Assisted Conception in Israel* (Durham and London: Duke University Press, 2000).

93. Davey et al., "Identity."

94. Nathan Drazin, *History of Jewish Education From 515 B.C.E. to 220 C.E.* (Baltimore, MD: Johns Hopkins University Press, 1940).

95. M. Holzman, *G'varim: Resources for Jewish Men* (New York: National Federation of Temple Brotherhoods, 2003); Nancy Leffert and Hayim Herring, *Shema: Listening to Jewish Youth* (Minneapolis, MN: Search Institute, 1998); Reichert and Ravitch, "Defying."

96. "Jewish Nobel Prize Winners," JINFO.org, 2015, http://jinfo.org/Nobel_Prizes.html.

97. Friedlander et al., "Introducing"; Peter F. Langman, "Including Jews in Multiculturalism," *Journal of Multicultural Counseling and Development* 23 (1995): 222–36; Peter F. Langman, *Jewish Issues in Multiculturalism* (Northvale, NJ: Jason Aronson, 1999); Irwin D. Rinder, "Mental Health of American Jewish Urbanites: A Review of Literature and Predictions," *Journal of Social Psychiatry* 9 (1963): 104–09; Schlosser, "Affirmative."

98. Friedlander et al., "Introducing."

99. Ibid.

100. Reichert and Ravitch, "Defying."

101. Ibid.

102. Ibid.

103. Ibid.

104. Ibid.

105. Ibid.

106. Ibid.

107. Breger et al., "Moment"; Schaefer, *Racial*.

108. Kaplan, "Freud, Jews, and Judaism"; Rabbi Jeffrey K. Salkin, "Seven Rebellious Jews You Should Know," Martini Judaism: For Those Who Want to Be Shaken and Stirred, April 9, 2015, http://jeffreysalkin.religionnews.com/2015/04/09/ seven-rebellious-jews-know/; Shmuel Feiner, "Seductive Science and the Emergence of the Secular Jewish Intellectual," *Science in Context* 15, no.1 (2002): 121–35; Michael P. Steinberg, "Jewish Identity and Intellectuality in Fin-de-Siècle Austria: Suggestions for a Historical Discourse," *New German Critique* 43 (1988): 3–33.

109. Davey et al., "Identity."

110. Breger et al., "Moment."

111. Jonathan Chaves, "Confucianism: The Conservatism of the East," *Intercollegiate Review* 38, no. 2 (2002): 44–50; Chaihark Hahm, "Law, Culture, and the Politics of Confucianism," *Columbia Journal of Asian Law* 16, no. 2 (2002): 253–91; Andrew Eungi Kim and Gil-sung Park, "Nationalism, Confucianism, Work Ethic and Industrialization in South Korea," *Journal of Contemporary Asia* 33, no. 1 (2003): 37–49; Zhenzhong Ma et al., "Confucian Ideal Personality and Chinese Business Negotiation Styles: An Indigenous Perspective," *Group Decis Negot* 24 (2015): 383–400.

112. Steven Greer and Tiong Piow Lim, "Confucianism: Natural Law Chinese Style?" *Ratio Juris* 11, no. 1 (1998): 80–89; Krista Millay and Carla Mae Streeter, "Implicit Harmony: An Overview of Confucianism and Taoism and Their Gift to the Christian Faith," *Chinese American Forum* 19, no. 3 (2004): 2–6.

113. Betty Kelen, *Confucius: In Life and Legend* (Camden, NJ: Sheldon, 1974).

114. Millay and Streeter, "Harmony."

115. Greer and Lim, "Confucianism"; Millay and Streeter, "Harmony."

116. Sally Chan, "The Chinese Learner—A Question of Style," *EduKelencation + Training* 41, no. 6/7 (1999): 294–304; Arif Dirlik, "Confucius in the Borderlands: Global Capitalism and the Reinvention of Confucianism," *Boundary 2*, 22 no. 3 (1995): 229–73; Richard B. Freeman and Wei Huang, "China's 'Great Leap Forward' in Science and Engineering," in *Global Mobility of Research Scientists: The Economics of Who Goes Where and Why* (London: Elsevier, 2015), 155–75.

117. Maris G. Martinsons and Aelita Brivins Martinsons, "Conquering Cultural Constraints to Cultivate Chinese Management Creativity and Innovation," *Journal of Management Development* 15, no. 9 (1996): 18–35; Xinzhong Yao, "Confucianism and Its Modern Values: Confucian Moral, Educational and Spiritual Heritages Revisited," *Journal of Beliefs and Values* 20, no. 1 (1999): 30– 40.

118. Dirlik, "Confucius"; Hahm, "Law."

119. William A. Callahan, "Negotiating Cultural Boundaries: Confucianism and Trans/National Identity in Korea," *Cultural Values* 3, no. 3 (1999): 329–64; Ji-Sun Chung, "Women's Unequal Access to Education in South Korea," *Comparative Education Review* 38, no. 4 (1994): 487–505; Dirlik, "Confucius"; Kim and Park, "Nationalism"; Yao, "Confucianism"; Soon Hyung Yi, "Transformation of Child Socialization in Korean Culture," *Early Child Development and Care* 85 (1993): 17–24.

120. Callahan, "Negotiating"; Chung, "Women's"; Hahm, "Law"; Yi, "Transformation."

121. Guo-Ming Chen and Jensen Chung, "The Impact of Confucianism on Organizational Communication," *Communication Quarterly* 42, no. 2 (1994): 93–105; Geert Hofstede and Michael Harris Bond, "The Confucius Connection: From Cultural Roots to Economic Growth," *Organizational Dynamics* 16 (1988): 5–21; KH Kim, "Cultural Influence on Creativity: The Relationship between Creativity and Confucianism" (PhD diss., University of Georgia, 2004); KH Kim, "Exploring the Interactions between Asian Culture (Confucianism) and Creativity," *Journal of Creative Behavior* 41, no. 1 (2007): 28–53; KH Kim et al., "Creativity and Confucianism among American and Korean Educators," *Creativity Research Journal* 23, no. 4 (2011): 357–71.

122. Ruiping Fan, "Reconsidering Surrogate Decision Making: Aristotelianism and Confucianism on Ideal Human Relations," *Philosophy East and West* (2002): 346–72; Ranjoo Seodu Herr, "Is Confucianism Compatible with Care Ethics? A Critique," *Philosophy East and West* (2003): 471–89; Hofstede and Bond, "Confucius"; Kwang-Kuo Hwang, "Filial Piety and Loyalty: Two Types of Social Identification in Confucianism," *Asian Journal of Social Psychology* 2 (1999): 163–83; Kwang-Kuo Hwang, "The Deep Structure of Confucianism: A Social Psychological Approach," *Asian Philosophy* 11, no. 3 (2001): 179–204; Anh Tuan Nuyen, "Confucianism, Globalisation and the Idea of Universalism," *Asian Philosophy* 13, no. 2–3 (2003): 75–86.

123. Cortney A. Evans et al., "Understanding Relations among Children's Shy and Antisocial/ Aggressive Behaviors and Mothers' Parenting: The Role of Maternal Beliefs," *Merrill-Palmer Quarterly* 58 (2012): 341–74; Cliff McKinney, Mary Catherine Milone, and Kimberly Renk, "Parenting and Late Adolescent Emotional Adjustment: Mediating Effects of Discipline and Gender," *Child Psychiatry and Human Development* 42 (2011): 463–81; Clea A. McNeely, and Brian K. Barber. "How Do Parents Make Adolescents Feel Loved? Perspectives on Supportive Parenting from Adolescents in 12 Cultures," *Journal of Adolescent Research* 25, no. 4 (2010): 601–31; Christian L. Porter et al., "A Comparative Study of Child Temperament and Parenting in Beijing, China and the Western United States," *International Journal of Behavioral Development* 29, no. 5 (2005): 541–51; L. Steinberg et al., "Authoritative Parenting and Adolescent Adjustment across Various Ecological Niches," *Journal of Research on Adolescence* 1 (1991):19–36.

124. Robert J. Englehart and David B. Hale, "Punishment, Nail-Biting, and Nightmares: A Cross-Cultural Study," *Journal of Multicultural Counseling and Development* 18, no. 3 (1990): 126–32.

125. Chen and Chung, "Confucianism"; Zoltan Bathory et al., "Profiles of Educational Systems of Countries Participating in Practical Skills Testing," *Studies in Educational Evaluation* 18 (1992): 301–18; Lucia French and Myung-Ja Song, "Developmentally Appropriate Teacher-Directed Approaches: Images from Korean Kindergartens," *Journal of Curriculum Studies* 30 (1998): 409–30; McNeely and Barber, "Parents"; Philippa Williams, Lesley Barclay, and Virginia Schmied, "Defining

Social Support in Context: A Necessary Step in Improving Research, Intervention, and Practice," *Qualitative Health Research* 14, no. 7 (2004): 942–60.

126. Kim, "Developing"; Kim et al., "Creativity"; Scott A. Shane, "Why Do Some Societies Invent More Than Others?" *Journal of Business Venturing* 7, no. 1 (1992): 29–46; Scott A. Shane, "Cultural Influences on National Rates of Innovation," *Journal of Business Venturing* 8, no. 1 (1993): 59–73.

127. "Confucian World Order," Korea Society, July 2, 2015, http://chosonkorea.org/index.php/society/confucian-world-order.

128. Ibid.

129. Joseph R. Levenson, *Confucian China and Its Modern Fate*, vol. 3, *The Problem of Historical Significance* (London, UK: Routledge and Kegan Paul, 1965).

130. Chaves, "Confucianism"; Hwang, "Deep"; Byeong-Chul Park, "An Aspect of Political Socialization of Student Movement Participants in Korea," *Youth and Society* 25, no. 2 (1993): 171–80.

131. Malcolm Gladwell, *Outliers: The Story of Success* (New York: Little, Brown, 2008).

132. Chung, "Women's"; Yong Chen Fah, "The Spirituality of Chinese Social Obligations," *Transformation: An International Journal of Holistic Mission Studies* 19, no. 1 (2002): 34–36; Young-Shin Park and Uichol Kim, "The Educational Challenge of Korea in the Global Era: The Role of Family, School, and Government," *Chinese University Education Journal* 26/27, no. 2/1 (1999): 91–120; Linda K. Johnsrud, "Korean Academic Women: Multiple Roles, Multiple Challenges," *Higher Education* 30, no. 1 (1995): 17–35.

133. Chung, "Women's"; Johnsrud, "Academic"; Kim, "Cultural"; Kim, "Exploring"; Kim et al., "Creativity"; Park and Kim, "Challenge."

134. Levenson, *Confucian*; KH Kim, "Learning from Each Other: Creativity in East Asian and American Education," *Creativity Research Journal* 17, no. 4 (2005): 337–47; Scott D. Thomson, "How Much Do Americans Value Schooling?" *NASSP Bulletin* 73, no. 519 (1989): 51–67; Esther Lee Yao, and Fred D. Kierstead, "Can Asian Educational Systems Be Models for American Education? An Appraisal," *NASSP Bulletin* 68, no. 476 (1984): 82–89.

135. Richard M. Haynes and Donald M. Chalker, "World-Class Schools," *American School Board Journal* 184, no. 5 (1997): 20–26.

136. Haynes and Chalker, "World-Class"; Richard M. Haynes and Donald M. Chalker, "The Making of a World-Class Elementary School," *Principal* 77, no. 3 (1998): 5–6, 8–9; Taipei National Tax Administration, "Scope of Exemption," Ministry of Finance, 2012, http://www.ntat.gov.tw/county/ntat_ch/ntat_en/en9-02-3-10.jsp; Thomson, "How"; Yao and Kierstead, "Asian."

137. Thomson, "How."

138. Haynes and Chalker, "World-Class."

139. Z. P. Henderson, "Myth of Native Ability Hurts American Education," *Human Ecology* 19, no. 1 (1990): 29–30; Haynes and Chalker, "Making"; Clark W. Sorensen, "Success and Education in South Korea," *Comparative Education Review* 38, no. 1 (1994): 10–35.

140. Li-Rong Lilly Cheng, Kenji Ima, and Gene Labovitz, "Assessment of Asian and Pacific Islander Students for Gifted Programs," in *Addressing Cultural and Linguistic Diversity in Special Education*, ed. Shernaz B. García (Reston, VA: Council for Exceptional Children, 1994), 30–45; David Y. F. Ho, "Cognitive Socialization in Confucian Heritage Cultures," in *Cross Cultural Roots of Minority Child Development*, eds. Patricia M. Greenfield and Rodney R. Cocking (Hillsdale, NJ: Erlbaum, 1994), 285–313; Pew Research Center, "The Rise of Asian Americans," Pew Research Center: Social and Demographic Trends, April 4, 2013, http://www.pewsocialtrends.org/2012/06/19/the-rise-of-Asian Americans/2/; Harold W. Stevenson and James W. Stigler, *The Learning Gap: Why Our Schools Are Failing and What We Can Learn from Japanese and Chinese Education* (New York: Summit, 1992).

141. Bruce B. Henderson, Melvin H. Marx, and Yung Che Kim, "Academic Interests and Perceived Competence in American, Japanese and Korean Children," *Journal of Cross-Cultural Psychology* 30, no. 1 (1999): 32–50.

142. Chen and Chung, "Confucianism"; Dirlik, "Confucius"; Hahm, "Law"; Martinsons and Martinsons, "Conquering"; Paul Morris, "Asia's Four Little Tigers: A Comparison of the Role of Education in Their Development," *Comparative Education* 32, no. 1 (1996): 95–109; Sorensen, "Success."

143. Steven J. Heine and Darrin R. Lehman, "Culture, Self-Discrepancies, and Self-Satisfaction," *Personality and Social Psychology Bulletin* 25 (1999): 915–25; Steven J. Heine et al., "Is There a Universal Need for Positive Self-Regard?" *Psychological Review* 106 (1999): 766–94; Steven J. Heine, Shinobu Kitayama, and Darrin R. Lehman, "Cultural Differences in Self-Evaluation: Japanese Readily Accept Negative Self-Relevant Information," *Journal of Cross-Cultural Psychology* 32, no. 4 (2001): 434–43; Shinobu Kitayama et al., "Individual and Collective Processes in the Construction of the Self: Self-Enhancement in the United States and Self-Criticism in Japan," *Journal of Personality and Social Psychology* 72 (1997): 1245–67; Hazel Rose Markus and Shinobu Kitayama, "Culture and the Self: Implications for Cognition, Emotion, and Motivation," *Psychological Review* 98, no. 2 (1991): 224–53.

144. Steven J. Heine and Darrin R. Lehman, "Cultural Variation in Unrealistic Optimism: Does the West Feel More Invulnerable Than the East? *Journal of Personality and Social Psychology* 68 (1995): 595–607.

145. Steven J. Heine and Takeshi Hamamura, "In Search of East Asian Self-Enhancement," *Personality and Social Psychology Review* 11 (2007): 4–27; Heine, Kitayama, and Lehman, "Cultural."

146. Ibid.

147. Ibid.

148. Ibid.

149. Ronald S. Anderson, "An American View of Japanese Education," *Phi Delta Kappan* 39 (1957): 99–103; J. Chan and Y. Chen, "Processes and Outcomes of Encouraging Universities to Implement Creative Studies Colleges," in *Creative Education Programs in Taiwan: Development and Implementation*, ed. J. Chan (Taipei, Taiwan: Ministry of Education, 2008), 244–57; Edward Foster, "'Exam Hell' in Japan," *Change* 5, no. 6 (1973): 16–19; Martinsons and Martinsons, "Conquering"; Ju-min Park and Jane Chung "Military Discipline for 'Soldiers' on Korea Exam's Front Line," *Reuters*, November 5, 2012, http://www.reuters.com/article/2012/11/05/us-korea-exam-idUSBRE8A408Q20121105; Hoi K Suen and Lan Yu, "Chronic Consequences of High-Stakes Testing? Lesson from the Chinese Civil Service Exam," *Comparative Education Review* 50, no, 10 (2006): 46–65; Jean Wollam, "Equality versus Excellence: The South Korean Dilemma in Gifted Education," *Roeper Review* 14 (1992): 212–17.

150. Haynes and Chalker, "World-Class"; Park and Chung "Military."

151. Benjamin A. Elman, "Civil Service Examinations (Keju)," *Berkshire Encyclopedia of China* (Great Barrington, MA: Berkshire, 2009), 405–10; Suen and Yu, "Chronic."

152. Suen and Yu, "Chronic."

153. George A. Brown, Joanna Bull, Malcolm Pendlebury, *Assessing Student Learning in Higher Education* (New York: Routledge, 1997); Elman, "Examinations."

154. Elman, "Examinations"; Suen and Yu, "Chronic."

155. Ibid.

156. Suen and Yu, "Chronic."

157. Editorial Board, "Asia's College Exam Mania," *New York Times*, November 6, 2013, http://www.nytimes.com/2013/11/07/opinion/asias-college-exam-mania.html?_r=0; From the Print Edition, "Exams in South Korea: The One-Shot Society," *Economist*, December 17, 2011, http://www.economist.com/node/21541713; Jiyeon Lee, "South Korean Students' 'Year of Hell' Culminates with Exams Day," CNN, November 13, 2011, http://www.cnn.com/2011/11/10/world/asia/south-korea-exams/; Dexter Roberts, "China Exam System Drives Student Suicides, *Bloomberg*, May 15, 2014, http://www.bloomberg.com/news/articles/2014-05-15/china-exam-system-drives-student-suicides; Suen and Yu, "Chronic."

158. Chen and Chung, "Confucianism"; Amy Chua, *Battle Hymn of the Tiger Mother* (New York:

Bloomsbury, 2011); Dirlik, "Confucius," 229–73; Rob M. Fielding, "A Socio-Cognitive Perspective on Cross-Cultural Attitudes and Practices in Creativity Development," *Australian Art Education* 20, no. 1–2 (1997): 27–33; Hahm, "Law"; Martinsons and Martinsons, "Conquering"; Morris, "Asia's"; Elizabeth Rudowicz and Anna Hui, "The Creative Personality: Hong Kong Perspective," *Journal of Social Behavior and Personality* 12, no. 1 (1997): 139–48; Sorensen, "Success."

159. Wing Chung Lau, Antoinette Lee, and Lynda Ransdell, "Parenting Style and Cultural Influences on Overweight Children's Attraction to Physical Activity," *Obesity* 15, no. 9 (2007): 2293–2302; Junwei Yu and Alan Bairner, "Confucianism, Baseball and Ethnic Stereotyping in Taiwan," *International Review for the Sociology of Sport* 47, no. 6 (2011): 690–704.

160. Chua, *Tiger*.

161. Doyle W. Bishop and Charles A. Chace, "Parental Conceptual Systems, Home Play Environment, and Potential Creativity in Children," *Journal of Experimental Child Psychology* 12, no. 3 (1971): 318–38; Hazel Feldhusen, "Teaching Gifted, Creative, and Talented Students in an Individualized Classroom," *Gifted Child Quarterly* 25, no. 3 (1981): 108–11; Rob M. Fielding, "Creativity Revisited: Strategies for Developing Creative Potential," *Journal of the Institute of Art Education* 7, no. 2 (1983): 51–60; Beth A. Hennessey and Teresa M. Amabile, *Creativity and Learning* (Washington, DC: National Education Association, 1987); Ochse, *Excellence*; Ruth Richards, "Beyond Piaget: Accepting Divergent, Chaotic, and Creative Thought," *New Directions for Child and Adolescent Development* 72 (1996): 67–86; Dorothy G. Singer and Jerome L. Singer, *The House of Make-Believe: Children's Play and the Developing Imagination* (Cambridge, MA: Harvard University Press, 1990); Dorothy G. Singer and Jerome L. Singer, *Imagination and Play in the Electronic Age* (Cambridge, MA: Harvard University Press, 2005); Jerome L. Singer, *The Child's World of Make-Believe* (New York: Academic, 1973); Jerome L. Singer, "Researching Imaginative Play and Adult Consciousness: Implications for Daily and Literary Creativity," *Psychology of Aesthetics, Creativity, and the Arts* 3, no. 4 (2009): 190–99. Lev S. Vygotsky, "The Development of Imagination in Childhood," in *The Collected Works of L. S. Vygotsky*, vol. 2, eds. Robert W. Rieber and Aaron S. Carton (New York: N. Minick, Tranc., 1987); Lev S. Vygotsky, "Imagination and Creativity in Childhood," *Soviet Psychology* 28, no. 1 (1990): 84–96; Lev S. Vygotsky, "Imagination and Creativity of the Adolescent," in *The Vygotsky Reader*, eds. R. Van Der Veer and Jaan Valsiner (Cambridge: Blackwell, 1994), 266–88.

162. Chua, *Tiger*.

163. Karen Levin Coburn, "Organizing a Ground Crew for Today's Helicopter Parents," *About Campus* 11, no. 3 (2006): 9–16; Jessica M. Dennis, Jean S. Phinney, and Lizette Ivy Chuateco, "The Role of Motivation, Parental Support, and Peer Support in the Academic Success of Ethnic Minority First-Generation College Students," *Journal of College Student Development* 46, no. 3 (2005): 223–36; Marnie Hiester, Alicia Nordstrom, and Lisa M. Swenson, "Stability and Change in Parental Attachment and Adjustment Outcomes during the First Semester Transition to College Life," *Journal of College Student Development* 50, no. 5 (2009): 521–38; Juan-Claude Lemmens, Gerhard I. Du Plessis, and David JF Maree, "Measuring Readiness and Success at a Higher Education Institution," *Journal of Psychology in Africa* 21, no. 4 (2011): 615–21.

164. Chen and Chung, "Confucianism"; Hofstede and Bond, "Confucius"; Hwang, "Filial"; Qingping Liu, "Filiality versus Sociality and Individuality: On Confucianism as 'Consanguinitism,'" *Philosophy East and West* 53, no. 2 (2003): 234–50.

165. Pew Research Center, "The Rise of Asian Americans," Pew Research Center: Social and Demographic Trends, April 4, 2013, http://www.pewsocialtrends.org/2012/06/19/the-rise-of-Asian Americans/2/.

166. Mimi Bong, "Effects of Parent-Child Relationships and Classroom Goal Structures on Motivation, Help-Seeking Avoidance, and Cheating," *Journal of Experimental Education* 76, no. 2 (2008): 191–217.

167. Hofstede and Bond, "Confucius"; Hwang, "Filial."

168. Ruth K. Chao, "Beyond Parental Control and Authoritarian Parenting Style: Understanding Chinese Parenting through the Cultural Notion of Training," *Child Development* 65, no. 4 (1994):

1111–19; Ruth K. Chao and Stanley Sue, "Chinese Parental Influences and Their Children's School Success: A Paradox in the Literature on Parenting Styles," in *Growing up the Chinese Way*, ed. Sing Lau (Hong Kong: Chinese University Press, 1996), 93–120; Sunita Mahtani Stewart et al., "Does the Chinese Construct of Guan Export to the West?" *International Journal of Psychology* 37, no. 2 (2002): 74–82.

169. McNeely and Barber, "Parents."

170. David Y. F. Ho, "Fatherhood in Chinese Culture," in *The Father's Role: Cross-Cultural Perspectives*, ed. Michael E. Lamb (Hillsdale, NJ: Erlbaum, 1987), 227–45; David Y. F. Ho, "Filial Piety, Authoritarian Moralism, and Cognitive Conservatism in Chinese Societies," *Genetic, Social, and General Psychology Monographs* 120 (1994): 347–65; David Y. F. Ho, "Filial Piety and Its Psychological Consequences," in *The Handbook of Chinese Psychology*, ed. Michael Harris Bond (Hong Kong: Oxford University Press, 1996), 155–65.

171. Kim, "Developing"; Kim et al., "Creativity"; Seana Moran, "The Roles of Creativity in Society," in *The Cambridge Handbook of Creativity* (New York: Cambridge University Press, 2010), 74–90.

172. S. Sum Yeung, "The Dynamic of Family Care for the Elderly in Hong Kong" (PhD diss., University of Hong Kong, 1989).

173. Kim and Park, "Nationalism"; Liu, "Filiality."

174. Callahan, "Negotiating"; Chen and Chung, "Confucianism"; Chung, "Women's"; Dirlik, "Confucius"; Kwang-Kuo Hwang, "Confucian Thoughts and Modernization: Theory Analysis and Empirical Study," *China Tribune* 319 (1989): 7–24; Kim and Park, "Nationalism"; Roderick MacFarquhar, "The Post-Confucian Challenge," *Economist*, February 9, 1980, 65–72; Yao, "Confucianism"; Yi, "Transformation."

175. Chen and Chung, "Confucianism"; Hwang, "Filial"; June Ock Yum, "The Practice of Uye-Ri in Interpersonal Relationships," in *Communication Theory: Eastern and Western Perspectives*, ed. D. Lawrence Kincaid (New York: Academic, 1987), 87–100.

176. Chua, *Tiger*.

177. Michael Harris Bond, *Beyond the Chinese Face* (Hong Kong: Oxford University Press, 1991); Chan, "Chinese Learner," 294–304; Kai-ming Cheng, "Can Education Values Be Borrowed? Looking into Cultural Differences," *Peabody Journal of Education* 73, no. 2 (1998): 11–30.

178. John Biggs and David Watkins, "The Chinese Learner in Retrospect," in *The Chinese Learner: Cultural, Psychological and Contextual Influences*, eds. David Watkins and John Biggs (Melbourne: Australian Council for Educational Research, 1996), 269–85; Robert Briggs, "Shameless! Reconceiving the Problem of Plagiarism," *Australian Universities Review* 46, no. 1 (2003): 19–23; Glenn D. Deckert, "A Pedagogical Response to Learned Plagiarism among Tertiary Level ESL Students," *Guidelines* 14, no. 1 (1992): 94–104; Jiang Xueqin, "Chinese Academics Consider a 'Culture of Copying,'" *Chronicle of Higher Education* 48, no. 36 (2002): 45; Justin Zobel and Margaret Hamilton, "Managing Student Plagiarism in Large Academic Departments," *Australian Universities Review* 45, no. 2 (2002): 23–30.

179. James D. Alexander, "Lectures: The Ethics of Borrowing," *College Teaching* 36, no. 1 (1988): 21–24; John Biggs, "Asian Learners through Western Eyes: An Astigmatic Paradox," *Australian and New Zealand Journal of Vocational Education Research* 2, no. 2 (1994): 40; Niall Hayes and Lucas D. Introna, "Cultural Values, Plagiarism, and Fairness: When Plagiarism Gets in the Way of Learning," *Ethics and Behavior* 15, no. 3 (2005): 213–31; Ilona Leki, *Understanding ESL Writers: A Guide for Teachers* (Portsmouth, NH: Boynton/Cook, 1992); Alastair Pennycook, "Borrowing Others' Words: Text, Ownership, Memory and Plagiarism," *TESOL Quarterly* 30 (1996): 210–30.

180. Maud Mundava and Jayati Chaudhuri, "Understanding Plagiarism: The Role of Librarians at the University of Tennessee in Assisting Students to Practice Fair Use of Information," *College and Research Libraries News* 68, no. 3 (2007): 170–73.

181. Suen and Yu, "Chronic."

182. Michael Harris Bond, ed., *The Psychology of the Chinese People* (New York: Oxford University Press, 1986);Thomas O'Donoghue, "Malaysian Chinese Students' Perceptions of What Is Necessary for Their Academic Success in Australia: A Case Study at One University," *Journal of Further and Higher Education* 20, no. 2 (1996): 67–80.

183. Tom Bartlett and Karin Fischer, "The China Conundrum," *Chronicle*, November 3, 2011, http://chronicle.com/article/The-China-Conundrum/129628/; Bond, *Chinese*; Glenn D. Deckert, "Perspectives on Plagiarism from ESL Students in Hong Kong," *Journal of Second Language Writing* 2 (1993): 131–48; Peter Friedman, "China's Plagiarism Problem," *Forbes*, May 26, 2010, http://www.forbes.com/2010/05/26/china-cheating-innovation-markets-economy-plagiarism.html; Kim and Park, "Nationalism"; Louisa Lim, "Plagiarism Plague Hiders China's Scientific Ambition," *NPR*, August 3, 2011, http://www.npr.org/2011/08/03/138937778/plagiarism-plague-hinders-chinas-scientific-ambition; O'Donoghue, "Malaysian," 67–80; Raymond A. Schroth, "The Plagiarism Plague, America," *National Catholic Weekly*, May 14, 2012, http://americamagazine.org/node/150525; Zobel and Hamilton, "Plagiarism."

184. Hahm, "Law."

185. Bong, "Parent-Child."

186. Ge Gao, "'Don't Take My Word for It'—Understanding Chinese Speaking Practices," *International Journal of Intercultural Relations* 22, no. 2 (1998): 163–86.

187. Chen and Chung, "Confucianism"; Fan, "Reconsidering"; Herr, "Confucianism"; Hofstede and Bond, "Confucius"; Hwang, "Filial"; Hwang, "Deep"; Long-Chuan Lu, Ya-Wen Huang, and Hsiu-Hua Chang, "Confucian Dynamism, the Role of Money and Consumer Ethical Beliefs: An Exploratory Study in Taiwan," *Ethics and Behavior* 24, no. 1 (2014): 34–52; Ma et al., "Confucian"; Millay and Streeter, "Harmony."

188. Chen and Chung, "Confucianism"; Fan, "Reconsidering"; Herr, "Confucianism"; Hofstede and Bond, "Confucius"; Rudowicz and Hui, "Personality"; Hwang, "Filial"; Hwang, "Deep"; Josephine Chinying Lang and Chay Hoon Lee, "Workplace Humor and Organizational Creativity," *International Journal of Human Resource Management* 21, no. 1 (2010): 46–60; Lu, Huang, and Chang, "Confucian"; Ma et al., "Confucian"; Hae-Ae Seo, Eun Ah Lee, and KH Kim, "Korean Science Teachers' Understanding of Creativity in Gifted Education," *Journal of Secondary Gifted Education* 16, no. 2–3 (2005): 98–105.

189. Averill, Chon, and Hahn, "Emotions"; Jessie Ee and Tan Oon Seng, "Cultural Influences of the East and West: Implications on the Educational Reforms in the Singapore Context," *KEDI Journal of Educational Policy* 5, no. 1 (2008): 49–62.

190. Chen and Chung, "Confucianism"; Fan, "Reconsidering"; Herr, "Confucianism"; Hofstede and Bond, "Confucius"; Hwang, "Filial"; Hwang, "Deep "; Kim, "Cultural"; Kim, "Exploring'; Kim et al., "Creativity"; Liu, "Filiality"; Lu, Huang, and Chang, "Confucian"; Ma et al., "Confucian"; Millay and Streeter, "Harmony."

191. Kim, "Developing"; Kim et al., "Creativity"; Liu, "Filiality."

192. Kim et al., "Creativity."

193. Ibid.; Elisabeth Rudowicz and Teresa Ng, "On Ng's Why Asians Are Less Creative Than Westerners," *Creativity Research Journal* 15, no. 2–3 (2003): 301–302; Noriko Saeki, Xitao Fan, and Lani Dusen, "A Comparative Study of Creative Thinking of American and Japanese College Students," *Journal of Creative Behavior* 35, no. 1 (2001): 24–36.

194. Weihua Niu, "Confucian Ideology and Creativity," *Journal of Creative Behavior* 46, no. 4 (2013): 274–84.

195. Cheng-Hsien and Jing-Jyi Wu, "The Structural Relationships between Optimism and Innovative Behavior: Understanding Potential Antecedents and Mediating Effects," *Creativity Research Journal* 23 (2011): 119–28; Weihua Niu, "Development of Creative Research in Chinese Societies: A Comparison of Mainland China, Taiwan, Hong Kong, and Singapore," in *The International Handbook of Creativity*, eds. James C. Kaufman and Robert J. Sternberg (New York: Cambridge, 2006), 374–94; Seo, Lee, and Kim, "Korean."

196. Kim et al., "Creativity"; Ng Aik Kwang and Ian Smith, "The Paradox of Promoting Creativity in the Asian Classroom: An Empirical Investigation," *Genetic, Social, and General Psychology Monographs* 130, no. 4 (2004): 307–32.

197. Chua, *Tiger*.

198. Ibid.

199. Diana Baumrind, "Current Patterns of Parental Authority," *Developmental Psychology Monograph* 4, no. 12 (1971): 1–103.

200. David Brooks, "Amy Chua Is a Wimp," *New York Times*, January 17, 2011, http://www.nytimes.com/2011/01/18/opinion/18brooks.html?_r=0; Annie Murphy Paul, "Tiger Moms: Is Tough Parenting Really the Answer," *Time* 177, no. 4 (2011); Amy Chua, "Why Chinese Mothers Are Superior," *Wall Street Journal*, January 8, 2011, http://online.wsj.com/article/SB10001424052748704111504576059713528698754.html#articleTabs%3Dcomments.

201. Kim, "Learning."

202. Xinyin Chen, Qi Dong, and Hong Zhou, "Authoritative and Authoritarian Parenting Practices and Social and School Performance in Chinese Children," *International Journal of Behavioral Development* 21, no. 4 (1997): 855–73; Zahari Ishak, Suet Fin Low, and Poh Li Lau, "Parenting Style as a Moderator for Students' Academic Achievement," *Journal of Science Education and Technology* 21, no. 4 (2012): 487–93; Kim, "Learning."

203. Kathryn A. Price and Anthea M. Tinker, "Creativity in Later Life," *Maturitas* 78, no. 4 (2014): 281–86; Mark A. Runco, "Creativity," *Annual Review of Psychology* 55 (2004): 657–87; Mark A. Runco and Ruth Richards, eds., *Eminent Creativity, Everyday Creativity, and Health* (Norwood, NJ: Ablex, 1997).

204. Runco, "Creativity"; Dean Keith Simonton, "The Genetics of Giftedness: What Does It Mean to Have Creative Talent?" in *Creatively Gifted Students Are Not Like Other Gifted Students: Research, Theory, and Practice*, eds. KH Kim, James C. Kaufman, John Baer, and Bharath Sriraman (Rotterdam, The Netherlands: Sense, 2013).

Chapter 9: ION Thinking Skills (Inbox, Outbox, and Newbox) within the ACP (Apple-Tree Creative Process)

1. O. E. Ball, and E. Paul Torrance, *Streamlines Scoring Workbook: Figural A* (Bensenville, IL: Scholastic Testing Service, 1984); KH Kim, "Can We Trust Creativity Tests? A Review of the Torrance Tests of Creative Thinking (TTCT)," *Creativity Research Journal* 18, no. 1 (2006): 3–14; KH Kim, "Is Creativity Unidimensional or Multidimensional? Analyses of the Torrance Tests of Creative Thinking," *Creativity Research Journal* 18, no. 3 (2006): 251–59; KH Kim, Bonnie Cramond, and Deborah L. Bandalos, "The Latent Structure and Measurement Invariance of Scores on the Torrance Tests of Creative Thinking—Figural," *Educational and Psychological Measurement* 66, no. 3 (2006): 459–77; Bernard Nijstad et al., "The Dual Pathway to Creativity Model: Creative Ideation as a Function of Flexibility and Persistence," *European Review of Social Psychology* 21, no. 1 (2010): 34–77; Paul B. Paulus, Nicholas W. Kohn, and Lauren E. Arditti, "Effects of Quantity and Quality Instructions on Brainstorming," *Journal of Creative Behavior* 45, no. 1 (2011): 38–46; Paul B. Paulus et al., "Effects of Task Instructions and Brief Breaks on Brainstorming," *Group Dynamics: Theory, Research, and Practice* 10, no. 3 (2006): 206–19; Vicky L. Putman and Paul B. Paulus, "Brainstorming, Brainstorming Rules and Decision Making," *Journal of Creative Behavior* 43, no. 1 (2009): 29–40; Eric F. Rietzschel, Bernard Nijstad, and Wolfgang Stroebe, "Relative Accessibility of Domain Knowledge and Creativity: The Effects of Knowledge Activation on the Quantity and Originality of Generated Ideas," *Journal of Experimental Social Psychology* 43, no. 6 (2007): 933–46; Dean Keith Simonton, "Creativity and Wisdom in Aging," in *Handbook of the Psychology of Aging*, eds. James E. Birren and Klaus Warner Schaie (San Diego, CA: Academic, 1990), 320–29; E. Paul Torrance, *The Search for Satori and Creativity* (Buffalo, NY: Bearly Limited Creative Education

Foundation, 1979); E. Paul Torrance, *Guidelines for Administration and Scoring/Comments on Using the Torrance Tests of Creative Thinking* (Bensenville, IL: Scholastic Testing Services, 1987); E. Paul Torrance, *Creativity: Just Wanting to Know* (Republic of South Africa: Benedic Books, 1994); E. Paul Torrance, *Why Fly? A Philosophy of Creativity* (Norwoord, NJ: Ablex, 1995); E. Paul Torrance, *Research Review for the Torrance Tests of Creative Thinking Figural and Verbal Forms A and B* (Bensenville, IL: Scholastic Testing Services, 2000); E. Paul Torrance and Tammy Safter, *Making the Creative Leap Beyond* (Buffalo, NY: Creative Education Foundation, 1999).

2. Benjamin S. Bloom et al., *Taxonomy of Educational Objectives: The Classification of Educational Goals. Handbook I: Cognitive Domain* (New York: McKay, 1956); Alexandra Cole and Jennifer De Maio, "What We Learned about Our Assessment Program That Has Nothing to Do with Student Learning Outcomes," *Journal of Political Science Education* 5, no. 4 (2009): 294–314; Scott W DeWitt et al., "The Lower-Order Expectations of High-Stakes Tests: A Four-State Analysis of Social Studies Standards and Test Alignment," *Theory and Research in Social Education* 41, no. 3 (2013): 382–427; J. P. Guilford, "Creativity," *American Psychologist* 5 (1950): 444–54; Robert J. Marzano and Arthur L. Costa, "Question: Do Standardized Tests Measure General Cognitive Skills? Answer: No," *Educational Leadership* 45, no. 8 (1988): 66–71; Daniel L. McCollum, "The Deficits of Standardized Tests: Countering the Culture of Easy Numbers," *Assessment Update* 23, no. 2 (2011): 3–5; Kenneth A. Wesson, "The 'Volvo Effect'—Questioning Standardized Tests," *Young Children* 56, no. 2 (2001): 16–18.

3. Mary Ruth Coleman and James J. Gallagher, *Report on State Policies Related to Identification of Gifted Students* (Chapel Hill: University of North Carolina at Chapel Hill, 1992); Margie K. Kitano and Marcia DiJiosia, "Are Asian and Pacific Americans Overrepresented in Programs for the Gifted?" *Roeper Review* 24, no. 2 (2002): 76–80.

4. James C. Kaufman and John Baer, "An Introduction to the Special Issue: A Tribute to E. Paul Torrance," *Creativity Research Journal* 18, no. 1 (2006): 1–2.

5. E. Paul Torrance, *Guiding Creative Talent* (Englewood Cliffs, NJ: Prentice-Hall, 1962); E. Paul Torrance, *Creativity in the Classroom* (Washington, DC: National Education Association, 1977); E. Paul Torrance, *The Manifesto: A Guide to Developing a Creative Career* (West Westport, CT: Ablex, 2002).

6. KH Kim and Joyce VanTassel-Baska, "The Relationship between Creativity and Behavior Problems among Underachievers," *Creativity Research Journal* 22, no. 2 (2010): 185–93.

7. Lewis M. Terman, *Mental and Physical Traits of a Thousand Gifted Children* (Stanford, CA: Stanford University Press, 1925).

8. David H. Feldman, "A Follow-Up of Subjects Scoring above 180 IQ in Terman's Genetic Studies of Genius," *Exceptional Children* 50 (1984): 518–23.

9. Frank Barron, "Creative Vision and Expression in Writing and Painting," in *The Creative Person*, ed. Donald W. MacKinnon (Berkeley: University of California, 1961), 237–51; Jacob Getzels and Philip Jackson, "The Meaning of Giftedness—An Examination of an Expanding Concept," *Phi Delta Kappan* 40, no. 2 (1958): 75–77; Jacob Getzels and Philip Jackson, *Creativity and Intelligence* (New York: Wiley, 1962); Harrison G. Gough, "Studying Creativity by Means of Word Association Tests," *Journal of Applied Psychology* 61, no. 3 (1976): 348–53; J. P. Guilford, *The Nature of Human Intelligence* (New York: McGraw-Hill, 1967); J. P. Guilford and Paul R. Christensen, "The One-Way Relation between Creative Potential and IQ," *Journal of Creative Behavior* 7, no. 4 (1973): 247–52; Donald W. MacKinnon, "Creativity in Architects," in *The Creative Person*, ed. Donald W. MacKinnon (Berkeley: University of California, 1961), 291–320; Donald W. MacKinnon, "Educating for Creativity: A Modern Myth?" in *Education for Creativity*, ed. Paul Heist (Berkeley: University of California, 1967), 1–20; Donald W. MacKinnon, "Educating for Creativity: A Modern Myth?" in *Training Creative Thinking*, eds. Gary Davis and Joseph A. Scott (Melbourne, FL: Krieger, 1978), 194–207; Dean Keith Simonton, *Greatness: Who Makes History and Why* (New York, Guilford, 1994).

10. KH Kim, "Can Only Intelligent People Be Creative? A Meta-Analysis," *Journal of Secondary Gifted Education* 16 (2005): 57–66; KH Kim, "Meta-Analyses of the Relationship of

Creative Achievement to Both IQ and Divergent Thinking Test Scores," *Journal of Creative Behavior* 42, no. 2 (2008): 106–30.

11. David H. Feldman, "The Development of Creativity," in *Handbook of Creativity*, ed. Robert Sternberg (New York: Cambridge University Press, 1999), 169–86.

12. V. L. Dawson et al., "Predicting Creative Behavior: A Reexamination of the Divergence between Traditional and Teacher-Defined Concepts of Creativity," *Creativity Research Journal* 12, no. 1 (1999): 66–78; Howard Gardner, "Giftedness: Speculations from a Biological Perspective," *New Directions for Child and Adolescent Development* 17 (1982): 47–60; H. L. Kaila, "Democratizing Schools across the World to Stop Killing Creativity in Children: An Indian Perspective," *Counseling Psychology Quarterly* 18 (2005): 1–6; Kim, "Crisis; George Land and Beth Jarman, *Breakpoint and Beyond: Mastering the Future—Today* (New York: HarperCollins, 1993); Torrance, *Search*; Torrance and Safter, *Making*.

13. Bloom et al., *Taxonomy*. *Inbox and newbox thinking was modified from Bloom et al.'s *Taxonomy* and synthesized with my research.

14. Torrance, *Search*; Torrance and Safter, *Making*.

15. Guilford, "Creativity"; Jonathan, A. Plucker, "An Introduction to the Special Issue: Commemorating Guilford's 1950 Presidential Address— J. P. Guilford," *Creativity Research Journal* 13, no. 3–4 (2000): 247.

16. J. P. Guilford, "Structure of Intellect," *Psychological Bulletin* 53 (1956), 267–93; J. P. Guilford, *Personality* (New York: McGraw-Hill, 1959); J. P. Guilford, "Basic Conceptual Problems of the Psychology of Thinking," *Proceedings of the New York Academy of Science* 91 (1960): 6–21; Guilford, *Nature*; J. P. Guilford, *Creative Talents: Their Nature, Uses, and Development* (Buffalo, NY: Bearly Limited, 1986); Guilford and Christensen, "One-Way."

17. Yiling Cheng, KH Kim, and Michael F. Hull, "Comparisons of Creative Styles and Personality Types between American and Taiwanese College Students and the Relationship between Creative Potential and Personality Types," *Psychology of Aesthetics, Creativity, and the Arts* 4, no. 2 (2010): 103–12; Kim, "Creativity"; KH Kim, "Which Creativity Tests Can We Use?" *Creativity Research Journal* (in press); Kim, Cramond, and Bandalos, "Latent"; KH Kim et al., "Creativity and Confucianism among American and Korean Educators," *Creativity Research Journal* 23, no. 4 (2011): 357–71; Hangeun Lee and KH Kim, "Can Speaking More Languages Enhance Your Creativity? Relationship between Bilingualism and Creative Potential among Korean American Students with Multicultural Link," *Personality and Individual Differences* 50, no. 8 (2011): 1186–90; Torrance, *Search*; Torrance and Safter, *Making*. *Also, my analyses of the data sets from Kim, "Can Only"; Kim, Meta-Analyses"; Kim, "Crisis."

18. Bloom et al., *Taxonomy*.

19. Ibid.; Cole and De Maio, "Learned"; DeWitt et al., "Lower-Order"; Guilford, "Creativity"; Marzano and Costa, "Question"; McCollum, "Deficits"; Wesson, "'Volvo."

20. K. Anders Ericsson, "Expertise," *Current Biology* 24, no. 11 (2014): 508–10.

21. Bloom et al., *Taxonomy*.

22. Cheng, Kim, and Hull, "Comparisons"; Kim, "Creativity"; Kim, "Which"; Kim, Cramond, and Bandalos, "Latent"; Kim et al., "Creativity"; Lee and Kim, "Speaking"; Torrance, *Search*; Torrance and Safter, *Making*. *Also, my analyses of the data sets from Kim, "Can Only"; Kim, "Meta-Analyses; Kim, "Crisis."

23. Ball and Torrance, *Streamlines*; Torrance, *Search*; Torrance, *Guidelines*; Guilford, "Structure; Guilford, *Personality*; Guilford, "Basic"; Guilford, *Nature*; Guilford, *Talents*; Guilford and Christensen, "One-Way"; Torrance, "Nature"; Torrance, *Manual* (1990); Torrance, *Wanting*; Torrance, *Manual* (1998); Torrance, *Review*; Torrance, *Manifesto*; Torrance and Safter, *Making*.

24. Bloom et al., *Taxonomy*.

25. Robert S. Root-Bernstein and Michele M. Root-Bernstein, *Sparks of Genius: The Thirteen Thinking Tools of the World's Most Creative People* (Boston, MA: Houghton Mifflin, 1999).

26. Robert J. Sternberg and James C. Kaufman, "Constraints on Creativity: Obvious and Not So

Obvious," in *The Cambridge Handbook of Creativity*, eds. James C. Kaufman and Robert J. Sternberg (New York: Cambridge University Press, 2010), 467–82.

27. Colin Martindale et al., "EEG Alpha Asymmetry and Creativity," *Personality and Individual Differences* 5, no. 1 (1984): 77–86; Olga M. Razumnikova, Nina Volf, and Irina Tarasova, "Strategy and Results: Sex Differences in Electrographic Correlates of Verbal and Figural Creativity," *Human Physiology* 35, no. 3 (2009): 285–94.

28. Silvano Arieti, *Creativity: The Magic Synthesis* (Oxford, England: Basic, 1976).

29. Gjurgjica Badzakova-Trajkov, Isabelle S. Häberling, and Michael C. Corballis, "Magical Ideation, Creativity, Handedness, and Cerebral Asymmetries: A Combined Behavioural and fMRI Study," *Neuropsychologia* 49, no. 10 (2011): 2896–2903; Rosa Aurora Chávez-Eakle et al., "Cerebral Blood Flow Associated with Creative Performance: A Comparative Study," *Neuroimage* 38, no. 3 (2007): 519–28; Norbert Jaušovec, "Differences in Cognitive Processes between Gifted, Intelligent, Creative, and Average Individuals while Solving Complex Problems: An EEG Study," *Intelligence* 28, no. 3 (2000): 213–37; Yasuyuki Kowatari et al., "Neural Networks Involved in Artistic Creativity," *Human Brain Mapping* 30, no. 5 (2009): 1678–90; Annukka K. Lindell, "Lateral Thinkers Are Not So Laterally Minded: Hemispheric Asymmetry, Interaction, and Creativity," *Laterality: Asymmetries of Body, Brain and Cognition* 16, no. 4 (2011): 479–98; Elizabeth R. Shobe, Nicholas M. Ross, and Jessica I. Fleck, "Influence of Handedness and Bilateral Eye Movements on Creativity," *Brain and Cognition* 71, no. 3 (2009): 204–14.

30. Arieti, *Creativity*; Lindell, "Lateral"; Shobe, Ross, and Fleck, "Handedness."

31. *The Apple-Tree Creative Process was synthesized from (1) the creative problem solving discussed in Alex F. Osborn, *Applied Imagination: Principles and Procedures of Creative Problem Solving*, 3rd ed. (New York: Scribner's, 1963); (2) Sidney J. Parnes, *Creative Behavior Guidebook* (New York: Charles Scribner's, 1967); and (3) the future problem solving program discussed in Torrance, *Classroom* and in Pansy Torrance et al., *Handbook for Training Future Problem Solving Teams* (Athens: University of Georgia, 1977).

32. Torrance, *Classroom*; Torrance et al., *Handbook*.

33. Ericsson, "Expertise."

34. K. Anders Ericsson, "The Acquisition of Expert Performance: An Introduction to Some of the Issues," in *The Road to Expert Performance: Empirical Evidence from the Arts and Sciences, Sports, and Games* (Mahwah, NJ: Erlbaum, 1996), 1–50; K. Anders Ericsson, Neil Charness, Paul J. Feltovich, and Robert R. Hoffman, eds, *The Cambridge Handbook of Expertise and Expert Performance* (New York: Cambridge University Press, 2006); Howard Gardner, *Creating Minds* (New York: Basic Books, 1993); John R. Hayes, *The Complete Problem Solver* (Hillsdale, NJ: Erlbaum, 1989); Simonton, *Greatness*; Dean Keith Simonton, *Genius 101*, The Psych 101 Series (New York: Springer, 2009); Robert W. Weisberg, *Creativity: Beyond the Myth of Genius* (New York: Freeman, 1993).

35. Pierre Desrochers, "Local Diversity, Human Creativity, and Technological Innovation," *Growth and Change* 32 (2001): 369–94; Howard E. Gruber, *Darwin on Man: A Psychological Study of Scientific Creativity* (Chicago: University of Chicago Press, 1981); Hayes, *Complete*; Brian Knudsen et al., "Density and Creativity in U.S. Regions," *Annals of the Association of American Geographers* 98, no. 2 (2008): 461–78; Michael D. Mumford et al., "Process-Based Measures of Creative Problem-Solving Skills: II. Information Encoding," *Creativity Research Journal* 9, no. 1 (1996): 77–88; Michael D. Mumford et al., "Process-Based Measures of Creative Problem-Solving Skills: III. Category Selection," *Creativity Research Journal* 9, no. 4 (1996): 395–406; Andrea S. Vincent, Brian P. Decker, and Michael D. Mumford, "Divergent Thinking, Intelligence, and Expertise: A Test of Alternative Models," *Creativity Research Journal* 14, no. 2 (2002): 163–78; Weisberg, *Creativity*; Robert W. Weisberg, "Prolegomena to Theories of Insight in Problem Solving: Definition of Terms and a Taxonomy of Problems," in *The Nature of Insight*, eds. Robert J. Sternberg and Janet E. Davidson (Cambridge, MA: MIT Press, 1995), 157–96; Robert W. Weisberg, "Creativity and Knowledge: A Challenge to Theories," in *Handbook of Creativity*, ed. Robert J. Sternberg (Cambridge: Cambridge University Press, 1999), 226–50.

36. Arthur Cropley, "In Praise of Convergent Thinking," *Creativity Research Journal* 18, no. 3 (2006): 391–404; Willard L. White, "Interviews with Child I, Child J, and Child L," *Roeper Review* 12 (1990): 222–27; Vincent, Decker, and Mumford, "Divergent; Chen-Bo Zhong, Ap Dijksterhuis, and Adam D. Galinsky, "The Merits of Unconscious Thought in Creativity," *Psychological Science* 19, no. 9 (2008): 912–18.

37. Ronald A. Finke, Thomas B. Ward, and Steven M. Smith, *Creative Cognition: Theory, Research, and Applications* (Cambridge: Massachusetts Institute of Technology, 1992); Michael D. Mumford et al., "Process Analytic Models of Creative Capacities," *Creativity Research Journal* 4, no. 2 (1991): 91–122; Zhong, Dijksterhuis, and Galinsky, "Merits."

38. Bernard M. Bass, *Leadership and Performance beyond Expectations* (New York: Free Press, 1985); Elliott Jaques, *A General Theory of Bureaucracy* (London: Heinemann, 1977); Michael D. Mumford and Mary Shane Connelly, "Leadership," in *Encyclopedia of Creativity* eds. Mark A. Runco and Steven Pritzker (San Diego, CA: Academic, 1999), 139–46.

39. Mark A. Runco, "The Creativity of Children's Art," *Child Study Journal* 19 (1989): 177–89; Ellen Winner, *Gifted Children: Myths and Realities* (New York: Basic Books, 1996).

40. Saba Ayman-Nolley, "Vygotsky's Perspective on the Development of Imagination and Creativity," *Creativity Research Journal* 5, no. 1 (1992): 77–85; Lev S. Vygotsky, "Imagination and Creativity in Childhood," *Soviet Psychology* 28, no. 1 (1990): 84–96.

41. Ayman-Nolley, "Vygotsky's"; Lev S. Vygotsky, "Imagination and Creativity of the Adolescent," in *The Vygotsky Reader*, eds. Renee Van Der Veer and Jaan Valsiner (Cambridge: Blackwell, 1994), 266–88.

42. Arne Dietrich, "The Cognitive Neuroscience of Creativity," *Psychonomic Bulletin & Review* 11, no. 6 (2004): 1011–26.

43. K. Anders Ericsson, Kiruthiga Nandagopal, and Roy W. Roring, "Giftedness Viewed from the Expert-Performance Perspective," *Journal for the Education of the Gifted* 28, no. 3/4 (2005): 287–311.

44. Ibid

45. Ibid.

46. Betty Hart and Todd R Risley, "The Early Catastrophe: The 30 Million Word Gap," *American Educator* 27, no. 1 (2003): 4–9.

47. Benjamin S. Bloom, *Developing Talent in Young People* (New York: Ballantine Books, 1985); Ericsson, Nandagopal, and Roring, "Giftedness."

48. Ericsson, Nandagopal, and Roring, "Giftedness."

49. Ericsson, "Expertise"; K. Anders Ericsson, Ralf Th. Krampe, and Clemens Tesch-Romer, "The Role of Deliberate Practice in the Acquisition of Expert Performance," *Psychological Review* 100 (1993): 363–406; Ralf Th. Krampe and K. Anders Ericsson, "Maintaining Excellence: Deliberate Practice and Elite Performance in Young and Older Pianists," *Journal of Experimental Psychology: General* 125 (1996): 331–59; Gardner, *Creating*; Hayes, *Complete*; Hebert A. Simon and William G. Chase, "Skill in Chess," *American Scientist* 61(1973): 394–403; Simonton, *Greatness*; Simonton, *101*.

50. Ericsson, Nandagopal, and Roring, "Giftedness"; Edwin A. Locke and Gary P. Latham, *A Theory of Goal Setting and Task Performance* (Englewood Cliffs, NJ: Prentice Hall, 1990); Edwin A. Locke and Gary P. Latham, "Building a Practically Useful Theory of Goal Setting and Task Motivation: A 35-Year Odyssey," *American Psychologist* 57, no. 9 (2002): 705–17.

51. Ericsson, Nandagopal, and Roring, "Giftedness."

52. K. Anders Ericsson, "Basic Capacities Can Be Modified or Circumvented by Deliberate Practice: A Rejection of Talent Accounts of Expert Performance. A Commentary on Michael J. A. Howe, Jane W. Davidson, and John A. Sloboda, 'Innate Talents: Reality or Myth?'" *Behavioral and Brain Sciences* 21 (1998): 413–14; Andreas C. Lehmann and K. Anders Ericsson, "The Historical Development of Domains of Expertise: Performance Standards and Innovations in Music," in *Genius and The Mind: Studies of Creativity and Temperament in the Historical Record*, ed. Andrew Steptoe (New York: Oxford University Press, 1998), 67–94; Ericsson, Krampe, and Tesch-Romer, "Deliberate."

53. Ericsson, Nandagopal, and Roring, "Giftedness."

54. Ericsson, Krampe, and Tesch-Romer, "Deliberate;" Michael J. A. Howe, "Prodigies and Creativity," in *Handbook of Creativity*, ed. Robert J. Sternberg (New York: Cambridge University Press, 1999), 116–33; Runco, "Art"; Simonton, *Greatness*; Dean Keith Simonton, "Creativity and Genius," in *Handbook of Personality: Theory and Research*, eds. Oliver P. John, Richard W. Roberts, and Lawrence A. Pervin (New York: Gilford, 2008), 679–98; Ellen Winner, *Gifted Children: Myths and Realities* (New York: Basic Books, 1996).

55. Ericsson, Nandagopal, and Roring, "Giftedness."

56. Bloom et al., *Taxonomy*.

57. Ibid.; John F. Feldhusen, "The Role of the Knowledge Base in Creative Thinking," in *Creativity and Reason in Cognitive Development*, eds. James C. Kaufman and John Baer (New York: Cambridge University Press, 2006), 137–44; Jocelyn H. Newton and Kevin S. McGrew, "Introduction to the Special Issue: Current Research in Cattell-Horn-Carroll–Based Assessment," *Psychology in the Schools* 47, no. 7 (2010): 621–34.

58. Phillip L. Ackerman, "Individual Differences in Skill Learning: An Integration of Psychometric and Information Processing Perspectives," *Psychological Bulletin* 102 (1987): 3–27; Janet E. Davidson and Robert J. Sternberg, "The Role of Insight in Intellectual Giftedness," *Gifted Child Quarterly* 28 (1984): 58–64; Ronald A. Finke, Thomas B. Ward, and Steven M. Smith, *Creative Cognition: Theory, Research, and Applications* (Cambridge: Massachusetts Institute of Technology, 1992).

59. Bloom et al., *Taxonomy*.

60. Ibid.

61. Ackerman, "Differences"; Davidson and Sternberg, "Insight"; Finke, Ward, and Smith, *Cognition*.

62. Bloom et al., *Taxonomy*.

63. Ackerman, "Differences"; Davidson and Sternberg, "Insight"; Finke, Ward, and Smith, *Cognition*.

64. Vincent, Decker, and Mumford, "Divergent."

65. Mumford et al., "Measures II"; Mumford et al., "Measures III"; Vincent, Decker, and Mumford, "Divergent."

66. Simonton, *Greatness*; Simonton, *101*.

67. Ibid.

68. Ericsson, "Acquisition"; Ericsson et al., *Handbook*; Ericsson, Nandagopal, and Roring, "Giftedness"; Gardner, *Creating*; Hayes, *Complete*; Simonton, *Greatness*; Simonton, *101*.

69. Ericsson, Nandagopal, and Roring, "Giftedness."

70. Ericsson, "Basic"; Ericsson, Krampe, and Tesch-Romer, "Role"; Lehmann and Ericsson, "Historical"; Locke and Latham, *Theory*; Locke and Latham, "Building."

71. Ericsson, Nandagopal, and Roring, "Giftedness"; Elizabeth MacLeod, *Albert Einstein: A Life of a Genius* (Toronto, Canada: Kids Can, 2003).

72. Ericsson, "Acquisition"; Ericsson et al., *Handbook*; Gardner, *Creating*; Hayes, Complete; Simonton, *Greatness*; Simonton, *101*.

73. Ericsson, "Acquisition; Ericsson, Nandagopal, and Roring, "Giftedness."

74. Ibid.

75. Simonton, *Greatness*.

76. Ibid.; Simonton, *101*; Walberg et al., "Childhood Traits and Experiences of Eminent Women," *Creativity Research Journal* 9, no. 1 (1996): 97–102.

77. James Mackay, *Sounds out of Silence: A Life of Alexander Graham Bell* (Edinburgh, EH: Mainstream, 1997).

78. Matthew Josephson, *Edison* (New York: McGraw Hill, 1959).

79. David Herbert Donald, *Lincoln* (New York: Simon and Schuster, 1996).

80. Benjamin Franklin, *Autobiography of Benjamin Franklin with Introduction and Notes* (New York: Macmillan, 1913).

81. Ericsson, Nandagopal, and Roring, "Giftedness."

82. Mark Batey and Adrian Furnham, "Creativity, Intelligence, and Personality: A Critical Review of the Scattered Literature," *Genetic, Social, and General Psychology Monographs* 132, no. 4 (2006): 355–429; Edward De Bono, *New Think: The Use of Lateral Thinking in Generation of New Ideas* (New York: Basic Books, 1968); Guilford, "Creativity"; Arthur Koestler, *The Act of Creation* (New York: Macmillan, 1964); Jonathan W. Schooler and Joseph Melcher, "The Ineffability of Insight," in *The Creative Cognition Approach*, eds. Steven M. Smith, Thomas B. Ward, and Ronald A. Finke (Cambridge: MIT Press, 1995), 97–134; Sternberg and Kaufman, "Constraints."

83. Batey and Furnham, "Creativity"; De Bono, *New*; Guilford, "Creativity"; Koestler, *Act*; Schooler and Melcher, "Ineffability"; Sternberg and Kaufman, "Constraints."

84. Jack A. Goncalo and Barry M. Staw, "Individualism–Collectivism and Group Creativity," *Organizational Behavior and Human Decision Processes* 100, no. 1 (2006): 96–109; Simonton, *Greatness*.

85. Bloom, *Developing*; Ericsson, Nandagopal, and Roring, "Giftedness."

86. Bernstein and Root-Bernstein, *Sparks of Genius*; Twila Z. Tardif and Robert J. Sternberg, "What Do We Know about Creativity?" in *The Nature of Creativity*, ed. Robert J. Sternberg (New York: Cambridge University Press, 1999), 429–40.

87. Bernstein and Root-Bernstein, *Sparks*; Tardif and Sternberg, "Know"; Uzzi Brian Uzzi and Jarrett Spiro, "Collaboration and Creativity: The Small World Problem," *American Journal of Sociology* 111, no. 2 (2005): 447–504.

88. Koestler, *Act*.

89. Ibid.

90. Parnes, *Guidebook*; Torrance, *Classroom*; Torrance, *Search*; Torrance et al., *Handbook*; Torrance and Safter, *Making*.

91. Ibid.

92. Ball and Torrance, *Streamlines*; Torrance, *Search*; Torrance, *Guidelines*; Torrance, "Nature"; Torrance, *Manual* (1990); Torrance, *Wanting*; Torrance, *Manual* (1998); Torrance, *Review*; Torrance, *Manifesto*; Torrance and Safter, *Making*.

93. Ibid.

94. Parnes, *Guidebook*; Torrance, *Classroom*; Torrance, *Search*; Torrance et al., *Handbook*; Torrance and Safter, *Making*.

95. Ball and Torrance, *Streamlines*; Torrance, *Search*; Torrance, *Guidelines*; Guilford, "Structure"; Guilford, *Personality*; Guilford, "Basic"; Guilford, *Nature*; Guilford, *Talents*; Guilford and Christensen, "One-Way"; Torrance, "Nature"; Torrance, *Manual* (1990); Torrance, *Wanting*; Torrance, *Manual* (1998); Torrance, *Review*; Torrance, *Manifesto*; Torrance and Safter, *Making*.

96. Torrance manual, Zhong, Dijksterhuis, and Galinsky, "Merits."

97. Ball and Torrance, *Streamlines*; Kim, "Trust; Kim, "Creativity"; Kim, Cramond, and Bandalos, "Latent"; Nijstad et al., "Dual"; Paulus, Kohn, and Arditti, "Quantity"; Paulus et al., "Instructions"; Putman and Paulus, "Brainstorming"; Rietzschel, Nijstad, and Stroebe, "Accessibility"; Simonton, "Wisdom"; Torrance, *Search*; Torrance, *Guidelines*; Torrance, *Manual* (1990); Torrance, *Wanting*; Torrance, *Fly*; Torrance, *Manual* (1998); Torrance, *Review*; Torrance, *Manifesto*; Torrance and Safter, *Making*.

98. Kathleen Krull, *Albert Einstein*, Giants of Science Series (New York: Viking, 2009).

99. Ball and Torrance, *Streamlines*; Torrance, *Search*; Torrance, *Guidelines*; Guilford, "Structure"; Guilford, *Personality*; Guilford, "Basic"; Guilford, *Nature*; Guilford, *Talents*; Guilford and Christensen, "One-Way"; Torrance, "Nature"; Torrance, *Manual* (1990); Torrance, *Wanting*; Torrance, *Manual* (1998); Torrance, *Review*; Torrance, *Manifesto*; Torrance and Safter, *Making*.

100. Torrance, *Search*; Torrance and Safter, *Making*.

101. Ball and Torrance, *Streamlines*; Torrance, *Search*; Torrance, *Guidelines*; Torrance, "Nature"; Torrance, *Manual* (1990); Torrance, *Wanting*; Torrance, Manual (1998); Torrance, *Review*; Torrance, *Manifesto*; Torrance and Safter, *Making*.

102. Morris I. Stein, *Stimulating Creativity: Individual Procedures* (New York: Academic, 1974).

103. George de Mestral, Alexander Fleming, and Henri Becquerel examples: K. F. Haven *Marvels of Science: 50 Fascinating 5-Minute Reads* (Westport, CT: Libraries Unlimited, 1994); Rothman, *Everything's Relative: And Other Fables from Science and Technology* (New York: Wiley, 2003); T. Stephens, "How a Swiss Invention Hooked the World," 2007, http://www.swissinfo.ch/eng/Home/Archive/How_a_Swiss_invention_hooked_the_world.html?cid=5653568.

104. Ball and Torrance, *Streamlines*; Torrance, *Search*; Torrance, *Guidelines*; Guilford, "Structure"; Guilford, *Personality*; Guilford, "Basic"; Guilford, *Nature*; Guilford, *Talents*; Guilford and Christensen, "One-Way"; Torrance, "Nature"; Torrance, *Manual* (1990); Torrance, *Wanting*; Torrance, *Manual* (1998); Torrance, *Review*; Torrance, *Manifesto*; Torrance and Safter, *Making*.

105. Nijstad et al., "Dual."

106. Ibid.

107. Rietzschel, Nijstad, and Stroebe, "Accessibility."

108. Nijstad et al., "Dual."

109. Koestler, *Act*; Mark A. Runco, "Creativity," *Annual Review of Psychology* 55 (2004): 657–87; Sternberg and Kaufman, "Constraints."

110. Jennifer S. Mueller, Shimul Melwani, and Jack A. Goncalo, "The Bias against Creativity: Why People Desire but Reject Creative Ideas," *Psychological Science* (2012): 13–17; Eric F. Rietzschel, Bernard Nijstad, and Wolfgang Stroebe, "The Selection of Creative Ideas after Individual Idea Generation: Choosing between Creativity and Impact," *British Journal of Psychology* 101, no. 1 (2010): 47–68; Jennifer A. Whitson and Adam D. Galinsky, "Lacking Control Increases Illusory Pattern Perception," *Science* 322, no. 5898 (2008): 115–17.

111. E. Paul Torrance, "A Longitudinal Examination of the Fourth-Grade Slump in Creativity," *Gifted Child Quarterly* 12, no. 4 (1968): 195–99.

112. Christine Charyton and Glenn E. Snelbecker, "Engineers' and Musicians' Choices of Self-Descriptive Adjectives as Potential Indicators of Creativity by Gender and Domain," *Psychology of Aesthetics, Creativity, and the Arts* 1, no. 2 (2007): 91–99; Hans J. Eysenck, *Genius: The Natural History of Creativity* (Cambridge, UK: Cambridge University Press, 1995); Gregory J. Feist, "A Meta-Analysis of Personality in Scientific and Artistic Creativity," *Personality and Social Psychology Review* 2, no. 4 (1998): 290–309; Jacob W. Getzels and Mihaly Csikszentmihalyi, "Scientific Creativity," *Science Journal* 3 (1967): 80–84; Ravenna Helson, Brent Roberts, and Gail Agronick, "Enduringness and Change in Creative Personality and the Prediction of Occupational Creativity," *Journal of Personality and Social Psychology* 69, no. 6 (1995): 1173–83; Anne Roe, *The Making of a Scientist* (New York: Dodd, Mead, 1953).

113. Cheng, Kim, and Hull, "Comparisons"; Kim, "Cultural"; Garnet W. Millar, *E. Paul Torrance: The Creativity Man* (Norwood, NJ: Ablex, 1995); Noriko Saeki, Xitao Fan, and Lani Dusen, "A Comparative Study of Creative Thinking of American and Japanese College Students," *Journal of Creative Behavior* 35, no. 1 (2001): 24–38.

114. Brian Mullen, Craig Johnson, and Eduardo Salas, "Productivity Loss in Brainstorming Groups: A Meta-Analytic Integration," *Basic and Applied Social Psychology* 12, no. 1 (1991): 3–23; Paulus et al., "Instructions"; Paul B. Paulus and Huei-Chuan Yang, "Idea Generation in Groups: A Basis for Creativity in Organizations," *Organizational Behavior and Human Decision Processes* 82, no. 1 (2000): 76–87.

115. Paulus, Kohn, and Arditti, "Quantity"; Paulus et al., "Instructions"; Putman and Paulus, "Brainstorming."

116. L. Mabel Camacho and Paul B. Paulus, "The Role of Social Anxiousness in Group Brainstorming," *Journal of Personality and Social Psychology* 68, no. 6 (1995): 1071–80; Paul B. Paulus and Mary T. Dzindolet, "Social Influence Processes in Group Brainstorming," *Journal of Personality and Social Psychology* 64, no. 4 (1993): 575–86.

117. Paulus and Yang, "Generation."

118. Camacho and Paulus, "Anxiousness"; Michael Diehl and Wolfgang Stroebe, "Productivity

Loss in Brainstorming Groups: Toward the Solution of a Riddle," *Journal of Personality and Social Psychology* 53, no. 3 (1987): 497–509; Osborn, *Applied.*

119. Mullen, Johnson, and Salas, "Productivity"; Paulus et al., "Instructions"; Paulus and Yang, "Generation."

120. Paul B. Paulus, Timothy S. Larey, and Anita H. Ortega, "Performance and Perceptions of Brainstormers in an Organizational Setting," *Basic and Applied Social Psychology* 17, no. 1–2 (1995): 249–65.

121. Adrian Furnham, "The Brainstorming Myth," *Business Strategy Review* 11, no. 4 (2000): 21–28; Nicholas W. Kohn, Paul B. Paulus, and YunHee Choi, "Building on the Ideas of Others: An Examination of the Idea Combination Process," *Journal of Experimental Social Psychology* 47, no. 3 (2011): 554–61; Paulus et al., "Instructions."

122. Knudsen et al., "Density."

123. Ronald S. Burt, "Structural Holes and Good Ideas," *American Journal of Sociology* 110, no. 2 (2004): 349–99; Lee Fleming, Santiago Mingo, and David Chen, "Collaborative Brokerage, Generative Creativity, and Creative Success," *Administrative Science Quarterly* 52, no. 3 (2007): 443–75; Szabolcs Kéri, "Solitary Minds and Social Capital: Latent Inhibition, General Intellectual Functions and Social Network Size Predict Creative Achievements," *Psychology of Aesthetics, Creativity, and the Arts* 5, no. 3 (2011): 215–21; Simon Rodan and Charles Galunic, "More Than Network Structure: How Knowledge Heterogeneity Influences Managerial Performance and Innovativeness," *Strategic Management Journal* 25, no. 6 (2004): 541–62; Manuel E. Sosa, "Where Do Creative Interactions Come From? The Role of Tie Content and Social Networks," *Organization Science* 22, no. 1 (2011): 1–21; Uzzi and Spiro, "Collaboration."

124. Mullen, Johnson, and Salas, "Productivity"; Paulus et al., "Instructions"; Paulus and Yang, "Generation."

125. Solomon E. Asch, "Opinions and Social Pressure," *Scientific American* 193, no. 5 (1955): 31–35.

126. Ball and Torrance, *Streamlines*; Torrance, *Search*; Torrance, *Guidelines*; Torrance, "Nature"; Torrance, *Manual* (1990); Torrance, *Wanting*; Torrance, *Manual* (1998); Torrance, *Review*; Torrance and Safter, *Making*; A. W. White, "The Effects of Movement, Drawing, and Verbal Warm-Up upon the Performance of Fourth Graders on a Figural Test of Creative Thinking," *Dissertation Abstracts International* 37A: 4248 (PhD diss., University of Georgia, 1976).

127. Eric F. Rietzschel, Carsten K. W. De Dreu, and Bernard Nijstad, "Personal Need for Structure and Creative Performance: The Moderating Influence of Fear of Invalidity," *Personality and Social Psychology Bulletin* 33, no. 6 (2007): 855–66.

128. Alan R. Dennis et al., "Process Structuring in Electronic Brainstorming," *Information Systems Research* 7 (1996): 268–77.

129. Rietzschel, De Dreu, and Nijstad, "Need."

130. Hamit Coskun et al., "Cognitive Stimulation and Problem Presentation in Idea-Generating Groups," *Group Dynamics* 4 (2000): 307–29.

131. Nijstad et al., "Dual."

132. Camacho and Paulus, "Anxiousness"; Diehl and Stroebe, "Loss"; Osborn, *Applied*; Paulus and Dzindolet, "Influence." Paulus, Kohn, and Arditti, "Quantity"; Paulus et al., "Instructions"; Paulus and Yang, "Generation"; Putman and Paulus, "Brainstorming."

133. Randy O. Frost et al., "The Dimensions of Perfectionism," *Cognitive Therapy and Research* 14, no. 5 (1990): 449–68; Nicholas T. Gallucci, George Middleton, and Adam Kline, "Perfectionism and Creative Strivings," *Journal of Creative Behavior* 34, no. 2 (2000): 135–41.

134. Osborn, *Applied.*

135. Burt, "Structural"; Fleming, Mingo, and Chen, "Collaborative"; Rodan and Galunic, "More"; Sosa, "Where."

136. Richard Florida, "The Economic Geography of Talent," *Annals of the Association of American Geographers* 92, no. 4 (2002): 743–55; Kéri, "Solitary."

137. Carsten K. W. De Dreu, Fieke Harinck, and Annelies EM Van Vianen, "Conflict and Performance in Groups and Organizations," in *International Review of Industrial and Organizational Psychology*, vol. 11, eds. Cary L. Cooper and Ivan T. Robertson (Chichester, UK: Wiley, 1999), 367–405; Robin Martin and C. M. Noyes, "Minority Influence and Argument Generation," *British Journal of Social Psychology: Special Issue on Minority Influence* 35, ed. Charlan J. Nemeth (1996): 91–103; Frances J. Milliken and Luis L. Martins, "Searching for Common Threads: Understanding the Multiple Effects of Diversity in Organizational Groups," *Academy of Management Review* 21 (1996): 402–33; Gabriel Mugny, *The Power of Minorities* (London: Academic, 1982); Charlan J. Nemeth, "Dissent as Driving Cognition, Attitudes and Judgments," *Social Cognition* 13 (1995): 273–91; Charlan J. Nemeth, "Managing Innovation: When Less Is More," *California Management Review* 40 (1997): 59–74; Charlan J. Nemeth, "Minority Dissent and Its 'Hidden' Benefits," *New Review of Social Psychology* 2 (2003): 11–21; Charlan J. Nemeth, Keith Brown, and John Rogers, "Devil's Advocate vs. Authentic Dissent: Stimulating Quantity and Quality," *European Journal of Social Psychology* 31 (2001): 707–20; Charlan J. Nemeth, "The Liberating Role of Conflict in Group Creativity: A Study in Two Countries," *European Journal of Social Psychology* 34, no. 4 (2004): 365–74; Charlan J. Nemeth and Barry M. Staw, "The Tradeoffs of Social Control and Innovation within Groups and Organizations," in *Advances in Experimental Social Psychology*, vol. 22, ed. Leonard Berkowitz (New York: Academic, 1989), 175–210; Tom Postmes, Russell Spears, and Sezgin Cihangir, "Quality of Decision Making and Group Norms," *Journal of Personality & Social Psychology* 80, no. 6 (2001): 918–30; Linn Van Dyne and Richard Saavedra, "A Naturalistic Minority Influence Experiment: Effects on Divergent Thinking, Conflict, and Originality in Work-Groups," *British Journal of Social Psychology* 35 (1996): 151–68; Katherine Y. Williams and Charles A. O'Reilly III, "Demography and Diversity in Organizations: A Review of 40 Years of Research," *Research in Organizational Behavior* 20 (1998): 77–140.

138. Serge Moscovici, "Towards a Theory of Conversion Behavior," in *Advances in Experimental Social Psychology*, vol. 13, ed. Leonard Berkowitz (San Diego, CA: Academic, 1980), 209–39; Charlan J. Nemeth and Brendan Nemeth-Brown, "Better Than Individuals? The Potential Benefits of Dissent and Diversity for Group Creativity," in *Group Creativity*, eds. Paul B. Paulus and Bernard Nijstad (Oxford: Oxford University Press, 2003), 63–84; Nemeth, "Conflict."

139. Osborn, *Applied*; Paul B. Paulus, V. Brown, and Anita H. Ortega, "Group Creativity," in *Social Creativity*, vol. 2, eds. Ronald E. Purser and Alfonso Montuori (Cresskill, NJ: Hampton, 1999), 151–76; Paulus and Dzindolet, "Influence."

140. De Dreu, Harinck, and Van Vianen, "Conflict"; Karen Leggett Dugosh et al., "Cognitive Stimulation in Brainstorming," *Journal of Personality and Social Psychology* 79, no. 5 (2000): 722–35; Milliken and Martins, "Searching"; Moscovici, "Conversion"; Nemeth, "Dissent"; Nemeth, "Managing"; Nemeth, "Minority"; Nemeth and Nemeth-Brown, "Better"; Nemeth and Staw, "Tradeoffs"; Van Dyne and Saavedra, "Naturalistic"; Williams and O'Reilly, "Demography."

141. Nemeth, "Conflict."

142. Nemeth, Brown, and Rogers, "Devil's."

143. Karen A. Jehn and Elizabeth A. Mannix, "The Dynamic Nature of Conflict: A Longitudinal Study of Intragroup Conflict and Group Performance," *Academy of Management Journal* 44, no. 2 (2001): 238–51; Nemeth, "Conflict."

144. Kohn, Paulus, and Choi, "Building"; Parnes, *Guidebook*; Torrance, *Classroom*; Torrance et al., *Handbook*.

145. Matthijs Baas, Carsten KW De Dreu, and Bernard Nijstad, "A Meta-Analysis of 25 Years of Mood-Creativity Research: Hedonic Tone, Activation, or Regulatory Focus?" *Psychological Bulletin* 134, no. 6 (2008): 779–806; De Dreu, Baas, and Nijstad, "Hedonic"; Jens Förster, Kal Epstude, and Amina Özelsel, "Why Love Has Wings and Sex Not: How Reminders of Love and Sex Influence Creative and Analytic Thinking," *Personality and Social Psychology Bulletin* 35, no. 11 (2009): 1479–91; Alice M. Isen et al., "The Influence of Positive Affect on the Unusualness of Word Associations," *Journal of Personality and Social Psychology* 48, no. 6 (1985): 1413–26; Alice M. Isen, Kimberly A. Daubman, and Gary P. Nowicki, "Positive Affect Facilitates Creative Problem Solving," *Journal*

of Personality and Social Psychology 52, no. 6 (1987): 1122–31; Nijstad et al., "Dual"; Sandra W. Russ, *Affect and Creativity: The Role of Affect and Play in the Creative Process* (Hillsdale, NJ: Erlbaum,1993).

146. F. Gregory Ashby, Alice M. Isen, and A. U. Turken, "A Neuropsychological Theory of Positive Affect and Its Influence on Cognition," *Psychological Review* 106 (1999): 529–50; De Dreu, Baas, and Nijstad, "Hedonic"; Russ, *Affect*.

147. Shelly H. Carson, Jordan B. Peterson, and Daniel M. Higgins, "Decreased Latent Inhibition Is Associated with Increased Creative Achievement in High-Functioning Individuals," *Journal of Personality and Social Psychology* 85 (2003): 499–506; Jonathan D. Cohen, Todd S. Braver, and Joshua W. Brown, "Computational Perspectives on Dopamine Function in Prefrontal Cortex," *Current Opinion in Neurobiology* 12 (2002): 223–29; Dreisbach and Thomas Goschke, "How Positive Affect Modulates Cognitive Control: Reduced Perseveration at the Cost of Increased Distractibility," *Journal of Experimental Psychology: Learning, Memory, and Cognition* 30, no. 2 (2004): 343–53.

148. Dreisbach and Goschke, "Positive."

149. Förster, Epstude, and Özelsel, "Love"; Geir Kaufmann and Suzanne K. Vosburg, "'Paradoxical' Mood Effects on Creative Problem-Solving," *Cognition and Emotion* 11, no. 2 (1997): 151–70.

150. Paul R. Christensen, Joy Paul Guilford, and R. C. Wilson, "Relations of Creative Responses to Working Time and Instructions," *Journal of Experimental Psychology* 53, no. 2 (1957): 82–88; Carsten KW De Dreu et al., "Working Memory Benefits Creative Insight, Musical Improvisation, and Original Ideation through Maintained Task-Focused Attention," *Personality and Social Psychology Bulletin* 38, no. 5 (2012): 656–69; Osborn, *Applied*; L. Sidney J. Parnes, "Effects of Extended Effort in Creative Problem Solving," *Journal of Educational Psychology* 52, no. 3 (1961): 117–22; Paulus, Kohn, and Arditti, "Quantity"; Paulus et al., "Instructions"; Putman and Paulus, "Brainstorming."

151. Ap Dijksterhuis and Teun Meurs, "Where Creativity Resides: The Generative Power of Unconscious Thought," *Consciousness and Cognition* 15, no. 1 (2006): 135–46; Ap Dijksterhuis and Loran F. Nordgren, "A Theory of Unconscious Thought," *Perspectives on Psychological Science* 1, no. 2 (2006): 95–109.

152. Ibid.; Koestler, *Act*; Laura J. Kray, Adam D. Galinsky, and Elaine M. Wong, "Thinking within the Box: The Relational Processing Style Elicited by Counterfactual Mind-Sets," *Journal of Personality and Social Psychology* 91, no. 1 (2006): 33–48; Schooler and Melcher, "Ineffability"; Thomas B. Ward, "Structured Imagination: The Role of Category Structure in Exemplar Generation," *Cognitive Psychology* 27, no. 1 (1994): 1–40; Zhong, Dijksterhuis, and Galinsky, "Merits."

153. Dijksterhuis and Meurs, "Where"; Dijksterhuis and Nordgren, "Unconscious"; Koestler, *Act*; Kray, Galinsky, and Wong, "Thinking"; Schooler and Melcher, "Ineffability"; Steven M. Smith and Steven E. Blankenship, "Incubation Effects," *Bulletin of the Psychonomic Society* 27, no. 4 (1989): 311–14; Ward, "Imagination."

154. Ibid.

155. Mihaly Csikszentmihalyi, *The Evolving Self* (New York: HarperCollins, 1993); Koestler, *Act*; Arthur I. Miller, *Insights of Genius* (New York: Springer, 1996); Simonton, *Greatness*; Dean Keith Simonton, "Significant Samples: The Psychological Study of Eminent Individuals," *Psychological Methods* 4, no. 4 (1999): 425–51; Torrance, *Fly*.

156. Sarnoff Mednick, "The Associative Basis of the Creative Process," *Psychological Review* 69, no. 3 (1962): 220–32.

157. Dijksterhuis and Meurs, "Where"; Dijksterhuis and Nordgren, "Unconscious"; Koestler, *Act*; Kray, Galinsky, and Wong, "Thinking"; Schooler and Melcher, "Ineffability"; Smith and Blankenship, "Incubation"; Todd M. Thrash et al., "Mediating between the Muse and the Masses: Inspiration and the Actualization of Creative Ideas," *Journal of Personality and Social Psychology* 98, no. 3 (2010): 469–87.

158. Ball and Torrance, *Streamlines*; Jaušovec, "Differences"; Kowatari et al., "Neural"; Lindell, "Lateral"; Shobe, Ross, and Fleck, "Handedness"; David J. Sill, "Integrative Thinking, Synthesis, and

Creativity in Interdisciplinary Studies," *Journal of General Education* 50, no. 4 (2001): 288–311; Torrance, *Search*; Torrance, *Guidelines*; Torrance, "Nature"; Torrance, *Manual* (1990); Torrance, *Wanting*; Torrance, *Manual* (1998); Torrance, *Review*; Torrance and Safter, *Making*.

159. Ball and Torrance, *Streamlines*; Jaušovec, "Differences"; Kowatari et al., "Neural"; Lindell, "Lateral"; Shobe, Ross, and Fleck, "Handedness"; Sill, "Integrative"; Torrance, *Search*; Torrance, *Guidelines*; Torrance, "Nature"; Torrance, *Manual* (1990); Torrance, *Wanting*; Torrance, *Manual* (1998); Torrance, *Review*; Torrance and Safter, *Making*.

160. Benjamin Baird et al., "Inspired by Distraction: Mind Wandering Facilitates Creative Incubation," *Psychological Science* 23, no. 10 (2012): 1117–22; De Dreu, Baas, and Nijstad, "Hedonic"; Dijksterhuis and Meurs, "Where"; Dijksterhuis and Nordgren, "Unconscious"; Koestler, *Act*; Kounios and Beeman, "Aha!"; Ut Na Sio and Thomas C. Ormerod, "Does Incubation Enhance Problem Solving? A Meta-Analytic Review," *Psychological Bulletin* 135, no. 1 (2009): 94–120; Jonathan Smallwood, "Mind-Wandering while Reading: Attentional Decoupling, Mindless Reading and the Cascade Model of Inattention," *Language and Linguistics Compass* 5, no. 2 (2011): 63–77; Jonathan Smallwood and Jonathan W. Schooler, "The Restless Mind," *Psychological Bulletin* 132, no. 6 (2006): 946–58; Zhong, Dijksterhuis, and Galinsky, "Merits."

161. Rosa Aurora Chávez-Eakle, "On the Neurobiology of the Creative Process," *Bulletin of Psychology and the Arts* 5, no. 1 (2004): 29–35; Koestler, *Act*.

162. Albert Bandura, *Self-Efficacy: The Exercise of Control* (New York: Freeman, 1997); Thrash et al., "Mediating."

163. Colin Martindale, "Biological Based of Creativity," in *Handbook of Creativity*, ed. Robert J. Sternberg (New York: Cambridge University Press, 1999), 137–52.

164. Dijksterhuis and Meurs, "Where"; Kounios and Beeman, "Aha!"; Schooler and Melcher, "Ineffability"; Karuna Subramaniam et al., "A Brain Mechanism for Facilitation of Insight by Positive Affect," *Journal of Cognitive Neuroscience* 21, no. 3 (2009): 415–32; Thrash et al., "Mediating."

165. Carson, Peterson, and Higgins, "Decreased"; De Dreu et al., "Memory"; Koestler, *Act*; Dijksterhuis and Meurs, "Where"; Dijksterhuis and Nordgren, "Unconscious"; Koestler, *Act*; Kray, Galinsky, and Wong, "Thinking"; Martindale, "Biological"; Nijstad et al., "Dual"; Jordan B. Peterson, Kathleen W. Smith, and Shelley Carson, "Openness and Extraversion Are Associated with Reduced Latent Inhibition: Replication and Commentary," *Personality and Individual Differences* 33 (2002): 1137–47; Schooler and Melcher, "Ineffability"; Smith and Blankenship, "Incubation"; Ward, "Imagination."

166. Benjamin Baird, Jonathan Smallwood, and Jonathan W. Schooler, "Back to the Future: Autobiographical Planning and the Functionality of Mind-Wandering," *Consciousness and Cognition* 20, no. 4 (2011): 1604–11; Jennifer C. McVay and Michael J. Kane, "Does Mind Wandering Reflect Executive Function or Executive Failure? Comment on Smallwood and Schooler (2006) and Watkins (2008)," *Psychological Bulletin* 136, no. 2 (2010): 188–97; Benjamin W. Mooneyham and Jonathan W. Schooler, "The Costs and Benefits of Mind-Wandering: A Review," *Canadian Journal of Experimental Psychology/Revue canadienne de psychologie expérimentale* 67, no. 1 (2013): 11–18; Jerome Singer and John S. Antrobus, "A Factor-Analytic Study of Daydreaming and Conceptually-Related Cognitive and Personality Variables (Monograph Supplement 3)," *Perceptual and Motor Skills* 17, no. 1 (1963): 187–209.

167. Baird et al., "Inspired"; Sio and Ormerod, "Incubation"; Smallwood, "Reading"; Smallwood and Schooler, "Restless," 946–58.

168. Baird et al., "Inspired"; Dijksterhuis and Meurs, "Where"; Dijksterhuis and Nordgren, "Unconscious"; 95–109; Simonton, "Samples"; Jerome Singer and Vivian G. McCraven, "Some Characteristics of Adult Daydreaming," *Journal of Psychology* 51, no. 1 (1961): 151–64.

169. Şenol Beşoluk, "Morningness–Eveningness Preferences and University Entrance Examination Scores of High School Students," *Personality and Individual Differences* 50, no. 2 (2011): 248–52; Senol Besoluk, İsmail Önder, and İsa Deveci, "Morningness–Eveningness Preferences and Academic Achievement of University Students," *Chronobiology International* 28, no. 2 (2011):

118–25; Markku Koskenvuo et al., "Heritability of Diurnal Type: A Nationwide Study of 8753 Adult Twin Pairs," *Journal of Sleep Research* 16, no. 2 (2007): 156–62.

170. De Dreu et al., "Memory"; Koestler, *Act*; Kounios and Beeman, "Aha!"; Sill, "Integrative"; Ullrich Wagner et al., "Sleep Inspires Insight," *Nature* 427, no. 6972 (2004): 352–55.

171. Ibid.

172. Nijstad et al., "Dual."

173. Dietrich, "Neuroscience."

174. Nijstad et al., "Dual."

175. Dietrich, "Neuroscience"; Rietzschel, De Dreu, and Nijstad, "Need"; Rietzschel, Nijstad, and Stroebe, "Accessibility."

176. Ibid.

177. Keith J. Holyoak and Paul Thagard, "The Analogical Mind," *American Psychologist* 52, no. 1 (1997): 35–44; Sternberg and Kaufman, "Constraints."

178. Nijstad et al., "Dual."

179. Bloom et al., *Taxonomy*.

180. Tardif and Sternberg, "Know";

181. Dreisbach and Goschke, "Positive"; Dietrich, "Neuroscience"; Severine Koch, Rob W. Holland, and Ad Van Knippenberg, "Regulating Cognitive Control through Approach-Avoidance Motor Actions," *Cognition* 109 (2008): 133–42.

182. Dreisbach and Goschke, "Positive"; Koch, Holland, and Van Knippenberg, "Control."

183. Kaufmann and Vosburg, "Paradoxical"; Nijstad et al., "Dual."

184. Kaufmann and Vosburg, "Paradoxical."

185. Andrea Abele-Brehm, "Positive and Negative Mood Influences on Creativity: Evidence for Asymmetrical Effects," *Polish Psychological Bulletin* 23 (1992): 203–21; Kaufmann and Vosburg, "Paradoxical"; Vosburg, "Positive"; Nijstad et al., "Dual."

186. Abele-Brehm, "Mood"; Baas, De Dreu, and Nijstad, "Meta-Analysis"; Kaufmann and Vosburg, "Paradoxical"; Vosburg, "Positive."

187. Roshan Cools, "Role of Dopamine in the Motivational and Cognitive Control of Behavior," *Neuroscientist* 4 (2008): 381–95; Dreisbach and Goschke, "Positive"; Gesine Dreisbach et al., "Dopamine and Cognitive Control: The Influence of Spontaneous Eyeblink Rate and Dopamine Gene Polymorphisms on Perseveration and Distractibility," *Behavioral Neuroscience* 119 (2005): 483–90; Johannes Muller et al., "Dopamine and Cognitive Control: The Prospect of Monetary Gains Influences the Balance between Flexibility and Stability in a Set-Shifting Paradigm," *European Journal of Neuroscience* 26 (2007): 3661–68; Nijstad et al., "Dual."

188. Newton and McGrew, "Special"; Torrance, *Classroom*;; Torrance et al., *Handbook.*

189. *Ibid.*

190. Torrance, *Classroom*; Torrance et al., *Handbook.*

191. Sternberg and Kaufman, "Constraints"; Ball and Torrance, *Streamlines*; Torrance, *Search*; Torrance, *Guidelines*; Torrance, "Nature"; Torrance, *Manual* (1990); Torrance, *Wanting*; Torrance, *Manual* (1998); Torrance, *Review*; Torrance and Safter, *Making.*

192. Ball and Torrance, *Streamlines*; Torrance, *Search*; Torrance, *Guidelines*; Torrance, "Nature"; Torrance, *Manual* (1990); Torrance, *Wanting*; Torrance, *Manual* (1998); Torrance, *Review*; Torrance and Safter, *Making.*

193. Root-Bernstein and Root-Bernstein, *Sparks.*

194. Kevin Brown, *Reflections on Relativity* (New York: MathPages, 2015).

195. Ball and Torrance, *Streamlines*; Torrance, *Search*; Torrance, *Guidelines*; Torrance, "Nature"; Torrance, *Manual* (1990); Torrance, *Wanting*; Torrance, *Manual* (1998); Torrance, *Review*; Torrance and Safter, *Making.*

196. Ronald A. Finke, "Creative Insight and Preinventive Forms," in *The Nature of Insight*, eds. Robert J. Sternberg and Janet E. Davidson (Cambridge, MA: MIT Press, 1995), 225–80; Kentaro Fujita et al., "Spatial Distance and Mental Construal of Social Events," *Psychological Science* 17, no. 4

(2006): 278–82; Lile Jia, Edward R. Hirt, and Samuel C. Karpen, "Lessons from a Faraway Land: The Effect of Spatial Distance on Creative Cognition," *Journal of Experimental Social Psychology* 45, no. 5 (2009): 1127–31; Nira Liberman, Yaacov Trope, and Cheryl Wakslak, "Construal Level Theory and Consumer Behavior," *Journal of Consumer Psychology* 17, no. 2 (2007): 113–17; Ido Liviatan, Yaacov Trope, and Nira Liberman, "Interpersonal Similarity as a Social Distance Dimension: Implications for Perception of Others' Actions," *Journal of Experimental Social Psychology* 44, no. 5 (2008): 1256–69; Evan Polman and Kyle J. Emich, "Decisions for Others Are More Creative Than Decisions for the Self," *Personality and Social Psychology Bulletin* 37 (2001): 492–501; Emily Pronin and Lee Ross, "Temporal Differences in Trait Self-Ascription: When the Self Is Seen as an Other," *Journal of Personality and Social Psychology* 90, no. 2 (2006): 197–209; Cheryl J. Wakslak et al., "Representations of the Self in the Near and Distant Future," *Journal of Personality and Social Psychology 95, no. 4 (2008)*: 757–73; Thomas B. Ward, "What's Old about New Ideas?" in *The Creative Cognition Approach*, eds. Steven M. Smith, Thomas B. Ward, and Ronald A. Finke (Cambridge, MA: MIT Press, 1995), 157–78.

197. Nijstad et al., "Dual."

198. Robert Root-Bernstein et al., "Arts Foster Scientific Success: Avocations of Nobel, National Academy, Royal Society, and Sigma Xi Members," *Journal of Psychology of Science and Technology* 1 no. 2 (2008): 51–63.

199. Ball and Torrance, *Streamlines*; Torrance, *Search*; Torrance, *Guidelines*; Torrance, "Nature"; Torrance, *Manual* (1990); Torrance, *Wanting*; Torrance, *Manual* (1998); Torrance, *Review*; Torrance and Safter, *Making*.

200. Miller, *Albert Einstein's Special Theory of Relativity: Emergence (1905) and Early Interpretation (1905–1911)* (Reading, MA: Addison-Wesley, 1981); Arthur I. Miller, "Scientific Creativity: A Comparative Study of Henri Poincaré and Albert Einstein," *Creativity Research Journal* 5, no. 4 (1992): 385–418; Rhona A. Ochse, *Before the Gates of Excellence: The Determinants of Creative Genius* (Cambridge, UK: Cambridge University Press, 1990); Albert Rothenberg, "The Janusian Process in Scientific Creativity," *Creativity Research Journal* 9, no. 2–3 (1996): 207–31; Robert S. Root-Bernstein, "Music, Creativity and Scientific Thinking," *Leonardo* 34, no. 1 (2001): 63–68; Robert S. Root-Bernstein, "The Art of Innovation: Polymaths and Universality of the Creative Process," in *The International Handbook of Innovation*, ed. Larisa Shavinina (Danvers, MA: Elsvier, 2003), 267–78; Robert S. Root-Bernstein, "Multiple Giftedness in Adults: The Case of Polymathy," in *The Handbook on Giftedness*, ed. Larisa Shavinina (New York: Springer Science, 2008), 853–70; Root-Bernstein and Root-Bernstein, *Sparks of Genius*; Robert S. Root-Bernstein and Michele M. Root-Bernstein, "Artistic Scientists and Scientific Artists: The Link between Polymathy and Creativity," in *Creativity: From Potential to Realization*, eds. Robert J. Sternberg, Elena L. Grigorenko, and Jerome Singer (Washington, DC: American Psychological Association, 2004), 127–51; Larisa Shavinina, "Explaining High Abilities of Nobel Laureates," *High Ability Studies* 15, no. 2 (2004): 243–54; Lewis Wolpert and Alison Richards, eds., *Passionate Minds* (Oxford, UK: Oxford University Press, 1997); Harriet Zuckerman, "The Scientific Elite: Nobel Laureates' Mutual Influences," in *Genius and Eminence*, ed. Robert S. Albert (Oxford, UK: Pergamon, 1983).

201. Miller, *Einstein's*; Miller, "Scientific"; Ochse, *Excellence*; Rothenberg, "Janusian"; Root-Bernstein, "Music"; Root-Bernstein, "Art"; Root-Bernstein, "Multiple"; Root-Bernstein and Root-Bernstein, *Sparks*; Root-Bernstein and Root-Bernstein, "Artistic"; Shavinina, "Explaining"; Wolpert and Richards, *Passionate*; Zuckerman, "Scientific."

202. Ball and Torrance, *Streamlines*; Torrance, *Search*; Torrance, *Guidelines*; Torrance, "Nature"; Torrance, *Manual* (1990); Torrance, *Wanting*; Torrance, *Manual* (1998); Torrance, *Review*; Torrance and Safter, *Making*.

203. Ibid.; Tardif and Sternberg, "Know."

204. Root-Bernstein and Root-Bernstein, *Sparks*; Ball and Torrance, *Streamlines*; Torrance, *Search*; Torrance, *Guidelines*; Torrance, "Nature"; Torrance, *Manual* (1990); Torrance, *Wanting*; Torrance, *Manual* (1998); Torrance, *Review*; Torrance and Safter, *Making*.

205. Crystal Gibson, Bradley S. Folley, and Sohee Park, "Enhanced Divergent Thinking and

Creativity in Musicians: A Behavioral and Near-Infrared Spectroscopy Study," *Brain and Cognition* 69, no. 1 (2009): 162–69; Jay Woodward and Paul L. Sikes, "The Creative Thinking Ability of Musicians and Nonmusicians," *Psychology of Aesthetics, Creativity, and the Arts* 9, no. 1 (2015) 75–80.

206. Jacob Getzels and Mihaly Csikszentmihalyi, *Creative Thinking in Art Students: An Exploratory Study* (Chicago: University of Chicago Press, 1964).

207. Ball and Torrance, *Streamlines*; Torrance, *Search*; Torrance, *Guidelines*; Torrance, "Nature"; Torrance, *Manual* (1990); Torrance, *Wanting*; Torrance, *Manual* (1998); Torrance, *Review*; Torrance and Safter, *Making*.

208. Bernstein and Root-Bernstein, *Sparks*.

209. Rothenberg, "Janusian."

210. Dean Keith Simonton, "The Genetics of Giftedness: What Does It Mean to Have Creative Talent?" in *Creatively Gifted Students Are Not Like Other Gifted Students: Research, Theory, and Practice*, eds. KH Kim, James C. Kaufman, John Baer, and Bharath Sriraman (Rotterdam, The Netherlands: Sense, 2013).

211. Ball and Torrance, *Streamlines*; Torrance, *Search*; Torrance, *Guidelines*; Torrance, "Nature"; Torrance, *Manual* (1990); Torrance, *Wanting*; Torrance, *Manual* (1998); Torrance, *Review*; Torrance and Safter, *Making*.

212. Tardif and Sternberg, "Know."

213. George Lakoff and Mark Johnson, *Philosophy in the Flesh: The Embodied Mind and Its Challenge to Western Thought* (New York: Basic Books, 1999); Barbara J. Phillips and Edward F. McQuarrie, "Impact of Advertising Metaphor on Consumer Belief: Delineating the Contribution of Comparison versus Deviation Factors," *Journal of Advertising* 38, no. 1 (2009): 49–61.

214. Alex Marin, Martin Reimann, and Raquel Castaño, "Metaphors and Creativity: Direct, Moderating, and Mediating Effects," *Journal of Consumer Psychology* 24, no. 2 (2013): 290–97; Alexander M. Rapp et al., "Neural Correlates of Metaphor Processing," *Cognitive Brain Research* 20, no. 3 (2004): 395–402.

215. Lakoff and Johnson, *Philosophy*; Phillips and McQuarrie, "Impact."

216. Chun-Tuan Chang and Ching-Ting Yen, "Missing Ingredients in Metaphor Advertising: The Right Formula of Metaphor Type, Product Type, and Need for Cognition," *Journal of Advertising* 42, no. 1 (2013): 80–94.

217. Lakoff and Johnson, *Philosophy*; Phillips and McQuarrie, "Impact."

218. Chang and Yen, "Missing."

219. Ball and Torrance, *Streamlines*; Tardif and Sternberg, "Know"; Torrance, *Search*; Torrance, *Guidelines*; Torrance, "Nature"; Torrance, *Manual* (1990); Torrance, *Wanting*; Torrance, *Manual* (1998); Torrance, *Review*; Torrance and Safter, *Making*.

220. Ibid.; Kim, "Which"; Razumnikova, Volf, and Tarasova, "Strategy"; Root-Bernstein and Root-Bernstein, *Sparks*.

221. Ball and Torrance, *Streamlines*; Torrance, *Search*; Torrance, *Guidelines*; Torrance, "Nature," 43–75; Torrance, *Manual* (1990); Torrance, *Wanting*; Torrance, *Manual* (1998); Torrance, *Research Review*; Torrance and Safter, *Making the Creative Leap*.

222. Betty Edwards, *Drawing on the Artists Within* (New York: Simon and Schuster, 1986); Root-Bernstein and Root-Bernstein, *Sparks of Genius*.

223. Simonton, *Greatness*; Ball and Torrance, *Streamlines*; Torrance, *Search*; Torrance, *Guidelines*; Torrance, "Nature"; Torrance, *Manual* (1990); Torrance, *Wanting*; Torrance, *Manual* (1998); Torrance, *Review*; Torrance and Safter, *Making*.

224. Angela K.-Y. Leung et al., "Embodied Metaphors and Creative 'Acts,'" *Psychological Science* 23, no. 5 (2012): 502–509.

225. Leung et al., "Embodied"; Torrance, *Search*; Torrance and Safter, *Making*.

226. Ball and Torrance, *Streamlines*; Torrance, *Search*; Torrance, *Guidelines*; Torrance, "Nature"; Torrance, *Manual* (1990); Torrance, *Wanting*; Torrance, *Manual* (1998); Torrance, *Review*; Torrance and Safter, *Making*.

227. Ibid.

228. Bloom, *Developing*; Oya Gürdal Tamdogon, "Creativity in Education: Clearness in Perception, Vigorousness in Curiosity," *Education for Information* 24, no. 2 (2006): 139–51; Torrance, *Search*; Torrance and Safter, *Making*.

229. Walter Isaacson, *Steve Jobs* (New York: Simon and Schuster, 2011).

230. Chávez-Eakle, "Neurobiology"; Ball and Torrance, *Streamlines*; Torrance, *Search*; Torrance, *Guidelines*; Torrance, "Nature"; Torrance, *Manual* (1990); Torrance, *Wanting*; Torrance, *Manual* (1998); Torrance, *Review*; Torrance and Safter, *Making*.

231. Jack A. Chambers, "Relating Personality and Biographical Factors to Scientific Creativity," *Psychological Monographs: General and Applied* 78, no. 7 (1964): 1–20; Ericsson et al., *Handbook*; Hayes, Complete; Simonton, *Greatness*; Simonton, *101*.

232. Cheng, Kim, and Hull, "Comparisons"; Kim, "Is Creativity"; Kim, "Developing"; Kim, Cramond, and Bandalos, "Latent"; Kim et al., "Creativity"; Lee and Kim, "Speaking"; Razumnikova, Volf, and Tarasova, "Strategy."

233. Torrance, *Search*; Torrance and Safter, *Making the Creative Leap*.

234. Ball and Torrance, *Streamlines*; Cools, "Role"; Dreisbach and Goschke, "Positive"; Dreisbach et al., "Dopamine"; Muller et al., "Dopamine"; Nijstad et al., "Dual"; Torrance, *Search*; Torrance, *Guidelines*; Torrance, "Nature"; Torrance, *Manual* (1990); Torrance, *Wanting*; Torrance, *Manual* (1998); Torrance, *Review*; Torrance and Safter, *Making*.

235. Cools, "Role"; Dreisbach and Goschke, "Positive"; Dreisbach et al., "Dopamine"; Muller et al., "Dopamine"; Nijstad et al., "Dual."

236. Dreisbach and Goschke, "Positive."

237. Cools, "Role"; Dreisbach and Goschke, "Positive"; Dreisbach et al., "Dopamine"; Muller ct al., "Dopamine"; Nijstad et al., "Dual."

238. Vincent, Decker, and Mumford, "Divergent."

239. Ball and Torrance, *Streamlines*; Torrance, *Search*; Torrance, *Guidelines*; Torrance, "Nature"; Torrance, *Manual* (1990); Torrance, *Wanting*; Torrance, *Manual* (1998); Torrance, *Review*; Torrance and Safter, *Making*.

240. Isaacson, *Jobs*.

241. Walter Isaacson, *Einstein: His Life and Universe* (New York: Simon and Schuster, 2007).

242. Chávez-Eakle, "Neurobiology."

243. Stacy R. Finkelstein and Ayelet Fishbach, "Tell Me What I Did Wrong: Experts Seek and Respond to Negative Feedback," *Journal of Consumer Research* 39, no. 1 (2012): 22–38; Kéri, "Solitary."

244. Dijksterhuis and Meurs, "Where"; Torrance, *Search*; Torrance and Safter, *Making*.

245. Miller, *Einstein's*; Miller, "Scientific"; Muller et al., "Dopamine"; Ochse, *Excellence*; Rothenberg, "Janusian"; Root-Bernstein, "Art"; Lev S. Vygotsky, "The Development of Imagination in Childhood," in *The Collected Works of L. S. Vygotsky*, vol. 2, eds. Robert W. Rieber and Aaron S. Carto, trans. Norris Minick (New York: Plenum, 1987).

246. Ball and Torrance, *Streamlines*; Torrance, *Search*; Torrance, *Guidelines*; Torrance, "Nature"; Torrance, *Manual* (1990); Torrance, *Wanting*; Torrance, *Manual* (1998); Torrance, *Review*; Torrance and Safter, *Making*.

247. Isaacson, *Jobs*.

248. Jan Garden Castro, *The Art and Life of Georgia O'Keeffe* (New York: Crown, 1985).

249. Nelson Mandela, *Long Walk to Freedom: The Autobiography of Nelson Mandela* (New York: Little, Brown, 1994).

250. Anthony Sampson, *Mandela: The Authorized Biography* (New York: Vintage Books, 1999).

251. Isaacson, *Einstein*; Krull, *Einstein*.

252. Brown, *Reflections*; Isaacson, *Einstein*; Tardif and Sternberg, "Know."

253. Freeman J. Dyson, "The Radiation Theories of Tomonaga, Schwinger, and Feynman," *Physical Review* 75, no. 3 (1949): 486–582; Freeman J. Dyson, "The S Matrix in Quantum Electrodynamics," *Physical Review* 75, no. 11 (1949): 1736–75.

254. Kendall Haven, *Marvels of Science: 50 Fascinating 5-Minute Reads* (Westport, CT: Libraries Unlimited, 1994); Simonton, *Greatness*; Simonton, *101*; Tardif and Sternberg, "Know."

255. Richard Florida, "Bohemia and Economic Geography," *Journal of Economic Geography* 2 (2002): 55–71; Florida, "Economic"; Richard Florida, *The Rise of the Creative Class: And How It's Transforming Work, Leisure, and Everyday Life* (New York: Basic Books, 2002); AnnaLee Saxenian, *Silicon Valley's New Immigrant Entrepreneurs: Skills, Networks, and Careers* (Berkeley: University of California at Berkeley, Public Policy Institute of California, 1999); Scott Andrew Shane, *General Theory of Entrepreneurship: The Individual-Opportunity Nexus* (Northampton, NY: Edward Elgar, 2003); Kay Slama, "Rural Culture Is a Diversity Issue," *Minnesota Psychologist* 1 (2004): 9–13; Pascal Zachary, *The Global Me: New Cosmopolitans and the Competitive Edge—Picking Globalism's Winners and Losers* (New York: Perseus Books, 2000).

256. Ball and Torrance, *Streamlines*; Tardif and Sternberg, "Know"; Torrance, *Search*; Torrance, *Guidelines*; Torrance, "Nature"; Torrance, *Manual* (1990); Torrance, *Wanting*; *Torrance, Manual* (1998); Torrance, *Review*; Torrance and Safter, *Making*.

257. Ball and Torrance, *Streamlines*; Torrance, *Search*; Torrance, *Guidelines*; Torrance, "Nature"; Torrance, *Manual* (1990); Torrance, *Wanting*; Torrance, *Manual* (1998); Torrance, *Review*; Torrance and Safter, *Making*.

258. Eysenck, *Genius*; Feist, "Meta-Analysis"; Tardif and Sternberg, "Know"; Torrance, *Search*.

259. Chambers, "Relating"; Mihaly Csikszentmihalyi, *Flow: The Psychology of Optimal Experience* (New York: Harper and Row, 1990); Hans J. Eysenck, "Creativity and Personality: Suggestions for a Theory," *Psychological Inquiry* 4 (1993): 147–78; Feist, "Meta-Analysis"; Roe, *Making*; Simonton, *Greatness*.

260. Fariborz Damanpour, "Organizational Innovation: A Meta-Analysis of Effects of Determinants and Moderators," *Academy of Management Journal* 34, no. 3 (1991): 555–90; David A. Gilliam and Karen E. Flaherty, "Storytelling by the Sales Force and Its Effect on Buyer–Seller Exchange," *Industrial Marketing Management* 46 (2015): 132–42; Anna S. Mattila, "The Role of Narratives in the Advertising of Experiential Services," *Journal of Service Research* 3 (2000): 35–45; Dan Padgett and Douglas Allen, "Communicating Experiences: A Narrative Approach to Creating Service Brand Image," *Journal of Advertising* 26 (1997): 49–62.

261. Karl Albrecht, *Executive Tune-Up: Personal Effectiveness Skills for Business and Professional People* (Englewood Cliffs, NJ: Prentice-Hall, 1980); William F. Chaplin et al., "Handshaking, Gender, Personality, and First Impressions," *Journal of Personality and Social Psychology* 79, no. 1 (2000): 110–17; William W. Maddux, Elizabeth Mullen, and Adam D. Galinsky, "Chameleons Bake Bigger Pies and Take Bigger Pieces: Strategic Behavioral Mimicry Facilitates Negotiation Outcomes," *Journal of Experimental Social Psychology* 44, no. 2 (2008): 461–68; Greg L. Stewart et al., "Exploring the Handshake in Employment Interviews," *Journal of Applied Psychology* 93, no. 5 (2008): 1139–46; Lawrence E. William and John A. Bargh, "Experiencing Physical Warmth Promotes Interpersonal Warmth," *Science* 322, no. 5901 (2008): 606–607.

262. Ball and Torrance, *Streamlines*; James Hartley, "Planning That Title: Practices and Preferences for Titles with Colons in Academic Articles," *Library & Information Science Research* 29 (2007): 553–68; Torrance, *Search*; Torrance, *Guidelines*; Torrance, "Nature"; Torrance, *Manual* (1990); Torrance, *Wanting*; Torrance, *Manual* (1998); Torrance, *Review*; Torrance and Safter, *Making*; Cynthia Whissell, "The Trend Towards More Attractive and Informative Titles: American Psychologist 1946–2010," *Psychological Reports* 110, no. 2 (2012): 427–44.

263. Hartley, "Planning"; Whissell, "Trend."

264. Gilliam and Flaherty, "Storytelling"; Alexander Haas, Ivan Snehota, and Daniela Corsaro, "Creating Value in Business Relationships: The Role of Sales," *Industrial Marketing Management* 41 (2012): 94–105.

265. Stavroula Kalogeras, "Storytelling: An Ancient Human Technology and Critical-Creative Pedagogy for Transformative Learning," *International Journal of Information and Communication Technology Education* 9, no 4 (2013): 113–22.

266. Ball and Torrance, *Streamlines*; Joan Joesting and Robert Joesting, "Correlations of Scores on Full-Range Picture Vocabulary Test, Three Measures of Creativity, SAT Scores, and Age," *Psychological Reports* 33, no. 3 (1973): 981–82; Torrance, *Search*; Torrance, *Guidelines*; Torrance, "Nature"; Torrance, *Manual* (1990); Torrance, *Wanting*; Torrance, *Manual* (1998); Torrance, *Review*; Torrance and Safter, *Making*.

267. Albrecht, *Executive*; Ball and Torrance, *Streamlines*; Cheng, Kim, and Hull, "Comparisons"; Feist, "Meta-Analysis"; Colin Robert R. McCrae, "Creativity, Divergent Thinking, and Openness to Experience," *Journal of Personality and Social Psychology* 52, no. 6 (1987): 1258–65; Russ, *Affect*; Torrance, *Search*; Torrance, *Guidelines*; Torrance, "Nature"; Torrance, *Manual* (1990); Torrance, *Wanting*; Torrance, *Manual* (1998); Torrance, *Review*; Torrance and Safter, *Making*.

268. Albrecht, *Executive*; Gilliam and Flaherty, "Storytelling"; Melanie C. Green and John K. Donahue, "Simulated Worlds: Transportation into Narratives," in *Handbook of Imagination and Mental Simulation*, eds. Keith D. Markman, William MP Klein, and Julie A. Suhr (New York: Psychology, 2009); Richard G. McFarland, Goutam N. Challagalla, and Tasadduq A. Shervani, "Influence Tactics for Effective Adaptive Selling," *Journal of Marketing* 70 (2006): 103–17; Kawpong Polyorat, Dana L. Alden, and Eugene S. Kim, "Impact of Narrative versus Factual Print Ad Copy on Product Evaluation: The Mediating Role of Ad Message Involvement," *Psychology & Marketing* 24 (2007): 539–54; Shu-Mi Yang et al., "Knowledge Exchange and Knowledge Protection in Interorganizational Learning: The Ambidexterity Perspective," *Industrial Marketing Management* 43, no. 2 (2014): 346–58.

269. Gilliam and Flaherty, "Storytelling."

270. David Ballantyne et al., "Value Propositions as Communication Practice: Taking a Wider View," *Industrial Marketing Management* 40 (2011): 202–10; Jennifer Edson Escalas, "Self-Referencing and Persuasion: Narrative Transportation versus Analytical Elaboration," *Journal of Consumer Research* 33 (2007): 421–29; Gilliam and Flaherty, "Storytelling"; Haas, Snehota, and Corsaro, "Creating"; Tom van Laer et al., "The Extended Transportation-Imagery Model: A Meta-Analysis of the Antecedents and Consequences of Consumers' Narrative Transportation," *Journal of Consumer Research* 40, no. 5 (2014): 797–817.

271. Ballantyne et al., "Value"; Damanpour, "Organizational"; Escalas, "Self-Referencing"; Gilliam and Flaherty, "Storytelling"; Green and Donahue, "Simulated"; Haas, Snehota, and Corsaro, "Creating"; Kalogeras, "Storytelling"; Mattila, "Role"; McFarland, Challagalla, and Shervani, "Influence"; Padgett and Allen, "Communicating"; van Laer et al., "Extended"; Yang et al., "Knowledge."

272. Jim Corrigan, *Business Leaders: Steve Jobs* (Greensboro, NC: Reynolds, 2009); Isaacson, *Jobs*.

273. Isaacson, *Jobs*.

274. Yeshua Adonai, "Apple's Think Different Campaign," November 2013, https://www.academia.edu/5471103/Apples_Think_Different_campaign;

275. Mandela, *Freedom*.

276. Ibid.

277. "Steve Jobs," interview by Daniel Morrow, Computerworld Information Technology Awards Foundation, April 1995, http://www.computerworld.com/s/ article/9220609/Steve_Jobs _interview_One_on_one_in_1995?taxonomyId=214and pageNumber=; Ward, Smith, and Finke, "Creative Cognition," 189–212.

278. Steven J. Heine and Takeshi Hamamura, "In Search of East Asian Self-Enhancement," *Personality and Social Psychology Review* 11 (2007): 4–27; Steven J. Heine, Shinobu Kitayama, and Darrin R. Lehman, "Cultural Differences in Self-Evaluation: Japanese Readily Accept Negative Self-Relevant Information," *Journal of Cross-Cultural Psychology* 32, no. 4 (2001): 434–43.

279. Charles S. Carver and Michael F. Scheier, *On the Self-Regulation of Behavior* (New York: Cambridge University Press, 1987); Ayelet Fishbach, Tal Eyal, and Stacey R. Finkelstein, "How Positive and Negative Feedback Motivate Goal Pursuit," *Social and Personality Psychology Compass* 4, no. 8 (2010): 517–30; E. Tory Higgins, "Self-Discrepancy: A Theory Relating Self and Affect," *Psychological Review* 94 (1998): 319–40; Avraham N. Kluger and Angelo DeNisi, "The Effects of

Feedback Interventions on Performance: A Historical Review, a Meta-Analysis, and a Preliminary Feedback Intervention Theory," *Psychological Bulletin* 119 (1996): 254–84; Daniela J. Owen, Amy M. S. Slep, and Richard E. Heyman, "The Effect of Praise, Positive Nonverbal Response, Reprimand, and Negative Nonverbal Response on Child Compliance: A Systematic Review," *Clinical Child and Family Psychology Review* 15, no. 4 (2012): 364–85.

280. De Dreu, Baas, and Nijstad, "Hedonic"; Kounios and Beeman, "Aha!."

281. Bloom et al., *Taxonomy*; Cole and De Maio, "Learned"; DeWitt et al., "Lower-Order"; Guilford, "Creativity"; Marzano and Costa, "Question"; McCollum, "Deficits"; Wesson, "'Volvo."

282. Dawson et al., "Predicting"; Gardner, "Giftedness"; Guilford, "Creativity"; Kaila, "Democratizing"; Kim, "Crisis"; Land and Jarman, *Breakpoint*; Torrance, *Search*; Torrance and Safter, *Making*.

283. College Board, "About Us," June 2016, https://www.collegeboard.org/about.

284. Blaire Briody, "SAT Test: Another Drain on the Family Budget," *Fiscal Times*, May 1, 2013, http://www.thefiscaltimes.com/Articles/2013/05/01/SAT-Tests-Another-Drain-on-the-Family -Budget; Janet Lorin, "Nonprofit Head of College Board Paid More Than Harvard's Leader," *Bloomberg*, August 26, 2011, http://www.bloomberg.com/news/articles/2011-08-26/nonprofit -head-of-college-board-paid-more-than-harvard-s-leader; Valerie Strauss, "How Much Do Big Education Nonprofits Pay Their Bosses? Quite A Bit, It Turns Out," *Washington Post*, September 30, 2015, https://www.washingtonpost.com/news/answer-sheet/wp/2015/09/30/how-much-do-big -education-nonprofits-pay-their-bosses-quite-a-bit-it-turns-out/.

285. Carol Costello and Bob Ruff, "Educating America: The Big Business of the SAT," *CNN*, December 29, 2009, http://am.blogs.cnn.com/2009/12/29/educating-america-the-big-business-of-the-sat/; Lorin, "Nonprofit"; Strauss, "Nonprofits."

286. Costello and Ruff, "Educating America."

287. KH Kim and Michael F. Hull, "Effects of Motivation, ACT/SAT, GPA, and SES on College Choice for Academically Advanced Students and Other Students," *World Journal of Educational Research* 2, no. 2 (2015): 140–67; KH Kim and Michael F. Hull, "Effects of Intrinsic and Extrinsic Motivation, Self-Efficacy, and Educational Expectations on Students' Post-Secondary Institutional Choice," *World Journal of Behavioral Science* 1, no. 1 (2015): 31–46.

288. Hunter M. Breland et al. "Trends in College Admission 2000: A Report of a National Survey of Undergraduate Admissions Policies, Practices, and Procedures," Joint ACT, AIR, College Board, ETS and NACAC Research Report March, 2002, http://www.ets.org/research/policy_research _reports/publications/report/2002/cnrr; David A. Hawkins and Jessica Lautz, *State of College Admission* (Alexandria, VA: National Association for College Admission Counseling, August, 2007), http://www.nacacnet.org/research/research-data/documents/07stateofadmission.pdf.

289. Kim and Hull, "Effects"; Kim and Hull, "Intrinsic."

290. Hawkins and Lautz, *College Admission*.

291. Thomas R. Coyle and David R. Pillow, "SAT and ACT Predict College GPA after Removing g," *Intelligence* 36, no. 6 (2008): 719–29; Meredith C. Frey and Douglas K. Detterman, "Scholastic Assessment or g? The Relationship between the Scholastic Assessment Test and General Cognitive Ability," *Psychological Science* 15, no. 6 (2004): 373–78.

292. Coyle and Pillow, "SAT and ACT"; Katherine A. Koenig, Meredith C. Frey, and Douglas K. Detterman, "ACT and General Cognitive Ability," *Intelligence* 36, no. 2 (2008): 153–60.

293. ACT, "Facts About the ACT," http://www.act.org/news/aapfacts.html.

294. Briody, "SAT"; Jennifer L. Kobrin, Wayne J. Camara, and Glenn B. Milewski, *The Utility of the SAT I and SAT II Admissions Decisions in California and the Nation* (New York: College Entrance Examination Board, 2002), https://research.collegeboard.org/sites/default/files/publications/2012/7/ researchreport-2002-6-utility-sat-i-ii-admissions-decisions-california-nation.pdf; Wesson, "Volvo."

295. KH Kim and Robert J. Kipper, "Creativity and Gangs: Who Joins Gangs and Why? A Critical Review of the Literature," *World Journal of Behavioral Science* 2 (2016): 12–18.

296. Andrew Salute, Kristin M. Murphy, and Brittany Aronson, "What Can We Learn from the Atlanta Cheating Scandal?" *Phi Delta Kappan* 97, no. 6 (2016): 48–52.

297. Bonnie Cramond, "The Torrance Tests of Creative Thinking: From Design through Establishment of Predictive Validity," in *Beyond Terman: Contemporary Longitudinal Studies of Giftedness and Talent*, eds. Rena F. Subotnik and Karen D. Arnold (Norwood, NJ: Ablex, 1993), 229–54; Thomas P. Hébert, Bonnie Cramond, Kristie L. Speirs Neumeister, Garnet Millar, Alice F. Silvian, *E. Paul Torrance: His Life, Accomplishments, and Legacy* (Storrs, CT: National Research Center on the Gifted and Talented [NRC/GT], University of Connecticut, 2002); Torrance, *Wanting*.

INDEX